Classical
Film
Violence

Classical Film Violence

Designing and Regulating
Brutality in Hollywood
Cinema, 1930–1968

Stephen Prince

Rutgers University Press
New Brunswick, New Jersey, and London

Library of Congress Cataloging-in-Publication Data

Prince, Stephen, 1955–
    Classical film violence : designing and regulating brutality in Hollywood cinema, 1930–1968 /
Stephen Prince.
        p.   cm.
Includes bibliographical references and index.
    ISBN 0-8135-3280-9 (cloth : alk. paper)—ISBN 0-8135-3281-7 (pbk. : alk. paper)
    1. Violence in motion pictures.   2. Motion pictures—United States.   3. Motion pictures—
Censorship—United States—History.   I. Title.
    PN1995.9.V5 P75 2003
    791.43′6—dc21   2002015870

British Cataloging-in-Publication information is available from the British Library.

The publication program of Rutgers University Press is supported by the Board of Governors of
Rutgers, The State University of New Jersey.

Design by Karolina Harris

Manufactured in the United States of America

This one is for Kim

Contents

Classical
Film
Violence

"They [the public] want red meat and they want it raw."

—A FILM EXCHANGE MANAGER, 1910

"To avoid unnecessary cruelty, we earnestly suggest you reconsider the killing of the little child."

—PCA SCRIPT EVALUATION LETTER, 1958

Introduction

After the bombing of the World Trade Center on September 11, for a brief moment Hollywood seemed to rethink its love affair with movie violence. Studio executives worried that action movies featuring an arsenal of weapons and big buildings exploding were a tainted commodity. Their fears were short-lived, however; after a few weeks, it was business as usual.

If movie violence today is an inescapable part of the film business, what about the earlier period of classical Hollywood, in the 1930s and 1940s, when the studios made movies on their sound stages and backlots? That was an era of regulated screen content. Before a project went into production, the content of a script was carefully scrutinized for problematic religious and moral elements. Where did violence fit into this regulated screen world? And how does that compare with our own time?

In Hollywood lingo, this book is a "prequel" to *Savage Cinema: Sam Peckinpah and the Rise of Ultraviolent Movies.* My earlier book studied the turn toward ultraviolence in American cinema after 1968, chiefly by examining the work of Peckinpah, modern cinema's most famous practitioner of screen violence, and that of filmmakers inspired by him.

The present volume examines violence in Hollywood film during the era of the Production Code: from 1930, when the industry adopted the Code, until 1968, when the last vestiges of the Code were abolished. During this period, filmmakers had to get the sexual, moral, religious, and violent material in their scripts formally cleared before they could start production.

Much is to be learned by looking at this earlier period. The explosion of graphic violence on-screen after 1968 can seem very disjunctive compared to previous decades of filmmaking. After 1968, for example, gunshot victims explode in showers of blood; they did not do so in earlier decades. Looking

1

closely at this earlier period, however, some surprising discoveries await us, and they make the relationship of the eras before and after 1968 seem less stratified and more of a continuum.

How did the industry regulate screen violence in the Hollywood period? Did the term "violence" have the same meanings in industry discourse that it does today? To what extent were Hollywood filmmakers drawn to hard violence? Did they try to "push the envelope"—try to expand the boundaries of the violence they could depict—or is this interest more purely a manifestation of post-sixties filmmaking? How was screen violence stylized, aestheticized, in the Hollywood period? What contribution did sound make to this aestheticization? In what ways can we compare and describe screen violence in the Code and post-Code eras?

These are some of the questions that I explore in the following chapters. The book is not meant to be an encyclopedic history of film violence. Its scope is limited by the methodology I chose to employ and, as such, there are bound to be some films that I do not discuss that an exhaustive history might cover. I offer instead an account of the stylistic development of American screen violence that is grounded in industry documentation about its negotiated depictions.

I will be looking very closely at film style, at the ways filmmakers use the elements of cinema to design screen violence within the constraints that were imposed on them by the Production Code. This emphasis on style will enable us to reveal some key features in the history of American screen violence that a more strictly ideological or social history approach would not. Indeed, this study is *not* a social history of movie violence, nor does it frame violence primarily in terms of ideology, race, class, gender or other macro-level kinds of variables. The sociological or social history approach generates many fine insights, but I propose instead to look at the *cinematic* components of film violence because these reveal a significant history and a striking relationship between screen violence in the era of the Production Code and in our own time.

Except in a few instances, this book does not examine movie violence in relation to big historical events that occurred within the time frame of the Production Code. These would include such things as the Great Depression, the Cold War and the Civil Rights movement. World War II will concern us in chapter four, but these other events will not.

I have several reasons for bracketing these things off from the discussion. (Numerous other scholars writing on film violence have dealt with them.)[1] First, I am interested in exploring film violence as a *primary* condition and element of cinema. The social history or ideological approach to movie violence tends to treat screen violence as a symptom of some larger condition, whether it be war, depression, ideology, gender, or race relations. Screen violence is responsive to such conditions. It would be foolish to deny this. But the social history approach can run the risk of treating movie violence as a dependent variable, as a subset of the larger social or historical categories that have pride of place in the analysis. According to this approach, as they change, so, too, does movie violence. Thus, gangster movies and the appeal of their lawless heroes reflect or embody public antipathy for Prohibition. The graphic violence of *The Wild Bunch* reflects the savagery of the Vietnam War. And so on.

These are perfectly fine propositions, but they tend to relegate movie violence to a back seat and reactive role in cinema. It is forever responding to noncinematic social categories or conditions. In contrast to this view, I regard violence as an essential component of cinema: part of its deep formal structure, something that many filmmakers have been inherently drawn toward and something that cinema does supremely well. Some important consequences follow from this view, the chief one being that whereas the social history approach will tend to regard movie violence as a kind of mask worn by the particular organization of power relations within a given period, with the masks changing as the configuration of power relationships changes, I am more interested in the enduring elements of movie violence. These can be located chiefly in the ways that filmmakers have approached violence at the level of cinematic form.

This consideration—the cinematic expression of violence in picture and sound—furnishes a compelling reason for bracketing off the social history approach from this study. Because it treats movie violence as a dependent variable, the social history approach runs the risk of abstracting screen violence from its cinematic context. Violence becomes a theme, an idea, or furnishes a proposition about society. It is taken to a second-order level of existence, removed from the primary material of the films themselves.

But it is this primary material—the formal organization of violence in picture and sound—that is cinema's unique inflection of violent subject matter. Violence, after all, exists in literature, painting, theater, in all of the representational arts. Cinema, arguably, represents violence in the most vivid terms. Why? Because it deals with screen violence as a proposition about society, as abstraction rather than material form, the social history approach does not enable us to answer this question.

Furthermore, it is the opportunity to create screen violence through the manipulation of cinematic form that draws filmmakers to gun battles, fistfights, and other forms of movie mayhem in the first place. At a basic level of craft, they learn how to do this mayhem, how to choreograph it for the screen, and how to build on and better the work of earlier colleagues. Viewers, too, become proficient at evaluating and responding to the conventions of movie violence within any given period. Screen violence has a history that exists not just at the more abstracted level of film as society's mirror but within the formal language of cinema, as filmmakers assimilate existing approaches and then seek to extend them. Without attending to the distinctive features of violence manifest at the level of film style, we miss this history and underestimate the importance for censorship battles and social controversy of cinema style and especially of what I refer to in this book as *stylistic amplitude*, the way that violent acts on-screen are elaborated by cinematic form. Stylistic amplitude is deeply implicated in the history of screen violence and the controversies over its nature. Because existing scholarly accounts of movie violence have tended to take a social history approach, they have typically minimized the importance of the stylistic domain.

This book, therefore, emphasizes the stylistic construction of screen violence by filmmakers working within the permissible creative boundaries of their periods. This emphasis provides a third reason for bracketing the social history approach. Because it tends to lift violence out of the material structure of a given film and take it to a more general level where violence becomes symptom, theme, or proposition, this approach may jump ahead of where historical analysis needs to be. Before we can know what screen violence means at the level of big social themes, we ought to know what filmmakers did at the level of individual films: how and why the violent material in shots was lit, how it was choreographed in scenes, and how the sequences were edited. By documenting this kind of formal design and the reasons behind it, I hope to offer not just a stylistic history of American screen violence but also a trove of information that a social historian of screen violence can build upon. Thus, though I am not using a social history approach, the material that I provide in this study can constitute the necessary foundation for such an approach.

I hope that the reader, therefore, will understand that the subject of this book is the "movie" in *movie* violence.

I move between two domains in the pages that follow. One domain is the area of cinematic design, composed of formal elements such as camera placement, lighting, editing, blocking of the action, and sound. How did filmmakers working in the Hollywood period use these elements of design when depicting scenes of violence? Did they establish conventions over time, comparable to such editing conventions as shot–reverse shot cutting in conversation scenes? Do these design elements change over time, and do they vary according to director or genre?

The other domain is composed of the industry records collected in the files of the Production Code Administration (PCA). These case files are organized by film and contain the record of negotiations between PCA officials and film-makers working on a given production. Thus, the *White Heat* case file contains correspondence documenting the PCA's evaluation of the script for this 1949 James Cagney gangster movie, its detailed feedback about the scripted elements of crime and violence, and the filmmakers' responses.

I am interested, then, in design and regulation. In going between the two domains, I have sought to tie the design issues to the regulatory ones. Holly-wood filmmakers were not free to create any cinematic design they wanted, to film scenes without constraints. To what extent, then, did an aesthetics of screen violence evolve in response to regulatory pressures? Looking closely at the formal design of violent scenes in films of this period, we will find that many of the choices about camera position, editing, blocking, or sound are functional responses by filmmakers to the constraints on content that they faced in clearing release approval from the PCA and then in surviving scrutiny by the nation's state and municipal censor boards. Certain lighting effects, for example, had proven utility in getting otherwise objectionable violence past the PCA and the regional censors. At the same time, filmmakers show an inherent interest in expanding their repertoire of stylistic tools for depicting violence, and this goal was somewhat antithetical to the objectives of regulation.

The several excellent histories of the PCA—Gregory Black's *Hollywood Censored* and *The Catholic Crusade Against the Movies,* Leonard Leff and Jerold Simmons's *The Dame in the Kimono,* Frank Walsh's *Sin and Censorship: The Catholic Church and the Motion Picture Industry*—have tended to focus on the content that the PCA regulated. What, for example, did Mae West *do* on-screen that aroused local censor action?

Correspondingly less attention has been paid to the relationship of PCA regulation to the formal structure of film within a specific topic area, such as violence. Violence, in fact, has rarely been studied in detail as it relates to the PCA. This is the first book to look at the subject. Studies of the agency have tended to focus on issues of sex, morals, religion, and profanity. A number of authors have examined the PCA and its efforts to regulate gangster movies, but these analyses tend to be pitched within the frame of historical sociology and to focus on the content of the movies, specifically the PCA's effort to clean up that genre's sociological messages about lawbreaking. Richard Maltby's superb account of the production and regulation of Howard Hawks's *Scarface* supplements its sociological focus with some attention to the film's stylistic depiction of violence.[2] Lea Jacobs's *The Wages of Sin* gives close attention to the formal designs that surrounded the contested subject matter in films about "fallen women."[3] She examines the cinematic marks in films with regulated subject matter in ways that are similar to what I will be doing with screen violence.

My analyses are based on a primary sample of sixty-five films for which I examined the PCA case files. These case files are housed in the Margaret Herrick library at the Academy of Motion Picture Arts and Sciences in Beverly Hills. The PCA maintained case files on the films that it reviewed, and into these went correspondence about scripts and script revisions, along with an array of other material. This included a synopsis of the film story that was provided by the studio, a credit list, a content analysis chart, the certificate letter, reports on trims ordered by local and overseas censor boards (the boards would send elimination reports to the film industry's New York office, which would forward them to the PCA in Los Angeles), interoffice correspondence regarding censor activity, letters of complaint from viewers, and correspondence about reissue of the film in later years. This reissue correspondence is especially interesting for revealing changes in public taste and PCA operating philosophy. On a number of occasions, films approved for release in the early 1930s were denied reissue certificates, or had trims ordered so as to qualify for re-release in the later 1930s or mid-1940s.

The sample of films used in this study is displayed in Appendix A. I selected the sample based on a number of criteria. I wanted films that were already notorious for their violence (e.g., *Kiss of Death,* which includes a famous scene where a psycho throws an invalid mother down a flight of stairs) or which, going in, I knew to contain a high incidence of violence (e.g., *Brute Force*). I wanted films across the three principal decades of the study's focus (1930s, 1940s, 1950s), and I wanted to draw from genres featuring violence as a basic staple—in this case, horror, Western, war, and adventure.

I used the case files to examine the issues, decisions, compromises, and controversies that arose during the script negotiation process over the depiction of violent material, and then I looked to see whether a given film's design carried audiovisual traces of this process. Did the negotiations described in the case files leave "marks" in the camerawork, the lighting, editing, or sound design of a picture? It seemed likely that regulatory constraints would show up at a formal level, inside the films, in their design. As, frequently, they do.

As I began to uncover the aesthetic patterns in the depiction of violence in classical Hollywood film, I expanded the range of films under consideration by including a secondary sampling of pictures whose case files I did not examine. This sampling helped to enlarge discussion of key topics, such as violence in film noir and the World War II pictures. The reader will therefore note that the discussion ranges between these two samples. I examined the aesthetics of screen violence in all the films that are included in the following chapters. I examined PCA case files only for those films in the primary sample.

Though this is not a social history approach, tracing the intersection of film design and screen regulation will occasionally take us into the realm of ideology, and this should not be surprising given the primal nature of the issues that are most deeply addressed by screen violence. Hollywood's regulatory policies, and the dominant aesthetic patterns that they influenced, express clear notions about the philosophical issues raised by violence—the nature and meaning of physical suffering and psychological pain, the relation of mind and body, the existence of cruelty in a "just" world. These ideas inform the aesthetics of violence in Hollywood film. By elaborating these ideas, the cinematic designs give expression to underlying assumptions about the nature of violence.

In writing this stylistic history, it has been necessary to engage at some length with two topic areas that are not themselves violence-specific but which bear in major ways on the subject. One is the Production Code Administration, which was charged with enforcing the Code and which worked with filmmakers in pre-production to iron out troublesome areas of content in scripts. The other is the now somewhat-distant phenomenon of regional censorship. Were it not for the existence of local censor boards scattered around the country in the Hollywood period, there would have been no Production Code or Production Code Administration. Getting films cleared by the regional censors was an ongoing headache for the industry, and it was a problem the PCA aimed to address. The story of screen violence in this period cannot be told without some attention to these two topic areas.

Thus, the study begins with a look at the phenomenon of regional censorship and the early controversies over movie violence that ensnared the medium shortly after its inception. Chapter one examines the growth of the regional censors and the court decisions that went against the film industry, limiting its freedom of expression, and upholding the prerogative of local communities to pass legislation restricting the exhibition of certain categories of film. These included films that depicted violence, and I examine some of the ways that screen violence instigated censor action. I end the chapter by profiling the kinds of violence—the weapons, the acts, the responses by victims—that censors were apt to cut. These prohibitions continued into the Hollywood period and helped to influence the Production Code.

Focusing on censorship issues in the silent period, and their relation to screen violence, Chapter one gives us a prelude to the study. Chapter two moves us into the time period proper of the book and begins with an extended discussion of the Production Code Administration and how it operated. This will be essential for the reader to grasp in order to understand the aesthetic discussions that follow. While I've tried not to duplicate material that is available elsewhere, my perspective on the PCA is more sympathetic than it seems is common to much of the scholarly and popular literature. A common take on the PCA sees the agency as one that interfered with the work of film-makers, often making it more fit for children than adults. In contrast, I do *not* treat the PCA as a censor.

Based on the case files, I offer a view that sees the PCA as working *for* film-makers and *against* regional censors. Moreover, framing the discussion this way allows us to pose a question that rarely seems to get asked: Was American film better off in some ways under the PCA than without it? In terms of screen violence, what was gained and what was lost under the PCA and then afterward?

After this profile of the PCA, I move into the extended analyses of style that occupy the remainder of the book. The rest of chapter two examines the developing aesthetics of violence as they play out in early and mid-1930s horror films. These films often depicted gruesome medical tortures or sadistic torments inflicted on captive victims, and they collectively show how filmmakers and the PCA grappled with overt imagery of sadism and the sounds of pain and suffering. The arrival of sound in the late 1920s reconfigures the aesthetics of violence in American film, taking filmmakers deeper into an exploration of its cinematic styling. Thirties horror films provide a vivid record of these explorations.

So do gangster and crime films, which I examine in chapter three. Numerous studies have been published on the classic gangster movies, some of which draw from scholarly study of PCA case files. In general, however, these studies have concentrated on the films' depictions of criminal behavior, often from a sociological perspective that looks at the public controversies surrounding the pictures. What were the messages about lawbreaking that elicited controversy? I am less interested in this kind of question because it has been well covered by others. What has not been covered so extensively is the kind of aesthetic analysis that I propose here, one that centers on the cinematic stylization of gun violence.

How did filmmakers integrate sound into the cinematic design of movie gunplay and use lighting and editing to amplify the force and impact of gun battles? Filmmakers quickly learned how they could increase what I call the stylistic amplitude of screen violence, and gun violence furnished a prime vehicle for these experiments. This elaboration of gun violence establishes clear continuities between classical Hollywood and our own period. The PCA tried to restrain the rising arc of carnage in thirties crime films, even to the point of suppressing gangster pictures for a while, but what filmmakers had learned in the early years of sound they could not unlearn. The die for the future had been cast.

Accordingly, chapter four examines the progressively deepening defiance of the PCA by filmmakers from the 1940s onward, filmmakers who were intent on bringing a harder violence to the screen than what the PCA would officially accept. The extent of this defiance is a largely untold story of PCA history, and it suggests a more limited view of the agency's authority than is popularly held. The films examined in this chapter show that filmmakers were putting on the screen acts of brutality and cruelty that the PCA had specifically prohibited. As a result the boundaries of acceptable screen practice began to expand, and this helped to erode the agency's ability to restrain what filmmakers could show. Like the design of gun violence, this development points to the linkages between classical and post-classical Hollywood.

As I noted earlier, some published works on the PCA seem to imply that American film would have been better off had the agency not existed, that it hobbled and crippled artistic expression. That this is a false question is demonstrated by the regional censor boards—the ultimate control of film content and cause of industry regulation lay there. In those times and under those conditions, the PCA couldn't not have existed. But, to put all of this more positively, what did regulation help *give* to American film?

Chapter five examines the system and forms of screen rhetoric—the figurative devices—that classical Hollywood filmmakers used to suggest acts or categories of violence that they could not, or chose not to, depict directly. These forms of visual rhetoric are based on a logic of substitutional value whereby unacceptable types of violence could be depicted through various kinds of image substitution. By replacing the offensive or impermissible image or action with a less offensive substitute, the substitute could be used to evoke the more problematic, and censorable, representation. I examine five devices used by filmmakers to elide a presentation of hard violence. The availability and effectiveness of these devices show a positive contribution by the regulatory atmosphere of the times to the stylistic vocabulary of American cinema. Our screen poetics would be the poorer without them.

Chapter six brings the discussion of classical Hollywood into our own period by examining the ways that screen violence has changed since the period of the Production Code. It compares the regulation of violent screen *behavior* in classical Hollywood (e.g., no automatic weapons to be shown in the hands of criminals) with the emergence in our own period of violence as a *category in itself*. The emergence of this supra-category, which does not exist in this fashion in classical Hollywood, helped to symbolize the end of the Production Code Administration, which had never formulated a philosophy for regulating screen violence. The chapter examines the effort to develop such a philosophy with the inception of the Code and Rating Administration (CARA), with its

G-M-R-X schema, and examines the situation of filmmakers who, by the late 1960s, could put graphic violence on-screen but faced a new arena of PCA-like negotiation when their films were picked up by network television. The chapter compares the restricted nature of screen violence in the Hollywood period with its proliferation in graphic and hard forms in our own. I conclude with some reflections on the place that violence holds in the deep structure of cinema and has held throughout its history, as this study of the classical Hollywood period will show.

I want to extend my warmest thanks to Barbara Hall and Val Almendariz at the Margaret Herrick Library. Barbara especially went out of her way to assist with various last minute requests for material and clarification about points of information. Her work in support of my scholarship is greatly appreciated. Thanks also to Michelle LeCompte and Margaret J. Cline for their valuable research assistance.

1
Censorship and Screen Violence before 1930

In 1910, the Chicago police department, charged with enforcing the city's film censorship ordinance, banned *Final Settlement* (Biograph Co.) because it depicted killing, robbery, and an attack on a woman. It also banned *An Eye for an Eye* (Vitagraph Co.) because it depicted two strangulations. It passed *The Third Degree* (Actophone Co.), *Treasure of the Girl* (Carson Co.), *Pirate's Fiancée* (Lux Co.), and *New Marshal at Gila Creek* (Lubin Co.) provided the hold-ups, burglaries, kidnapping, robberies, and murders were cut out.[1]

That same year, in her letter of resignation from New York's Board of Censorship (also known as the National Board of Censorship), Josephine Redding condemned the film industry's exploitation of violence and crime, arguing that it damaged the industry economically and ethically. She specifically cited a Selig film, *The Indian's Way,* which depicted fistfights, an attempted murder and a revenge killing. "Violence is the predominating note," she wrote. "Pistol shooting, murder of the girl through physical brutality, the torture of the culprit, the struggle and finally the second murder. Some of us are disturbed by the effect of having such a cruelly shocking story put out at any time but especially now when local magistrates are denouncing motion pictures from the bench because of the violence they portray."[2]

The New York Board of Censorship had tried to formulate a policy for dealing with film violence. In 1909, its general secretary sent a letter to the Motion Picture Patents Co., which represented the leading production companies, suggesting some guidelines the Board would use in evaluating pictures. "Criminal acts which are too violent or gruesome, or which are in no way essential to the working out of the story, are to be deprecated. Scenes which directly suggest the committing of crimes, e.g., the manner of picking a lock or of holding up a person on a highway, are equally objectionable; finally, the

Board desires to express disapproval of scenes which represent the mixing of potions of poisons for the purpose of committing murder."[3]

In 1909 cinema was still a very new medium, barely moving beyond its nickelodeon phase. And yet, as these actions suggest, it was already embroiled in controversy over its depictions of violence. These controversies should look very familiar to us today because they have changed little over the decades. But cinema itself has changed. It is doubtful, for example, that today's viewer, seeing *An Eye for an Eye* or *The Indian's Way,* would be scandalized or disturbed by the fights or shootings contained in these films. Much film violence throughout the silent period has an overtly theatrical quality and mode of presentation. It is shown in full-figure framings, with the camera at a comfortable distance from the action, and the victims of punches or gunshots behave as they might on the stage. They flail about and then fall to the ground. The interval between the production of two classic Westerns, *The Great Train Robbery* (1904) and *The Toll Gate* (1920), shows a tremendous development in narrative complexity and the use of editing and cinematography for narrative purposes. But the two films show a correspondingly less striking disparity in their aesthetics of violence. In both films, the fisticuffs and shootings are stiff and unelaborated. As cinematic events they are brief, and neither the camerawork nor the editing embellishes the violence in much detail. The coming of sound did much to change the orientation of filmmakers to the presentation of violence. Sound stimulated them to search more intensively for uniquely cinematic inflections and thereby helped to shed the conventions of stage melodrama. Sound made violence palpable, gave it texture and rhythmic form, made it sensuous, and overcame the abstracting effects of the silent image. It put the cries of victims and the bark of weapons inside of the image.

But filmmakers who were excited about the revolution in the medium brought by sound and attracted to the prospect of exploring its potential for stylizing violence could not work freely; limitations were imposed upon their range of expression. Although this book is principally about screen violence during the era of the Production Code in classical Hollywood, we need to begin by taking a brief look at the period that preceded the inception of the Code in 1930. This chapter, therefore, is intended to give the reader a quick profile of the inception of film censorship and the way that depictions of violence helped to instigate that growth. We cannot talk about film violence without talking about regional film censor boards—what filmmakers could and couldn't show was always a function of these forces. Moreover, it is instructive to see how far back in motion picture history the controversies about movie violence go. Before we can get to the mayhem examined in subsequent chapters, then, we need to take a quick trip to the medium's infancy.

Almost as soon as the new medium appeared, social authorities and other custodians of public welfare and morality regarded motion pictures with great suspicion and anxiety. They feared that cinema would bypass existing institutions of socialization such as the church, schools, and the family. As a result state, municipal, and county agencies across the country worked actively to shape and control the conditions of motion picture representation.[4]

LEGAL AND ECONOMIC DIMENSIONS OF CENSORSHIP

Censorship of motion pictures quickly became a fixture of reform efforts. The city of Chicago passed the nation's first movie censorship ordinance on November 4, 1907, and the city's police department, charged with enforcing it, became movie censors. Unlicensed films could not be shown in Chicago, and no film would get a license that was "immoral or obscene, or portrays depravity, criminality or lack of virtue . . . or tends to produce a breach of the peace or riots, or purports to represent any hanging, lynching or burning of a human being."[5]

As this passage indicates, the ordinance made specific reference to certain kinds of violent material that would be outlawed. A group of nickelodeon operators promptly tested the ordinance by exhibiting films that had been denied a license. The case—*Block v. the City of Chicago* (1909)—became the first court-adjudicated censorship case in American movie history, and the films in question—*The James Boys in Missouri* (1908) and *Night Riders* (1908)—had been rejected for licensing because of their violence. The first movie censorship case to reach the courts, then, involved the issue of film violence. These films apparently do not survive, and it is unlikely that they contained any violence that would appear extreme or shocking to a cinema viewer of today.

Jake Block and five other nickelodeon operators filed suit, stating that the ordinance discriminated against them because stories of the James brothers (Jesse and Frank James, the famous bandits) were being concurrently presented in Chicago in other visual media (in stereopticons and as "stationary pictures," as well as on the stage), that it was unconstitutional because it delegated judicial powers to the police chief, took away property rights without due process of law, and was unreasonable and oppressive.[6]

In the first instance of a soon-to-be-well-established pattern in which courts of appeals deferred to local censors, the Supreme Court of Illinois found in favor of the City of Chicago, and its reasoning reveals significant assumptions about the nature of cinema and its audience that, as subsequent court cases showed, were entrenched in the judiciary and in public sector reformers. The court sidestepped the clear evidence that other pictorial media were presenting accounts of the James brothers' banditry by pointing to "the distinction between a failure to provide punishment for an act and the sanction of it." The ordinance, in other words, did not sanction the presentation of immoral or obscene pictures in other visual media, and, since it applied equally to everyone in the motion picture business, it was no grounds for objection to claim that other people were violating the law by other means.

But why single out the film business? Chief Justice Cartwright, writing the opinion of the court, found that the medium was more likely than other forms of entertainment to appeal to persons of "weak and immature minds." He wrote that film "audiences include those classes whose age, education and situation in life specially entitle them to protection against the evil influence of obscene and immoral representations."[7]

Cartwright wrote that depictions of crime that present only the action of the criminal "are . . . immoral and their exhibition would necessarily be attended with evil effects upon youthful spectators." Therefore, he continued, the chief of police was to be commended for denying permits for the exhibition of these and similar films. Such films "necessarily portray depictions of crime, and pictures of the 'Night Riders' can represent nothing but malicious mischief, arson and murder."

Cartwright's opinion resonates with the procedures later used by the Production Code Administration (PCA) in assessing crime films, whereby the PCA wanted to see compensating moral values to offset the charisma of the criminal. Cartwright raised the issue of moral balance in filmic depictions of violence by implying that *The James Boys* and *Night Riders* were immoral not simply because they concentrated on the exploits of outlaws but because they did so exclusively, without a corresponding depiction of law-abiding characters. This notion that films ought to strike a balance in their dramatic content—that they ought to offer morally admirable characters and behavior as a counterweight to depictions of crime—would have lasting duration and influence on American filmmaking. In this regard, the social attitudes enshrined in the Production Code, which are sometimes attributed to the preponderant Catholic influence on the Code, have clear historical antecedents.

The Block case reveals other continuities between this early period of motion picture history and our own. These demonstrate that a core question about film violence, from the standpoint of social policy, has deep roots in the medium and, as we shall see in later chapters, has never really gone away from the history of cinema. That question is a familiar one to us today: Do film images of violence or crime sway some viewers to commit acts similar to those they witnessed on-screen? Already, at the time of *Block*, the "evil influences" of cinema were being construed in terms of this issue, and Cartwright found that the films were potential threats to society. At least two years before the *Block* decision, accounts of movie-induced crime were being reported in news media. In May 1907, *Motion Picture World* warned about the dangers of children being allowed to see crime films by reporting on the case of two adolescent girls arrested for shoplifting after seeing a movie about a thief.[8]

The history of cinema is rife with such incidents. While the shoplifting in question was not a violent act, many copycat incidents are. I will review the scope of violent "copycat crimes" in chapter six and indicate the way in which they appear across the decades of the medium's history. Violent copycat crimes are frequently assumed to be exceptional or singular incidents, in this sense atypical of the medium's impact on viewers, and yet, as we will see in the final chapter, they seem always to have been co-present with the exhibition of films and, in this regard, may demonstrate a more systematic, rather than atypical, effect of cinema.

In respect of this, the court's concern with copycat crime prefigures our own worries about the medium. Viewed this way—with a measure of historical empathy—Justice Cartwright's defense of social morality against the insurgency of moving picture entertainment seems perhaps less quaint and unenlightened than it otherwise might. At the time of the ruling, this concern was part of the general Progressive effort to protect the weak and vulnerable members of society.[9] The notion of "weak" minds is a discourse bound to the Progressivism of the period. But the persistence of questions about the modeling of behavior by screen characters, and the persuasive appeal of film images and stories, has led contemporary researchers to a different manner of framing the problem. In place of "weak minds," contemporary research examines personality factors such as trait hostility, or the priming effects of film violence on a viewer's cognitive and emotional responses. I review some of these frameworks in chapter six.

At the present juncture, I want to identify the historical continuity of this core concern about the movies and emphasize the way that its initial surfacing in legal efforts to restrict film content occurs in terms of violent imagery. It has remained tied to film violence ever since. Furthermore, while the social anxiety has remained startlingly similar across different historical periods, the representation of screen violence has not. It has changed in a significant manner that requires us to map this public concern in relation to early cinema somewhat differently than in relation to post-1968 cinema.

One last point about the Block decision needs to be mentioned. The Court ruled that the ordinance needed no formal definition of obscenity and immorality because the concepts were clearly fixed in the minds of all citizens of "healthy and wholesome mind." The concept of obscenity was vested in the

15

public conscience. It would be half a century before the courts began to specify and narrow the legal concept of obscenity (e.g., in *Roth v. United States,* 1957) and then with reference to books, not films.[10]

Block told reformers that the medium was dangerous, that their fears were justified, and that vigilant scrutiny of motion picture content would be needed to protect society from the erosion of its moral base. This outlook, in turn, became the template through which movie censorship operated and in response to which the Production Code was framed.

Throughout its history the film industry has feared three basic types of threat: threats to box-office receipts from other, competitive forms of entertainment, threats of outside censorship from any source, and threats of public protest over the morality of the industry and its films.[11] The Block decision had played to two of those fears.

Immediately following the ruling, the film industry made a large-scale effort to disarm its critics by engaging in a program of voluntary self-censorship. Longstanding tensions between New York's clergy and the city's film exhibitors led to the formation in March 1909 of the National Board of Censorship, which become the first national organization to be affiliated with the film industry in a program of voluntary self-censorship.[12]

The Board was part of the Progressive agenda of its sponsoring organization, the People's Institute, whose leaders were keenly interested in the cause of child welfare and in the role that film could play in fostering the development of children.[13] A cooperative effort between public welfare organizations and the film industry, the Board was designed to counteract increasing regional efforts to regulate film content. The Motion Picture Patents Company, composed of the industry's leading production companies, agreed to submit its films to the Board, which in June 1909 began reviewing films for release throughout the country. In 1909, it claimed that it reviewed seventy-five percent of all films exhibited in the country.[14]

The Board's main efforts were directed at films containing obscenity and crime. For example, it refused to pass the Pathé film *Rat D'Hotel* (1909) because it showed burglars succeeding in their crime by chloroforming the victim.[15] The Board's censors worried that, by virtue of showing a successful crime and its method of accomplishment, the film might prove to be too influential and instructive in the ways of lawbreaking for its audience.

As was apparent in the *Block* ruling, the National Board's censuring of *Rat D'Hotel* focused on the *referential* aspect of depictions of crime and violence. The depiction itself, independent of the visual design or cinematic style given to it, was sufficient cause for alarm. For the medium's critics, to depict a crime on film was tantamount to endorsing the act itself. Motion pictures lacked the constitutional protections accorded to such symbolic mediums of communication as speech and writing; indeed, cinema would soon explicitly be denied such protection by the highest court in the land. In the prevailing view of the period, cinema was not a symbolic medium of expression. It was powerful in its realism, instructive in its ability to concretely picture crime and sexuality, and persuasive in its ability to photographically reference the unwholesome social conditions of the big cities, conditions that Progressive reform aimed to improve. Through its photographic realism, it was concretely a part of the social world of its spectators; it depicted that world rather than standing symbolically apart from it. It is reference, not style, which is at stake in the efflorescence of censorship energy around the motion picture medium in its first decades. And, as we will see in subsequent chapters, this would have major consequences for the representation of film violence.

Despite the efforts of the Board of Censorship to defuse tensions, state censorship laws were passed in Pennsylvania (1911), Ohio and Kansas (1913), Maryland (1916), New York (1921) and Virginia (1922), as well as laws in numerous municipalities. A landmark ruling in 1915 by the U.S. Supreme Court, *Mutual Film Corporation v. Industrial Commission of Ohio*, compounded the industry's vulnerability. The decision upheld state censorship and specifically excluded motion pictures from the constitutional protections on freedom of the press and publication.

Mutual was a film distributor required by Ohio law to submit its films for review to the state board of censors. Mutual felt this restricted its ability to engage in interstate commerce (its distribution center for Ohio was based in Detroit) and film production. In its appeal to the Court, Mutual offered an intelligent argument that motion pictures were not just a business but also a medium of culture and communication, conveying ideas regarding "every kind of political, educational, religious, economic and social question."[16] Mutual argued that the Ohio censorship law violated this freedom, as well as Ohio's own state constitutional guarantee of freedom for citizens to speak, write, and publish, and that constitutional guarantees "are not limited to forms of publication known at the time the Constitution was adopted." Thus, although the Constitution says nothing about cinema, films were a contemporary form of publication and the new medium of cinema performed many of the informational functions that have traditionally been accorded to the press.

The Court rejected the idea that cinema was a medium of speech. Films "are mere representations of events" and ones that are "capable of evil." Furthermore, motion picture exhibition "is a business pure and simple, originated and conducted for profit, like other spectacles" and therefore failed to qualify for protection under the Bill of Rights. Because films might exert evil effects

on their viewers, especially on women and children, the Court sustained police powers to regulate motion picture exhibition.

The nation's highest court had found state censorship of motion pictures to
be lawful. Moreover, the Court suggested that the medium of cinema was dangerous to society. This reasoning would have lasting consequences. For the
next thirty-six years, until 1952's *Burstyn v. Wilson*, when the Court reversed
the Mutual ruling, American film was running scared and tried to placate censor boards and public watchdog groups by monitoring the type and quantity
of violence that its films contained (along with sexual material and other
provocative content areas).

The representational constraints resulting from this, and faced by filmmakers, are the single most important factor distinguishing the aesthetic design
and emotional meaning of screen violence in the Hollywood period. As we
will see, these constraints also helped to order and regulate film design in a
manner that encouraged the emergence of normative patterns of imagery that
evolved in response to the pressures about what could and could not be
shown and to stand in for those dimensions of represented violence that exceeded the existing screen boundaries.

Regional film censorship thrived in the wake of the Mutual ruling, and the
industry had no defense. Fox's Western *The Deadwood Coach* (1922), starring
Tom Mix, for example, aroused the wrath of Chicago censors because they
considered its violence to be excessive and "obnoxious." They felt that the film
contained too many shootings and refused to license it for exhibition. Writing
for the Illinois Court of Appeals, Justice Taylor described the action of the film:

> The picture portrays, first, a killing, then a fight with the Indians and a stage-
> coach holdup, and an attempt to kill, then the shooting up of some kind of
> eating house, and a diving from a window, then a holdup of the Deadwood
> coach and its destruction, then a killing of the guard, the driver being beaten
> and tied to a tree, then an arrest, then a breaking of the jail by the rougher
> element of the town, then a release of a prisoner, and, finally, a so-called
> desperate fight to hold up the stage, then an attempt to escape, and, finally,
> a man plunges 1,000 feet to his death on the rocks.[17]

Based on this summary, Taylor noted that the film viewer's "chief source of
interest must be the repeated shooting at or of one man by another" and that
such films might actually instigate murder by stimulating the violent appetites
of the viewer. In language that might be written today, Taylor noted that "one
of the most conspicuous crimes today is indiscriminate shooting, the statistics

of which, we all know, are appalling." Films that present "to the imagination of the spectators constant scenes of shooting" should not be exhibited unless it can be shown that they are plainly harmless. The judge clearly had his doubts that such a case could be made, indicating that "where 'gun-play,' or the shooting of human beings, is the essence of the play and does not pertain to the necessities of war, nor to the preservation of law and order, is for personal spite or revenge, and involves taking the law into one's own hands, and thus becomes a murder, the picture may be said to be immoral; it inculcates murder."[18]

In the early 1920s, when Taylor wrote his opinion, six states and more than two hundred municipalities had censor boards in operation. The regional boards presented financial and distribution headaches for the industry because films had to be submitted separately to each of them, and they typically requested lists of trims that varied from region to region. The studios had to transport films to and from the boards—or, in cases where a board did not have projection facilities, to and from an exhibition location that board members could attend—and see to it that each print was cut according to a given board's specifications. The material inconveniences this arrangement imposed on the industry incited its willingness to fight the forces of censorship and also to confront the regional boards when they contemplated making extensive trims to a film.

What were the quantitative dimensions of state and municipal censorship? How many films were affected? Systematic and reliable figures are hard to come by, and conflicting accounts exist about the extent of censored material. Richard Randall reports that from 1932 to 1952, the New York Motion Picture Division examined 33,084 films, of which eight percent were approved with trims being requested.[19] Between 1922 and 1958, Virginia examined 49,592 films and requested changes in five percent of these. By contrast with these seemingly low figures, a study published in 1930 by filmmaker Pare Lorentz and Morris Ernst compiled figures on the number of cuts ordered by state censor boards in New York, Pennsylvania, Maryland, Kansas, Virginia, and Ohio in 1928. According to Lorentz and Ernst, out of 579 features reviewed that year, only 42 were passed uncut.[20]

Whatever the actual magnitude of censor action, the *symbolic* dimension of this threat was great. The censor boards represented a force outside of the industry that regulated the content of American film, and as long as the Mutual decision was the law of the land, the industry would not be the arbiter of its own work. It had to acknowledge the indirect, and sometimes quite direct, participation of regional censorship in the production of films. It had to be responsive to the grassroots anti-film pressures that had led to the inception of the regional boards.

Hollywood Creates the Production Code

To protect itself from this pressure and to intercede with the boards, the industry formed a trade group—the Motion Picture Producers and Distributors of America (MPPDA)—in 1922 and appointed former Postmaster General Will Hays at its head. Hays had the public mandate of cleaning up the industry's films. In 1924, Hays introduced "The Formula," a set of guidelines that filmmakers were asked to observe in order to tame the ire of censors and public pressure groups and a request that studios submit synopses of literary properties that they were thinking of adapting to the screen. This provision anticipated the subsequent policy of script vetting by the Production Code Administration.

In 1927, Hays created the Studio Relations Committee (SRC), with Jason Joy at its head. This agency represented the industry before regional censor boards and also functioned as an intermediary between Hays's reform policies and the studio infrastructure. The SRC studied the kinds of deletions typically made by regional censors and compiled a list of the most common. These data then became the "Don'ts and Be Carefuls," which Hays unveiled in 1927—a list of eleven topics off-limits to filmmaking and twenty-five additional subjects that required great care in order to be shown on-screen. The "Don'ts and Be Carefuls" were the forerunner of the Production Code and, in fact, were subsequently incorporated into the Code as examples of specific applications of the Code's general principles.

Not a single one of the eleven prohibited areas in the "Don'ts and Be Carefuls" deals with violence of any kind. They cover such things as profanity, nudity, the drug trade, prostitution, miscegenation, and ridicule of the clergy. Violence does appear in connection with the longer list of twenty-five subjects requiring careful attention. Specified items include the use of firearms, third-degree methods, "brutality and possible gruesomeness," hangings and electrocutions, cruelty to children or animals, branding of people or animals, rape, and murder. Thus, no aspect of violence was deemed sufficiently disturbing or objectionable to ban entirely from the screen, as had been done with profanity, prostitution, and the drug trade. Filmmakers instead were asked to be careful in their depictions of violent behavior. Like the subsequent Production Code, the "Don'ts and Be Carefuls" explicitly accept not just the place of violence in motion picture entertainment, but also a broad spectrum of imaginable violent behaviors from which no single behavior was deemed reprehensible enough to exclude.

The industry apparently did not consider movie violence to be a content area requiring special prohibitions. How can that be, it is justifiable to wonder, given the censorship activity that surrounded crime films and Westerns? Don't the reactions to pictures like *The James Boys, The Indian Way,* and *The Deadwood Coach* demonstrate that violence was a trouble spot for the industry? They certainly do, but in most instances the violence in question was entangled with categories of behavior that were considered morally inappropriate for film to portray: theft, outlawry, disrespect for law and order. The behavior of criminals on-screen furnished viewers with poor role models. Issues of violence were involved in this screen behavior, but it was the behavior that frequently was seen as being at the root of the social problem posed by cinema. The *gangsters* had the machine guns and the charisma, not the police, and the industry would try to solve this problem in the 1930s by putting federal agents with machine guns at the center of crime stories. The G-man pictures were violent, but the violence was acceptable in behavioral terms because it was force wielded by agents of law and order.

The "Don'ts and Be Carefuls" failed to constrain censor action and grassroots opposition to the movies. By the latter 1920s, Catholic groups were replacing cinema's Protestant opponents, whose opposition to the medium had been so decisive during its first two decades of existence. Catholic officials were willing to work with the industry to achieve reform and proposed a solution that would have enduring efficacy. This solution was the Production Code. Martin Quigley, a lay Catholic and publisher of a film industry trade journal, felt that outside censorship could be defeated if the industry would essentially suppress censurable material from its films during production. To the extent that this could be accomplished the regional censors would have no work to do, and in the meantime, films could come closer to exemplifying the moral standards that Catholics could endorse. His ideas conformed to Hays's own conviction that a more rigorous practice of self-regulation was needed than what the "Don'ts and Be Carefuls" had provided. In cooperation with Quigley and Hays, Father Daniel Lord, a university dramatics professor, drafted the document that became the Production Code. It welded motion picture content to Catholic philosophy and the conviction that art should instill a voice for morality in its audience. The result was a document that enshrined the ideals of family and marriage, religion and country and abhorred behaviors that were sinful to the religious mind. These included adultery, sexual relations outside of marriage, abortion, homosexuality, the drug traffic, and prostitution. All of these topics would be taboo areas under the Code and were generally suppressed from the screen during the tenure of the Production Code Administration. As Gregory Black writes, regarding the Catholic philosophy within the Code, entertainment films "should reinforce religious teachings that deviant behavior, whether criminal or sexual, cost violators the love and comforts of home, the intimacy of family, the solace of religion, and the protection of law. Films should be twentieth-century morality plays that illustrated proper behavior to the masses."[21]

The industry adopted the Code in 1930, but filmmakers would never wholly subscribe to such a restrictive philosophy, and the Studio Relations Committee found great difficulty in getting filmmakers to work within the Code. As a result, the great change in motion picture content, anticipated by the drafters of the Code, failed to occur. Disappointed, in 1933 Father Lord broke with the MPPDA, which had retained him as a special consultant. That same year the Payne Fund Studies were published, a nine-volume social scientific investigation of the influence of films on young viewers. While the authors of the studies reached relatively qualified conclusions about the influence of films, a best-selling summary of the work presented the findings in more inflammatory terms. Titled *Our Movie-Made Children,* the book's author argued that Hollywood films were producing a generation of juvenile delinquents, drawn to sex and crime. As Ruth Vasey notes, "the industry's main public relations problem in the twenties and thirties was the widespread conviction that children would be 'coached' in sophisticated, violent or antisocial behavior through their attendance at motion pictures."[22]

Disappointed at Hollywood's output during the first years of the Production Code, national Catholic organizations threatened a blacklist and boycott of the movies and in 1934 formed the Legion of Decency, which would screen and rate films for Catholic viewers. The objective was to spotlight problem films and pressure the industry to curb their production by threatening it with the loss of the Catholic audience, twenty million strong. The creation of the Legion of Decency was a key factor that prodded the industry to form the Production Code Administration in the same year as a means of "enforcing" the Production Code.

Joseph Breen, an Irish Catholic who had been involved in the Quigley-Lord discussion and drafting of the Code, was appointed to head the PCA. In the PCA, the industry had a mechanism to enforce the Code, one that remained in operation for thirty-four years. As I discuss in the next chapter, the prevailing view of the so-called "Breen Office" has seen it as a rigid and repressive agency. Jonathan Munby, for example, writes that the PCA had an "essentially prohibitive character."[23] Gregory Black describes Breen as "an extreme anti-Semite" who was opposed to movie portraits of divorce and birth control.[24] Black's description carries the implication that the PCA itself reflected this rigidity and intolerance and maintained tight control over movie content during the years of its peak power. Indeed, Black writes that in the late 1930s, the PCA was reviewing one to three thousand scripts per year, and that "PCA views prevailed in all cases."[25] J. David Slocum paints a similar portrait, writing that "the Code succeeded in circumscribing images of violence."[26]

This view of an all-powerful Code, and agency to back it up, tends to be the received wisdom on the subject. I'll be offering a rather different view. In the next chapter, I will suggest that the relations between the PCA, filmmakers, and studios were actually more fluid and open to compromise. While prohibitions on certain kinds of content—abortion or homosexuality, for example—may have been relatively firm, it was definitely not the case with film violence. With regard to depictions of violent behavior, under no circumstances is it true that PCA views "prevailed in all cases." In fact, the PCA seemed always to have had great difficulty in restraining filmmakers from intensifying their depictions of violence.

TYPES OF VIOLENCE TARGETED BY CENSORS

The PCA's efforts to regulate screen content built on the record of censorship established at the state and municipal level. As I mentioned previously, data from this record were incorporated into the Code, and the motion picture case files in the PCA archive in Los Angeles demonstrate a strong continuity between those aspects of violence that concerned the PCA and those that drew the ire of regional censors in the years preceding the Code. The regulation of film violence at the regional level before 1930, and its regulation by the industry after 1930, focuses on similar issues involving weapons, the type and nature of the assault, and depictions of suffering or pain. Because I give these issues detailed attention in the next chapters from the standpoint of industry self-regulation, it will be helpful here to indicate some parameters of the regional regulation of screen violence.

The New York market was a critical one for the industry, and, as a result, the New York board was especially comprehensive in the number of films that it screened for licensing. As Richard Randall writes, "of the 1,000–1,300 films released in the United States in any given year, probably all but fifty or fewer were examined by the New York Division of Motion Pictures."[27] The following examples of censored violence derive from the board's eliminations reports for the years 1927–1928 and provide a sampling of the kinds of violent screen content that repeatedly drew censor activity.[28] Guns were a great problem. Their mere depiction on-screen was the source of much censor activity, even if the weapons were not being fired. Merely pointing a gun at the camera was often sufficient to provoke a censor board's request that the scene be trimmed.

1. During the silent era, censors routinely cut imagery of characters flourishing guns. *The Great Train Robbery* famously concludes with this shot of a bandit pointing his gun at the camera. Though the film was released before the advent of regional censorship, this kind of image was often targeted. With its inception in 1934, the PCA inherited the gun problem.

For example, the New York board requested that "all views of gun pointed directly at camera" be eliminated from *Vanishing Trails #14* (Canyon, 1928), *Vanishing Trails #11* (New Cal, 1928), *Law of Fear* (F.B.O., 1928), *Partners in Crime* (Paramount, 1928), *Chicago after Midnight* (F.B.O., 1928), *Chinese Parrot* (1927), *Desperate Courage* (1927), *The Boss of the Rustler Roost* (1927), *Apache Raider* (1928) and numerous other films. In each of these cases, the board specified that it was the flourishing of a firearm—pointing it at the camera—that was the objectionable component in the scenes.

The New York board also commonly deleted action that showed guns being pointed at or into the body of another character. *The Night Flier* (De Mille, 1928) elicited the request to "eliminate close views of guns pressed against Jimmy's side and stomach, while men force him to drink in saloon." In *Desperate Courage* (Action, 1927), "in scene where girl is confined in room, eliminate view of Wally with gun pressed against back of 'the Dude.'"[29] *Blood Will Tell* (Fox, 1927) lost a shot of a gun being discharged and "all views of Cowan holding gun pressed against Buck's stomach."[30] *Back to Liberty* (Excellent, 1927) had to lose "all views of Devan, with gun pressed against Gabler's side."[31] On *Shootin' Irons* (Paramount, 1927), the board ordered the elimination of "close views of Pan with gun pressed against Hardman's body before and after fight."[32] Other films with this type of deletion included *The Irresistible Lover* (Universal, 1927), *Naughty* (Chadwick, 1927), *Black Jack* (Fox, 1927), *Partners in Crime* (Paramount, 1927), and *Vanishing Trails #9* (Canyon, 1928).

Later, the PCA would spend much time dealing with the display of guns by criminals, and its problems in that regard are clearly presaged by the censor board activity surrounding the display of firearms in the pre-Code era. The PCA was also plagued with the problem posed by machine guns in crime pictures—a problem that shows up previously in the regional censor reports. From *The Drag Net* (Paramount, 1928), the New York board ordered the elimination of "two views of Trent standing in shadow with machine gun in action, firing directly at café owner, killing him."[33] From *The Cop* (De Mille, 1928), the filmmakers were ordered to "eliminate view of crook adjusting machine gun, in taxi. Eliminate view of crook examining and setting machine gun, in hotel room."[34] From *City Gone Wild* (Paramount, 1927), they were told to "eliminate all near views of gun fire and machine-gun fire in battle of crooks on city's thoroughfare."[35]

The PCA would struggle with depictions of criminals shooting police and law-enforcement agents and would eventually ban them from pictures entirely. In this regard, they inherited an existing problem, as the New York board's reports demonstrate. From *Mark of the Frog #1* (Pathé, 1928), the filmmakers were directed to "eliminate all direct shots fired at police by thugs."[36] From *The Cop* (De Mille, 1928), the board asked them to "eliminate views of 'Scar' deliberately shooting at Policeman Coughlin, lying wounded on sidewalk. Eliminate views of crook hitting policeman Smith on head three times with gat."[37] From *City Gone Wild*, the order was to "eliminate scene of hand with gun through curtain, firing directly at District Attorney, killing him."[38]

While a provision was written into the Production Code governing the display of guns, the PCA closely scrutinized other types of weapons and was especially concerned with bladed instruments, such as knives and spears. As we will see, the PCA seemed to feel that the potential for brutality or gruesomeness—terms that were foundational concepts in its regulation of violence—was greater with this category of weapon than with guns. Some interesting empirical work validates this perception. A British study looked at the effects of genre and type of weapon on viewers' perceptions of film violence and found that viewers rated stabbings as more disturbing than shootings. "Shootings were perceived as significantly the most violent portrayals, but stabbings as significantly the most frightening and personally disturbing."[39] These overall results were modified by genre, with stabbings being seen as the most violent and disturbing in contemporary crime dramas and somewhat less so in Westerns. When we examine in the next chapters the PCA's efforts to restrict violence committed with knives or spears, it will be helpful to recall this empirical evidence that the type of weapon employed can have a significant impact on a viewer's perception of the overall level of violence on-screen and its emotional tone. Otherwise, the PCA's efforts might seem eccentric or overly concerned with odd details when, in fact, the agency was responding to a real phenomenological difference in the range of violent behaviors—as were, apparently, the regional censors in the years before the Code.

Regional censors did not like violence involving knives and other categories of bladed weapons. From *Vanishing Trails #14*, the New York board ordered the elimination of "all views of Mexican menacing girl who is tied and bound to tree, with knife—this includes scenes of Mexican throwing knife at girl. Eliminate view of Mexican where knife is shown distinctly sticking in his back."[40] From *Black Ace* (Maloney, 1928), the directive was to "eliminate close views of knife in Kaul's hand pressed against his breast in fight."[41] From *Buckskin Days* (Universal, 1928), at issue was the scene "where Indian holds knife over man in fight, including one view of knife pressed against throat of man."[42] In *The Triumph of a Rat* (Bradford, 1927), the board required the elimination of "all close views of knife in fight between Pierre and gangleader, leaving flash of blood on Pierre's breast."[43] From *The Masked Menace* (Pathé, 1927), the report directed the filmmakers to "eliminate all distinct views of knife when Job attacks Stillface after killing cat."[44] The board eliminated all views of a knife being thrown in *Andy Nose His Onions* (Universal, 1927) and of stabbings in *The Betrayer* (U.C.I., 1927) and *The Vampire* (U.C.I., 1927).

Other kinds of violent behavior spawned censor action because of the amount of brutality that was involved. Whippings, for example, were, prima facie, instances of sadism. Such scenes antagonized censors in the pre-Code period, and the PCA struggled with depictions of whipping as late as the early 1960s. From *The Haunted Ship* (1928), the New York board directed the elimination of "all views of skipper lashing boy with whip where lash touches flesh."[45] From *The Gaucho* (United Artists, 1928), filmmakers were told to "shorten prolonged view of Padre and girl, bound together on scaffold, after whips are brandished."[46] From *Within Prison Walls* (Portsmouth, 1928), the directive was to "eliminate scene showing prisoner being flogged."[47] From *Winds of the Pampas* (Superlative, 1927), filmmakers were ordered to "eliminate view of Mariquita actually striking her Father in face with whip."[48] Similar scenes to these were eliminated from *Born to Battle* (Cody, 1927), *The Broken*

Mask (Schlark, 1928), *Honor Bound* (Fox, 1928), *The Cossacks* (MGM, 1928), and *Hawk of the Hills #8* (Pathé, 1927).

Other forms of proscribed violence, carried over into the sound era and that the PCA regularly prohibited, included kicking and choking. The New York board, for example, ordered filmmakers to "eliminate all scenes of choking in fight between Le Busard and Ranger" from *Red Riders of Canada* (F.B.O., 1928).[49] From *Heroes in Blue* (Rayart, 1927), they were told to "eliminate view of Garrett choking old man, on floor in hallway."[50] Choking scenes were cut from *Man without a Face #10* (Pathé, 1927), *Roaring Broncs* (Action, 1927) and *Law of the Range* (MGM, 1928). The PCA was quite consistent in its efforts to remove kicking and choking actions from Hollywood fight scenes, and the agency seemed to share the conviction of the regional censors that such tactics were an unfair and possibly sadistic form of assault.

More extreme forms of violence included branding of people or animals with a hot iron, torture, and electrocution. A branding scene, for example, was removed from *Death Signal* (1928) and torture with a burning sword was cut from *The Cossacks*. "Eliminate scene where red hot sword is drawn across Altaman's eyes. Eliminate all views showing hot coals being placed in victim's hands. Eliminate views showing eyes being burned out by red hot sword."[51] Scenes showing prisoners walking toward, standing beside, or sitting in an electric chair were cut from *The Girl from Chicago* (Warner Bros., 1927), *Within Prison Walls* (Portsmouth, 1928), *Come to My House* (Fox, 1927), *Mark of the Frog #9* and *#10* (Pathé, 1928), and *The Hawk's Nest* (First National, 1928).

An important component of all forms of physical violence on the screen is the behavior of the victim—specifically, whether or not the victim is shown as suffering pain or anguish. In the last chapter of this book, I review evidence demonstrating an overwhelming trend in contemporary film and television of showing pain-free violence, in which there is no depiction of a suffering victim and therefore, in this regard, no suggestion that violence has bodily and emotional consequences. This property of contemporary screen violence, however, has deep roots in American cinema. As we will see in the next chapter, the PCA worked to suppress from the screen extended depictions of pain and suffering, and in doing so, it was following the lead of regional censors who removed such scenes from the films that they reviewed. Possibly, the censors and the PCA felt that expressions of pain would be disturbing for viewers and would be in poor taste and therefore should be suppressed. If so, they were acting with the best of intentions, but they wound up helping to instigate a trend toward whitewashed violence—toward a screen violence that provided pleasant entertainment rather than an honest depiction of the consequences of fights and shootings.

The New York board cut an extended whipping scene from *The Haunted Ship* (1927) in which a boy is strung up by his arms and whipped, then thrown into a cell below deck. The board was especially directive with regard to images that depicted the victim's response to this ordeal. "Eliminate all views of boy strung up with arms over head, excepting views in connection with subtitles; where no suffering is shown."[52] It also ordered the elimination of "views of boy's agonized face as skipper takes whip and approaches him" and "view of boy sinking into unconsciousness." Similar details of pain were removed from a whipping scene in *Winds of the Pampas* (1927). "In scene where Don Emmelio lashes Rafael, eliminate all views where whip is shown wrapping around face and body of Rafael and all views of Rafael's agonized face with blood streaming down it and views of him biting flesh on his arms in agony."[53] Compared with this detailed elimination order, the response to *The Road to Romance* (1927) was terse indeed: "Eliminate that part of the pirate in pain."[54]

In closing this profile of violence censorship by the New York board, I should mention that another large category of deletions involved scenes depicting details of crime, such as lighting dynamite fuses or breaking into safes. Examples include, from *His Day Off* (1927), the elimination of "all views of holdup of couple in car and all views of thieves taking jewelry from man's coat pockets and taking jewelry from woman" and, from *Dummies* (1927), "view of gangster actually lighting fuse on can of dynamite."[55] These eliminations do not involve violence per se, but rather depictions of criminality that the board deemed to be unnecessarily detailed and potentially influential on impressionable viewers. The PCA followed suit, and in its years of operation worked to apply sections of the Production Code that prohibited scenes detailing the methods of crime.

As these examples demonstrate, local censorship of screen violence showed clear patterns. Censor boards eliminated scenes in which guns were flourished on-screen (pointing at the camera was flourish enough), especially when crooks and gangsters used guns and when police were targets of violence. Violence that smacked of sadism—fights that involved choking or kicking—was actionable, as well as extreme forms of torture and scenes showing the response of the victims of violence. These patterns of censorship suggested clear policy guidelines. The Studio Relations Committee, and subsequently the Production Code Administration, would replicate the broad outlines of this approach to regulating screen violence and would be attentive to both the amount and the character of the mayhem in Hollywood movies.

But the SRC and the PCA were not dupes of the regional censors, nor did they see themselves as operating to censor films. They were there to serve the industry, not the censors. This divergence of mission—the censors were to be placated but the industry was to be protected and film production facilitated—helped to create a set of ongoing ambiguities and conflicts within the institution of the PCA and its relationship to the filmmakers whose work it evaluated. Moreover, filmmakers were not silent or passive partners in the work of managing screen violence. From the beginning of the sound era, and the start of the SRC/PCA's operation, filmmakers were drawn to screen violence. Its dynamics fascinated them, especially when transformed into the plastic properties of cinema. They learned quickly how to use lighting, editing, and the choreography of motion to transfigure violence and to extend and intensify its presence on-screen.

In this regard, they were racing ahead of the Production Code and the regional censor boards. These were still focused on the categories of behavior, while the filmmakers were rapidly learning how to amplify the stylistic coordinates of screen violence. On the one hand there were a character's actions, which were scripted and described verbally in negotiation with the PCA; on the other hand there was style, which arose during the actual making of the film. The PCA's operating procedures ensured that it would always be more sensitive to content—and better equipped to intervene—than it could in response to style. Filmmakers learned to elaborate the stylistic expression of violent character behavior partially as a means of getting around PCA proscriptions. In this, the filmmakers of classical Hollywood were truly the forebears of our contemporary cineastes of ultraviolence.

We are not yet in a position to see this. It will take several chapters to demonstrate this relationship. But, as we now turn to an extended examination of the PCA's negotiations with filmmakers over screen violence, it is essential to realize that the agency presided over a fissured community and that its efforts to hold the line on screen violence were doomed. Filmmakers would be pushing in the other direction, and it was only a matter of time before a changing culture, the extension of free speech protection to cinema, and a narrowing of the scope of legalized censorship would permit them to burst the boundaries that had restrained their filmmaking. The next two chapters examine these boundaries, and chapter four examines the breaking of those bonds. The PCA held a losing hand. It didn't look that way in 1930 or 1934, but in another thirty-four years the trajectory of screen violence was clear and unmistakable and it had led inexorably toward the graphic ultraviolence of our own period.

2
Cruelty, Sadism, and the Horror Film

Violence, in our contemporary sense of the term, does not exist in Hollywood cinema before the late 1960s. Signaled by *Bonnie and Clyde* in 1967 and the inauguration of the Code and Rating Administration's G-M-R-X scheme for rating film content in 1968, the new film violence that emerged in these years differed from the shootings, beatings, and other mayhem in the films of classical Hollywood because it was far more graphic. This new level of explicitness helped to put motion picture violence, as an idea and a topic, on the nation's agenda and gave it a visibility it had not previously possessed. Prior to that time, "violence" did not exist as a "thing-in-itself," perceived as an irreducible feature of cinema irrespective of considerations such as genre or the dramatic content of a given scene. There are, for example, no sections of Hollywood's Production Code that deal with what we now call "violence." Indeed, the word itself does not appear in the Code or its numerous revisions over the years.

The first section of the 1930 Code, General Principles, lists the fundamental moral and artistic obligations of acceptable screen entertainment, which are, generally, to uphold correct standards of life, provide moral uplift, and avoid inflaming unruly passions. (The Production Code appears in Appendix B.) The abstractions of this first section are made more specific with reference to film content in the second section, the Working Principles. Here, the Code makes reference to "crime," "wrong-doing," "criminal," and "evil" and cautions that films should not enlist audience sympathy for any of these elements of a story. The section on Principles of Plot makes reference to "murder," "cruelty," "brutality," and "repellent crimes" and cautions filmmakers not to give these such attention as to make viewers "accustomed" to them. The subsection on Plot Material refers to "brutal killings," which are not to be shown in detail; "revenge killings," which are not to be shown as justified; "criminals," who should not be heroized; and "methods of committing crime," which should not be dwelt upon lest some viewers learn techniques of law-breaking.

An addendum to the 1930 Code dealt with specific kinds of scenes and situations that were prohibited or were to be carefully regulated. Called "Particular Applications of the Code," this section evolved from the list of "Don'ts and Be Carefuls," assembled by Will Hays and the Studio Relations Committee (SRC) in 1927. According to Production Code Administration (PCA) staff member and, and later the organization's chief, Geoffrey Shurlock, the list was created by the staff of the Studio Relations Committee based on their experiences dealing with local censor boards. SRC head Jason Joy dealt with censors who had rejected a film or were threatening it with excessive cuts. "If there was trouble in Pennsylvania with an MGM picture, he was expected to go there . . . and try to get the picture out of hock. And the items that he found that were most commonly objected to, and were deleted [became the Don'ts and Be Carefuls]."[1] The SRC saw that particular kinds of material would tend to run into censor trouble on a regular basis. (The SRC and its successor, the PCA, maintained records of the cuts ordered by U.S. and overseas censors. These records enabled them to perceive the patterns that linked responses among the regional censor boards.) "These people had to deal with censor boards and knew where a picture got into trouble with, let's say, the Pennsylvania Censor Boards, who maybe hated scenes of trains being dynamited and regularly cut them out."[2] Based on this experience with local censors, the "Particular Applications" that were not to be shown explicitly on-screen or in detail included "brutal killings," "theft," "robbery," "safe-cracking," "dynamiting of trains, mines, buildings," "arson," and "the use of firearms."

Over the years, the PCA passed periodic amendments to the Code that sought to tighten some of its provisions (and, alternatively, in the 1950s, to loosen them). In the wake of wide-scale censor activity and a public outcry over the early 1930s cycle of horror pictures, the PCA passed an amendment dealing with "Brutality, Horror, and Gruesomeness," advising filmmakers that "scenes of excessive brutality and gruesomeness must be cut to an absolute minimum." In the wake of widespread public opposition to the industry's gangster pictures, in 1938 the PCA passed an amendment dealing with "Special Regulations on Crime." It prohibited the kind of large-scale killing typically found in these films: "Actions suggestive of wholesale slaughter of human beings . . . will not be allowed." It prohibited "excessive brutality," banned depictions of suicide (a subsequent revision permitted it when absolutely necessary to the story), held that depictions of murder be kept to a minimum, prohibited the display (including off-screen sound effects) of machine guns and other illegal weapons in the hands of criminals, prohibited "the flaunting of weapons by gangsters" and outlawed scenes showing the death of police or other law enforcement officers at the hands of criminals. In the wake of the Lindbergh case, the PCA prohibited depictions of kidnapping as the main theme of a film, when a child is involved or when the kidnappers profit from the crime or go unpunished.

Thus, there is abundant material in the Code and its amendments dealing with crime, criminals, murder, weapons, and brutality, but there is nothing on "violence," a category that does not exist in the Code. One might object, however, and claim that violence is indeed covered. If it is not named directly, the Code's terminology and particular applications nevertheless point to it. After all, cruelty, brutality, murder, and machine-gun killings are quite clearly violent acts, and plenty of movies over the years have shown these. The Code has a lot to say about such acts, and the PCA was extremely attentive to their depiction in classical Hollywood film because censor boards routinely cut this material. Moreover, viewers and representatives of public organizations (e.g., church groups and parent–teacher associations) regularly sent protest letters to the PCA about such material in films that were playing on neighborhood screens.

But more than mere terminology is at work here. The Code does not refer to "violence" because the term and the idea were not part of industry and public discourse as they are today. One reason for this is that filmmakers had not yet begun the intensive stylistic elaboration of violence that would become normative beginning in the late 1960s. As I will point out later, it is this amplification of style that has worked to define violence for the modern sensibility. By contrast, the violence in classical Hollywood film is inscribed within categories of reference that are deemed, in the views of the period, to be objectionable—guns in the hands of criminals, gruesome experiments conducted by mad scientists, brutal killings carried out by monsters or mobsters. Protests against the violence in classical Hollywood pictures centered on these referents—gangsters and ghouls, criminals, law-breakers, monsters, and the *crimes* they perpetrated. Crime and horror films, for example, were routinely attacked because of the referential frame within which the violence occurred. Protesters considered those frames to be unhealthy and unwholesome and to undermine social values and the public order. In filing a complaint with Warner Bros. about the violence and horror in *Mystery of the Wax Museum* (1933), for example, the Ohio Department of Film Censorship focused on the referents that it considered to be unhealthy: arson, drugs, and the provision of information about how a poison works. Department director B. O. Skinner wrote that the film "contains so many elements we find objectionable, as setting fire to the museum to obtain insurance, naming a poison and telling how it could be taken to produce death, using of dope and also the general theme of horror. I feel it would be much better for all of us if the production of this type of film would be discontinued."[3]

STYLISTIC AND BEHAVIORAL COMPONENTS OF SCREEN VIOLENCE

Violence in classical Hollywood film was less the issue than the behaviors to which it was attached and the moral example that these provided to viewers. Violent crime films were bad because criminals provided poor role models. The PCA behaved accordingly. By contrast, the violence that occurred in war films or Westerns was often recuperated by the genre. It did not seem as subversive as the violence in crime or horror pictures. It was susceptible to moralistic rationalization (e.g., the good guys vs. the bad guys, war is hell), which enabled it to be depicted as a form of entertainment to which few might object.

The violence in Westerns and war films is typically presented as a kind of righteous violence, carried out by heroes of strong moral purpose rather than the dubious role models supplied by gangsters and other criminals or monsters. Accordingly, the PCA was relatively more permissive and less worried about the shootings or killings that occurred in these genres. The combat films produced during World War II, for example, became a vital part of the home front, helping to rally the public around the moral cause of fighting the Germans and Japanese. As we will see in chapter four, the violence in many of these films was more sustained, graphic, and brutal than what would be tolerated in a gangster film. The righteousness of Western and war violence, and the moral appeal of the heroes who enacted it, helped to make it relatively safe and unobjectionable compared to the "problem" genres of crime and horror.

Reflecting these ideas, the PCA felt that some genres required less scrutiny than others and acted on this conviction when script assignments were made. PCA staff member Albert Van Schmus pointed out that scripts for problem pictures (e.g., crime films) were given for evaluation to staff members who were known to be careful and tough readers, whereas musicals or Westerns were typically assigned to readers known to be less stringent and less assertive in dealing with filmmakers and studio liaisons.[4] The PCA's internal documents also reflect this orientation, for example, in the content analysis that it compiled for each film. The PCA analyzed the content of each film it passed for exhibition and recorded the quantity and types of violent acts (among many other categories of nonviolent content) found in each picture. The notations on the analysis chart for the World War II picture *Objective, Burma!* (1945), an action blockbuster starring Errol Flynn, list the number of killings simply as "many" and, under the heading "other violence," simply "war."[5] The generic rationalization—war is hell—that appears on the analysis chart for *The Dirty Dozen* (1967) produces some unintentional comedy because of its juxtaposition with graphically violent content. The chart lists as forms of violence in the picture "shooting, knifing, fistfight, war" and, under "other," "German women and officers burned alive (war is hell)."[6] The "war is hell" descriptor excuses the brutality of the action.

This relative tolerance for violence within a frame of reference supplied by war was longstanding. In 1929 SRC head Jason Joy wrote to Universal studio's Carl Laemmle, Jr. regarding potential censor problems with Universal's anticipated production of the World War I drama *All Quiet on the Western Front* (1930), and remarked that the story's "preachment against war" would "make it possible for you to treat the various episodes which occur in the book with a boldness and truthfulness which I think you would be unwise to employ in a story of less merit."[7] In 1968, the Code and Rating Administration (CARA), which had replaced the PCA, was scrambling to formulate a policy statement on film violence, in preparation for MPAA president Jack Valenti's testimony before the National Commission on the Causes and Prevention of Violence (in 1947, the MPPDA had changed its name to the Motion Picture Association of America). Internal discussion, reflected in memos and notes, sought to differentiate "personalized" from "impersonal" forms of violence, with the latter being more acceptable and held to relatively less scrutiny and a looser standard. War films were cited as a preeminent example of impersonal violence: "Impersonal violence has traditionally been accepted as acceptable screen fare for audiences generally. War films have always fallen into this category. . . . Even the dreadful slaughter of the cavalry charge of the Light Brigade can be taken in stride. It would therefore be permissible for such films to be classified for general audience consumption."[8]

Like censor boards, citizens groups, and other critics of the film industry, the PCA tied violence to behavior. This is why the word "violence" does not appear in the Code. What does appear are lists of numerous referential categories where violence was impermissible, or types of violent *acts* forbidden to be depicted or for which depiction must be held to a minimum level of detail. What so strongly differentiates classical Hollywood under the Production Code from American film today is the relative degree of emphasis given to referentiality on the one hand, and to style on the other. In classical Hollywood, the stylistic means for representing violence were held to a minimum; in film today, these have expanded tremendously.

Screen violence is the stylistic encoding of a referential act. Thus, one can speak about the act, the behavior, the referent, and one can speak about the stylistic encoding. If we approach the difference between the eras in terms of these two dimensions, we could graph the relationship in ways that would picture the change that has occurred. The referential component of violence—the behavior that is depicted—is the x-axis, while its cinematic treatment—the stylistic design—is the y-axis. In classical Hollywood cinema, the x-axis is more extended than the y-axis. This is because Hollywood filmmakers could depict a relatively broad range of violent acts including beatings, shootings, hanging, knifing, and so on.

The y-axis registers what I will call *stylistic amplitude*, and its scale in classical Hollywood was not comparable to the x-axis. Amplitude is a function of two elements—graphicness and duration. The more graphic a violent act, the more detailed its depiction and the greater its stylistic amplitude becomes. The degree of graphicness is directly related to film technique. In many Hollywood movies, a character is shot and simply falls over or sinks out of the frame. This is an example of what, later in the book, I call the clutch-and-fall aesthetic; it has minimal stylistic amplitude. Cinematically, little occurs that could not be portrayed on the stage. By contrast, if the actor is squibbed to show the bullet strike or reacts with convulsions and spasmodic movements, or the compositional design of the frame works to emphasize the shooting and its point of impact, then the stylistic amplitude of the violence has increased. Duration, the other component of amplitude, is also a function of cinema technique. The more camera set-ups that a filmmaker uses to convey a violent act and incorporates into the editing, the more extended the screen time of that violence. If a filmmaker shoots a violent act with multiple cameras and edits among the footage captured by those cameras to provide a series of views on the violence, its screen duration—and stylistic amplitude—have expanded. Alternatively, within one camera set-up, a shooting might simply go on and on, with obvious consequences for its screen duration.

The relationship of these dimensions—behavior and stylistic amplitude—changes greatly after the Production Code is abolished. Both the x- and y-axis have expanded, and there is no longer such a discrepancy between the two. The behavioral axis expands because filmmakers since 1968 can show things that earlier directors could not. In *Once Upon a Time in the West* (1968), for example, Sergio Leone can have a character gun down a little boy at point-blank range. Slasher films can picture mutilation and dismemberment, acts that were not possible to show in classical Hollywood. A severed head, still alive and guided by the arms of the body to which it was once attached, can rape a woman, as in *Re-Animator* (1985).

And it is not just that a greater range of violent acts can be depicted; they can be extended, prolonged, and detailed, using the stylistic tools of montage, slow motion, or graphic effects work. In American film after 1968, therefore, both axes expand, and because the *y*-axis now catches up to the *x*, the greatest rate of change occurs there. Films are more violent today not just because they can show more violent behaviors than before but also because their stylistic design makes those behaviors more insistent and emphatic.

In classical Hollywood, the referential component of violence (the *x*-axis) elicited tremendous concern and vigilance. In post-classical Hollywood, it is the styling of violence (the *y*-axis), the extension of violence in time and space to graphic effect, which has helped to fuel debates over the social effects of violent movies. "Violence" emerges as a thing-in-itself in the contemporary sensibility when and because the links to reference, which oriented the public and industry discourse of classical Hollywood, have been augmented by expansion in the stylistic domain. This domain, and its changes, is central to understanding the history of American screen violence.

An important set of questions now arises from this view of the history of screen violence. If the PCA worked to limit filmic expressions of violence, in what ways did it do so? What was the discourse about the range and character of the material that could be shown? How did the PCA negotiate with filmmakers about the nature of what they would be permitted to film? To what extent did the PCA engage issues of stylistic amplitude? More positively, what stylistic possibilities were available to filmmakers working in classical Hollywood? What, in other words, was the cinematic "language" or rhetoric of screen violence in that period? Finally, why did this rhetoric change when and as it did, in such a way as to demark post-sixties cinema from classical Hollywood?

OPERATION OF THE PRODUCTION CODE ADMINISTRATION

To begin, we must first understand how the PCA operated within the institutional settings of Hollywood. This will enable us to place the negotiations over screen violence in their proper context. As I noted in the previous chapter, the popular conception of the PCA sees it simply as a rigid in-house censor for the film industry. Thus, lawyer Alan Dershowitz calls the Code "a pervasive system of censorship, micro-managed by right-wing religious zealots with moralistic agendas."[9] Film scholars are somewhat divided. Gregory Black tends to emphasize the rigidity of Joseph Breen and the PCA, while Leonard Leff and Jerold Simmons suggest they "were less doctrinaire than historians and others have painted them."[10] Leff has pointed out that the PCA would intercede with censors on behalf of controversial films and might even, at times, work to facilitate the production of such films.[11]

As most people know, the objectives of the Code and the PCA were to regulate screen content in the troublesome areas of sex, religion and crime. The agency accomplished this by reviewing scripts submitted by member companies of the Motion Picture Producers and Distributors of America (MPPDA), the umbrella trade association composed of major and minor Hollywood studios. (Beginning in 1930, the Code was implemented by the Studio Relations Committee under Jason Joy. In 1934, the Studio Relations Committee became the PCA, headed by Joseph Breen. In 1954, Geoffrey Shurlock succeeded Breen as PCA head.) Staff members of the PCA provided detailed feedback about acceptable and unacceptable elements in the scripts to film producers, or to studio liaisons who then forwarded the information to the film's producer or director. Each script was read by at least two PCA staff members. After reading, they would confer to reach an agreement about whether the script as a whole was approvable under the Code and about whether particular scenes or lines of dialogue, as written, might constitute problems. Albert E. Van Schmus, who joined the PCA in 1949, recalled this process:

> There were usually two readers, and if those two readers felt they needed more opinion, they would ask for a couple more readers. You'd discuss there anything that might be a problem under the Code, as a group, and then come to a position, an agreement. Then one of the two first original readers would write a letter to the company, say that it either met the requirements of the Production Code or did not.[12]

These letters about the script material, authored by staff readers, would go out under Joseph Breen's signature, and they would go out quickly. (Breen did not write all of the letters on which his name appears, a fact that sometimes is minimized by the existing histories of the PCA, which routinely refer to the letters as Breen's correspondence. This tends to make him seem omnipresent and the agency merely an extension of him.) The turnaround time between the submission of a script, or revised script pages, and the response letters was often just a few days. The speed with which the PCA responded demonstrates its desire not to be a source of delay for film projects, impeding them unnecessarily.

This detail about the timing of the letters is significant because it contravenes the popular perception of the agency as a repressive force in the industry. The PCA did not operate to block film production, nor did it have its institutional identity invested in doing so. On the contrary, the agency saw itself as working for filmmakers. Van Schmus recalled that Shurlock would say, " 'we work for the production-distribution people.' "[13] In their oral histories, both Van Schmus and Shurlock took pains to differentiate the PCA from the regional censors outside of the industry. They did not regard the agency as just another censor. For Shurlock, the Code was not there to protect the public from being harmed by filmmakers but the reverse. "I have never felt the American public cannot take care of itself viz a viz [sic] any given movie. . . . I am protecting the industry from being harmed by outraged viewers."[14] The Motion Picture Association, Van Schmus said, "spent millions and millions of dollars fighting the censorship boards and getting them declared unconstitutional. We would fight the laws which created censor boards in various states, and spend a lot of money preventing further legislation, enforcing or re-enforcing those censor boards."[15] Breen's objective was "to knock off the censor boards. . . . He was there to solve the dilemma that the picturemakers had, which was critical."[16]

That dilemma—the regional censorship of motion pictures—threatened creative expression and imposed substantial operating costs on the film industry. These costs included the licensing fees paid to the regional censors to cover their expenses and those consumed by the logistical operations needed to route film prints to the censor boards, costs exacerbated when a board required that its seal be attached to every duplicate print appearing in a geographical area.[17] PCA staff member Jack Vizzard wrote that it cost the industry more than a quarter of a million dollars a year in fees toward the New York state censor board. Were the number of existing state and municipal censor boards to increase, he wrote with some hyperbole, "it is conceivable that a film would have to weather several hundred censor boards before it could be exhibited. The cost would be utterly fantastic."[18]

The promptness, then, with which the PCA gave filmmakers its feedback is a significant indicator of where its allegiances lay. The speed at which the letters were completed is especially impressive, given that staff members were reading multiple scripts and given the length and detail present in many of the letters. Each letter would begin with a general assessment of the overall acceptability, or lack thereof, of the script under the Code. The agency, for example, rejected an initial script for Fritz Lang's *The Big Heat* (1953) in these terms: "We have read the script dated January 20th, 1953, for your proposed production *The Big Heat*, and regret to advise that this basic story is in violation of the Production Code, and a motion picture based upon it could not be approved by us."[19]

When scripts were rejected, as in this instance, the door was *not* closed on a production. The letter would go on to specify the material in violation of the Code, and negotiations would begin about how to modify it. A week after this letter rejecting the script, PCA staff members Eugene Dougherty and Van Schmus went to Columbia Pictures and met with producer Robert Arthur, writer Sidney Boehm, and director Fritz Lang and reached an agreement about story modifications that allowed the filmmakers to find an acceptable path toward the screen representations they sought. Then, as now, negotiation—not fiat—was the lifeblood of Hollywood, and it was the operating procedure of the PCA. I will have more to say on this point in a moment.

Another and common variation of response letter would begin with a statement that the script met the provisions of the Production Code, but directed the recipient's attention to specific problem areas. A sometimes-lengthy listing of specific scenes and pages from the script would follow, identifying material containing objectionable action or dialogue and with suggestions about how to fix it. It was expected that the filming of a script would follow the PCA's script evaluation and recommendations, and the evaluation letters would always end with the qualification, "you understand, of course, that our final judgement will be based on the finished picture."

A screening and evaluation of the completed picture constituted the second point at which the PCA could intervene to regulate content. This checkpoint in the regulatory process—the screening—is sometimes given too much weight by commentators wanting to stress the power of the PCA; in fact, there were clear limits to the agency's authority at this end point in the process. A studio, for example, would not conform a negative to an edited workprint until the PCA had signed off on a production by granting a seal. Thus, the PCA screened films that were still in workprint form rather than prints struck from a cut negative. Because the negative still had to be cut, filmmakers were working on picture and sound elements past the point at which the PCA had given its clearance. The agency had to trust that its wishes would be followed. In many of its letters to studio liaisons granting a seal of approval, the PCA stipulated that a film had to go into release with picture and sound elements in the version that it saw in a screening. However, there was no way for the agency to verify this. As Van Schmus remarked, "one of the problems we always had was we could never police the theaters to see if the prints were actually exactly the same that we had given approval to. . . . It was a voluntary system of self-regulation. . . . we had to assume that they were being, well, honest, and putting out the films as we approved them."[20]

If there were still problem areas in the picture at the time of the screening, the PCA might request trims—but, in fact, this rarely happened. Altering picture and sound elements at this late point could be expensive and detrimental to the coherence and structure of a given film. For these reasons, the PCA was actually quite loathe to request such changes from filmmakers. Robert Vogel, who was the PCA liaison at MGM in the 1950s, described the screenings as a courtesy extended by the studios to the PCA and said that major changes in picture and sound were not made. "There was never a major matter by that time."[21] As Van Schmus noted, "most of it [i.e., problems] was taken care of at the script level."[22] The PCA's process of review and clearance was front-loaded; it was heavily weighted at the scripting stage as a strategy for avoiding problems in the finished film that could crop up at the time of screening. Accordingly, the PCA devoted its greatest scrutiny to the screenwriting stage of pre-production, as Van Schmus said, to "cure the problems before you get into the ghastly expense of dealing with a finished picture."[23] In other words, changes arising at the time of the final screening were minimal to nonexistent, and in this regard the screenings often did amount to a courtesy rather than a stringent mechanism of clearance.

When post-production trims were needed after the clearance screening, they tended to be small. MGM's grim World War II film *Bataan* (1943) contains some of era's most vivid and intense violence and was subjected to relatively extensive cutting by some state censor boards and by overseas censors. Yet in granting its certificate of approval, the PCA asked for only a modest trim in the finished picture: "This certificate is issued on the understanding that you have deleted the close-up bayonet scenes agreed upon by Mr. Rapf and Mr. Breen, over the long distance telephone."[24] Throughout PCA correspondence, the term "scene" is typically used to designate a "shot" as well as what would more properly be known as a scene. In this case, coupled with the qualifier "close-up," the term almost certainly refers to shots and not to scenes and thus requests only that several shots giving close views of bayoneting during the film's extended fight scenes be excised. Note also the "gentlemen's understanding" that prevails. The PCA granted its approval of the finished film *before* the requested cuts were made and trusted that the studio would make them. This was not an isolated case. Many letters granted certificate approval before specified cuts were made.

The James Cagney gangster film *White Heat* (1949) got its certificate of clearance from the PCA contingent on an audio trim, as an agency memo documented. "We asked [Warner Bros.] assurances, and received them, that the sound effects of the gun shooting in the final big battle be kept as they are in the print we saw this afternoon. We told him it would be a Code violation if the sound effects of an automatic gun were substituted for what was used in the print we saw, in the case of the guard's gun, which is picked up in the offices of the refinery."[25] The PCA's Regulations on Crime forbid depictions of automatic weapons in the hands of criminals, and this included even an audio reference.

Nicholas Ray's gangster film *Party Girl* (1958) was granted its certificate contingent on the understanding that "in the gang warfare montage, two changes are to be made: (a) the killing of the girl in the hotel hallway will be cut out, and (b) the excessively long machine-gunning of the man on the apartment steps is to be considerably reduced."[26] These, and some dialogue adjustment to eliminate an implication of adultery, would be easy edits to accomplish.

In the case of the killing in the hotel hallway, the alteration left a scar on the film, a trace of the regulatory process. In the scene, mobster John Ireland ambushes a hood and his girlfriend in the hotel. Ireland guns the hood, and the woman runs off screaming. She disappears around a corner in the hallway, and Ireland starts after her. In the print screened for the PCA, he kills her, and the action dissolves to the next scene in the montage, another gangland killing, taking place on the steps outside a building. Because the policy was to keep post-production trims to a minimum, the dissolve stayed where it was in the film. This meant keeping the outgoing shot from the scene in the hallway, the shot over which the dissolve begins. This shot shows the body of the woman (or yet another woman, as the costuming is slightly different) that Ireland has killed, lying on the floor, and his lower legs as he steps closer to verify that she is dead. The revised action cuts from his pursuit of the woman in the hallway to the tail end of the shot showing her dead body that dissolves to the next scene. The killing is eliminated, but not all of its traces. We do still see the body, if only for a moment. From the standpoint of continuity, it would have been better to create a new dissolve from the point in the scene where Ireland runs after her, but this would have required more work. It was easier

---

2.   The arm chopping scene in *Spartacus*. In a rare instance of post-production trimming mandated by the PCA, it was shortened slightly, but the hewing of the limb remained on-camera.

simply to drop one or a few shots and keep the dissolve in its original location. This was a less effective way of omitting the woman's killing (we get a glimpse of her corpse), but it was an easier and less extensive edit to accomplish. That difference says everything about how the PCA handled post-screening trims.

Upon-screening Kirk Douglas and Stanley Kubrick's gladiator epic *Spartacus* (1960), the PCA requested some modest deletions—two shots with a nude Jean Simmons and the infamous "snail scene" between Laurence Olivier and Tony Curtis. In addition, mixing up the terminology of shot and scene, the agency ordered Universal Pictures to "eliminate the scene in which a soldier's arm is cut off and blood spurts."[27] This is one of the more startling moments of violence in the film and, indeed, in American cinema of the early sixties. It's a graphic, explicitly detailed mutilation of a Roman soldier by Spartacus (Kirk Douglas), who hacks off his forearm during a desperate battle that finds Spartacus and his army of rebel slaves outmatched and engulfed by the superior numbers of a huge Roman army.

This is not an incidental piece of violence that goes on in the background of the action or which only attentive viewers will catch. The shot is composed for maximum visual and emotional impact. Spartacus has been knocked from his horse and is shown fighting at close quarters in a series of crowded widescreen compositions. Then follows a shot whose frame is not cluttered with soldiers, the better for us to see what is about to happen. One Roman soldier stands in the foreground with his outstretched arm extended across the center of the frame. Spartacus looms up from the background and severs the outstretched arm. Three arterial spurts arc from the stump as Spartacus glares at his victim. The shot is composed to heighten and emphasize its violence by putting the arm chopping up front and in the center of the frame. Furthermore, such explicit detailing of extreme physical trauma was unusual in film prior to the late 1960s. Despite all of this—the flamboyant violence, an attack on what was still in cinema the inviolability of the human body, and the careful choreography of bloodshed to maximize its visceral impact—the PCA relented from its directive that the shot be cut. Upon discussion with Universal, in the end it asked only that the shot be shortened: "Modification of the battle scene in which an arm is severed, so that it will be reduced by nine frames at its very end. This scene from beginning to end was originally two feet, four frames long, the last twenty frames of which showed blood spurting. This portion has now been reduced by approximately one-half."[28]

The PCA rejected Alfred Hitchcock's *Psycho* after screening it on Feb. 19, 1960, citing Code violations. None of these, however, had to do with violence; all involved sexual imagery. The opening hotel room lovemaking included an open-mouthed kiss; the shower scene had some shots with nudity; and the agency felt the Peeping Tom shot, where Norman watches Marion Crane undress, went on too long.[29] From an editing standpoint, these are all minor trims that could be easily accomplished and are, therefore, consistent with the manner in which post-production revisions were handled within this regulatory system.

This fact is clarified through its contrast with another set of post-production trims that beset *Psycho* and originated from outside the industry and the PCA. The Catholic Legion of Decency requested precisely the kind of cuts the PCA avoided inflicting on Hollywood filmmakers. The Legion required three trims for the film to earn a B rating rather than a C (Condemned). In the scene where detective Arbogast is killed, Hitchcock was asked to eliminate two of the four knife blows at the foot of the stairs. (The killer knocks the detective down the stairs and attacks him as he lies stunned on the floor. The actual stabbing is off-camera, but we see the killer's hand with the knife as it plunges out of frame.) The film now survives with only one knife blow fully shown; the second is only suggested, because the scene quickly fades out before the

---

3. Although *Psycho* had been cleared by the PCA, the Catholic Legion of Decency intervened and asked that most of the violence be removed from the film's second murder scene, the killing of Arbogast.

second blow is delivered. This cut created major, serious consequences for the overall design of the film and the place of violence in that design. Critics—and Hitchcock himself—have used claims about the film's *decreasing* amount of violence to illustrate Hitchcock's command of suspense. The idea is that Hitchcock made the first killing in the film—of Marion in the shower—the most horrifically violent in order to grab the audience with such fright and intensity that it would take less violence throughout the remainder of the film to keep his audience hooked.

There is certainly some truth to this claim, but had the Legion not required deletion of more than half of the knife blows in the killing of Arbogast, that murder would be considerably more savage than it now appears and with a significantly different impact on the viewer and the choreography of violence and suspense over the course of the picture. Had Arbogast been permitted to die under a frenzy of knife blows, as Hitchcock had filmed it and the PCA approved it, the scene would more closely resemble the shower killing in its ferocity and cruelty, rather than constituting such a decrease in the intensity of the film's violence. As filmed and approved by the PCA, *Psycho* was an even more violent film than is now supposed.

In this regard, the design of the film does not reflect the "authorship" of Hitchcock so much as the forces of censorship, which were still powerful in 1960s America even though the PCA was then in a period of decline. By triggering censorship at municipal, state and national levels, screen violence operated to create a dispersal of creative expression, a disassembling of the unitary form which expression is commonly thought to achieve in the body of a finished film. Because it was subjected to numerous review boards and vetting procedures, screen violence in classical Hollywood makes ever more salient the longstanding objection to, and problem with, the auteur theory. Adjudicating violence entailed that films would have numerous authors rather than just a single author. As a site of adjudication and negotiation in classical Hollywood, screen violence is antithetical to orthodox auteurist notions of directorial control and creative expression. In this regard, the violence in *Psycho*, as we now have the film, is rather different in this crucial scene than it was in the picture as Hitchcock made it.

Another trim required by the Legion proved to be especially difficult to make. The Legion wanted the studio to remove a glimpse of blood on Norman's hands in the scene where he cleans the bathroom after murdering Marion in the shower. The Legion did not want any blood visible on Norman until that point in the scene where he stands at the sink and washes his hands. The problem is that the offending glimpse occurred in the middle of a more lengthy shot that showed Norman moving around the bathroom. This edit would be harder to carry out because the whole shot could not be dropped without damaging the scene. The offending frames could not be deleted without having some other action to cut to; otherwise, the edit would produce an unsightly jump cut. New footage had to be added as a cutaway. As PCA internal correspondence notes, "to eliminate blood on hand no direct positive cut is possible. We must supply new film which will consist of close-up Perkins head going into bathroom, hands below frame so no blood is seen on them at any time until the latter part of his washing his hands."[30] To make these changes, the film negative and fine-grain protection print would have to be recut.[31] This was precisely the kind of expensive and aggravating change that the PCA system of negotiating film content in advance of production was designed to avoid, and, significantly, the request for the change did not originate from a PCA directive but from the Legion of Decency. The PCA and the Legion worked closely with one another throughout the history of classical Hollywood, but the Legion took a much harder line with *Psycho*.[32]

It is true that most of the examples just cited come from films made in the 1950s, when PCA power was in decline. But case files from the 1930s and 1940s also bear out the general policy of seeking only minimal changes in post-production. They are changes that serve production, in that they permit the PCA to approve the films for release; the emphasis here is to be placed on *approve*. Along with the case cited earlier of the agency's rejection of the script for *The Big Heat* (a film not only approved and completed but now a classic film noir), they demonstrate the inaccuracy of claims like Gerald Gardner's, in his book *The Censorship Papers*, "when Joe Breen wrote to a producer that a film . . . could not hope to receive a seal, a vaultlike door slammed shut."[33]

One of the most striking features of the PCA's review process should now be evident: it did not include film *production*. This provides one of the clearest signs of the agency's limited reach. It did not watch over the actual production of a film. PCA staff did not go on set during filming to ensure that shooting was proceeding as per the Code. The agency lacked the resources to do this and the inclination. Everyone realized that this would be a dangerous usurpation of a filmmaker's creative prerogatives. As Van Schmus noted in strong terms, "we never, *never* insisted on being present at the shooting of any material . . . we would *never* call up and say, 'We must watch how you do this,' we'd never dream of that. Joe Breen would've fired anybody who did that."[34] On rare occasions and at the request of studio executives, a studio liaison to the PCA might visit the set, but it would not be the agency itself. Its involvement in a project was constrained and came at the beginning (script evaluation) and at the end (screening for a certificate).

Because the PCA did not oversee production, it was not in a position to vet a filmmaker's stylistic inflections of the scripted action. Its attentions were principally focused on the *x*-axis of screen violence. This is a significant point, and I will provide numerous examples as we go along of the way that film style could escape scrutiny. A brief one here will help clarify this phenomenon. A remarkably sadistic piece of violence in *The Man from Laramie* (1955) features Alex Nicol, playing a psychopath, shooting James Stewart in the hand at point-blank range. Nicol's men restrain Stewart and force his gun hand away from his side, where Nicol blasts a hole in it, cruelly maiming him. Phil Hardy has called this "one of the most brutal scenes in the American Western."[35] The PCA was worried about this action in the script because it seemed "excessively brutal." The agency advised, "if it is to be retained in the picture, it should be done off-screen, and not in any objectionable detail."[36] Director Anthony Mann keeps the camera off Stewart's hand during and after the shooting, which therefore occurs off-screen, honoring the PCA's script suggestion, but he includes a strong audio depiction of Stewart's pain. After he is shot, Stewart's whimpering and moaning go on at some length and are given clarity and prominence in the sound mix. This audio information increases the stylistic amplitude of the violent act, giving the violence a tangible form that it does not have visually. The PCA did not request that the audio be removed following the screening for clearance. The filmmakers gave the PCA what it wanted in the script negotiation (an indirect portrayal of the shooting) but then used style (the audio design) to get what they wanted all along: a visceral, brutally depicted scene of violence.

NEGOTIATING VIOLENCE UNDER THE PRODUCTION CODE

As this example suggests, the authority wielded by the PCA was relatively paradoxical: It was a powerful agency, and yet it was constrained by its very role as a gatekeeper in its own industry. The industry's distribution–exhibition pipeline needed a continuing flow of production, and the PCA was unwilling to disrupt this flow in any serious or ongoing manner. Thus, all of its decisions were constrained by its need to serve Hollywood's distribution and exhibition sectors. These contradictions—between the agency's function in the economic workings of the industry, the necessity of not subverting the industry's business structure, and the PCA's public relations mandate to keep objectionable material off the nation's movie screens—help to account for the primacy of negotiation in its dealings with filmmakers. As Lea Jacobs points out, "the Code was [not] simply 'enforced' in the manner of a law through the exercise of the power of restraint."[37]

At the same time, the agency's authority was vested securely in the corporate organization of the industry. Movies were the premiere and unchallenged mass medium of the 1930s and 1940s, and Hollywood had a lock on the manufacture and consumption of film entertainment. Until the 1950s, when the agency began to weaken, films were not distributed without certificates of approval, and the industry's vertical integration—the corporate control of production, distribution, and exhibition—enabled it to coordinate the content of films at the scripting stage with their downstream distribution and exhibition. (The industry's loss of its first-run theaters in the late 1940s, the severing of production and distribution from exhibition, was the beginning of a series of factors that would undermine the operation of the PCA in the following decade.)

It is important to stress the paradoxical and constrained nature of the agency's authority, because it has often been misinterpreted. David J. Skal, for example, in his otherwise excellent cultural history of horror movies, describes the Breen Office as trying to "bowdlerize" films.[38] He writes that the PCA could "stop a film from being exhibited. Finally, the code had teeth."[39] The Code may have had teeth, but the gums were soft. Filmmakers had plenty of room to maneuver their projects through to completion. The image of the PCA blocking films from exhibition conjures up a repressive, authoritarian agency hostile to production. Blocking a film from exhibition would constitute an absolute failure of the system. The front-loading (at the scripting stage) of the PCA review process was designed to avoid post-production trims, let alone the apocalyptic scenario of suppressing an entire film from exhibition.

As Lea Jacobs noted, the PCA did not issue edicts or rule by fiat, telling filmmakers in an authoritarian way what they could and could not show or say on-screen. Negotiation was the whole basis of the system, with the objective being to get films made. Van Schmus says, "when people write about the Production Code as just something that was *imposed* on the producers, they're kind of missing the point."[40] Geoffrey Shurlock stated, "we never refused seals. We were in the business of granting seals. The whole purpose of our existence was to arrange pictures so that we could give seals. You had to give a seal."[41] Van Schmus points out that letters from the Breen office saying that something was unacceptable under the Code were actually the starting points for negotiations.[42] Filmmakers did not take the rejections literally, according to Van Schmus, and, in any case, the rejections were usually qualified in some manner. A commonly used qualification was a phrase noting that a Code problem exists in a script or scene "as written." Van Schmus notes that "you had to be careful you did not wield too much power carelessly. It put the director in a bad situation by telling somebody, some creative person, that it's just impossible, you can't do that. . . . You had to be careful and avoid stubborn, obtuse positions like that."[43]

Joseph Breen was appointed to apply the Code as PCA head in 1934, in part because James Wingate, his predecessor as head of the SRC, had not worked effectively with filmmakers. Shurlock has pointed out that Wingate was not very skilled at dealing with creative people and that he had a censor's approach. Note the significance of this observation: Shurlock is drawing a distinction between the PCA and its staff and the censors empowered around the country at state and urban levels. Wingate had been a censor, the head of the New York state censor board. Shurlock describes how Wingate's inflexible censor's approach, simply mandating cuts and deletions, clashed with what filmmakers wanted and with the purpose and functioning of the PCA. "He'd say 'no, no, cut it out.' And what [filmmakers] wanted was not to cut it out but to do it differently. That is what was the purpose of this office finally."[44] In Shurlock's view, the purpose was to negotiate ways of showing problematic things so that they could pass under the Code. This is what he meant when he talked about "arranging" films so they could get a seal.

Rather than following a common tendency to describe the Breen office as "enforcing" the Code, I believe it is better and more accurate to speak of it as negotiating applications of the Code. A negotiated application gives filmmakers wiggle room in making their movies and gives PCA staff members space to maneuver in their dealings with filmmakers. For all concerned, this would be a more congenial and rewarding way of transacting their relationships. In a small community like that of Hollywood, professional relationships count for a lot—and maintaining good ones is essential to professional survival and to the business of making films and getting them cleared for exhibition. Van Schmus describes the way PCA staff members would reach out in a personal manner to filmmakers, producers, and studio liaisons when their projects were running into problems with the Code:

> There were occasions when you'd read a script and in order to show your concern about getting *along* with the company and trying to reason the thing out, solve the problem, you'd call them on the phone first, before writing the letter. And say, "look, you're going to get a strong letter from us on this property. There are some problems. But take a look at the letter, and call us back and we can get together and have a discussion." That would *often* be the step before writing the letter.[45]

PCA staff regularly met with filmmakers to discuss problem areas in a script. These story conferences enabled filmmakers to describe their approach to a scene in ways that often worked to their benefit. Van Schmus points out, "something in print might look a little startling, but when you sit down and talk with the man who's actually going to put it up there on the screen and he describes *how* it's going to be done, that can make a tremendous difference."[46]

The story conferences and other personal contacts between the PCA and filmmakers sustained the relationships so essential to filmmaking and helped to institutionalize the relative flexibility of the system. Even negotiations over difficult material might be conducted on a cordial basis. Aubrey Schenck, who was producing *Raw Deal* (1948), a tough and violent crime film directed by Anthony Mann, wrote to Breen to say how helpful he found the PCA staff members to be. His remarks are significant because (as detailed in a later chapter) this was a film on which the writer, producer and director prodded the PCA to accept specific acts of violence that it had initially prohibited. "Frequently, in the producing of motion pictures, due to our efforts to meet deadlines and to achieve better results, we fail to express our appreciation for the good rendered us by your organization . . . Although we cannot honestly admit that we liked all the changes that had to be made in the story, nevertheless we do wish to say that we admire the cooperative spirit and desire to help expressed by [PCA staff members]. They have been very helpful to us and we feel that due to their efforts . . . we will have a much better story."[47] Breen replied, "I hasten to thank you very cordially for your gracious letter with the little which we were able to do in helping out on your production . . . I want you to know that all hands here do appreciate your kindness."[48] Contrast with the formality of this exchange PCA staff member Eugene "Doc" Dougherty's friendly note to Robert Aldrich, handwritten on MPAA stationary, about their negotiations over the extensive profanity in the script for *The Dirty Dozen*. "Dear Bob: If you think I am going to have anything to do with approving the line 'wop bastard' *now*, you're crazy as hell. Best always, Doc."[49] Aldrich wrote a joking reply, and he also sent a note to Shurlock: "Because of the nature of our relationship there are many things that one cannot properly say 'thank you' for but that doesn't necessarily mean the silent partner is not appreciative. So, instead of saying 'thank you' let me say how much I appreciate the kind things . . . you had to say about *Dirty Dozen*. Okay? Okay!"[50]

Because the Code was applied in a negotiated fashion, rather than "enforced," PCA staff members could treat it as a flexible document rather than as a series of laws that were set in stone. As Van Schmus noted, "the phrases in the Code are open to interpretation. You can be very strict after you read it or you can be reasonably liberal."[51] Staff members might draw a distinction between the letter and the spirit of the Code. "There were so many things that did not come under the *letter* of the Code. That you could say, well, it doesn't violate the letter. Under the spirit of the Code, it's okay, as long as we don't actually violate this particular clause, specifically, we can let it go by.

4. The PCA's tolerance for violence varied according to genre. It permitted more graphic violence in the war film than it did in crime and gangster films. In *All Quiet on the Western Front*, a hand grenade blows a soldier apart, and all that remains are his hands clutching a barbed wire fence.

That kind of thinking did come up several times. Quite often."[52] Not surprisingly, staff members differed in their degrees of strictness or liberality, with Shurlock and Van Schmus being somewhat more liberal than Breen and Jack Vizzard.

The flexible and negotiated basis on which the Code was applied is most vividly apparent in the many disparities between what the PCA requested filmmakers to do and what they actually did. Many accounts of the PCA describe it as forcing filmmakers to remove material from films. But, as noted above, the PCA's authority was circumscribed, and its case files strikingly document instances in which filmmakers simply disregarded the PCA's recommendations or negotiated their way around them. I examine a number of these cases in chapter four, but it may be useful to quickly note a few occasions here, where material that the PCA explicitly forbid shows up quite plainly in the finished film.

One of the most vivid and haunting images from *All Quiet on the Western Front* (1930) is the mutilation that results when a soldier, charging into German machine-gun fire, reaches for a barbed wire fence separating him from the entrenched German lines. He is hit by a hand grenade, and after the explosion all that remains are his two hands, severed at the wrists, clutching the barbed wire. The MPPDA's Studio Relations Committee was worried about this scene in the script and recommended that it be omitted. An internal memo to SRC head Jason Joy cautioned against "any close-up scenes accenting gruesomeness" and two days later Joy wrote to Universal Pictures listing troublesome scenes in the script: "Scene 34-D: A wounded Frenchmen is shown lying on a barbed wire fence. An explosion occurs and blows his body away, leaving his hands clutching the wire. Gruesomeness of this kind is invariably eliminated by all censors and I should omit these scenes entirely."[53] Joy's recommendation is based on his anticipation that regional and foreign censor boards will delete the scene. Indeed, the SRC and PCA's rationale for existing was to, as Shurlock said, head the censors off at the pass.[54] The SRC had less authority in Hollywood than did the PCA, but, even so, the way this scene of violence bypassed agency objections and made it to the screen is very typical of cases that occurred during PCA tenure.

In the wake of public outcry and regional and foreign censorship of Hollywood's 1930s gangster films, the MPPDA revised the Code to forbid scenes showing police or other law authorities being killed by criminals. It was an explicit injunction against specific content. The PCA gave producer Mark Hellinger script approval for his prison break drama *Brute Force* (1947) with the admonition, "throughout the picture, please bear in mind the clause in the Code which forbids the showing of policemen, guards, etc., dying at the hands of criminals."[55] In the finished film, Burt Lancaster, leading a prison rebellion, machine-guns two guards (two more are killed by another inmate), and Lancaster beats the new prison warden unconscious and throws him to his death from the guard tower.

In Anthony Mann's *Raw Deal* (1948), gangster Raymond Burr throws a flaming fondue into a woman's face. It appears in the film, but the PCA had forbidden it: "The action of him throwing the flaming casserole at the girl and the horrible reaction of screaming and groaning on her part is unacceptably gruesome and could not be approved."[56] The initial scripts for Fritz Lang's *The Big Heat* were rejected by the PCA for scenes of excessive brutality, including the most famous one that made it into the finished picture—Lee Marvin hurling boiling coffee into Gloria Graham's face and her subsequent revenge by doing the same to him.[57]

As these instances demonstrate, the PCA's responses were not necessarily the last word on the matter; even when it had specifically warned against particular acts of violence, those very acts nevertheless might appear on-screen. We have, then, an agency whose authority, pertaining to screen violence at least, was circumscribed, and this will have numerous consequences for depictions of violence.

Violence in the Horror Film

With these essentials in mind about the manner in which the PCA worked, let us now examine how the agency negotiated the representation of violence with filmmakers. After the passage of the Code in 1930, two categories of film—horror and crime movies—were especially rife with instances of brutality and violence. These were the problem genres. They aroused considerable opposition by regional censor boards, angry viewers, and citizens groups, and challenged the PCA to adjust its standards about the thresholds of acceptability on-screen and to provide closer scrutiny of such films. The remainder of this chapter examines the horror film, and the next chapter deals with gangster movies. There was a tremendous amount of output in the horror genre in the 1930s, and the time and space limitations of this study do not permit a systematic analysis of every film made in the genre during this period. I will, instead, try to isolate significant issues in the representation of violence with reference to some of the classic pictures from that period.

A second caveat is in order regarding the horror films. Some of them, such as *Frankenstein*, have little of what might strike a contemporary viewer as excessive violence or even much violence of any kind. But we must be careful here not to become blinkered by our contemporary sensibility and frames of reference. The extreme amount of violence in films today has made viewers, in general, somewhat less sensitive to its depiction. It has made the real hardness and brutality of classical Hollywood film violence almost invisible to many contemporary viewers. This was not true for audiences in earlier decades and, as a result, displays that would strike a modern viewer as containing minimal violence were often sufficient to provoke angry backlashes from offended viewers and extreme fright reactions in children. Furthermore, the violence in the films was often implicit, pointed to by action on-screen that was itself nonviolent. And, in addition, in the horror films, it was entangled within situations that were morbid and horrific, such as grave robbing. We will need, therefore, to disentangle violence, implicit and overt, from these other elements.

The most striking thing about the first wave of horror movies in the early sound period is that the SRC underestimated its impact on public sensibilities. As a result, the agency gave the scripts for these pictures relatively cursory treatment and quick approval, only to find itself confronting a firestorm of controversy when the pictures played on neighborhood screens throughout the nation. David Skal writes that the horror film was the most lasting and influential invention of 1931, the year of *Dracula* and *Frankenstein*.[58] These films about monsters and mad scientists unleashed a new wave of imagery depicting cruelty, torture, pain, and murder and disseminated it en mass to the nation's movie screens. The avuncular and even campy tone that today surrounds Lugosi's Dracula or Karloff's Frankenstein monster is a measure of the extent to which these figures have become icons of popular culture. But the campiness distorts the way these films appeared to early audiences. They were quite popular and had good box-office returns, but they brought new levels of sadistic violence to popular culture. For viewers disturbed by this new imagery of cruelty, the films raised anxieties about the ability of this mass medium to insinuate itself into all strata of society and to undermine the values and mores that held communities together.

The SRC seems to have badly misjudged the degree of antagonism these films would arouse, and this is one reason that rigorous script evaluations became such an important part of PCA operating procedure. With reference to *Dracula*, Skal explains, "Colonel [Jason] Joy . . . seemed to find nothing in *Dracula* except a novelty entertainment. Since supernatural movies did not yet exist in Hollywood, they had never created controversy. And there was nothing in the Production Code about vampires."[59] Furthermore, as Black and Leff and Simmons have pointed out, Joy was relatively broad-minded and took a more liberal view of screen content than the regional censors. Accordingly, he at first saw little to worry about in the new horror films, as he also did with the initial gangster movies.

With regard to *Frankenstein*, the SRC wrote producer Carl Laemmle, Jr. a mild and relatively undetailed script evaluation letter that raised only general cautions about some of the horror imagery, such as the hanging of the dwarf by the monster. "[We] are of the opinion that the only incidents in it about which to really be concerned are those gruesome ones that will certainly bring an audience reaction of horror."[60] This—creating a reaction of horror—was the objective of the picture, of course, but it was inseparable from depictions of cruelty.

When *Frankenstein* was completed and screened for SRC approval, it seems to have easily passed, with only the suggestion that the dialogue references to "playing God" be deleted. The SRC wrote Laemmle, "we have seen your picture, *Frankenstein,* and believe it is satisfactory under the Code and, unless some of the official censor boards consider it gruesome, reasonably free from censorship action."[61] In retrospect, the SRC's complacency seems remarkable. Certainly, it seemed to have little sense that *Frankenstein* represented a significant escalation of screen violence that was likely to elicit considerable censor difficulty.

As I noted, it is perhaps difficult today—with more than seventy years of intervening movie mayhem—to appreciate how disturbing the gruesome imagery in *Frankenstein* was to its contemporary viewers, an impact that was accentuated by the sophisticated visual design of many of the film's sequences. (Other scenes, by contrast, are flat and stagy; the film's design is intriguingly bifurcated in this way.) The film opens with a grave robbery as Henry Frankenstein and his humpbacked assistant, Fritz, dig up a coffin in a twilit cemetery, surrounded by crucifixes, statuary, and iron fence posts skewed at wild Expressionist angles. The grave robbing is a perfect example of implicitly referenced violence. Nothing violent occurs in the first scene, and yet they intend to hack and saw apart the corpses that they are stealing. This is not murder, but it is violent desecration of the dead. In addition to the extraordinary morbidity of this opening scene, it was the implicit connection between stealing and violating the corpses that motivated many regional censor boards to recommend deleting it.

As Henry raises the coffin from the grave, a dissolve takes us to a long shot that shows Henry and Fritz hauling it on a cart through a desolate mountain landscape. There, they spy the body of a hanging victim and try to retrieve it as well. Fritz climbs the scaffold and is shown in a striking wide-angle shot that accentuates his deformity as he creeps along the top of the scaffold, moving directly toward the camera, which is placed at the end of the cross-beam along which he is crawling. The shot's design serves to bring this grotesque character, in a steadily encroaching manner, ever closer to the camera's eye and to the viewer. The sound information heightens the morbidity of his effort to free and then steal the hanging victim. Fritz pants for breath under his exertion, a striking sound effect that is given an unusual prominence for a film of this period. As he cuts the rope, the viewer can hear the knife sawing through the fibers, and the body lands with a dull and pronounced thud. Director James Whale, cinematographer Arthur Edeson, and the film's sound editor have made brilliant choices in their orchestration of picture and sound to give an intensely sensual detailing to the corpse-robbing scenes that open the film. Moreover, the framing of the action and the sound work operate to flaunt the grotesque action of the scene and its implied violence. It is not just that the setting—a graveyard– and the characters—an obsessed scientist and his disfigured assistant—are horrific. It is, crucially, that they are engaged in the theft and mutilation of once-living beings. Although it is implied, the violence lurking below the surface of the film's opening scenes was very much a factor in the emotional impact of the film on its viewers and the censor activity that surrounded it.

Whale, Edeson, and the sound editor give subsequent horrific scenes a cinematic treatment that is equally sophisticated. These include the sequence in which the monster first appears, in a flurry of disorienting edits, and the monster's makeup, with a scarred face and visible incisions where severed hands were attached to forearms—a scarring that points to the ripping and dismemberment of joint and flesh that were required for his creation. Because it gets so much screen time in the movie, the action where Henry uses an electric storm to animate the monster looms disproportionately large in the set of procedures whereby he is created.

By contrast, the work that took Henry the greatest amount of time and effort is not depicted directly on-screen. This is the work of chopping up bodies, sewing parts together, and disposing of the waste organs, limbs, and fluids. Except that he doesn't actually murder his victims, there is little that distinguishes the frenzy of abuse that he directs on their bodies from the serial killers portrayed in such films as *Henry: Portrait of a Serial Killer* (1986) and *Se7en* (1995). Though we don't see this on-screen, Henry's work is saturated with violence. We must infer its presence from the artifacts it has left behind, such as the scarring and incision marks on the monster.

The scene in which Fritz torments the monster with whip and torch is given exceptionally vivid cinematic treatment. As it begins, the monster is chained in a sloping Expressionist dungeon, and cries out with anger and confusion. Fritz, whose own deformity has perhaps filled him with a corresponding hatred for the monster, a kindred freak, bursts into the room and screams at the monster to be quiet and then proceeds to whip him. Whale films this action with the camera at some distance from the characters, framed in a long shot. When Fritz picks up a torch, however, and thrusts it into the monster's face, Whale and Edeson go in to an exceptionally tight framing of the action that serves to emphasize the monster's terror and Fritz's sadism. As Fritz waves the torch before his face, the monster collapses in a frenzy of terror in a tiny corner between a bench and the wall, and it is here that Whale and Edeson cut in to the tighter framing. It shows us the spastic acceleration of the monster's efforts to beat the torch away with his hands and his animal fear of the fire. The next shot is a subjective, moving camera shot, from the monster's point of view. The torch is thrust up into the lens of the camera, and Fritz's leering face hovers just beyond the fire as he tries to burn the monster and provoke real pain, not just fear. Fritz grins with the sadist's pleasure in the torment of his victim. The next cut is to an even tighter framing of the monster's face as he tries to elude the flame. These tight framings put the viewer inside the action, from the sadistic point of view of Fritz and the anguished view of his victim. Whale and Edeson then return to the previous long-shot framing of the action as the monster rises and tries to grab the torch. The scene fades out on this action, and the monster's anguished cries linger over the dark screen past the fade-out.

5–6. Cinematography and editing evoke the monster's torment by placing the viewer inside the sadistic action. We see the evil Fritz from the monster's view and then the creature's frenzied response. The scene visualizes the interior components of violence as well as its physical action. Regional censors were especially upset by the creature's "horrible animal sounds."

The significance of this scene lies in its shrewd use of the elements of cinema, chiefly framing, editing, and sound in conjunction with Karloff's performance, to accentuate the experience of torture as it registers on the victim. Had Whale filmed all of the action using the camera set-up that opens and closes the scene—the long-shot framing—the violence would have had minimal stylistic amplitude. The closer framings and the subjective view not only heighten the experience of the depicted violence, they also magnify the visual context in which the sound information occurs and therefore increase the force of that information. In these ways, the scene's design moves toward an amplification of the stylistic means for enhancing the depiction of violence.

Symptomatic of the period, however, the stylistic amplitude quickly reaches its upper limit. The cut-ins from the master shot are relatively brief, and the visual and aural elaboration of violence does not occupy much screen time. Stylistic amplitude in this period has clear limits on its duration. Segments of movie violence are not extended in time, as they are today. Their stylistic design, however shrewd—and the filmmaking here is very shrewd—is constrained by the limited duration. However, Whale's filmmaking has grasped essential techniques for interiorizing violence and registering suffering. The distance between then and now is merely a matter of the extension in space and time that more elaborate designs can accomplish. Elaborating the techniques, though, was not a possibility for Whale or the film. The forces of regional censorship, and the industry's own evolving efforts at self-regulation, saw to that.

The construction of the scene accentuates the pain and fear of the monster in a manner that does not just impress them intellectually upon the viewer but renders them with a tangible and sensory power. It then juxtaposes this suffering with the delight and pleasure that the tormentor takes in his action. Much film violence throughout the silent period was enacted in a theatrical manner and photographed by a camera that stayed outside the action. Whale and Edeson, by contrast, have put the viewer inside the action—inside the violence—and placed the pain of the monster at the center of the design. A critical ingredient of the design in accomplishing this is the use of sound. The monster's cries give the emotional coordinates of the violence a concrete presence in the scene. They give the violence its sharp edge, its ability to hurt. No wonder this sequence would be widely cut by censor boards, with Karloff's cries cited as a factor. Sound brought to cinema many new avenues of expression, from the slang of everyday speech to the song that made musicals possible. It also brought the capability to heighten violence by giving it an aural presence in the depiction of anguish and pain.

Fritz's death—killed by the enraged monster—is conveyed entirely through

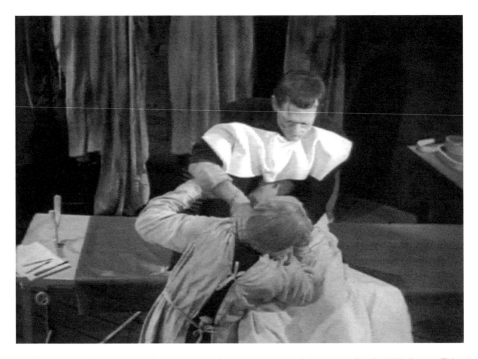

7. The sounds of pain and death were among the most controversial aspects of early 1930s horror. This strangulation scene was widely cut by censors because of the victim's lengthy, audible gasping and retching.

sound. He dies offscreen, while the camera is on Henry and another doctor who is assisting him. A long, pained scream signals Fritz's end. The doctors rush to the monster's dungeon and find Fritz hanging grotesquely from a wall, like a slab of meat on a hook. When, in a subsequent scene, the monster kills the other doctor, it is presented as a lengthy strangulation scene, filled with the victim's extended choking sounds. These go on for a full ten seconds as the monster chokes the life out of his victim. In these murders of Fritz and the doctor, the sound of violence is an integral part of the design. While protest from censors and viewers over the gruesomeness of the early sound horror films centered on the acts of murder or torture that were being committed on-screen, or were pointed to by acts like the grave robbing, these acts and the protest that they inspired were not inseparable from the cinematic expression filmmakers gave to them. This is why an understanding of violence needs to include both components, referent and style. In the early horror and gangster movies, we find filmmakers exploring—albeit tentatively—the camera set-ups, lens choices, lighting effects, editing choices, and sound designs that could accentuate moments of brutality and grotesquerie and make them more sensual as cinema and more emotional for viewers to experience. They left these designs as a legacy for subsequent filmmakers to elaborate upon and, with more immediate effect in their own period, as an incitement to the entrenched forces of censorship around the country.

THE REGIONAL CENSORS RESPOND

These forces were quick to react. *Frankenstein* ran into numerous problems with censor boards, the most severe and protracted of which were in Kansas. Initially Kansas banned the film entirely, charging that the picture was cruel and tended to debase morals, and then relented but imposed a long list of eliminations that the censors surely knew would gut the film. Universal certainly felt the deletions would destroy the film's coherency, and Carl Laemmle, Jr. requested that Joy and the SRC intercede and try to get the film passed with fewer cuts.[62] Their willingness to do so is a clear demonstration of what Geoffrey Shurlock said, namely, that the SRC and the PCA worked for filmmakers and the industry, not the regional censors. As Leonard Leff has pointed out, "the intercession of the PCA with municipal, state, and especially international censors on producers' behalf was far more common than has been reported."[63]

The eliminations report that the SRC received from Kansas provides a concrete illustration of the types of violence and horror that were troubling to the regional censors and that many felt ought to have no place on cinema screens. These included imagery of corpses, physical scarring, whipping, surgical injection, strangulation, and the sights and sounds of fear and physical pain:

Reel 1: Digging up casket.

Reel 2: View of body swathed and covered lying on table.
 (2) Conversation about the body.
 (3) Close-up of scar on wrist where hand is sewed on.

Reel 3: Close-up of body being uncovered and of the body uncovered. Also view of body being raised to the point where only the apparatus shows.
 (2) Words by Frankenstein describing how he made the body.
 (3) Words by Frankenstein, "Now I know what it feels to be like God."

Reel 4: Close-up of the creature as it enters the room.
 (2) Close-up as it sits in chair.
 (3) Close-up as it lifts arms.
 (4) Close-up of head and hands.

(5) Close-up of creature in den with Fritz beating it with a whip, and deviling it with a fire torch.

(6) Close-up of the injection of hypodermic into monster and struggle with Doctor and Frankenstein.

(7) Close-up of the creature's face as it falls.

(8) Horrible animal sounds made by creature.

(9) Dead screams by Fritz.

Reel 5: View of creature on table with doctor working over it and preparing for dissection.

(2) Two close-ups of face of creature as it lies on table.

(3) Close-up of creature's hand as it grabs toward Doctor's neck.

(4) Entire scene of Doctor's murder.

Reel 6: Close-up of face.

(2) Close-up of face.

(3) Close-up of face.

(4) Entire episode of monster with child, Maria.

(5) Entire episode of monster in Elizabeth's room.

(6) Child in father's arms being carried through the streets.

Reel 7: Close-up of face of monster.

(2) Struggle between monster and Frankenstein.

Reel 8: View of creature dragging Frankenstein up the stairs.

(2) Close-up of face of creature snarling at Frankenstein.

(3) Entire struggle of creature and Frankenstein.

(4) View of creature throwing Frankenstein from the windmill roof.

(5) View of Frankenstein catching on windmill blades.

(6) Entire episode of burning of mill in which monster is destroyed, including all views of him and sounds he makes as he tries to escape the flames and as he is pinned down in flames by falling beam.[64]

A moment's pause to reflect upon the nature of these eliminations reveals how integrally connected they are with issues of violence. While the eliminated footage might not contain overt acts of violence, it often clearly referenced it. Thus, the deletion marked "digging up casket" was objectionable because of the profanity that grave robbing represented and also because of the subsequent act of violence which it suggested—namely, Frankenstein's intent to violate the corpse by cutting it into pieces and surgically attaching these pieces to parts of other corpses in order to make his artificial man. The elimination marked "view of body swathed and covered lying on table" was footage that pictured the results of Frankenstein's violence upon the corpses he had stolen, as did the numerous close-ups of the creature that were deleted. The monster's elaborate scarring visualized the result of Frankenstein's assaults on the bodies of the dead, with the most explicit of these images marked as the third deletion in reel two. The first four eliminations in reel four were evidently marked for a similar reason. The monster's halting, awkward movements, brilliantly enacted by Boris Karloff, are the responses of a creature whose body is a patchwork of limbs that have no organic unity, as they are derived from the partial bodies of other beings.

Thus, many of the eliminations which at first seem to be free of violence, and therefore to have been deleted for other reasons, turn out to point to violent acts as the antecedents or consequents of the eliminated footage. This feature of images—their ability to "point to" some condition which they themselves do not directly depict—is an extremely significant characteristic of the discourse of violence in classical Hollywood films. As we will see in chapter five, the visual rhetoric that emerged in this period for depicting violence makes extensive use of different types of visual displacement—that is, the creation of images that employ different strategies for pointing to a violent act that often could not be represented directly.

Other eliminations demanded by the Kansas censors involved footage that clearly contained violent acts. Elimination five in reel four—footage showing Fritz tormenting the creature with a burning torch—involves the relatively extended ordeal of suffering. Karloff's facial expressions, his panicky efforts to escape Fritz, and his cries of pain and terror are vivid elements in the scene. Depictions of physical suffering, with the body marked as lacerated and in pain, would be relatively rare throughout the classical Hollywood period, but the early sound horror films were significant exceptions to this rule. It is in this context, where screen violence was predominantly pain-free, that the Kansas censors found the sound work in the film to be disturbing and censurable. They referred to "the horrible animal sounds made by [the] creature."

The strangulation of the doctor in reel five, marked for deletion, not only showed his slow demise but marked it aurally with the sounds of his death—his choking, retching effort to breathe. The sound information conveys the experience of dying in close physical detail, and this way of marking the body in distress was too much for Kansas. So, too, was the footage showing the monster caught in the burning windmill. Being burned alive is an inherently terrifying manner of violent death, and while the scene never shows this actually occurring, the monster is clearly trapped by the spreading fire and is eventually pinned beneath a burning beam that falls from the ceiling. Perhaps the imagery alone, suggesting his impending death, was sufficiently shocking for the censors to mark it for deletion. But the images didn't work alone. Once again, sound information marked the violence as intensely physical and depicted the character's suffering. As in the scene with Fritz, the monster vocalizes his fear of fire, making "horrible animal sounds" which tell the viewer that this is a sentient, suffering being that is perishing.

The film's physical detailing of violence, its marking of pain and rage as an emotional and bodily experience, and its placement of this detailing within a morbid story of grave robbing and vivisection, are what elicited the Kansas censors' judgment that *Frankenstein* was a film of 'cruelty' and the ensuing protest action by other censor boards and community organizations. In the end, the Kansas censors relented. Following efforts by Joy and Breen to overturn the ban and then the long list of eliminations, Kansas passed the film with a smaller but still relatively extensive series of cuts. Joy and Breen's "victory" in this regard was greeted with industry-wide relief. The episode had aroused considerable animosity among studios toward the regional censors. As a PCA memo noted regarding the Kansas victory, "this, of course, pleases us very much, as it does Universal. This news will be happily received by the other companies too, because the trade papers carried the word of the original rejection which created a wave of acrimonious anti-censor feeling among the folks of the industry."[65]

Frankenstein also encountered a great deal of trouble with Quebec censors, who initially banned the film: along with *Murders in the Rue Morgue* (1932), it was also banned in several Massachusetts towns. Universal again called on the SRC to overturn these bans, pointing to a large revenue loss if the picture could not be released in those markets. In contrast to the problems in Quebec and Kansas, censors in Chicago, Ohio, and Virginia passed the film with no eliminations. This disparity in the responses of regional censors emphasizes the dilemma faced by the industry when it brought violent films to market. The communications by Joy and Breen with local censor boards, the field trips to visit with them, and the compilation of data on eliminations were efforts to rationalize and make predictive judgments about a process that had fundamentally irrational components. The disparity among the responses by local censors presented the industry with an extremely difficult demand. Despite the SRC and, later, the PCA's best efforts, how could they help filmmakers design a picture whose violence would satisfy standards of censorship that shifted from region to region and might even change within a region over time? When *Frankenstein* was reissued in 1938, for example, Kansas censors passed it without any eliminations.

In negotiating with filmmakers over depictions of violence, the SRC and PCA were walking a tightrope from which they were bound to fall. They might be knocked off by filmmakers determined to push for greater amounts of violence or for its more explicit depiction, as occurred with the sequel *Bride of Frankenstein* (discussed below). Alternatively, they might receive a body slam by one or more regional censor boards. While the SRC and PCA could hope to influence filmmakers through the script negotiations that preceded production, trying to craft a picture that would satisfy censors everywhere was an often impossible undertaking. As such, the national release of a picture such as *Frankenstein* required a terrific amount of work, time, and money from the SRC to get the picture into badly needed markets that were often blocked by the decisions of local censors. Movie violence in the classical Hollywood period could be a tremendously desiccative element, tending to scatter integral parts of films onto the cutting room floor as mandated by regional censor boards and to fragment the markets in which a picture might be exhibited. It is not surprising, therefore, that the PCA would closely scrutinize the violence in scripts. This effort to fix problems in advance was really the most rational part of the irrational business of putting films, with no Constitutional free speech protection, into national release.

When *Frankenstein* was reissued in 1938, the PCA insisted on eliminating the dialogue about playing God in reel three, the drowning of the child, Maria, in reel 6; the shot of the Doctor jabbing the syringe into the monster's back in reel 4; and shortening the shots that show Fritz tormenting the monster. Even so, the rerelease triggered a furor in White Plains, New York, a town of 50,000 people some twenty miles from Manhattan. The events in White Plains illustrate the impact of the new level of violence and morbidity that *Frankenstein* and the other horror pictures had brought to the screen. Of particular interest here are the reactions of the White Plains school children. They responded with anxiety and agitation to *Frankenstein* and apparently became so worked up that local authorities sent protest letters to the PCA, asking how it could release such material to neighborhood screens where impressionable children would see it. The responses of the children provide an indicator of the degree of violence in *Frankenstein*, as it appeared to its period audience, in contradistinction to the tendency for viewers today to see it in campy and inoffensive terms.

Katherine Vandervoort, the Director of Attendance for White Plains public schools, was distressed by the fright reactions she witnessed in children who had attended a double bill of *Dracula* and *Frankenstein* in a town theatre. She sent a letter to the MPPDA and to the PCA describing her encounter with a nine-year-old boy who had become anxious during a screening of *Frankenstein* and rushed out of the theater. "A small boy came running up Main Street looking wildly up into the faces of pedestrians. He stopped in front of me and begged to be shown the way to Grant Avenue. I could see that he was hysterical."[66] When Vandervoort offered to take the boy home, "he appeared pitifully relieved," and during the ride home, "he kept on chattering more or less incoherently." Slowly, she says, the source of his agitation became clear: "At last, however, I began to listen to what he was saying and to one remark he kept repeating over and over again, 'I *know* he was going to kill her! I *know* he was!' 'Kill whom,' I asked. Then he babbled on about a little girl and a man and finally I got out of him that 'Frank somebody was going to kill a pretty little girl.' Then, of course, I realized that he had attended the show at Keiths [theater]."[67] He was apparently describing the sequence in the film where the monster plays with Maria, a little girl. The studio had deleted the footage showing the monster throwing her into a lake, where she drowns, but the boy seemed to have inferred what was going to happen despite the deletions.

The next day, Vandervoort visited several elementary school classrooms and found that a great number of the children had seen the horror double feature. She also found that they exhibited a variety of jittery emotional responses. "Some of them were still wide-eyed with excitement and wanted to tell the whole story in detail. Others appeared more anxious not to talk about it." One girl "has cried at night ever since. Many other children said they wouldn't go to sleep when they got home."

Vandervoort asked the industry to take steps to stop the production of films that could have such effects on children—who,under the conditions of that time, could go to theaters and "feast on horror, murder, crime and loose morals." She pointed to the larger implications of the situation she had described. "The small picture I have given you of what happened in White Plains this week could be multiplied by volumes from all over the United States and possibly Canada and other lands." If the film industry did not change its ways, she said, legislative remedies and action by the National Federation of P.T.A. might be necessary.

While Vandervoort clearly had an anti-horror film agenda, her descriptions of the children are quite compelling. In fact, they are consistent with the findings of empirical studies of fright reactions among children to horror media. Cantor and Oliver describe how these responses vary along developmental lines, according to the age of the viewer. Viewers at different ages are likely to find different aspects of the films frightening. Young children, for example, are likely to find purely fantastic elements like monsters more frightening than are adult viewers—and especially so if those elements are visually grotesque. Summarizing the results of numerous studies, they state that "children up to age 8 should be especially terrified by the fantastic and grotesque monsters that populate such films—even if they do not understand critical elements of the plot."[68] Part of what is involved here is the ability to make the distinction between fantasy and reality, which is easier for older viewers to do.

> Before a child understands the distinction, he or she will be unable to comprehend that something that is not real cannot pose a threat, and thus, the reality or fantasy status of a media depiction should have little effect on the fear it evokes. As the child comes increasingly to understand this distinction and increasingly appreciates the implications of real-world threats, depictions of real dangers should gain in fear-evoking potential relative to depictions of fantasy dangers.[69]

They cite a viewer's recollections of being terrified by the witch in *The Wizard of Oz:* "'That old witch scared me so much that I had recurring nightmares about her for about three or four weeks after each showing . . . The dream would always climax with my perspective being that of Dorothy's and the Witch saying in an extremely grotesque way, 'come my prittee [sic].' I would awake screaming and crying.'" Cantor and Oliver present evidence that some of the fright reactions may be long lasting, enduring for years. Of Hitchcock's *The Birds,* a viewer said, "the movie has instilled a permanent fear in me. . . . I like to hunt [but] I am perpetually afraid to grab any duck or goose that isn't absolutely dead. I keep picturing the birds in the movie . . . biting people." Another viewer attributes "my phobia of taking a shower without anyone in the house" to having seen *Psycho.* Five years later, "I still find myself peering around the shower curtain in fear of seeing the beholder of my death."[70]

Unlike Vandervoort, Cantor and Oliver do not suggest that children should be spared exposure to horror films. They point out that many children like such films and do not want their viewing restricted and that even innocuous films have been shown to elicit intense fright reactions. Nevertheless, they conclude, "emotional reactions can endure well beyond the time of viewing, and . . . these reactions can involve intense negative affect and, at times, the avoidance of activities that would otherwise be deemed nonthreatening."[71]

Even if we grant the possibility that Vandervoort may be exaggerating to some degree the condition of the children she observed, the situation that she describes does not seem at all unlikely. The empirical literature has documented fright responses of just the sort she mentions. As we examine the evolving abilities of filmmakers to depict violence in vivid terms, we would do well to remember that it can have consequences for viewers and for the communities in which they live. Films in distribution do not simply disappear into a void: they leave emotional and cognitive traces in their viewers.

The PCA, in fact, received numerous letters over the years from viewers outraged over screen violence and concerned about its effects on society (I will cite from several of these letters in the last chapter when we look at indicators of the effects on viewers of violent films). The PCA could not resolve the conflict between filmmakers and these sectors of the viewing audience. The agency was hamstrung by the competing demands of filmmakers who wanted to put the extra bit of gore on-screen, the censors and community groups who agitated against this, and the robust box-office that horror films were earning. *Variety*, the film industry trade paper, estimated that horror films had given Universal Pictures a $10 million profit during in the decade that elapsed since the premiere of *Frankenstein*.[72] PCA head Joseph Breen could only respond to Vandervoort in terms of these contradictions. He sent copies of her letter to the PCA staff and a number of studio liaisons, and he wrote her in reply, expressing his "considerable alarm" about the situation she described and confessed, "personally, I dislike these pictures very much."[73] There was, however, he pointed out, "a very substantial market for these films, both in this country and abroad." While he promised to make use of her letter in discussions with studios that were planning to produce horror films, it was clear that the industry would respect the "very substantial market" that existed.

In response to the furor over the first wave of horror films, the PCA tried to exercise greater care with future productions. But as *Frankenstein* premiered, there were several more horror pictures in the works whose scripts the SRC quickly approved, seriously misjudging their likelihood to arouse controversy and censor trouble. Requesting few rewrites, the SRC approved the script for Universal's *Murders in the Rue Morgue* (1932), finding that it was acceptable under the Code "and reasonably safe from censorship difficulties."[74] Paramount was planning a production of *Dr. Jekyll and Mr. Hyde* (1931). While concerned about the brutality and sexual suggestiveness in the script, the SRC nevertheless felt that the novel's stature might enable the filmmakers "to go a step further in both dialogue and action than would ordinarily be the case."[75] When the finished picture was screened, Joy expressed a qualified confidence in its public reception but admitted that it was too early to know how it or the other horror pictures would fare: "Because it is based on a well established literary classic, the public and the censors may overlook the horrors which result from the realism of the Hyde make-up, though we are frank to say we cannot estimate what the reaction will be to this, or to the other horror pictures."[76]

Paramount also was preparing *Island of Lost Souls* (1933), based on the H. G. Wells novel about a scientist surgically transforming animals into human beings—a theme that worried the SRC with its potential for sacrilege. Despite this, the script quickly passed scrutiny, with a remaining reservation expressed only about a line of dialogue: "With regard to official censorship it is very likely that you will lose the line on Page D-35 in which Moreau says: 'Do you know how it seems to feel like God' since a similar line in a recent picture [i.e., *Frankenstein*] was eliminated by a majority of the boards. Aside from this we see no other details to which there could be any reasonable objection."[77] When the finished picture was screened, the SRC wrote that it should "cause very little difficulty from a censorable standpoint. . . . we see nothing in the picture to which any objection could be made. Incidentally, we enjoyed this picture thoroughly."[78]

The SRC's ready tolerance for these pictures, and its optimistic predictions for their success, contrast starkly with their reception by regional and overseas censors. *Island of Lost Souls,* for example, was banned in Singapore, New Zealand, Holland, Tasmania, Germany, India, Hungary, Italy, South Africa, the Netherlands, and Latvia, a fate that influenced the PCA's own subsequent view of the film. In 1935, it refused to grant a reissue license for *Island of Lost Souls* because of the film's "extreme horror," with Joseph Breen noting "the picture has been rejected in toto by fourteen censor boards."[79] In 1941 Paramount tried again to reissue the film and was again turned down, with Breen noting that the picture could not be approved under the Production Code because of the blasphemy of Moreau's experiments and "the general flavor of excessive gruesomeness and horror," which made the picture "quite definitely repulsive."[80] The PCA finally relented and granted a reissue certificate contingent on trims of dialogue dealing with the creation of life, with God, with the panther-woman's sexuality, and, crucially, the elimination of the "beastman on table and groans," a scene that had been widely cut by censor boards. The problems posed by this scene are directly tied to its aesthetic rendering of violence and link it with another widely deleted scene, in *Murders in the Rue Morgue,* of a woman tied to a cross and subjected to a gruesome medical experiment. In 1936, the PCA granted a reissue certificate for *Murders* provided this scene was mostly eliminated.

SOUND AND THE AMPLIFICATION OF PAIN

Both scenes are quite disturbing: they achieve this effect principally through the use of sound, in a manner that demonstrates the new ability that sound gave filmmakers to aesthetically stylize acts of cruelty and violence and to make these vivid and disturbing at a new and evocative sensory level. Both of these films were produced quite early in the sound era, and the two scenes show how the addition of audio information augments a viewer's impression of the overall level of violence on-screen relative to what a silent film image

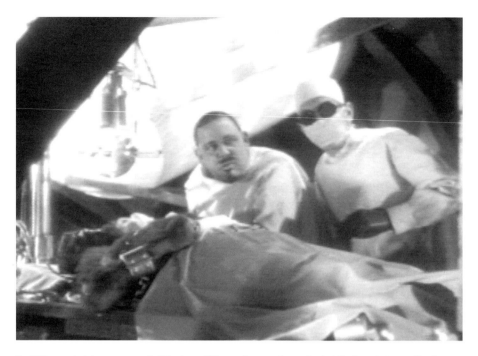

8. Little overt violence occurs in this view of Moreau's operating suite, but the beast strapped to the table is moaning in constant pain, and his crying (from off-screen) leads into this shot and extends beyond it.

can achieve. In both scenes, the audio conveys the sounds of suffering, alerting the viewer to the presence of *pain* in the depicted action—a component that little in the images is actually denoting. It is the sound of pain that takes the action in the scenes to such heights of violence that each scene became quite dangerous, in the eyes of censors upon the films' release and for the PCA when contemplating the pictures' subsequent reissue.

In *Island of Lost Souls,* ordinary guy Edward Parker is shipwrecked on Moreau's island and slowly learns of the doctor's fiendish surgeries upon the local wildlife. While speaking with Lota, a panther-woman whom Parker erroneously believes is human, they hear moaning and screaming from another part of Moreau's compound. Tracing the screams to their source, Parker finds himself at the door to Moreau's surgery, where he sees the doctor, in surgical garb, standing over a beast in human form, which is strapped to a table. The cries are coming from the captive beast. Horrified, Parker rushes away as the screams continue.

The moment of revelation—the shot inside the surgery that shows the beastman strapped to the table—is merely a moment of punctuation in a longer sequence, which begins with the onset of the crying and Parker's rush to investigate and ends with his dash away from the surgery and the gradual cessation of the cries. The revelation of Moreau's ghastly business—which Parker calls "torture" and "vivisection"—occupies just one shot (the view of the surgery), which lingers on-screen for nearly five seconds. The shot contains no overt violence. The beastman rolls his head back and forth on the table, and Moreau shouts for Parker to get out, but we never actually see Moreau doing anything to his victim. The shot, however, sits inside the framing material provided by sound—the screams that lead into and out of the view of the surgery. This audio information is much longer in duration. It lasts for forty seconds, which is an extraordinarily long time to be subjected to a character's suffering. Empirical studies of viewer reactions to screen violence have shown that when expressions of pain and suffering are present in a scene, viewers tend to attribute a greater level of violence to the depicted action.[81] That seems unquestionably to operate in the design of this scene: without the sound of the beastman's pain, the scene would contain virtually nothing disturbing or horrible. It was the sound of pain in this scene that motivated the censor action.

Those struggles are evident in connection with the offending scene in *Murders in the Rue Morgue*, where the insane Dr. Mirakle (Bela Lugosi) has bound a woman to a large cross in his laboratory and is subjecting her to repeated injections of blood from an ape. As in the scene from *Island of Lost Souls*, the audio information consists largely of sustained screaming, in terror and pain. The imagery in this case, however, is more overtly gruesome, with shadowy lighting and the evocation of sexual bondage and fetishism (the victim is bound in her underwear). She struggles against her bonds, and her hands twist violently against the restraints while she continuously moans and shrieks.

Much of the scene is shot as an extended, lengthy take that starts as a medium shot framing Mirakle as he injects her with ape blood. The camera then dollies back as he crosses to his desk and microscope, his victim framed prominently in the background. There are no cutaways to other objects or action that would serve to place the victim offscreen; she remains on-camera. The sustained framing of the distraught victim and her continuing cries are precisely the kind of intensive and unremitting focus on violence and cruelty that the PCA would work very hard henceforth to expunge from scripts and films, as will be evident in its handling of the torture scenes contained in *The Black Cat* (1934) and *The Raven* (1935). The visual and audio attention to torture in *Murders*, by contrast, is remarkably unimpeded. Worse yet, from the standpoint of censors and PCA authorities concerned about setting limits on the depiction of screen violence, Mirakle's victim succumbs to her ordeal

9. This torture and execution scene in *Murders in the Rue Morgue* is one of the most shocking instances of violence in early sound horror. The victim stays on-camera and, until her death, never
stops screaming.

and dies. She has been tortured to death. More remarkably yet, she dies on-
camera: there is no resort to off-screen discretion. Mirakle callously cuts her
body from the cross and dumps it into the river below his lab, like so much of-
fal. Within the space of a single shot, we witness the victim's anguish, her
death, and her transfiguration into waste material. This scene is the most hor-
rendous depiction of violence in the first wave of thirties horror films and af-
fords the viewer little respite from its sustained cruelties.

To its credit, the PCA was very concerned about the scene—so much so
that, following the screening for clearance, it required additional audio editing
to tone down the violence before the picture could qualify for a seal:

> Our feeling is that the screaming of the woman of the street in the scene in
> which she is being subjected to a test by Dr. Mirakle is over-stressed, not
> only from the standpoint of possible audience reaction but also censorship

objection. Because the victim is a woman in this instance, which has not heretofore been the case in other so-called "horror" pictures recently produced, censor boards are very likely to think that this scene is over done in gruesomeness. We therefore suggest that you ought to consider making a new soundtrack for this scene, reducing the constant loud shrieking to lower moans and an occasional modified shriek.[82]

As the scene now survives, the woman begins shrieking quite loudly as it opens, and then her cries drop to a lower level for the remainder of the action. Universal's audio re-mixing, however, failed to prevent widespread censor action on the film. Censor boards in Pennsylvania, Chicago and New York eliminated the scene. Virginia and Massachusetts permitted only a short flash of the woman tied to the cross, and Kansas allowed only the very end, where Mirakle is shown in close-up after disposing of the body as he says, "will my search never end?" By contrast with these regions, Ohio passed the film with no eliminations. The head of its censor board, however, issued a stern warning to the SRC, specifically citing the scene where Mirakle "has a woman tied with her hands above her head and is threatening and torturing her." Ohio's chief censor warned:

Up to the present we have permitted some of these sequences to be shown and have reduced the footage of others. I wish to advise you, however, that in the future we are going to take more drastic action concerning such scenes of horror and realism to which we have found the public is reacting unfavorably. In this I am asking for the cooperation of the Producers not to include such sequences in pictures so it will not be necessary for us to cut into the plots to remove them.[83]

Overseas, the picture was banned in Hungary. The SRC also had a difficult time with the censors in Canada; British Columbia had condemned and banned the picture from exhibition in Vancouver. Upon appeal the censor board approved the film with eliminations, which, not surprisingly, included Mirakle's torture of the woman. The SRC dispatched Jason Joy on a series of visits to regional censor boards to calm them regarding the brutal material appearing in the horror films and in other pictures generally. It wrote to express its gratitude to the British Columbia censors for reconsidering their decision to ban the film. "I am glad you saw fit to pass *Murders in the Rue Morgue*. It seemed to me imaginative and fantastic, and I felt that no-one could be seriously affected by the incidental idea of the doctor's experiments."[84] This is a curious and self-serving response. The doctor's experiments are hardly "incidental"—they are basic to the story. Their depiction involved the film's most sustained scene of brutality, one consistently involved in censor action.

The escalation of violence in horror films, which sound was helping to make possible, exposed the industry to serious risk. Rejection by a regional censor board meant the loss of playoff sites for exhibition and the revenue these would generate. Horror was big box office, but it carried substantial cultural and economic danger to the extent that these films alienated regional censors and citizens groups. Accordingly, in its message to the Canadian censors, the SRC tried to alleviate their concerns about upcoming films in the horror cycle and to remind them that their actions directly affected the welfare of the industry, especially in a time of global economic crisis: "You will soon probably be worrying about Metro-Goldwyn-Mayer's feature, *Freaks*. I understand the censor board has rejected it but I feel sure the company will make a sincere effort to eliminate every objectionable feature in order to save its play date in Vancouver. In these times of depression the loss of one play date for a picture is a matter of serious money."[85]

The industry had to weigh the risks and benefits of a continuing investment in the cycle of horror. Even as the SRC was giving relatively lax scrutiny to the violence in the first wave of horror pictures, Jason Joy was privately worrying about the moral and financial harm these pictures might do to the industry. In December 1931, Joy wrote to Will Hays, "perhaps it would be wise to obtain an early estimate of the audience reaction and critical opinion concerning *Dracula* and *Frankenstein* by Universal, *Dr. Jekyll and Mr. Hyde* by Paramount, and *Almost Married* by Fox, all of which are in distribution or are about to be distributed. Paramount has another 'gruesome' picture about to be put into production and Metro-Goldwyn-Mayer has *Freaks* which is about one-half shot."[86] He asked, "is this the beginning of a cycle which ought to be retarded or killed?"

He wrote again to Hays in early January urging that something be done about the horror pictures, worrying that the violence in the films would continue to escalate until the cycle wore itself out. He predicted that the films would be "straining for more and more horror until the wave topples over and breaks."[87] But the SRC's warnings to the studios about horror were not having much effect, Joy wrote, in a context where "*Frankenstein* is staying for four weeks and taking in big money at theatres which were about on the rocks." He suspected that the sampling of letters protesting the pictures reflected a more general public attitude. "If the scattered and more or less individual instances that come to our attention reflect the general attitude, resentment is surely being built up. How could it be otherwise if children go to these pictures and have the jitters, followed by nightmares? . . . Not only is there a future economic consideration, but maybe there is a real moral responsibility involved to which I wonder if we as individuals ought to lend our support."

The history of screen violence shows at least two constants. One the one hand, it plays out primarily as a *y*-axis phenomenon, as filmmakers continually amplify the stylistic inflection of mayhem. On the other, it rarely involves moments in which the industry queries its own moral responsibility for peddling violence and ramping up mayhem. Economic considerations tend to carry more weight than moral issues, as Breen's reply to Vandervoort essentially pointed out. Thus, Joy's question is itself a remarkable one, but as the $10 million profit that accrued from a decade of horror demonstrates, it had little effect on the proliferation of these pictures.

THE PCA TAKES A HARDER LINE

Profits aside, the violence in the first wave of horror films pointed to the region of crisis in which the SRC and the industry itself operated. The SRC was caught between the interests of the studios to exploit the box-office potential of these films, the desire of filmmakers to explore the capability of cinema for depicting gore and grotesquerie, and the demands of regional and overseas censor boards opposed to this material. There was no easy resolution of these competing imperatives. The industry did not act as radically toward horror films as it did with the gangster cycle, where it essentially renounced the production of the genre. But it did move more aggressively to scale down the violence in subsequent horror pictures, paying close scrutiny to scripted material and to finished scenes that it thought were too horrific.

A case in point is Universal's production of *The Black Cat*, which underwent script review by the PCA early in 1934. Writer-director Edgar G. Ulmer was fashioning a remarkably morbid tale about the clash between two twisted survivors of World War I. Vitus Werdegast (Bela Lugosi) is a psychiatrist with a morbid fear of cats and a consuming hatred for Hjalmar Poelzig (Boris Karloff), an architect who stole Werdegast's wife and daughter and left him for dead on the battlefields of Turkey. Poelzig has built an enormous mansion on the site of a Turkish fort where prisoners were tortured and executed, and in the basement of his mansion he keeps the bodies of women he has killed, storing them upright in bizarre glass coffins. One among them is Werdegast's wife, and as the psychiatrist arrives at the mansion, Poelzig is preparing the daughter for sacrifice in a black mass.

The climax of the film depicts the psychiatrist's ghastly vengeance. Werdegast and his hulking assistant seize Poelzig and tie him to an embalming rack. Werdegast gleefully announces to his victim that he plans to skin Poelzig alive and then he proceeds to do just that. The scene invites comparison with the torture scene in *Murders in the Rue Morgue*. Both feature a victim in bondage, strapped to a wooden apparatus with Lugosi as their tormentor. Yet the differences in their degree of explicitness, and their audiovisual design, point to the heightened degree of scrutiny that the PCA was giving to grotesque scenes in the horror genre by mid-decade. Compared with the scene in *Murders in the Rue Morgue*, the flaying scene in *The Black Cat* is handled more discretely, with a more oblique visual and audio presentation—in part because the idea of what is being depicted (flaying alive as opposed to forcible injection) is more extreme and ghastly.

The PCA expressed grave concerns about this scene during its review of the Peter Ruric script, due to the censorship and community protest aroused by *Frankenstein, Murders in the Rue Morgue, Island of Lost Souls* and other early horror pictures. While giving the script an overall approval, the PCA felt that the chief danger in the proposed film was the flaying scene: "The major difficulty on this score is indicated by the gruesomeness, which is suggested by the script, dealing with the scenes of the action of skinning a man alive. It is our understanding that you propose to suggest this merely by shadow or silhouette, but as we suggested this morning, this particular phase of your production will have to be handled with great care, lest it become too gruesome or revolting."[88]

After going on in the script review letter to mention other potential problem areas—several scenes in which cats were to be killed, the display of corpses of women in glass coffins—Breen again emphasized the seriousness of the problem that the flaying scene represented. "This entire sequence is a very dangerous one and it would be advisable for us to discuss them [sic] thoroughly before any further preparation is made." The PCA correctly anticipated that this scene would be ripe material for the regional censors and would be widely eliminated—actions that would be accompanied by a foreseeable amount of protest from viewers upset over the film's morbid and horrific material. And all of this would threaten the film's viability in badly needed markets.

The PCA did not suppress the scene in the script nor force the filmmakers to excise it from the picture. But it did work to encourage the filmmakers to adopt a more oblique approach to its representation. Thus, from the point where Poelzig is strapped to the rack, the scene is considerably shorter than the comparable torture action in *Murders in the Rue Morgue*. There the viewer has a continuous, unobstructed view of Mirakle's victim for the length of the scene and can plainly see and hear her struggles: her hands twisting against the restraints, and, of course, her ongoing screams. By contrast, the audio of the flaying is quite muted and conveys little sense of Poelzig's agonies. The

10. Silhouette lighting provided filmmakers with an effective means for indirectly showing prohibited kinds of violence. In *The Black Cat,* the skinning of Poelzig (Boris Karloff) appears as a shadow play.

viewer hears a only few quiet moans, nothing at all like the screaming that signaled the suffering in *Murders* and *Island of Lost Souls.* The evolving politics of screen violence were working, by mid-decade, to suppress the use of sound to delineate physical suffering. This suppression would have lasting consequences for American film, helping to make screen violence into the largely pain-free phenomenon that it remains even today.

With a similar logic—this time working toward the omission of visible cruelties—the scene shows very little of the flaying action. As soon as Werdegast begins slicing away at his victim, the film cuts to a shot of the action as suggested by Werdegast and Poelzig's shadows silhouetted against the wall. The silhouettes provide the viewer with quick glimpses of the flaying action, and they are the chief means by which the viewer can observe it. The silhouettes also take the viewer out of the action, at least as an event that is directly depicted for the camera. The viewer sees what is happening but only obliquely and briefly. Silhouetted depictions of violence are a major and recurring visual code in films of the 1930s, providing an indirect means for depicting acts of brutality. Silhouetted action also figured in the medical torture in *Murders in the Rue Morgue*, but there the silhouettes—shadows on the wall of Mirakle working on his bound victim—served to *introduce* the scene. The scene opens with the silhouettes, and the camera then dollies from them to the actual figures and stays on them for the remainder of the action, until Mirakle dumps the woman's body in the river. The trajectory of the visual design of violence in the Mirakle scene moves from the oblique to the explicit, whereas in *The Black Cat* it moves from explicit to oblique. This reversal of emphasis was a consequence of the changed political situation of movie violence by mid-decade, when the PCA was struggling to move filmmakers toward a more conservative presentation of gruesome material.

Despite its efforts, however, the PCA's initial sense that the scene was "dangerous" proved accurate. Numerous censor boards eliminated it. Maryland, Ohio, Ontario, and Chicago deleted all or a portion of it, while the picture was wholly banned in British Malaya, Italy, Sweden, Austria, and Finland.

When Lugosi and Karloff again teamed up in another adaptation of Poe, *The Raven* (1935), Breen wrote to Universal to caution it about "the current accumulation of horror in motion pictures," and the PCA was even more stringent in its efforts to restrain the filmmakers.[89] In *The Raven* Lugosi plays Dr. Vollin, a surgeon with an obsession for Poe and a basement full of torture devices, the most elaborate being a huge pendulum with a sharpened blade that slowly descends toward a victim strapped to a slab below. Vollin surgically disfigures the face of a criminal, Bateman (Karloff), so as to blackmail him into carrying out Vollin's wishes. These involve exacting an elaborate revenge upon a judge, Thatcher, who has crossed him. Vollin lures the judge to his estate, whereupon Bateman seizes him and straps him to the slab. Vollin then starts the descending pendulum.

Examining the script for the proposed film, the PCA drew an immediate line in the sand, advising "great care" in handling scenes of "excessive horror and brutality."[90] These included the operation upon Bateman (only the resulting disfigurement appears in the finished film), the various torture devices in Vollin's basement, and the knife blade sweeping down on Thatcher. At an ensuing script conference, the filmmakers and the PCA agreed that "no detail of the actual operation upon Bateman will be shown," and "Bateman's appearance will never be unhumanly repulsive." To ensure this, Universal shot some test footage of Karloff made up as the disfigured Bateman and screened it for approval by the PCA—a highly unusual procedure that departed from the agency's normative methods of evaluating only scripted material.

The other conditions for depicting the film's horrors were that "the instruments of torture will be passed in review, as if in a museum," "blood will not be shown," and "the pendulum knife will not touch Thatcher's body."[91] Not only that, the knife never even gets close to touching him, a development that also seems to have been stipulated in the agreement between the filmmakers and the PCA. These conditions, of course, preclude the film from developing much suspense about whether Thatcher will be harmed. His torture provides the climax to the film, and the now-tame manner in which it appears tends to rob the film of tension and impact. The swinging pendulum stays at a discreet and never-terribly-exciting distance. The tortures that filmmakers had depicted in the first wave of horror films were now deemed too dangerous for the industry, and, while they were not excised from the screen, their depiction lacked even the suggestion of a hard edge. Despite these efforts, however, censors in New York, Ohio, Pennsylvania, and Virginia deleted some or all of the pendulum torture, and censors in Pennsylvania removed the close-ups of Bateman's face following the operation.

THE LIMITS OF PCA POWER

The PCA felt that its negotiations on *The Raven* and *The Black Cat* had been productive and satisfactory and that the filmmakers had been cooperative in toning down material that would otherwise have been provocatively explicit. After a screening of *The Black Cat* and its certification for release, the PCA wrote to Universal, saying, "we are particularly pleased with the manner in which your studio and director have handled this subject, and we congratulate you."[92] By contrast, the agency's experience with Universal over the long-awaited sequel to *Frankenstein* was considerably less harmonious. This case shows the agency's limited ability to overrule filmmakers and studio executives when they were really determined to push screen violence past a point the PCA felt was safe. It came to feel that Universal was ignoring its admonitions over the violence in the script for the *Frankenstein* sequel, with results that the agency believed were both dismal and predictable.

The Return of Frankenstein (the title later changed to *Bride of Frankenstein*) underwent script review in December of 1934, and while the PCA approved it overall under the Code, the agency was very concerned about what appeared to be a lot of murders and a high body count in the scenes as scripted:

One of the principal elements which we believe needs further attention is the number of killings which this present script indicates. We counted ten separate scenes in which the monster either strangles or tramples people to death—this, in addition to some other murders by subsidiary characters. In a picture as basically gruesome as this one we believe such a great amount of slaughter is unwise, and we recommend very earnestly that you do something about toning this down.[93]

Directly following the studio's receipt of this letter, director James Whale met with the PCA's Geoffrey Shurlock and Iselin Auster and assured them that he would handle the killings in the script in a discreet manner and would not dwell unduly on their details. Hearing the filmmaker describe how he intended to shoot the material served, at the time, to allay the PCA's concerns. Whale also conveyed his intentions in writing to Joseph Breen, telling him, "the killings will all be minimized in the photographing of the scenes, most of them being in one little sequence to describe the reign of terror, and the whole of the film on this will be very short." He added the assurance, "I note what you say about shooting the picture with the utmost care and good taste and I assure you that this is my intention."[94] The PCA formalized this understanding in another letter to the studio, a missive that served to clarify the common ground the agency thought it had reached with the filmmakers. "It is our understanding that Mr. Whale intends to shoot the various killings in this picture in a decidedly impressionistic manner, without devoting much footage to them, and in such a way as to avoid the gruesome details."[95]

The film then went into production, and a warning sign soon emerged that the filmmakers might be contemplating additional horrific material beyond what was scripted. Lillian Russell, with the Office of the Censor at Universal Pictures, telephoned to ask how the PCA would regard new material that would involve mutilating one of the main characters—who was, making the idea more severe yet, a woman. The PCA quickly vetoed the idea. As Geoffrey Shurlock recorded in a memo, Russell "called about the proposed sequence dealing with grafting of heroine's heart onto female monster. I suggested that the script was already heavy with gruesome elements and expressed fear that any further exaggeration along this line might make the finished picture unacceptable screen fare. Miss Russell indicated that the studio was not at all committed to the idea themselves."[96] The last remark is an interesting one and suggests that the query may have been a trial balloon, to see what would happen—that is, to gauge how the PCA would respond and what the filmmakers might get away with.

When the PCA finally saw the finished picture, it seemed to realize that Whale's assurances of discretion had not served to keep the material as filmed within acceptable limits. Moreover, in reaction to the censor action elicited by the first wave of horror pictures, the PCA took a hard line with the violence and gruesome imagery in *The Bride of Frankenstein*. The agency rejected the film as a violation of the Production Code "because of its excessive brutality and gruesomeness."[97] As was customary in the PCA's dealings with studios, however, a rejection did not close the door to a negotiated solution to the problem that would enable the picture to pass certification. Accordingly, the PCA's rejection letter went on to suggest specific material that might be eliminated from the film. Were they to be wholly enacted by the filmmakers, the recommended cuts would have excised from the film virtually all of the elements qualifying as horror. Furthermore, some of the recommended excisions were of material that was hardly emphasized in the visual design of a scene. An example is the deletion of the monster's bloody hands in the hermit's hut (see list item number 6). The camera pans down from the monster's face to his outstretched arms—outstretched in friendship for the blind hermit—and several rivulets of blood can be seen on his hand, a wound likely incurred in a scuffle with gypsies in a preceding scene. The blood is not excessive, but it does represent a wounding to the body—and in the 1930s visible trauma to bodily tissue was treated with great caution by filmmakers and the PCA because of its predictable excision by regional censors. Thus, Breen on principle recommended its deletion, in spite of the relatively minor nature of the visible bleeding.

The extent of the recommended deletions and the attention given to relatively minor details like the blood on the monster's hand suggests that they were a tactical, not strategic, maneuver by the PCA. It is likely that the letter was meant to serve as an opening gambit in the negotiations that would surely follow. Granting this likelihood, however, does not diminish the agency's conviction that the film, as completed, contained an abundance of horror elements that would elicit too much action by regional censor boards. The subsequent antipathies in the dealings between the PCA and Universal confirm that at the time Breen sent the rejection letter, the agency was firm in its belief that this picture was a dangerous one from the standpoint of the political and economic losses that would ensue for the studio. Addressing the Universal studio liaison, Breen wrote, "I respectfully suggest that you suggest to Mr. Laemmle his consideration of the following recommendations:"[98]

1. Delete all the offensive "breast shots" in reel one.
2. Delete the shots of the monster in the pool actually drowning Hans;
3. Delete shot of monster actually pushing Hans's wife into the cistern;
4. Delete the shots of the little girls coming out of church in their white dresses and discovering the body of the little girl lying on the ground;
5. Delete the shot of the mother carrying the child's dead body in her arms;
6. Delete the shot of the bloody hands of the monster in the hermit's hut;

7. Delete entirely the sequences of the idiot nephew strangling his uncle;
8. Delete the close-up shot of the monster as he falls, crashing the lid of a coffin and later seems to fondle the head of the corpse;
9. Cut the entire sequence of the deserted street and the murder of the woman by the half-wit;
10. Cut the shot of the heart being taken from a jar with the forceps;
11. Cut the shot of the monster throwing the man over the roof.[99]

Two days after the PCA's rejection of the screened film, Breen went to Universal and met with Carl Laemmle, Jr., James Whale, and Harry Zehner, and the group thrashed out their differences over how much violence could remain in the finished film. Universal resisted making the cuts that the PCA had recommended, and, faced with the studio's unwillingness to remove as much material as the PCA wanted, Breen compromised and allowed most of the recommended deletions to stand. The only recommended cuts that were agreed to and accepted were those numbered 1, 5, and 7 in the rejection letter. Deletion number 2, showing the monster drowning Hans, would remain in the film but would lose its details, namely, shots showing the bubbling of the water and the monster laughing. A cutaway to an owl serves to cover the deleted footage in this drowning scene. The monster advances on Hans in long-shot and then, in medium-shot, grabs him and pushes him below the water. The cutaway to a close-up of an owl then follows, serving to leap over the shots that were omitted of the water frothing with Hans's struggles and the monster laughing. Following the shot of the owl, a close-up of the monster indicates that the struggle is over and Hans is dead. Viewing the scene from an editing standpoint and in light of the PCA correspondence, one can see clearly that there is missing material: shots of the death that the studio agreed to lose.

Gone now also is the shot of the mother carrying her dead child, identified in Breen's letter as suggested deletion number five. The children run from the church in their white dresses, and they discover the corpse, discretely hidden by some shrubbery, but the action cuts away to another location before the mother can pick up her dead child. How the child died is left unexplained. Thus, from a narrative and an editing standpoint, the action is choppy and unsatisfactorily enigmatic.

The murder scene, identified as deletion number nine, which Breen had recommended losing entirely, would now be shortened in the following way: "The shot on the deserted street, in which the half-wit throws the blanket over the head of the woman is to be cut from the spot where he actually covers the woman's head with the blanket."[100] As the scene exists in the finished film, Karl reaches for his victim with the scarf. He is using it to blind her, which will en-

11. Because of censor action on the first wave of horror films in the sound period, the PCA tried to take a harder line with subsequent pictures. It recommended that much of the violence be deleted from *Bride of Frankenstein,* including some of the details in this drowning scene, but Universal resisted making all of the cuts.

able him to kill her more easily. In action that the narrative suggests will occur but which happens offscreen, he will rip open her chest and cut the heart from her body and then give the organ to Frankenstein for use in vivifying the bride. It was probably this suggested violation of a corpse that motivated the PCA to recommend trimming the scene and motivated censor boards to trim the action even further. As the film now exists, as soon as Karl reaches for the woman with his scarf, a quick dissolve takes the viewer out of the scene, omitting the ensuing violence.

The other recommended deletions were not carried out, the picture remaining as it was. However, it is likely that some trimming occurred with the shot designated as elimination number ten. As soon as Dr. Frankenstein's assistant lifts the heart out with forceps and it appears on-screen, a fast dissolve to another location takes the viewer away from the scene and the disembodied organ. The placement of this dissolve, coming so abruptly, suggests that some frames of the shot in which the heart is displayed were dropped.

After negotiating these cuts, everyone at the meeting agreed that the PCA would re-screen the film before giving a final decision about its release certificate. Even so, Universal had won a significant victory—preserving many of the shots the PCA wanted cut from the film—and had done so in a context unlike the early 1930s, where the political response of local communities to films of gruesome horror was all too clear. By agreeing to Universal's position of minimizing cuts to the picture prior to release, the PCA was tacitly agreeing to weather the storm of protest and censor action that horror films were by then routinely arousing.

But it did so reluctantly, as subsequent correspondence about the reaction to the picture by censor boards confirms. Before the picture was released, the PCA warned Universal that it was facing virtually certain action by censors, and the agency reiterated its view that this was a dangerous picture. The warning carried an implicit scolding, as the PCA viewed Universal's determination to disregard its recommendations as a foolish course of action. Writing to Universal to convey his judgment that the picture was acceptable under the Code, Breen warned, "it is more than likely that this picture will meet with considerable difficulty at the hands of political censor boards, both in this country and abroad. The very nature of the production is such as to invite very critical examination on the part of these censor boards and you may well expect difficulty with it wherever the picture is shown."[101] He closed by emphasizing the volatility of the censorship climate in the country and the limited ability of the Production Code to protect filmmakers. "It is the kind of a picture which is acceptable under the *letter* of our Production Code, but very dangerous from the standpoint of political censorship."

Although censors in Kansas, New York, and Massachusetts approved the picture without eliminations, it ran into trouble with the Ohio Board of Censors. (Overseas, it was banned in Hungary, Palestine and Trinidad and was passed in Japan and Sweden but with eliminations numerous enough to require two pages for listing.) The eliminations ordered in Ohio were especially galling to the PCA because many pertained to scenes the agency had originally asked Universal to cut. These included the drowning of Hans, the monster pushing the woman into the cistern, the entire episode of the discovery of the murdered girl, the half-wit attacking the woman, and the monster throwing the man from the roof.

Faced with these cuts before the picture could enter markets in Ohio, Harry Zehner, at Universal, wrote to Breen asking his help in getting the Ohio censors to reinstate some of the deleted material. Although the SRC and the PCA had traditionally done just this—interceded for studios with local censor boards—Zehner's request was infuriating in light of Universal's intransigence in its pre-release negotiations with the PCA. Zehner's request occasioned an outburst of anger and frustration from Breen, which he expressed in a letter to Will Hays.

He began by recounting the history of the agency's dealings with Universal over the picture, emphasizing the agency's concern that the script included too much brutality and the studio's reluctance to follow the agency's advice about material to eliminate. When the finished picture was screened, "we told the studio that it was unacceptable, and succeeded in getting them to make a number of eliminations."[102] Breen pointed out that the PCA cautioned Laemmle, Whale, and Zehner that even though it had approved the picture for release, local censors would surely demand cuts. "All three of the Universal executives waved aside our decision in the matter and told us they were willing 'to take a chance' on these eliminations." Breen continued, "curiously enough, of the (9) eliminations ordered by the Ohio Board (6) of them—definitely—were eliminations which we warned the studio would be made."

Breen then raised the fundamental issue. How ought the PCA to behave, with regard to political censorship, when studios defied its recommendations? Studios that did so were failing to support the system that had mandated a Code and an agency empowered to apply it. In light of that, what obligations did the PCA have? Did a studio's intransigence lessen the agency's obligation to intercede on its behalf with regional censors? Breen wrote,

> The point in this whole discussion is this: what responsibility, if any, have we to defend a picture before political censor boards, where the studio deliberately refuses to accept our counsel in the matter and risk mutilation?
>
> In making the eliminations, the Ohio censor board has run true to form. Six of the eliminations are of the exact kind which censor boards, everywhere, almost invariably delete from pictures. We expected these eliminations, and now we have them.
>
> This whole matter is important because, as you know, I have been trying to bring it about that, when we approve a picture under the Code, it is our responsibility to defend our decision against censor mutilation at all costs. But with these borderline cases—instances where scenes, or lines, or episodes in the picture, are acceptable under the Code—how far ought we to go?[103]

As I noted earlier, the dilemma was irresolvable because the interests of filmmakers and the PCA did not necessarily coincide. The agency was a braking mechanism—not an industry censor—designed to inhibit, but not expunge, depictions of violence and brutality. The filmmakers, studio executives, and PCA staff involved agreed that violence was an inextricable part of certain kinds of stories. These included horror films, crime pictures, Westerns, adventure films, and war films. Violence was an integral and inherent part of the American screen, and the issue became one of finding its acceptable limits. The regional censors helped determine these limits. The PCA well knew the type of material that censors rejected, and this guided the agency's negotiations with filmmakers. The problem was that the objectives of filmmakers and the PCA were different. Filmmakers often desired to push against the restraints on screen expression—tried to accelerate against the brakes the PCA sought to apply. When this happened, the PCA could find itself in a lose-lose situation, compelled to relent and allow more brutality on-screen than it wanted and then to face action by local censors and complaints by studios and their requests for assistance. A genre like horror accelerated the development of these tensions because horror, and the violence it involves, is a cumulative experience. Audiences become accustomed to existing thresholds of violence and morbidity, and filmmakers then find that they have to go further to evoke the same level of response.

Conclusion

Bride of Frankenstein today has the reputation of being a harmlessly campy film, in part due to a critical tendency to view James Whale as a filmmaker who subverted the norms of the period by injecting a gay sensibility into the picture and enlivening the comedy with attitudes that today are recognized as camp. To be sure, the film is comical, often to the detriment of its horror elements. But what has seemingly vanished from our contemporary understanding of the picture is how dangerous this film was regarded to be: how Whale, and the picture's screenwriters and the executives at Universal, pushed for more violence and brutality than the PCA thought was safe. Indeed, today the picture is hardly thought of as being violent at all; film scholars almost universally regard it as a comedy. But the PCA's struggle with Universal over the production and release of this film shows clearly how volatile, tense, and fragile were the relationships that bound studios to the agency and how relative was the agency's authority, with respect both to filmmakers and to the regional censors.

This struggle also demonstrates how charged the political atmosphere surrounding horror had become by 1935—so much so that the agency was willing to countenance the removal of virtually all of the horrific elements from the film. In light of this, it should not surprise us that the genre, as practiced by Universal and other majors, would eventually devolve into safe adolescent programming (e.g., *Frankenstein Meets the Wolf Man, House of Frankenstein, House of Dracula*). This devolution is usually attributed to an exhaustion of the genre's classical monsters and narrative formulae. But it also stems at least in part from the suppression of violence, instigated by the reactions of regional censors to the horror pictures and the PCA's increased scrutiny of the genre.

In this regard, violence is the great ghost in the genre, lurking behind its controversies. Although many of the period's horror pictures are strong on atmosphere and minimize overt violence, its implicit presence in the morbid story situations helped fuel the attacks on the genre by the regional censors. Moreover, the genre's violence wasn't always implicit. When it was overt it assumed blatantly cruel forms, mixed with sadism and torture, and swiftly provoked efforts to limit the ability of filmmakers to evoke these qualities. It is striking how quickly violence in early thirties horror films moved toward extreme forms of physical assault and violation and how essential sound was in the evocation of these portraits of atrocity. The modern viewer who believes that there isn't much violence in the old Hollywood films, or much cruelty or sadism, needs to take a closer look at the films examined in this book. In this chapter alone we have seen a woman kidnapped, tortured, and executed, transformed on-camera from a human being to waste matter dumped in a river. We've seen directly (or through implied action) characters skinned alive, burned alive, murdered and their hearts ripped from their bodies, and the killing of children.

This is a remarkable amount of brutality, made more striking by its inability to move or affect many modern viewers, for whom these old pictures might seem quaint, charming, campy or boring. The violence in classical Hollywood film can seem transparent, invisible, and hardly worth remarking on compared with films today. It often provokes laughter. Rather than providing an accurate portrait of the older films, however, this response may serve only to indicate how far culture has traveled in its ability to assimilate increasingly violent forms of popular entertainment. For in their day, these pictures were dangerous for the industry to make.

The SRC underestimated the strength of the dark currents of violence coursing through the horror film and the speed at which these would grow. Faced with the efflorescence of especially cruel forms of violence, the industry was swift to intervene and place a ceiling on the efforts of filmmakers to push violence further. We will see exactly this pattern replicated in the films of gun violence examined in the next chapter. The fact that this struggle was playing out in the industry across different genres suggests how fundamental the lure of violence was for many of Hollywood's directors. The result of their work was the rapid archiving among creative artists of knowledge about how to do violence for the movies. In a more negative direction, the lessons of horror demonstrated that depictions of violence could have markedly destructive effects upon a film, inciting cuts by regional censors, and suggested that film violence could become one of the industry's most dangerous problems. As it would, and it would be an insoluble one.

Nowhere was the drive toward harder-edged violence more visible than in the crime film, and specifically in the gangster film. The industry had fought an extended series of skirmishes over the censorship of its popular horror pictures. Those battles were nothing compared to the explosions that surrounded the escalating violence in crime and gangster movies. Moreover, the elaboration of violence in those pictures far exceeded what had been accomplished in the horror films. It was more extensive and was embedded in more complex structures of picture and sound. The real love affair of filmmakers in American cinema is with gun violence. We turn now to an examination of those pictures in which it flourished.

3
Elaborating Gun Violence

As a roadster speeds around the corner, the police wait in ambush, armed with Tommy guns. The car races up the street, its door flies open, and a body spills out and bounces on the pavement. The cops open up with pistols and machine-guns, and the staccato popping of the weaponry blends with the sirens of motorcycles in pursuit of the speeding car. Cops swarm the concrete streets. A close-up shows the lifeless face of Gimpy, a local mobster. He stares open-eyed at nothing, blood streaming from his nose and both sides of his mouth.

Doorway to Hell (1930) has been called the prototype of the classic gangster film, and while much of the violence in the picture is awkwardly staged, this scene is uncommonly vivid.[1] In the rattling of Tommy guns and the wailing of sirens, it shows the new sensuousness that sound technology brought to screen violence and the sudden flurry of brutality—violence hopped-up on speed—that would be most at home in the gangster film.

Doorway to Hell was released a few months before *Little Caesar* and has been eclipsed by that picture and those it helped to spawn. But this scene and another—the drive-by machine-gunning of a mobster—show very clearly what is coming in the nascent gangster genre: outbursts of gun violence that would bring the sadism of horror pictures down to street level, situated in more immediately familiar settings. Perhaps because their violence belonged to a recognizably real world of urban streets, rather than ancient castles in Europe or uncharted tropical islands, the gangster films ignited a level of controversy that surpassed what surrounded the horror films. *Little Caesar* was part of the triumvirate of gangster movies, along with *Public Enemy* (1931) and *Scarface* (1932), that helped to spawn the classic phase of the genre. These pictures became so dangerous for the industry that it shut down their production in 1935 and shifted to crime pictures extolling the exploits of federal agents fighting the gangsters.

Curtailing the production of gangster pictures was only the most visible and radical sign of the industry's effort to respond to its critics. Less obviously, and of longer-lasting duration, were the policies adopted by the Production Code Administration (PCA) for dealing with gun violence and the depiction of armed conflict with the law that was endemic to crime films. These policies guided the PCA's evaluation of scripts for more than two decades, and they stemmed from the state of crisis in which the gangster cycle had thrown the industry. Widespread censor action on these films threatened to undermine the integrity of the newly passed Production Code, and the accelerating vividness of the violence in these films challenged the Studio Relations Committee (SRC) to formulate a set of policies to deal with the essential problem they posed: the attractions of violence dispensed by antisocial and sociopathic characters.

As it did with horror pictures, in the 1930s the PCA cracked down on violent crime films. By the 1940s, however, filmmakers were making a concerted effort to push against the existing restraints, and they brought a tide of brutality and explicitness to the screen that surpassed the violence of the classic gangster films. By that time, however, the PCA was less aggressive and effective, and the result helped to mark the beginning of the end for the agency. It was also the start of a more explicit and hard-edged violence that prefigures, and helped to precipitate, the modern screen violence that begins in earnest with *Bonnie and Clyde* and the Code and Rating Administration (CARA) system of 1968. In this chapter, I examine the styling of violence in gangster and crime films and the policies surrounding the depiction of guns and gun violence and the duration of these policies. In the next chapter, I examine the push toward harder violence that began in the 1940s.

ON THE LOW RANGE OF STYLISTIC AMPLITUDE

The early thirties gangster films have a varying and inconsistent degree of stylistic amplitude. A single film like *Doorway to Hell* may show strikingly disparate degrees of sophistication in its styling of violence from scene to scene. This variation suggests that the awareness among filmmakers of how to style violence for the camera was a rudimentary one, inconsistently grasped and unevenly executed. While the dumping of the body from the roadster gets a strong cinematic treatment, a subsequent scene showing a large-scale, gang war shoot-out at a brewery is choreographed quite poorly. Filmed almost entirely in long-shot, the blocking of the action is awkward and clumsy, the compositions are disorganized, and the sound of gunfire conveys little sense of perspective or direction. It is difficult to look at the images and know who is doing what to whom. The only composition that is not a long-shot framing is a medium close-up of a cop calling the station on his phone box. He takes a slug, but the viewer really has to infer this. It is more implicit than explicit. The soundtrack is unorganized; no gunshot is given sufficient prominence to suggest that a bullet has struck him. Based on what the viewer sees, the character seems to be suddenly overcome with lassitude and sinks out of the frame, as if he has fallen asleep. The shooting lacks physicality, as does all of the violence in this big action set-piece. Ironically, a montage of newspaper headlines had introduced the scene, heralding a gang war reign of terror. Because the scene that follows lacks sufficient stylistic amplitude, the viewer sees nothing so exciting as a reign of terror.

In the following discussion of the early gangster films, I want to examine the variations in their stylistic amplitude and show what filmmakers were realizing about the contribution that different elements of cinema—lighting, editing, performance, the choreography of movement—could make in the styling of violence. Of supreme importance is sound—and, arguably, this component played the role of catalyst, stimulating filmmakers to take the other components of cinema to a higher level of contribution. The lesson for the stylistic history of screen violence that emerges from the varying amplitude of these pictures is that once filmmakers learn compelling ways of styling violence, the methods can't be unlearned. They go into the storehouse of cinema syntax and stay there, available to subsequent filmmakers whose interests incline them in this direction.

Of those films in the classic triumvirate, *Little Caesar* is actually the least violent. It contains none of the gruesome or grotesque elements that can be found in *Public Enemy* and *Scarface*. *Public Enemy,* for example, ends with memorably brutal imagery. A rival gang kills Tom Powers (James Cagney) and leaves his body at his mother's home. Tom is trussed up on a stretcher and swathed in gauze like a mummy, except for his ravaged face. The mobsters prop the stretcher against the front door, so that it falls forward and into the room when his brother opens the door. A low-angle camera frames the action, and Tom's corpse falls into the face of the camera. It's a sudden, jarring end to the film, and it was a scene widely deleted by censors. *Scarface* has innumerable killings, the most savage of which occur in the montage of Tommy gun murders, with men convulsing before flame-spouting machine-guns.

By contrast, the violence in *Little Caesar* is less stylish—that is to say, is less attuned to the cinematic properties that could make it arresting and hypnotic. In this regard, it is very similar to the zero-degree level of amplitude found in the brewery shoot-out in *Doorway to Hell*. At the beginning of the film when Rico (Edward G. Robinson) is a just small-time punk, he sticks up a gas station; the camera stays outside and the viewer sees none of the violence that occurs, only hears the popping of a pistol. The elision of violent action, of course, can be a very effective strategy (and we will explore this strategy in depth in chapter five), but here it isn't. For it to work well, the viewer needs to have a well-developed sense—and, often, a dread about—the specific nature of the violence transpiring off-camera. The viewer here has neither kind of investment in the action, and, as a result, the elision of the gas station shooting is merely an unsatisfying way of leaping over the violence.

When Rico is a big-time gangster, his enemies try to take him out with a machine-gun ambush, firing from a passing wagon on the street. The bullet hits on the storefront are vivid—they ought to be, since real bullets were used to knock out chunks of masonry—but Rico's wounding is depicted in an almost off-hand manner. The framing and editing of the action virtually occlude the wounding instead of centering it and clarifying it. It becomes apparent that Rico has been hit only because Robinson can be seen holding his upper arm. This casual depiction is not at all like the details of death in *Public Enemy* and *Scarface,* where we see what bullets and beatings will do to a body. Rico's end—cut down by a cop's machine-gun—is a legendary scene mainly because of his great exit line, "Mother of Mercy, is this the end of Rico?" As violence, however, the staging is clumsy, and it is badly choreographed from one edit point to the next.

The film nevertheless elicited considerable action by censor boards, but they seemed relatively indifferent to the stylistic dimensions of gun violence. The backlash against the genre was a function of its representational content—that is, the fact that the films were built around bad-guy characters who achieve great wealth and success by being ruthless and violent. The problem the gangster film posed for the industry principally lay here, in putting the gun in the hand of the criminal. It didn't always matter whether the gun was fired or with what cinematic gusto. Merely brandishing the gun was enough for censors to delete the image. By putting guns in the hands of criminals and building pictures around those characters and their bloody deeds, the industry, to its critics, was making pictures that lacked a voice for morality. The violence on-screen could be stagy and theatrical, as in *Little Caesar,* or fluid and cinematic, as in *Scarface*—either way, it was the x-axis, the behavioral referent, which was considered so dangerous in the discourse of the period. As Richard Maltby points out, "concerns about the representation of violence . . . formed part of a broader disquiet about the representation of criminality."[2]

The release of *Little Caesar* was greeted with the kind of censor action that had surrounded gun imagery in the 1920s, when, it will be recalled from chapter one, the mere display of guns was sufficient to prompt elimination. This was a prime example of the dominance of referential content over style. The Pennsylvania board, for example, deleted virtually all of the film's gunplay except for the last scene in which the police machine-gun Rico. The Pennsylvania eliminations report collected by the PCA listed as deletions:

Reel 1—views of man standing with his hands up in doorway and backing into doorway

Reel 3—views of men holding guns on others in café

Reel 4—views of Rico shooting from car

Reel 5—views of shooting from wagon as it passes along street

Reel 5—views of man holding gun on man at outer door of café

Reel 5—views of man holding gun on man at inside door of café

Four of these deletions involve no gun violence, no discharge of a weapon. They involve the brandishing of guns, which, as in the 1920s, the censors considered volatile material. Furthermore, these scenes have minimal stylistic elaboration. The camera set-ups are functional, and little is done with composition, camera movement, or editing to make the violence more vivid. The Pennsylvania censors were not acting against shockingly stylized screen violence. The danger of the film lay in the referential acts to which the images pointed—criminals using guns—and not in their stylistic embodiment. This danger was compounded by the charismatic performance of Robinson and by the centrality of his character in the film's plot. Rico became the picture's hero, and his unregenerate qualities, his refusal to knuckle under to anyone, were shown as admirable.

In this regard, it is significant that the Pennsylvania board did not require any trims of the police ambush that concludes the film. Guns were brandished here, too, but the censors did not deem Rico's shooting by law authorities to be threatening to the public order because of the moral value of showing the police prevail. Even if Rico remains unrepentant, the police catch and execute him. In this regard, it could be said that the picture asserted the moral voice for legal authority. The PCA's great ideological struggle with the genre lay in trying to balance the sociopathic charisma of the gangster with the moral voice of legal authority. The PCA expended considerable effort to develop an appropriate moral voice within the brutality and violence of crime pictures— even to the point of bolstering the Code with new amendments stipulating how weaponry or law officers had to be depicted. The lure of violence, though, would prove to have its own siren call.

Perhaps in response to that call, censors in Alberta, Canada, rejected the film entirely, finding its referencing of crime and violence to be too dangerous to public order. They condemned the film as "an unrelieved crime picture, in which there was nothing but the plotting to commit a crime, or actually carrying it out." In their view, "a picture of this kind had two functions—one was to teach young criminals how to commit crime, and secondly to stimulate them to become heroes by doing these things."[3]

SRC head Jason Joy tried to outmaneuver the censor boards by positioning the film as a picture against gangsters, which aimed to dramatize their danger to society. This stratagem had an element of duplicity. It is doubtful that many viewers of *Little Caesar* came away from the film more impressed with the blank, cardboard figures of the police, who figure in only a few scenes, than with the flamboyance of Rico. Nevertheless, in its effort to locate an acceptable moral voice within the gangster cycle, the PCA would aim to position all three early classics—*Little Caesar, Public Enemy* and *Scarface*—as exposes of the criminal menace to society.

Hoping to get *Little Caesar* past the Vancouver Board of Censors, which had rejected the picture, Joy wrote its chief censor, "in my opinion, if there ever was a production against crime and gangsters, it's this picture."[4] He enclosed a letter from a criminologist, who consulted on occasion for the SRC and who evaluated the film and believed that it showed "the alertness of the police" in pursuing Rico and the "the supremacy of law and order."[5]

In his battle with the New York censor board, Joy claimed that the film had to show the violence and ruthlessness of Rico and his gang in order to emphasize the need to combat them. "The description of the lawless acts of the gangsters in 'Little Caesar' is necessary in order that the audience may understand for what acts the characters are being punished and may have therefore the opportunity to compare the profitableness of the acts with the punishment finally received."[6] Joy continued, "the more ghastly, the more ruthless the criminal acts of these gangsters are shown on the screen, the stronger will be the audience reaction against men of their kind and organized crime in general." In this regard, he argued, the depiction of violence and brutality was absolutely necessary for the film's ability to morally instruct its viewers. Censor action aimed at reducing the depiction of criminal behavior by removing its details worked to "reduce and even destroy the moral value of the picture as a whole."

As Joy worked feverishly to appeal the censor bans, he worried about the effects on the industry of the backlash that *Little Caesar* was generating. His remarks provide another demonstration that the SRC's fundamental alliance lay with filmmakers and the studios and not with the regional censor boards.

The SRC acted as a pubic liaison for the industry, but at times like these, in battling for a controversial film, its antipathy for regional censors and their hobbling effects on creative expression plainly emerged. Of the New York censor board, he wrote, "they are riding hell out of us."[7] He derided the British Columbia censors as "probably the most exacting and fault-finding of any censors in the world."[8] After a year during which the British Columbia censors showed cooperation with films made within the strictures of the Production Code, Joy lamented that they "have reverted to their former small, narrow, picayunish fault-finding attitude, with their eyes so firmly glued on little details that they are unable to see the picture as a whole and judge it accordingly."[9]

Joy's greatest fear was that widespread censor action on *Little Caesar* would undermine the newly passed Production Code and the efforts of the SRC to encourage filmmakers to abide by the Code. "It is really too bad to allow censors to reject or mutilate pictures that are conscientiously and sincerely made within the Code," he wrote. "The inevitable result of this will be the complete downfall of the Code."[10] In other correspondence he worried, "when [filmmakers] see their careful work destroyed by vigorous censorship with eyes glued on details, nothing can result but their utter discouragement and a dissipation of the results of the constant and painstaking work this Association is doing."[11] Battles with the censors over a picture like *Little Caesar* thus acquired greater significance, symbolizing a larger struggle over who would control the representational content of American cinema. Joy urged aggressive action. "This censor business is going to need some careful and strong methods if we are not to allow production to be taken entirely out of our hands and placed in those of the censors. . . . We ought to fight for every picture and every single situation in every picture whenever we feel the slightest justification for it."[12] At stake and at risk of being lost was "our right to make and exhibit pictures which conform to the standards of good taste among reasonably intelligent people."[13]

AN UPSURGE IN STYLISTIC AMPLITUDE

While *Little Caesar* was embroiled in its censor battles, the Warner Bros. script for *Public Enemy* was undergoing review by the SRC. Cognizant of the criticism that the police did not get enough screen time relative to the gangsters in *Little Caesar*, Joy encouraged Warners to beef up their role in *Public Enemy*. "At present, they always seem to be rushing in after the deed has been committed."[14] He also cautioned the studio about likely censor action in scenes depicting machine-guns "and other weapons when they appear overabundantly" and noted the inevitability of "controversy with the censors."

When the completed picture was screened for the SRC, Joy found it "entirely satisfactory" under the Code.[15] But he warned the studio again that it faced likely censorship action. "If any of the censors believe the final shot of the boy is too gruesome, that, too, will be eliminated. There is always the chance that machine-guns in the hands of other than law enforcement officers may be eliminated. You will have to take your chances on all of these. I hope you may be very successful."[16]

Joy's worries about censorship of the machine-guns were prescient. Censors did attack these images, and in a few years the PCA would move to scrutinize the display of weaponry in crime films and to specifically ban any depiction of criminals in possession of illegal weapons. Compared with *Little Caesar*, the violence in *Public Enemy* was harsher, more sadistic, and given a more flamboyantly cinematic treatment. Indeed, the arc of violence across these three pictures shows an increase in ferocity and vividness, and *Public Enemy* had upped the ante on *Little Caesar* in less than a year. This development is symptomatic of the historical process underlying violence in the American cinema—namely, an inexorable movement to breach existing barriers and content restrictions. *Little Caesar* helped to mark the low amplitude point of this rise in the genre's mayhem. Despite the censor anger over its depiction of guns and violence, compared with subsequent pictures it was the zero point from which they calibrated their escalation of the stylistic amplitude of screen violence.

Public Enemy's first shooting is more dynamic than anything in *Little Caesar*. Under cover of darkness, Tom Powers (Cagney) and a gang rob a fur company, but the effort fails and they scatter in panic from the encroaching police. A cop shoots one of the fleeing gang members, and the killing is choreographed with great visual skill. The gangster and the pursuing cop run toward the camera. The movement is fast, and it's placed on an axis converging at the camera and viewer. The cop fires once; his victim convulses, but doesn't fall. When the cop fires again the crook is hit, staggers against a lamppost, and collapses like a rag doll. Because the action is staged in a rush at the camera and the viewer, the violence is choreographed so that it, too, is aimed at the viewer. By shooting at the gangster, the cop also sights the viewer. Framing the action in extreme long-shot, however, undercuts the effectiveness of this design. Bringing the camera closer to the action would magnify the force of the design, but the principle—setting an axis for violent action that will increase its impact on the viewer—is clearly grasped by the filmmakers.

Furthermore, the scene's lighting helps to compensate for the somewhat distanced framing of the action. To accentuate the shooting, the cinematographer has placed lights at right angles to the path along which the cop and his

12. The lighting design in *Public Enemy* makes the gun smoke erupt behind the victim like a geyser of blood. The action is dynamically staged, on a diagonal toward the camera. The stylistic amplitude of gun violence quickly increased.

prey are running. The cop fires the first shot when he crosses the beam of light placed at his right, which lights up the burst of smoke from his gun and makes it into an erupting bright cloud surrounded by the darkness of the night. When the cop shoots again, he is illuminated by the second right-angled light source, and the effect this time is even more dramatic. The fleeing gangster is center screen, the better to display what happens next. Because the cop is directly behind the gangster, with the second shot a huge cloud of bright white smoke explodes around the figure of the victim—seemingly explodes out of him—and he crashes into the lamppost. Although the filmmakers do not show bullet strikes on the body, the lighting of this action uses gun smoke to visualize the physical violence in a way that suggests the bodily damage and, at the same time, creates a compelling pictorial effect. The choreography of violence in this brief scene shows a sophisticated grasp of cinema, making the action far more exciting than the stiff, theatrical framings of *Little Caesar.*

But it is not just the staging of gun violence that *Public Enemy* accentuates beyond the accomplishments of *Little Caesar. Public Enemy* ramps up the attitudes that surround the violence. The violence in *Little Caesar* has few psychological attributes; it does not convey or signal emotion. In *Public Enemy* it does, and, as a result, the violent acts have richer coordinates. The killers in *Little Caesar* do not derive sadistic pleasure from their violence, but Tom Powers does—especially in the remarkably callous scene where he executes Putty Nose, an old crime boss who has known Tom since Powers was a boy. Putty helped start Tom on a life of crime, giving him his first gun. Tom and his partner, Matt, corner Putty Nose in his apartment, but Tom doesn't kill Putty right away. He toys with him, like a cat will do with a smaller animal, knowing that its ability to dispense death is secure. Tom knocks the older man to the ground, and Putty pleads for his life. Tom remarks gleefully, "oh, so you don't want to die!" The old gangster reminds Tom how he used to play piano for him. "Tommy, don't you remember? You and Matt, how you used to be just kids, and we were friends?" Desperate, he flings himself onto his knees and begs Matt not to let Tom kill him. He pleads for their old friendship. "Didn't I always stick up for you?" Tom responds by kicking the old man to the ground, knocking him away from Matt. But he scrambles back to his feet and clutches Matt's arm, begging both of them not to harm him. "Ain't you got a heart?" he asks Tom. "You remember that song I used to sing, that song I taught you? You remember, Tommy, back in the club, how you kids used to laugh at that song."

Putty goes to his piano and starts to play the old song, and Tom stands behind him. He smiles at Putty Nose, allowing him to play, allowing him to feel some relief that maybe Tom, convinced of their friendship, will spare his life. But as Putty plays, Tom reaches into his coat and pulls out a pistol. The camera pans away and dollies over to Matt, standing by the door. Offscreen, Tom fires two shots, and Putty makes a retching sound. Then, in action implied by the offscreen sound effects, Putty collapses upon the keyboard. As the camera remains on Matt, Tom walks into frame, pats Matt casually on the arm and says, "I guess I'll call up Gwen. She oughta be home by now." He walks out the door, and the scene ends with this powerful evocation of Tom's indifference to the murder he commits and to the victim's humanity, which the scene has worked to emphasize through his desperate pleas to live.

The execution of Putty Nose is a remarkably sadistic and brutal killing that takes *Public Enemy* far beyond anything *Little Caesar* had put on-screen. The focus of the scene is the attitude surrounding the violence, the pleasure in killing, the pride at humiliating the victim, and the willful extension of the victim's torment. The off-camera shooting is not nearly as disturbing as the sadism with which Tom tortures Putty. In these two scenes (the other being the shooting by the streetlamp following the robbery), *Public Enemy* brings a superb choreography to the exterior and interior components of violence—the exterior being its placement within the camera frame, the interior being the psychology of killing and the emotional interplay between killer and victim. Whereas *Little Caesar* offended censors by merely brandishing guns in the hands of its criminals, *Public Enemy* puts both sting and spectacle into its violence.

The other killings in the film are equally striking. Rival gangsters set up a pair of machine-guns in an apartment across the street from one of Tom's hangouts and ambush him and Matt as they pass by on the street. The scene makes an interesting comparison with the ambush of Rico in *Little Caesar*. In contrast to the woodenness of the staging in *Little Caesar, Public Enemy* explicitly references the new aesthetic of sound and builds this into its staging of the ambush. The film cleverly uses sound to set off a false alarm and trick the viewer—along with Tom and Matt—into relaxing just before the guns are fired. Tom and Matt hear a loud series of explosions that could be gunfire. They hit the ground, but it turns out to be a nearby coal truck unloading its cargo. Relieved, they continue on, and the ambush commences. The machine-gun kills Matt and blasts chunks of mortar out of the corner wall around which Tom has darted. As in *Little Caesar*, the filmmakers used a real machine-gun off-camera to blast the mortar with visible bullet strikes. Unlike *Little Caesar*, though, where the sound is merely a brute means of depicting the ambush, here it becomes a channel for organizing and heightening our perception of the violence. As a metaphor for gunfire, the crashing coal sets off a false alarm but fills the air with its suggestion of a violence that is incipient and inescapable. The outbreak of real violence validates the promise of the metaphor and makes it real.

From a filmmaking standpoint, the most strikingly visualized and fluidly choreographed scene of violence shows Tom's revenge on Schemer Burns and his gang for the killing of Matt. It's a one-man assault, a near-suicidal charge as Tom takes on the whole gang with just his grit and his gat. At night, in a heavy rainstorm, Tom waits outside their headquarters as the gang gathers. When they've assembled, he charges into their office for the kill. The heavy rain adds an undercurrent of visual energy to the scene, with its steady roar on the soundtrack and the reflective light effects of the falling water. But it is the camerawork and editing that make this scene so dynamic. While he waits outside Tom smiles defiantly, and when he starts his walk toward the office the camera frames him in a medium shot and begins a backward track, moving with him as he marches forward. The moving camera underscores the dramatic power of Tom's death march, the camera accompanying him on this mission. The shot ends in a striking use of depth of field. He walks up to the camera and sticks his face right in the lens, until the camera's shadow veils his face and ends the shot with a kind of fade-out.

13. Violence rendered in vivid cinematic terms. Wounded, Tom Powers staggers through the rain and is captured by a low-angle camera at curbside in a series of fluid, mobile framings.

The film then cuts to a long-shot framing of the office complex as Tom enters. The camera stays outside, and the soundtrack conveys the essential information of Tom's attack. We hear a flurry of shots, followed by the long dying wail of a gangster. This cry, like those in *Island of Lost Souls* and *Murders in the Rue Morgue*, is another example of the vocalized expression of pain that was soon to disappear from American film. Tom emerges, wounded and staggering. Cagney moves in a miniature ballet of pain and disorientation that shows his skills as a dancer. (Musical theater was his original career aim.) Once again, the film style visually embodies Tom's movements, cutting to a low-angle, moving camera shot at curbside, tracking backward through the rain as Tom staggers along the curb line. When he pitches forward, the film cuts to a closer view, a tightly framed telephoto shot that adds a spastic energy to his movements. The telephoto lens makes the camera's short, quick pans to reframe the action look jerky and violent.

In the tight telephoto composition, Tom's pitching and lurching seem ready to explode out of the frame.

THE CINEMATIC TRANSFIGURATION OF VIOLENCE

Lighting, sound, depth of field, framing, and camera movement—the film-making combines and exploits all of these parameters to make this scene the visual and kinetic climax of the film. All work to orchestrate the violence of the scene in memorable and cinematic terms and to demonstrate that screen violence was accelerating in its stylistic amplitude. And in this regard, the film had one more punch left to deliver its audience. This was the picture's penultimate scene, in which Tom's corpse is delivered to his mother's house bound with rope, swathed in bandages, with a bloody face and lifeless eyes. As his brother opens the door, Tom pitches forward, landing on his face with a dull thud, like so much dead meat. It's a shocking and grotesque conclusion to a film of considerable, masterfully executed violence.

Tom's death at the end enabled the filmmakers, the studio, and the SRC to claim that the film taught a moral lesson: namely, that crime does not pay. Of course, the film's stylistic accomplishments taught a somewhat different lesson—that screen violence was seductive and exciting, an attention-getting flourish, and that it could mobilize the most eloquently expressive powers of cinema. This lesson is the fundamental truth and motivating force behind the amplification of style in American screen history. The SRC, however, couldn't very well acknowledge this in its dealings with censor boards, so it pushed the importance of the film's ostensible moral lesson—one more example of how the period's discourse put reference ahead of style. As the SRC's Lamar Trotti explained in an evaluation of the film, "the end is rather horrible, and probably has a strong moral value. . . . One is left with the unspoken feeling of sorrow he has brought on his family, as well as with the idea that the hoodlum pays in the end."[17] As producer Darryl Zanuck put it, the film "punched over a moral." He said that "in *Public Enemy*, we also have a very strong moral theme, to wit: If there is pleasure and profit in crime . . . that pleasure and that profit can only be momentary, as the basic foundation of law violation, ultimately ends in disaster to the participant."[18]

The regional censor boards did not buy this argument; nor did they buy into Joy's claim, made earlier in connection with *Little Caesar*, that the moral voice in gangster films required the showing of much violence and brutality. There was some variation across regions in the response of the censor boards, but those who made cuts zeroed in on the picture's violence. Ohio and Maryland eliminated nearly all of the shots showing the machine-guns being placed in ambush and firing on Tom and Matt. New York permitted only a flash image (three feet of film) of the machine-guns at the window. Ohio and Maryland eliminated the penultimate shot "of Tom's dead body standing in doorway, swaying and falling to floor, allowing only scenes where he is lying face down on the floor." In the scene where Tom kills Putty Nose, Ohio eliminated the shot of Tom pulling the gun from his coat; Maryland cut the entire scene, along with assorted other material, such as the scene where Putty Nose gives guns to the boys and the famous grapefruit scene of sexual violence (where Tom crushes a grapefruit in his girlfriend's face).

Interestingly, none of the eliminations reports collected by the SRC specifies any censor action on what I have suggested is the most vividly filmed scene of violence: Tom's attack on Schemer Burns and his gang. Despite the exciting formal design of the scene, it does omit the actual violence, which takes place off-frame and is suggested only by the sound of guns popping and a dying gangster's cry. Thus, its offensive representational content was minimal. By contrast, images showing machine-guns being placed at a window overlooking the street, or Tom pulling a gun from his coat, or Putty Nose giving guns to boys, or Tom's corpse falling inside his mother's house—these images that had clear denotative content became the targets for censor action.

Filmmakers were becoming more proficient at staging and styling violence for the camera, but censors were relatively slow to catch on to this. While they were trimming shots of machine-guns, filmmakers were learning that a backwards-moving camera shot, or a radical change in lens perspective, could heighten the impact of violence as well as the surrounding narrative material—the dramatic lead in and out of the violent act itself. As Jason Joy had complained, the censors had their "eyes glued on details"—a body falling to the floor, an illegal weapon in the hand of a criminal—while filmmakers were transcending these isolated details by weaving them into whole sequences where picture and sound were orchestrated for maximum emotional impact. The elaboration of cinematic violence was engendering a stylistic treatment that encompassed more than the violent act itself—a treatment that wove the act into an elaborate tapestry of structure accentuating brutality by extending before it and beyond it. The only way that censorship could deal with this evolution was to order deletions of entire scenes, thereby risking a loss of narrative coherence. Filmmakers were moving toward more elaborated stylistic renderings of violence, while censors—and the SRC and then the PCA in responding to them—were fixating on content. For filmmakers it wasn't primarily the *act* of violence that they found interesting; it was the stylistic transfiguration of the act. It was putting the light at just the right angle to make the gun smoke bloom behind the victim like a spray of blood.

THE SRC CRACKS DOWN AS *SCARFACE* LOOMS

In a sign of the gathering storm, the SRC received a report that Wisconsin censors had rejected the film and had convened a meeting with representatives of the major theater circuits and independent theater owners. "At this meeting the [Wisconsin Motion Picture] Commission expressed itself as being opposed to the gangster pictures and they read numerous communications from other cities where such pictures were meeting with like objections."[19] The Commission forwarded a resolution against gangster pictures to Will Hays. When the Commission reversed a ban on *Public Enemy* and allowed it to be shown in the Wisconsin area, it did so only after exhibitors and distributors pledged to cooperate in helping to eliminate gangster films.

By June of 1931, the SRC was feeling the heat. Jason Joy remarked on the unprecedented nature of the outcry.

> In all my nine years of experience in our industry, no "cycle" has ever been criticized so severely and with such apparent feeling as the cycle of crime pictures. Despite the fact that two or three of the more recent gang pictures have achieved more than average returns at the box office, I have been told emphatically by censors, chiefs of police, newspaper editors, exhibitors and leaders among the citizenry that there is a vast growing resentment against the continued production and exhibition of this type of picture. Some of the people, especially those in places of authority, are almost fanatical in their desire to stop the further flow of these pictures.[20]

A vivid example of community opposition to the gangster cycle can be found in the reaction of Montclair, New Jersey in the aftermath of a notorious shooting said to have been inspired by movie violence. On June 23, 1931, twelve-year-old Winslow Elliott, the son of one of the community's prominent citizens, was shot and killed by a sixteen-year-old playmate who was acting out a scene from the MGM gangster movie *The Secret Six.* In comparison with *Public Enemy* or *Scarface,* this picture actually has very little gun violence, which makes its connection with this incident curious. Two hundred people attended the funeral service, and town civics clubs adopted a resolution opposing gangster movies which was sent to the town mayor, who threatened legal action to prevent further exhibition of gangster films. Warner Bros. announced that it would discontinue showing gangster movies at the two theaters it owned in town. The studio said, "there will be no more gangster pictures shown in Montclair in 1931. Such films are practically at the end of their cycle."[21]

In the wake of the public opposition, the SRC worked to persuade the major studios to curtail production of future gangster movies and to reduce the gangster elements of those pictures that were already in production. A number of projects were affected, involving a range of studios. Universal complied by inserting anti-gangster messages into *Homicide Squad,* and Warners postponed production of *The Gentleman from San Francisco* because of its sympathetic portrait of a criminal.[22] Warners also recut *Larceny Lane* and changed its ending. Tiffany eliminated all gangster references in *X Marks the Spot,* and RKO changed the emphasis in *The Tip-Off* from gangsters to prize fighting. RKO recalled and recut all prints of *Bad Company,* and Fox halted production on *Disorderly Conduct* so that gangster themes could be removed from the story. Columbia eliminated scenes glorifying gangsters from *The Guilty Generation.*

At the same time that the SRC was maneuvering to persuade studios to discontinue gangster productions, filmmakers were pushing the aesthetics of gun violence even further. The most notorious of the gangster pictures, and the SRC's biggest headache, was the Howard Hughes production *Scarface,* which Hughes intended to be the biggest and baddest gangster picture of them all. Worse yet from the standpoint of probable censor action, its gangster character, Tony Camonte, was based on a real figure, Al Capone, who was still very much in power and defying the legal authorities to take him down. The MPA tried to dissuade Hughes from pursuing the project, which it regarded as a danger to the entire industry. As the SRC noted in a memo on the history of the *Scarface* project:

> Immediately the association presented to Mr. Hughes all the available arguments as to why such a subject should not be brought to the screen. The principal reason was that public objection to gangster themes was at its height and that the official censor boards—strengthened by this public support—were openly announcing their unwillingness to accept any more gangster pictures. Moreover, agitation for further state and municipal control of pictures dealing with the subject was being considered as a direct consequence of the gang pictures, thus endangering the investments of all companies.[23]

The SRC was gravely worried about the flagrant cruelty and violence in the script of the proposed film and especially about the likelihood for the film to draw fire down upon the industry. Joy wrote, "believe story fundamentally offers greatest gangster problem so far, and every effort should be made to help studio see difficulties into which it is running head-on."[24] As initially written, the script pitted its gangster hero in a heroic battle against the police: it portrayed him as the underdog and glorified his lone stand. As the SRC viewed the script, "this glorification is emphasized by his final gesture of bravado, when he deliberately walks out into police gunfire, a lone man braving the world."[25] Moreover, "Camonte is shown as a home-loving man, good to his mother and protective of his sister. Murdering is more of a game than anything else, an outlet for his tremendous energy and ability." To rectify this unacceptably flattering portrait, the SRC recommended that Camonte should be shown at the end as a coward, as "a yellow dog." Hughes did not like this idea and resisted SRC efforts to alter the character of Camonte. Nevertheless, under continuing pressure from the SRC, he slowly modified his position; the SRC continued to worry, however, that the picture's violence would provoke public outcry and backlash from censors. Joy recorded in a memo the status of the script negotiations as of mid-June: "The treatment of the story is becoming more satisfactory. There [sic] still remains the most harsh and frank gangster picture we have ever had. We told [Hughes] that we did not expect it to pass any of the censor boards, and that it would probably have the effect of closing the door for any further possibilities in that direction."[26] In his resumes on the production throughout the remainder of the summer, Joy continued to warn of censor trouble and to express doubts about whether the picture would even be releasable. "It is our opinion that the picture will be able to play only in about 50 percent of the theaters of the country, unless radical revisions are made in the treatment."[27]

When the finished picture was screened on September 8, the SRC told Hughes that the film had to have a new ending that would remove the heroic spectacle of Camonte defying the police and dying like a brave underdog. Hughes consented, and portions of the film were reshot to replace deleted material that had been flattering to Camonte, to create a new ending in which Camonte "goes yellow," to strengthen the police presence in the film, and to add an anti-gun message. This last feature—the anti-gun preachments which show up in the film in a printed foreword and in scenes where law enforcement authorities comment on the need to keep guns out of the hands of criminals—was a late-in-the-game addition about which the SRC was especially enthusiastic. The idea seems to have originated in a story conference held in September, involving Joy and Lamar Trotti of the SRC, director Howard Hawks, and writer E. B. Derr. In a memo after the meeting, Trotti made note of the suggestion to emphasize the idea that the gangster is successful as long as he has a gun. Take away the gun, and he's a yellow rat. "The final message of the picture will be—not to let criminals get possession of guns."[28] Trotti noted that Hawks was enthusiastic for the idea and would try to sell Hughes on it.

To create the anti-gun messages in the picture, and to help sell it as an anti-gun movie, Trotti surveyed newspaper opinion on the topic. He asked the staff to gather newspaper coverage of New York's anti-gun Sullivan Law and editorials advocating that the way to fight gangsters was to deprive them of weapons.[29] About this ploy for promoting the film, he boasted, "I think we are going to pull a grand-stand stunt in connection with [*Scarface*]."[30] Jason Joy quickly came to share Trotti's enthusiasm for "the 'anti-gun' idea as the theme song in 'Scarface.'"[31] Joy wrote to Will Hays that the film "may very well become a great preachment which will help corral public support for the efforts of policemen to stop the sale of guns to hoodlums."[32] The SRC hoped to position the film, before it was released and submitted to censor boards, in terms of "the new theme of the picture with respect to the use of guns."[33]

SCARFACE AND THE CELEBRATION OF VIOLENCE

The picture abounds in vividly staged gun battles and visceral images of violent death. Camera set-ups, framing, editing and sound: all work to give the picture's violence a tremendous punch and power, due to the way that it is stylistically articulated. The power of the film's mayhem derives from the way the gun battles are defined in audiovisual terms. But the SRC, and even some of the censor boards, seemed not to grasp this fact and concentrated instead on the picture's dramatic content and how changing this might help solve the political problems the picture was facing. Thus the SRC advocated altering the referential coordinates of the narrative—making Camonte turn coward, and adding more scenes of police and public authorities lamenting the problem of gangsters and illegal weapons. It believed that the way to save the film lay in adding a "new theme" rather than addressing the tremendous visual attraction manifested in the filmmaking for guns and for the aesthetic display of their destructive force. It is this fascination with gun violence, expressed stylistically, which impresses a viewer today as that aspect of the film that seems most contemporary, most resistant to diminishing with time. This fascination with the cinematic styling of violence makes *Scarface* an enduringly modern film, despite the passage of more than seventy years since its release. And this love affair with gun violence, voiced at hundreds of points in the picture through the choices about camera, editing and sound, made it highly unlikely that a viewer would, as the SRC hoped, "leave the theatre with a definite impression of the anti-gun angle and no feeling at all that the gangster had been glorified."[34]

In fairness to the SRC they were attentive to some aspects of the film's style, even while failing to grasp the extent to which that style might influence a viewer's response. As I discussed in *Savage Cinema: Sam Peckinpah and the Rise of Ultraviolent Movies,* a filmmaker's love for creating screen violence manifests itself at the level of structure and is there transmitted to the viewer, who can be made to share the filmmaker's own relationship to the materials. A design, therefore, that makes violence exciting and hyperkinetic does not work very well for conveying anti-violence or anti-gun messages, as the SRC hoped to accomplish with the thematic revisions in *Scarface*. Those revisions would be superimposed onto a design that negated them. To the degree that it was attentive to the problem of the stylistic imperative, the agency tried to caution the filmmakers about the manner in which machine-guns would be filmed and in which shooting deaths would be framed. The agency wrote to Hughes, "shots of machine-guns in the hands of gangsters are invariably deleted by domestic censor boards, and any of the shooting affairs that are made too cruel and gruesome will be quite objectionable, and we suggest that you will use good judgment to keep the camera off the assailant and the victim, in each case, while the murder is being done."[35]

This suggestion that the camera not frame shooter and victim within the same shot at the moment of killing may have helped give rise to one of the more enduring myths about the PCA and American cinema. That myth is the idea that gun violence in the Hollywood period, as enforced by the PCA, required that shooter and victim appear in separate shots, with an edit point placed between them. Clint Eastwood explained the revolutionary effect of the violence in Sergio Leone's *A Fistful of Dollars* (1964) by claiming that Leone broke this rule because, as a European filmmaker, he had been unaware of it: "There were rules in Hollywood years ago, unspoken rules, that you never tied up shots of a person being shot. In other words, you never shot a tie-up shot of a man shooting a gun and another person getting hit. It's a Hays Office rule from years ago, a censorship deal. You'd cut to the guy shooting, and then cut to a guy falling."[36]

Discussing the classic gangster films of the 1930s, Richard Maltby writes, "a character could not normally shoot another character in a two-shot; the image of the gun being fired had to be separated from the representation of its impact by a cut."[37] This is not entirely true, as even *Scarface* demonstrates in some of its drive-by shootings where the killer and victim occupy the same frame. While many of the shooting deaths in Hollywood films are shown in accordance with this ostensible rule, there was apparently no absolute prohibition, written or unwritten, against showing the action within a single framing. Hollywood films from every decade prior to the fall of censorship in the late 1960s include dynamically staged or brutal killings in which killer and victim are framed together. In *G-Men* (1935) the gangster villain, Collins, shoots Ann Dvorak at point-blank range within one camera framing. A bit later, James Cagney guns a garage mechanic working for the gangsters. The composition is dynamic, with Cagney in the right foreground shooting diagonally across the frame and hitting the mechanic in the rear left of the frame. In *The Roaring Twenties* (1939), Cagney guns a thug on a staircase, and, in the same framing, the victim tumbles down toward the camera. In *This Gun for Hire* (1942), the professional hit man, played by Alan Ladd, takes three slugs at close range from a pair of cops, who burst into the room where he is holed up; the three share the camera frame. During a savage battle with enemy Japanese in the World War II drama *Bataan* (1943), Robert Taylor shoots a Japanese soldier lying prone at point-blank range, and the bullet and muzzle flash of his rife blow the man backwards. In *The Big Sleep* (1946) Bogie gets the drop on a thug and guns him three times, the darkness of the night accentuating the muzzle flash of his pistol. The thug takes the hits with an astonished look on his face. The violence is captured in one framing. In *House of Bamboo* (1955), Robert Ryan bursts into a room and pumps lead into a foe, the victim screaming as each bullet goes in. In *Machine-Gun Kelly* (1958), stoolie Morey Amsterdam takes a head shot at point-blank range from a shooter standing just behind and to the side of him. *Party Girl* (1958) features several flamboyant on-camera killings. John Ireland shoots a man three times in a hotel corridor, two of the shots occurring as the victim looks him in the eye while collapsing against a doorframe. Another victim is machine-gunned on a doorstep, the killers firing through a glass window. Still another victim is dispatched in a phone booth as the killer sprays it with machine-gun fire. Yet another gangland hit shows a machine-gun in the immediate foreground of the shot, mowing down a pair of fleeing hoods. In Richard Brooks's *The Last Hunt* (1958), Robert Taylor pivots in the background of a deep-focus shot and plugs Lloyd Nolan in the foreground of the frame. In *The Killers* (1964), assassins Lee Marvin and Clu Gulagher blast victim John Cassavetes numerous times at close range.

In all of these examples, the killer shares the frame with his victim as the on-camera violence is presented in the real time of a single shot. While the editing "rule" stipulating that shooter and victim be separated in different frames may have had some force, it clearly was not binding. Moreover, even in cases employing alternate camera set-ups to show shooter and victim, an enterprising filmmaker might stage the action so as to undercut the separation. When the psychopathic gangster Johnny Udo (Richard Widmark) shoots ex-con and cop informant Nick (Victor Mature) in *Kiss of Death* (1947), the action cuts between shots of Udo firing his pistol and shots of Nick taking the slugs. In the reverse-angles of Nick, smoke and sparks appear above the lower frame line, suggesting that Udo's gun is just barely outside the camera's view and giving the gun a presence within the shot that it does not explicitly have.

Compared with the gangster films that preceded it, *Scarface* represented a tremendous increase in the amount and ferocity of violence, backed up by an

14. Despite the myth that the PCA forbid the presentation of shooter and victim together in the frame, examples can be found in every decade before the fall of censorship. When Marlowe (Humphrey Bogart) guns Canino (Bob Steele) in *The Big Sleep*, the nighttime setting shows off the muzzle flash of his pistol.

impressive increase in its stylistic amplitude. Much of this increased ferocity was due to the film's prominent display of machine-gun killings, but this factor in itself is an insufficient explanation for the power of the film's violence. Machine-guns, after all, had figured prominently in gangster movies for years—so much so that censor boards began deleting frames from scenes as soon as they appeared on-screen. It wasn't just the guns that gave *Scarface* its punch; it was the picture's orchestration of violence. If *Little Caesar* occupies the base of the *y*-axis among the period's gangster films, *Scarface* occupies the uppermost range.

Beginning literally with a bang, *Scarface* introduces its gangster hero, Tony Camonte, in the act of committing murder. The film begins with Camonte's assassination of Big Louie Costillo, thus defining Camonte in terms of gun violence which he will continue to gleefully carry out against rivals and friends until he is cut down by police bullets. *Scarface* aestheticizes violence in a self-conscious way. Throughout the film, a cross-motif provides a kind of code or shorthand for announcing the onset of violent death, and its use begins in the first shot. From a low angle, the camera shows a streetlight bisected by a diagonal street sign; the pattern forms an X. When characters in the film die, the set design or the lighting creates a cross or X on-screen as a way of winking at the viewer and self-consciously weaving violence into the iconography of the film. This cumulative strategy leads the viewer to anticipate each new act of violence as an opportunity to search the screen for the motif within the composition. The Xs thus embellish the violence by making each killing part of a self-contained visual tableau and the narrative a means for connecting the violent tableaux and for leading the viewer from X to X.

In other respects, however, the visual design of this initial killing scene is less successful. It is presented as a single, extended shot, and the long-take design conflicts with the film's essentially hyperkinetic approach to violence. The montages of killing that appear later on are superb instigations of hyperkinesis—but not the slow, elaborate moving camera shot that connects the X outside the restaurant with the killing of Costillo inside. The camera tracks from the street sign into the restaurant in the early morning hours, where Big Louie and two friends are all that remain of a boisterous stag party. Louie and his pals talk about gang affairs and then say goodnight. Louie walks to a pay phone as the camera follows him and then tracks away to the right to reveal the silhouette of Camonte stalking toward the unsuspecting Louie, who is now off-frame. Whistling while he works, Camonte pulls a pistol and shoots Louie three times. He wipes the gun and walks off frame right. The camera then tracks left to reveal Louie sprawled on the ground. Offscreen, Tony's casual whistling continues as he exits the restaurant, an expressive use of sound to characterize his indifference to the violence he's committed.

The choreography of action for a single, extended moving camera shot is impressive, but there is no necessary connection here between this staging and the violence. The long take and the prowling camera are sophisticated cinematic accomplishments, but they do not render the violence more vivid or connect with it as organically as the film's subsequent montages do—or, to cite a different type of design, as the use of lighting to accentuate gunfire does in *Public Enemy*.

Another component of the scene's design bears mentioning because we are now in a position to appreciate its significance. We have seen it before, in the last chapter, but I have waited until now to give it its true weight and significance. That is the silhouette lighting of Tony, which connects the film to the cinematography of violence that developed in early thirties horror films. I call

15. The shadow plays enabled filmmakers to indirectly depict acts of violence and offered a strategy for evading the PCA and the regional censors. In silhouette, Tony Camonte (Paul Muni) guns Big Louie Costillo.

this use of silhouetted action a *shadow play* because it is invariably dynamic. It encodes an action violent in nature, in a manner that displaces its details from the direct view of the camera but plays them in general outline as silhouetted action. The silhouette figures are not static. They are not pictorial in a painterly fashion. They move in the discharging of a violent act. They are, therefore, a kind of play, a moving scenario of poetically displaced violence, thrust off-frame but leaving the trace of its shadows on-camera. The skinning of Poelzig in *The Black Cat* occurred as a shadow play, as did the introduction to the torture scene in *Murders in the Rue Morgue*. Subsequently in that film, when Mirakle's killer ape strangles him, the action plays in silhouette. We will have occasion to note instances of shadow-play imagery in other films in forthcoming discussion.

There seem to have been two reasons for the use of silhouetted figures in gangster and horror violence of this period, and they are somewhat contradictory. Unquestionably, there was a calculation that the silhouettes were more likely to slip past censors and thereby to meet with approval by the SRC because the manner of presentation was indirect. The viewer did not actually see the bodies of killer and victim, merely their shadows. Shown indirectly, the violence, it could be said, was merely suggested. Depicting troublesome subjects or acts by suggestion was a filmmaking strategy dearly beloved by the PCA, and silhouetted imagery was calculated to play to this bias. Thus, the shadow-play designs operated to lessen the gruesomeness of the dramatic action they accompanied.

On the other hand, the silhouettes arguably distilled the violence into a purer form. As a silhouette seen against a pure white background, Tony's gun leaps out at the viewer. Its shape and presence are insistent and inescapable. The ape's strangulation of Mirakle plays in a kind of digital format—it is either absolutely present (the silhouette) or absolutely absent (the blank wall surrounding the shadows). Because presence-absence is the only visual discrimination the shadow-play offers, the design distills its violence into a concentrated form. Other objects in the scenes do not distract the viewer's eye because all such detail is absent from the shadow-play. The shadow-plays were thus an ambivalent mode of presentation. They offered oblique and indirect depictions of violence but, in doing so, they concentrated the violent action into pure visual form. As a result, the shadow-plays were not always successful in escaping from censor action. New York and Pennsylvania censors, for example, deleted the silhouetted killing of Costillo from *Scarface*.

By contrast, the film's next extended scene of violence fared better with the censors. As part of their effort to corner the liquor business, Tony and his gang shoot up the Shamrock bar, whose owner has been resisting their cartel. The action is conceived almost exclusively in terms of sound. Like the design of Tom Powers's attack on Schemer Burns in *Public Enemy*, the camera stays outside the Shamrock so that sound can be used to convey the violence of the assault. A cacophony of shots and automatic weapons fire explodes on the soundtrack, and bullets shatter the bar's front window. As with the analogous scene in *Public Enemy*, this one tended to escape extensive censor action. Among the eliminations reports on the film collected by the SRC, the New York and Pennsylvania censor boards ordered the largest, most extensive deletions throughout the film. Both boards deleted a previous scene showing Tony hurling a bomb through the window of another establishment, but New York requested no deletion of any part of the Shamrock scene. Significantly, Pennsylvania ordered only that its conclusion—showing Tony and his gang running out of the Shamrock and getting into their car—be cut.

The censors' relative tolerance for these analogous scenes in *Public Enemy* and *Scarface* suggest a higher valence for visual elements that denote violence in comparison with its encoding as sound information, except when sound was used to denote the experience of pain. Unquestionably, the offscreen sound of gunfire in both scenes denotes the violent action that is occurring, but, in terms of censor action on these scenes, this sound was evidently taken as being less provocative than visually denoted violence. Thus, even though the conclusion of the Shamrock scene—Tony and his gang fleeing the bar—shows no violence, its proximity *as an image* to the action suggested by the soundtrack rendered it vulnerable to excision in Pennsylvania. The regional censors apparently weighed the encoding of violence as picture and as sound using different scales, and the weights assigned were not always consistent. As we have seen, the sounds of extended suffering, of vocalized pain, were essentially banished from American film after the early 1930s—while, in the same period, these scenes in *Public Enemy* and *Scarface* that displace violence from the visual to the sonic drew a relatively mild response from the censors.

New York and Pennsylvania both deleted the entire scene of the film's next killing, in which Tony and his gang force their way into a hospital and, in a dynamic staging, race down a corridor flinging open doors in search of their victim, a survivor of the Shamrock hit. Although the camera is off the victim when Tony shoots him—shoots not once but three times—the viewer does see the victim, prone in bed, just before and then just after the shooting, and an X prominently displayed in the shadows on the rear wall. (In the coming years the PCA would routinely try to persuade filmmakers to reduce the number of shots or punches delivered at the victim.) This scene plays in primarily visual terms, and with a clear referent, and thus drew censor action.

THE ONSET OF ULTRAVIOLENCE

From this point on, machine-gun violence comes to the fore in the picture, and the audiovisual design becomes markedly more hyperkinetic. A Slavko Vorkapitch–style montage showing a machine-gun blasting the pages off a calendar, marking the passage of time, follows the hospital killing. Warned to stay out of the north side of town, Tony and his friend Guino (George Raft) are ambushed in a scene that has become a staple of gangster movies. As they relax at a café a seemingly endless series of cars drive by and rake the establishment with machine-gun fire, and bullet hits are visualized in exploding glass, furniture, and fixtures. Tony decides he wants a machine-gun, and Guino gets him one by shooting a gangster off a passing car and rushing out to grab his gun.

New York and Pennsylvania censors ordered trims in the scene to reduce the duration of the drive-by shooting and to eliminate Guino's killing of the passing gangster. Significantly, they ordered a deletion in the following scene of an extreme close-up of the machine-gun in Tony's hands, when he says that the machine-gun is the only way to give orders. The film's most incendiary action then occurs—Tony in medium close-up, with an orgiastic grin, firing the machine-gun at the camera. His body jerks with the recoil, the gun spits fire, and a shroud of gun smoke rolls up over his figure. Two such close-ups are intercut with shots of bullets shredding the walls of the pool hall. Both censor boards eliminated the action, save for a brief flash of Tony holding the gun after the shooting is over. Given the furor in the period over crime films, the sequence is clearly inflammatory, its design visualizing the excitement of violence for Tony (and for viewers) and the incitement for Tony to kill that this pleasure provides. Along with the machine-gun killing that caps *Show Them*

16. Tony Camonte is about to shred the pool hall with his Tommy gun. The film's hyperviolence looks very contemporary.

No Mercy (1935), this is the most vivid close-quarter view of automatic weapons firepower in early thirties cinema.

What follows—a lengthy montage of drive-by shootings as Tony's gang puts its weapon to work—is the film's most kinetic, bravura display of machine-gun murder. Victims are gunned down inside hotels, on doorsteps, on the sidewalk, and escaping from cars, their deaths accentuated by physical convulsions under the impact of high velocity bullets and accompanied by a magisterial demonstration of the power of sound. Victims die with a cry forced from their lungs; glass shatters, police sirens scream, a dog whimpers, a hysterical woman shrieks, and car after car erupts with gunfire or smashes into a building, truck, or lamppost. The mayhem concludes with a re-enactment of the St. Valentine's Day massacre, visualized as another of the period's shadow-plays. Seven silhouetted shadows, lined up along a wall, fall to the off-screen sound of gunfire as smoke coils over the scene.

This sequence is the most extended slaughter scene in early sound film, and, from the standpoint of its audiovisual design, it is an expertly choreographed exercise in the cinematic rendering of violence. Every composition is dynamic, every action a vivid one, and every juxtaposition of picture and sound works to create a multiplicative effect. The sequence is a celebration of violence as only the cinema can do, magnifying its properties and pumping up the audiovisual expression into grandiloquent terms. The celebration is flamboyant and transgressive. The filmmakers are overjoyed at the plastic properties of cinema and the audiovisual combinations that enable them to make the violence sing and sting—and, at the same time, are excited by the naughtiness of it all, the in-your-face aggression of putting so much killing on-screen at once and doing it with such a cinematic flourish.

The excitement and the aggression manifested by the design of this sequence should strike today's viewer as very contemporary because it exhibits the kind of sustained, hypnotized fascination with violence that has become an everyday feature of contemporary film. This is, quite simply, ultraviolence of a very modern kind. The sequence shows no graphically detailed destruction of the human body. Visualizing bullet strikes on flesh and bone fell beyond the aesthetic and moral parameters of the period. But in terms of the duration of the violence, its ferocity, and the sheer body count, the sequence is thoroughly modern.

Scarface shows how quickly ultraviolence arrived in early sound cinema. Had the regional censors and other public authorities not attacked the film and motivated the PCA to crack down on this kind of hyperviolence, it would doubtless have become entrenched as a pervasive feature of American cinema long before it did. Early thirties cinema brought filmmakers very quickly toward an understanding of how to choreograph hyperviolence for the camera, and in the editing, and how to augment it with sound. The history of American screen violence subsequent to *Scarface* is a history of delaying the inevitable, of restraining filmmakers from crossing a threshold that they had shown great interest in breaching in the early horror and gangster pictures and, in *Scarface*, did in fact breach. In this sense, the PCA would wage a losing gambit because its efforts to negotiate a safe level of screen violence, in order to keep the censors off the industry's back, required that filmmakers unlearn, or not use, the knowledge about the choreography of strong screen violence that had accumulated rapidly in the early years of sound film. That the PCA would succeed at this as long as it did is a remarkable accomplishment, and it gave rise to an elaborate screen rhetoric of visual displacement—of visual tropes for suggesting that which is not shown directly—that substituted for graphic depiction and that became the normative language of screen violence in American cinema over the next decades.

---

17. In the glare of a spotlight, Tony Camonte jerks convulsively as machine-gun bullets hammer into him. As a stylistic device, Camonte's spasms prefigures modern depictions of violent death in films like *Bonnie and Clyde* and *The Wild Bunch*.

The machine-gun montage is the climax of violence in *Scarface*, and while there are plenty of shootings yet to come—a machine-gun ambush of Tony during a high speed car chase, Tony's shooting of Guino, and the finale in which Tony shoots it out with the police—none offers as intense or prolonged a choreography of gun violence. The finale, however, does include a significant detail that, like the hyperkinesis of the montage, anticipates the contemporary styling of gun violence. Tony is killed when he rushes out of his fortified mansion and is hit by two bursts of machine-gun fire from the police. The film quite clearly shows his body convulsing under the impact of the bullets. The bullet hits themselves are not visualized. There are no squibs as there would be in a contemporary film. However, Tony's jerky, stiff-limbed, awkward efforts to remain standing under the hail of fire unmistakably give us an early 1930s rendition of a physically violent death, with the pantomime conveying the multiple bullet hits.

Moreover, the moment acquires duration—extension in time that is comparable to the contemporary use of slow-motion. Tony does not fall immediately. A cross-cut series of four shots extends the moment and keeps him on his feet. Tony rushes out of the house, the police fire from offscreen, and he jerks spasmodically, stumbles and tries to keep his footing. The film cuts to the police, who stop firing, watch Tony offscreen, and then blast him again. The film cuts back to Tony, still doing his puppet's dance of death, and he then begins to pitch forward, at which point the film cuts to a new set-up showing him hit the ground. The editing prolongs the moment of violence to shift its emphasis in a significant and what feels now like a contemporary manner, from a depiction of violent death to an extended observation of violent passage, of *dying* as a process that takes time and that exhibits its own telltale visual signs. These are rendered commonly in the modern period as a spasmodic ballet of grotesque dance-like motion, presented using multiple camera editing and slow-motion intercut with normal speed footage. Tony's death scene does not feature multiple camera editing or any manipulations of film speed, but its presentation as an edited construction, working to extend the process of dying under violence, inflects it in a distinctively modern direction and helps to make it a prototype of the multi-camera montages that Arthur Penn, in *Bonnie and Clyde* (1967), and Sam Peckinpah, in *The Wild Bunch* (1969), helped to popularize.

Scarface showed in unmistakable terms what *cinematic* violence was all about, as distinguished from the staging conventions of theatrical melodrama that had influenced so many films. The film's excessive and flamboyant violence—more shrewdly and skillfully designed than in any previous picture—and the extraordinary controversy that engulfed it and the other gangster pictures prodded the industry to discontinue their production. *Scarface* would nearly become a suppressed film, but the filmmaking knowledge that went into its design of violence could not be suppressed. Now that it was manifest among filmmakers in the industry, it would find outlets in other productions even if they were not classically styled gangster films.

THE SPECIAL REGULATIONS ON CRIME

The industry's decision to curtail production of gangster movies proved to be temporary since their production, in fact, resumed later in the decade. A more lasting consequence of the upsurge of movie gangster violence in the early thirties was the passage of an amendment to the Production Code dealing with depictions of crime in motion pictures. The amendment contains a series of stipulations about how certain material is to be depicted, and all of the stipulations deal with the representational content of scenes rather than with issues of camera style, editing, or the marriage of image and sound. The PCA's response to the gangster controversy was to try to reduce the overall level of carnage on-screen and to regulate the dramatic content of crime pictures rather than the aesthetic elaboration of gun violence.

Excerpted from the MPA's Annual Report dated February 15, 1935, the guidelines regarding crime in motion pictures (see Appendix C) covered the following areas of content. The provisions were formally adopted as an amendment to the Code (Special Regulations on Crime) in 1938:

1. Detailed portraits of crime (e.g., hotwiring a car, robbing a bank) should never be shown in detail. This rule stemmed from concern that one of the untoward social effects of the gangster cycle was to teach impressionable viewers how to commit crimes.
2. The mass violence illustrated by the montage from *Scarface* was now off-limits. "Action suggestive of wholesale slaughter of human beings . . . will not be allowed."
3. Excessive brutality must not be portrayed.
4. Depictions of murder are to be kept to a minimum. The agency expressed concern about "the alarming increase in the number of films showing the taking of human life."
5. Suicide must not be portrayed unless absolutely necessary for the plot.
6. Machine-guns, sub-machine-guns, and other illegal weapons must not be shown in the hands of criminals, nor should their possession by criminals be suggested by off-screen sound (e.g., gunshots that are clearly from automatic weapons). This is virtually the only regulation

that addresses stylistic aspects, dealing as it does with the use of sound to suggest the existence of objects off-camera.

7. No unique or trick methods for concealing guns are to be shown.

8. Gangsters must not be shown flaunting weapons. This regulation has implicit stylistic components. The close-ups in *Scarface* of Tony blasting the pool hall with the machine-gun are attributes of visual style that fix the viewer's attention upon the weapon. It spits fire and smoke in close range at the camera. The flaunting of the weapon, therefore, is as much a matter of camerawork as of the character's behavior. But, in the discourse of the period, "flaunting" tended to refer to the behavior of displaying weapons. As we saw in chapter one, local censors routinely deleted on-camera depictions of guns.

9. Dialogue by gangsters about weapons should be kept to a minimum.

10. No scenes at any time should show law officers dying at the hands of criminals. "This includes private detectives and guards for banks, motor trucks, etc."

The disjunction between content and style ensured that these regulations would be effective only in a relative and limited way. A given film might satisfy the letter of the policy on crime while subverting it stylistically. A vivid example of this can be found in *Show Them No Mercy*, released later in the same year that the PCA promulgated the crime regulations.

While the film is not a gangster picture in the classical sense of *Scarface* or *Public Enemy*, it does deal with a gang of criminals who, as the film opens, have just collected a large ransom on a child whom they had kidnapped. In the wake of the Lindbergh case, the industry faced considerable pressure to eliminate kidnapping from its pictures and especially not to show successful kidnappings. Thus, during production, Breen wrote to reassure Will Hays that the film was not really a kidnapping story but one about how hard it is for criminals to dispose of marked bills. Indeed, the kidnapping is over and the child returned to its parents as the film begins, and much of the ensuing action involves the gang's effort to get rid of the ransom money that the feds have marked. In explaining this distinction to Hays, however, Breen conceded that the film was indirectly a gang picture. "The story is *not* a kidnapping story in any sense of the word. . . . The picture is, of course, one of the so-called 'left-handed gangster pictures' and will probably cause some unfavorable criticism [in that regard]."[38]

While it tries to outwit the authorities and escape with the ransom, the gang hides out in an abandoned house, but the crooks find themselves holding a set of hostages when a young couple with a baby seeks shelter in the house during a storm. The couple's car had broken down on the road outside. Most of the film deals with this hostage situation, which is resolved when the gang splits up, authorities ambush and kill several of its members, and Loretta—the demure, sweet wife and mother who, with her husband and child, is being held hostage—shoots the meanest and most violent member of the gang, Pitch, played by Bruce Cabot. This shooting is perhaps the most startling act of violence in all of thirties cinema.

The killing is noteworthy in several respects. First, it involves a machine-gun that belongs to the gang, and the PCA cautioned the studio on this point during the script review process. (Jason Joy had by now left the Code office and was working for Twentieth Century Fox. Thus, in this interesting change of affairs, Breen Office staff was now explaining to Joy how things ought to be depicted on-screen.) "As you know, the showing of machine-guns in the possession of gangsters and criminals is not acceptable. Since the gun used here by Loretta is an illegal weapon in the possession of criminals, our Code ruling applies to this material. All scenes, therefore, which show this machine-gun, should be changed to eliminate all objection." Furthermore, "care should be taken to avoid promiscuous showing of *any* weapons, especially in the hands of the criminal characters."[39]

The filmmakers get around the objection to the illegal weapon in the hands of criminals by not showing any of the gang using the gun. When the gang scatters, it is left behind in the house where Loretta can find it and use it. As for the injunction to avoid a "promiscuous" display of the weapon, this is one of many instances during the Hollywood era of a Breen office recommendation being overruled by filmmakers, who put on-screen precisely what the PCA had indicated they could not show. Loretta's use of the gun is highly promiscuous, if that term is taken to mean that the gun is fired excessively or that its display is emphasized on-screen.

In the action of the scene, Pitch tries to kill Loretta and Joe, her husband. Trying to draw Pitch away from Loretta, Joe runs outside, pursued by Pitch, who shoots him with a pistol. Pitch then turns to face the house, where he anticipates Loretta will be easy prey. His shirt is partially open, exposing his chest. He freezes with dismay, and a reverse-angle shot shows why: Loretta is standing in the doorway with the machine-gun. What now happens is astonishingly vivid. Loretta opens fire with the gun, and its recoil makes her body shudder, her jaw drop and her eyes blink, but she keeps on firing. The imagery clearly shows the physical effect on the shooter of firing a powerful automatic weapon. The gun spurts flame, and a cloud of smoke rises up around her. As in *Public Enemy*, the scene is lit to accentuate the smoke from the firing weapon. Loretta is cross-lit, from the side and from behind, which ensures that the smoke is illuminated from two angles, and it positively glows on the screen. The film then cuts to Pitch, and, in an extremely rare detail for the Hollywood era, the bullet strikes are visualized across his bare chest. A line of bloody holes appears as Loretta rakes the fire across his body. (The bullet hits are simulated by inked plugs fired at a transparent screen in front of actor Bruce Cabot.) The film cuts from this medium-shot framing to a long shot of Pitch as he falls to the ground, all while Loretta keeps on firing (off-camera) and gun smoke rolls into the frame. A reverse-angle view of Loretta now shows her pointing the gun downward and still shooting, blasting away at Pitch's corpse (off-camera). A thick cloud of gun smoke envelops her, and when she at last ceases fire, we hear the clink of metallic cartridges hitting each other and the wooden porch.

A more "promiscuous" instance of machine-gun murder would be hard to imagine. The scene is brutal and intense. Loretta until now has been a gentle and nonaggressive character, which makes the carnage all the more shocking. Moreover, she kills Pitch many times over (like the Texas Rangers do to their quarry in *Bonnie and Clyde*), firing with vengeance and bloodlust even after he goes down. Beyond this representational content, the stylistics of the scene make the violence concrete and sensual by emphasizing details not normally a part of gunplay in this period—the bullet strikes on the victim's body, the gun's recoil, the lighting of the gun smoke, the clink of discharging cartridges. Loretta's killing of Pitch satisfies the letter of the Code because the machine-gun is not in the hands of a criminal. It is in her hands, and she is using it to defend her family. But the style is absolutely promiscuous, and this vividness arguably overwhelms the referential distinctions that the PCA wished to maintain by distinguishing between lawful and unlawful possession of automatic weapons. The killing is a slaughter, and the weapon is flaunted not by a criminal character, but by the filmmakers and at the level of style.

CO-OPTING MACHINE-GUN VIOLENCE IN THE G-MAN FILMS

Show Them No Mercy was problematic in another respect. Because of the prominence that it gives to the gangsters, the film failed to exemplify the new direction that the PCA wanted to see in crime films. The most successful rehabilitation of crime pictures was achieved by another film released that year. *G-Men* (1935) was the beginning of a cycle of films celebrating the ingenuity and courage of Federal agents in combating gangsters. The government agents would get the screen time and prominence previously given to mobsters in the gangster genre. Other examples of the new trend, also released in 1935, were *Public Hero Number One*, *Men without Names*, *Let 'em Have It*, and *Counterfeit*, the latter film about treasury agents (T-men). More pictures followed in subsequent years. Instead of focusing on gangster characters and treating the police as supporting players who made occasional appearances, the new formula kept the story centered on law enforcement authorities and their methodical procedures for tracking down criminals. As the PCA remarked happily in its script review of the *G-Men* project, "this story sounds a new note in the general category of crime stories in that it so cleverly and artistically portrays the important part played by the Federal Government men in their attempts to stamp out nation-wide crime."[40] The finished pictured elicited similar praise from the PCA. "The Warner Brothers [sic] G-Man picture is a wow. It is very well done, with the Government men standing out as great heroes."[41] The PCA's injunctions against gangster movies had apparently succeeded in taking the referential content of crime films in a safer direction. But what of the stylistics of violence, which had evolved into such seductive and exciting terms? Given the context of my earlier remarks, the reader will not be surprised to learn that the PCA's reformist measures left the stylistics of violence relatively untouched. Thus, the inherent tendency for aestheticized gun violence to excite and arouse the viewer continued unabated. The split between style and content in the regulation of screen violence had never been so apparent as it was now with the onset of the G-man pictures.

The new regulations on crime were a major component of the PCA's strategy for reforming crime films. Thus, during the pre-production and production phases of *G-Men*, the PCA undertook extended evaluations of the script and script revisions and looked closely at the depiction of weapons and of gun battles between the Feds and gangsters. The initial script evaluation letter was four pages and contained a long list of potential problems and admonitions. These derived from the new regulations—for example, flaunting of weapons by gangsters, no trick methods of concealing weapons, no killing of law officers. Thus, on script page eleven, "there should be no shot showing the gangsters, in scene 18, wearing armpit gun holsters—this with a view to cutting down, wherever possible, the display of guns on the persons of criminals."[42] Similarly, "the action of Collins putting the muzzle of his automatic against Brick's upper lip and then shoving it against his nose is an unnecessary flaunting of a gun by a gangster and will have to be deleted. There is no objection in this same scene to the action of Collins actually pulling the gun and pressing it against Brick's chest. But the arrogant flaunting of the gun cannot be allowed."[43]

In addition to the display of weaponry, the PCA was very concerned that the storyline might dwell too much on lawbreaking rather than on law enforcement. Thus, it took a firm line that the crimes of the gangsters, such as bank robbery, not be shown on-screen in any detail. This concern was motivated by the common charge leveled at the gangster films that they taught viewers methods of lawbreaking. Accordingly, the PCA advised the studio

> There should be no details of crime shown at any time. The action of the gangsters entering the bank; holding up the clerk and bashing him over the head with the revolver; slapping the girl; getting the money and running away; as well as the use of machine-guns either by actual display or by inference from the sound track, will have to be *entirely* deleted. We suggest that you indulge yourselves in this connection in a series of so-called Vorkopitch shots merely suggesting the holdup, with the sound of shots from regular rifles or revolvers coming in, instead of the shots of machine-guns. This is important. There should be no definite details of a holdup at any time. Not only are the detailed methods of crime forbidden by our Code, but invariably they are deleted by censor boards everywhere—both in this country and abroad.[44]

In the film, when the Leggett gang goes on a spree of bank robberies the episode is handled as the Breen Office had advised. It appears as an abbreviated montage (this is what the PCA meant by the term "Vorkopitch shots") of newspaper headlines screaming "Bank Robbery Toll Mounts," "Cashier Murdered in Holdup," and "Crime Wave Sweeps Midwest," dissolved over quick shots of the gang running into or out of banks and being chased by police. During the car chases, the cops and the gang trade gunshots, and the audio track of the montage carries plenty of gunshot noise. At no point, however, does the montage actually show a robbery or any wounding or death by gunfire. Indeed, the police seem to have mysterious powers of survival. During one chase, the gangsters put several bullets through the front windshield of a car packed with cops without hitting any of them. Here, and elsewhere in the film, the gangsters are armed with pistols, repeating rifles, and shotguns—but not with machine-guns. Machine-guns appear only in the possession of the police.

One of the PCA's greatest concerns was to rid the film of any imagery showing law officers being killed by gangsters. This policy ran counter to the demands of good drama, where the tension of an action film like this one demanded that a sense of danger to the heroes be established. If the police and Feds seemed to be invulnerable, that would remove any real opposition or threat from the gangsters, and the drama would become flat. Thus, the ideological imperative that police not be killed had to give way to a negotiated solution that would allow some death in the interests of good drama, but

18.   The killing of the federal agent in *G-Men*, presented as a shadow play.

without giving it explicit visualization. While the PCA was against an early scene in the script showing the murder of a Federal officer by Collins, one of the film's chief villains, the scene survived and was filmed. The PCA had written, "we suggest that you delete entirely scene 26 which is the scene showing the Government officer falling in death as a result of the shot fired from the window. We cannot allow law-enforcing officers thus to be shown, and censor boards everywhere will delete this scene from your picture."[45]

This scene is a crucial one for the story. The murdered agent, Eddie Buchanan, is a close friend of Brick (James Cagney), the film's hero, and the killing motivates Brick to become a Federal agent. The issue in keeping the scene would be to find a way of staging the action so as to satisfy the PCA's injunction about no law officer killings and yet be clear enough about Buchanan's murder so as to motivate Brick's subsequent behavior. The compromise solution was to show and yet not show the killing, and this was achieved by using shadow-play imagery. Buchanan trails a counterfeiter, a member of the Leggett gang, and arrests him as he leaves the gang's hideout. Collins sees this from an upstairs window, grabs a rife, and fires it at the street below. The film then cuts to a shot of the silhouettes of Buchanan and the counterfeiter, projected on the asphalt of the street by the glow of a street-lamp. One shadow crumples, drops a pair of handcuffs, and collapses against the other shadow, and then falls below the frame line. The film cuts to the counterfeiter (not his silhouette), now alone in the frame, looking up at the window from which Collins fired.

The shadow-play is unambiguous. A gangster killed the Federal agent, which clearly was a violation of the letter of the Code regulations on crime. Yet, for the reasons I discussed in an earlier context, the PCA counted the use of shadow-play imagery as an acceptable way of getting around this regulation. Strictly speaking, the killing was not shown on-camera, but rather the shadows of the action as its displacement. By displacing the murder onto the silhouettes, the killing becomes an off-screen event—one from which the camera was turned away in a manner that might signal to viewers that this was an action sufficiently horrifying, for ideological reasons, as to be beyond the bounds of tasteful representation. The shadow-play imagery thus enabled the PCA to show some ideological flexibility, as required by the film's narrative, in permitting the killing of a law officer and providing the motivation for Brick's subsequent behavior.

Buchanan's murder is clearly evident. The shadow-play is a displacement of the action, but there is nothing ambiguous about it. By contrast, a subsequent scene, depicting the Leggett gang ambushing Federal officers at a train station, is a masterpiece of evasion and ambiguity. In this case, the narrative content of the scene is completely suppressed by the visual design. The design obfuscates the action, and the viewer only learns the terrible outcome—four officers slain and two wounded—in a brief flurry of newspaper headlines that follow the ambush, screaming "Railway Station Massacre" and "Machine-gunners Butcher Officers." This scene is more narrowly responsive to the new regulations on crime.

Once again, the PCA cautioned the filmmakers against explicit imagery showing law officers dying. "In this connection also, there should be no shot showing the guards actually dying as a result of their battle with the gangsters. It will be all right to indicate as you do now by a newspaper insert that the guards have been killed, but there must be no shot actually showing them falling."[46] The ambush is given a dynamic cinematic design with wide framings showing the two groups blasting away at each other, camera moves through the field of fire, blurred and partial views of fast moving action, and a flurry of close framings isolating individual shooters. But as exciting as all of this is, the images conceal significant parts of the action. The gangsters keep their guns hidden beneath overcoats, and the viewer glimpses a weapon only occasionally. These are pistols and shotguns, yet a remarkable ambiguity surrounds them. While the gangsters are never shown with a machine-gun, when they open up on the Feds the soundtrack contains automatic weapons fire, briefly, before the slower bursts of pistol and shotgun take over. These sound effects suggest that there are machine-guns among the gangsters, and the PCA apparently missed this detail because there is nothing about it in the otherwise quite detailed case file.

As the newspaper headlines specify afterward, in the narrative action of the scene the gangsters are machine-gunning the Feds—but the imagery contradicts this, and the fact is only established in the scene by the brief soundtrack information as the ambush begins. Image and sound contradict one another. We get pictures of single-shot weapons and sounds of machine-guns; the ambiguity is only resolved by the newspaper headlines, although these may raise questions in the viewer's mind about exactly what transpired during the ambush. Moreover, the gun battle is ferociously staged, yet the shooting inflicts virtually no damage on the police. One officer falls, but his comrades pull him to safety, and no gangsters are hit. Afterward, however, the newspapers announce a massacre and four dead officers, providing information that was not in the imagery. The

19. Brick and his Tommy gun in *G-Men*. Like *Scarface*, the filmmaking is in love with the excitement of gun violence. The PCA believed that content, not style, was the problem in crime films and could be fixed by giving automatic weapons to the Feds instead of the gangsters.

displacement here of the ideologically unacceptable event is complete, whereas in the Buchanan killing it was only partial. While the railway ambush is a terrific piece of filmmaking, the narrative events that it references—the killing of officers—were entirely purged from the scene as visualized.

The scene's design provides an archetypal illustration of the PCA's focus on representational content as the means of rehabilitating crime films. The agency kept reiterating this point to Warners: "Whenever it is necessary for your story, you will show policemen being hit by bullets and wounded, *but will in no case ever show actual scenes of these law enforcement officers dying at the hands of gangsters.* This, we believe, will not only be satisfactory as a matter of industry policy, but will also be an improvement from the standpoint of general audience reaction, as we are firmly convinced that scenes of indiscriminate slaughter have become very distasteful to the public."[47]

The agency repeated the warning about cop killing in a subsequent letter, adding, "our idea is that it will be important to avoid a general impression of slaughter, blood-shed, or scenes that would tend to lessen respect for human life in the minds of mixed audiences."[48] For the PCA, the violent action and mayhem of gangland pictures would be acceptable if it was the cops who used the machine-guns and the gangsters who were gunned down. The agency's expressed desire to minimize slaughter is especially curious since *G-Men* contains the most vividly staged mass gun battles since *Scarface*, one of which—the Feds' assault on a Wisconsin cabin where the Leggett gang is holed up—is quite literally a slaughter scene, as the Feds use machine-guns and tear gas to flush the gang out of the cabin and then gun them down as they try to escape.

The machine-guns wielded by the Feds dominate the action and are given an insistent visual emphasis. The Feds keep their trigger fingers tight, to ventilate the cabin and then its fleeing inhabitants. The stylistics of the action—the popping of automatic weapons fire on the soundtrack, the flash of muzzle fire, bullet sprays eating into wood and shattering glass—are indistinguishable from a picture like *Scarface*. The filmmaking rhetoric emphasizes the firepower of these combat-like exchanges. Ideologically, though, things had changed—or so the PCA believed, and counted as a great victory. The screen mayhem was now on the side of law and order. As Breen wrote to Will Hays, proudly recounting the victory that this new film cycle represented,

The half dozen so-called G-Men pictures . . . are coming through in grand style. . . . The two pictures we have seen present the crime angles in fine style. There is a conspicuous absence of the wholesale slaughter, excessive brutality, and over-gruesomeness which, unfortunately, characterized some of our pictures back in the days when we were struggling with the gangster cycle, so-called. In the present crop of pictures, the crime angle is carefully handled; there is nothing suggestive of any definitely antisocial reactions; and there is little, if anything, which should cause any worry when the pictures get into general circulation.[49]

Indeed, censor boards in Ohio, Kansas, New York, Massachusetts, Chicago, and Pennsylvania passed the film with little or no eliminations. From this standpoint the agency's strategy was an unqualified success. But the agency's apparent belief that *G-Men* showed "a conspicuous absence of wholesale slaughter" is quite astonishing, given the dynamically depicted massacres that occur at the train station and the Leggett cabin. Perhaps the agency was being less than honest in its appraisal of the film. Alternatively, a more likely explanation is that its assessment embodied a narrow focus on the ideological rehabilitation of the gangster cycle, one that obscured the startling stylistic continuities between the gangster and G-man films. Those stylistic continuities are most striking in the hyperviolence that distinguishes *Scarface* and *G-Men*, despite their thematic differences. This continuity is a reminder of the importance of that which seems to have eluded the PCA in its makeover of the gangster cycle—namely, cinema's ability to give violence an insistent, hypnotic fascination that transcends the details of plot, character or theme. This ability is the deep structure of cinematic form and the deep logic of its deployment by filmmakers, few of whom can resist its compulsive appeal. This deep structure can overwhelm narrative content when it inflects narrative with its own stylistic and emotional imperatives. This is a key point about film violence that reformers and even scholars can miss when their attention is directed, as it often is, solely to issues of content or ideology. What the PCA gave so much attention—finding the acceptable ideological method for depicting violence—was completely irrelevant, not to censorship certainly, but to the predominant formatting insisted upon by the stylistics of cinema. Exactly as Marx said, ideology was merely a superstructure that worked to mystify the reality of the base level of structure, in this case the plastic properties of the medium.

Despite the PCA's belief in the success of its effort to squash the traditional gangster formula, gangster films did not stay banished. By 1937, Edward G. Robinson was back as *The Last Gangster* and the following year Cagney played one of the most famous hoods of his career, in *Angels with Dirty Faces*. By decade's end, he squared off against Humphrey Bogart in Raoul Walsh's memorable *The Roaring Twenties* (1939). But though the PCA could not defeat the movie gangsters and banish them from the screen, it continued to try to apply many of its Special Regulations on Crime, especially those governing the display of weapons on-screen and the killing of police officers.

THE LONGEVITY OF THE SPECIAL REGULATIONS ON CRIME

It will be helpful here to provide two additional illustrations of the PCA's continued commitment to the Special Regulations. Each example provides a rather vivid illustration of the convoluted negotiations over screen violence that the Special Regulations left as their legacy in classical Hollywood cinema. The PCA took the regulations so seriously that their application threatened to scuttle one of Paramount's prestige productions of 1950: *Detective Story,* directed by William Wyler from a popular play by Stanley Kingsley. In its script review, the agency had deemed *Detective Story* unacceptable under the Code because, at the climax, a thug under arrest at the New York City precinct, where all of the film's action occurs, steals a detective's gun and kills the film's main character, detective Jim McLeod (Kirk Douglas). It's not a premeditated killing; it's an impulsive and panicky act.

The agency judged the film unacceptable under the Code for a second reason: a subplot involving abortion. McLeod has been obsessively pursuing an abortionist and learns that his wife, Mary (Eleanor Parker), had visited the doctor years ago, before McLeod met her. Along with references to homosexuality, abortion was one of the few firm bans that the PCA enforced in American film. Thus *Detective Story* was a threatened production since it included two elements vital to its plot that were subject to prohibition. The agency conveyed this information to Paramount in a letter of June 12, 1950, which called the story "thoroughly and completely unacceptable."[50]

A week after the PCA rejected the script, Breen and Dougherty met with Wyler and Paramount liaison Luigi Luraschi, and Wyler at that time promised to consider an alternative to the abortion subplot. This story problem, however, remained unresolved for the next four weeks, and Paramount informed the PCA that it was contemplating an appeal of the agency's rejection of the script. Studios had the prerogative of appealing PCA decisions to the MPA's Board of Directors in New York, and Paramount intended to argue that the film would present abortion as an evil and, more significantly, that there was no specific ban on abortion in the Production Code. Indeed, there was not. The Code mentioned such things as adultery, seduction, rape, and scenes of "sex passion," but it said nothing about abortion. Despite this, the agency had a long history of deleting references to abortion from films, a history that Breen recounted for MPA president Eric Johnston in a four page single-spaced letter alerting him to the Paramount problem and defending the agency's position on *Detective Story.* Breen worried that the MPA might approve Paramount's appeal. He wrote, "we feel that if once the subject [of abortion] is approved . . . we will thus open up a new area of subject matter, dealing with a great evil, which [ultimately] may result in our . . . offending a great number of people, and bringing down upon the industry very considerable critical condemnation."[51]

After Breen's letter of August 4, 1950 to Eric Johnston, a three-month gap appears in the correspondence gathered in the agency's case file. One of Breen's objectives when he became head of the PCA was to document the agency's dealings with studios and filmmakers, and these records were collected in the case files, organized by film. The files, however, typically contain gaps in the chain of letters and memos that began with a project's script review and concluded with data on censor activity on the released picture. The gaps are often the result of negotiations, deals, and agreements being conducted via telephone, which often did not become a part of the written record gathered in a case file. Thus, the next written communication in the *Detective Story* file is a letter from Breen to Luigi Luraschi, dated November 8, 1950, and in it all references to abortion are gone. The abortion problem has vanished completely from the agency's negotiations with Paramount. The cop killing has not, but the PCA now shows a remarkable spirit of cooperation and willingness to break precedent and create a special exemption to the Code for this film. Breen decides that the PCA will make a special appeal to the MPA's Board of Directors, on behalf of Paramount, to approve this scene. Breen writes to Luraschi that the cop killing is "vital to the dramatic integrity of the picture" and that, as far as the PCA is concerned, while it violates the letter of the Code, it does not violate the spirit or intent of the Code. In rendering this verdict, the agency's turnabout is remarkable. In abandoning its appeal of the abortion decision, did Paramount trade abortion for a cop killing? (In the finished film, though abortion is never mentioned by name, the veiled references to the doctor's operations are clear enough.)[52]

The following day, November 9, Breen wrote another lengthy letter to Eric Johnston, making the case that the MPA approve a special exemption on cop killing, which would be applicable for this film only. In the letter Breen iterates the agency's judgment that the scene does not violate the spirit of the Code, and he reviews the reasons why the Special Regulations on Crime were adopted.

At the time the regulations were set up, we were gravely concerned about the large number of crime pictures, most of them dealing with the conflict between American gangsters and the police . . . there were frequent scenes showing policemen and other law-enforcing officers, being murdered by the gangsters. . . . Our purpose was to put an end to what was the typical gangster film formula of violent conflict with the police, in which policemen were slaughtered.[53]

Breen went on to claim that when the Special Regulations were formulated, the PCA was not concerned with scenes where law officers were killed "aside and apart from the atmosphere of gangsterism." The killing in *Detective Story* was not such an instance. "The killing of the policeman by a criminal is not the result of any 'conflict'—as such—between the police and the criminal. The scene has nothing suggestive of the old gangster formula." The killing is unpremeditated and is carried out by a hotheaded street punk, not a gangster. Breen then provided a lengthy description of the action in the scene and stated that it is "the climactic punch of the story." He then asked for authorization from the Board of Directors to approve the scene, with the understanding that this special exemption was not to be taken as a precedent of any kind.

The MPA offered a counterproposal. It suggested that, rather than create an exemption for one film, the Regulations on Crime be amended so as to attach the phrase "unless such scenes are absolutely necessary to the plot" to the general ban on law officer killings.[54] The additional phrase would enable Paramount to produce the film with McLeod's murder at its climax, and, accordingly, the PCA issued its Code certification on May 9, 1951. The battle of abortion had been resolved in the PCA's favor (references to abortion were deleted from the script), while the agency went the extra mile to accommodate the studio's wishes in regards to McLeod's fate. The deliberations over how to handle this scene, and the agency's request for permission from the MPA to clear it, demonstrate the lingering effects of the controversy that surrounded the gangster cycle some two decades earlier. The policies adopted by the PCA in the wake of those controversies were still factors in its assessment of even non-gangster films like *Detective Story*. At issue in these policies were the unresolved problems over the proper display and use of weapons on-screen—problems that had stayed with American cinema since the silent period and would only vanish as a regulatory issue in the changed political context of post-sixties Hollywood.

While the scene of McLeod's murder was potentially dangerous in an ideological context—it is, after all, a cop killing—its stylistic design is remarkably unassertive. As a moment of screen violence, it lacks the visual poetry and power of the mayhem in *Scarface*, *Show Them No Mercy*, and *G-Men*. The visual design is quite conservative, which may in itself provide an indicator of the scene's inflammatory content. Given the protracted negotiations that were

129

necessary for it to be filmed at all, Wyler may have chosen to handle it in a tasteful manner. Certainly the visual rhetoric of screen violence, which had evolved to this point in time, made available to him a greater range of stylistic devices than he chose to use. But then he had never been one of cinema's great stylists of physical action.

Wyler was famous for his long takes and use of deep-focus, and he does stage many scenes in *Detective Story* in these terms, filling the frame with multiple areas of activity in the group shots of the detective precinct. It is, therefore, significant that he does not film McLeod's murder in the real time of an extended shot that frames both the victim and his assailant. There was ample precedent for approaching the staging that way. *G-Men, This Gun for Hire,* and the other films mentioned earlier show killer and victim within the same frame. Moreover, doing so would have been in keeping with Wyler's aesthetic preference for extended, master-shot framings.

Instead, and quite conventionally, Wyler cuts between the killer firing the pistol and McLeod taking the slugs. We see shooter and victim in separate compositions. By contrast, the well-known publicity photo of the scene is actually more powerful because it does show everything within one frame, the gun going off and Mcleod wincing from the bullet's impact. While the injunction against a master-shot framing of gun murders was never absolute, it did possess some force, and Wyler and the studio were probably not eager to take their special exemption for the scene and then stylize the action in a visually powerful or aggressive way. Moreover, McLeod reacts to the slugs with the kind of cosmetic death that typified most shootings during the Hollywood period. He grabs his chest and slowly falls over, without exhibiting any of the visceral, kinesthetic physicality of Tony Camonte's death in *Scarface*. McLeod dies in a peaceful and placid way. Apart from expiring, he shows no other physical response to the shooting, and the bullet strikes have no visual presence on-screen. In this sense, his murder was ideologically transgressive but not stylistically so.

Along with the prohibition on cop killing, one of the most important of the Special Regulations was banning the use of submachine-guns or other illegal weapons by criminals. Like the cop-killing ban, this provision about automatic weapons had lingering effects on American film. A full two decades after the inception of the gangster cycle and the adoption of the Special Regulations, the PCA was still attentive to this stipulation. Its application by the agency caused a flurry of correspondence with director Stanley Kubrick and his producer and partner, James B. Harris, over the design of an unusual weapon that was to be used in *The Killing* (1956). This drama about a racetrack robbery told its story using a series of nonchronological time frames that would, years later, come to influence Quentin Tarantino and the narrative design of *Reservoir Dogs* (1992). Moreover, *The Killing* is a key film in Kubrick's career, showcasing his developing mastery of wide-angle compositions and dynamic changes in depth of field.

Adapting the novel *Clean Break,* the script by Kubrick and novelist Jim Thompson called for the main character to use a sub-machine-gun during the robbery. Aware of the Special Regulations on Crime, producer Harris wrote Geoffrey Shurlock, now head of the PCA, a letter informing him about their intent to use a sub-machine-gun in the scene and inquiring about how this would be regarded by the PCA. "Having seen firearms handled in various motion pictures," Harris wrote, "we feel sure that this MPAA ruling does not outlaw the use of all weapons. Thus, since this sequence is essential to our film, would you forward a description of permissible automatic weapons?"[55]

Shurlock replied with a strict reading of the Special Regulations, denying the filmmakers' request to use automatic weapons in the scene. "The code permits the use of any weapon that is not classified as an *illegal* weapon. This means that it permits the use of any weapon for which a license can be obtained—thus legalizing its possession. This eliminates machine-guns, sub-machine-guns, etc., but leaves a very large choice open to the producer." He added, "if you would indicate in your script what weapons you propose to use, we will then be able to report in detail as to their final acceptability."[56]

Faced with this rejection of their plan to use an automatic weapon, Kubrick and Harris slyly attempted to disguise a shotgun so as to look like a submachine-gun. They were betting that this would satisfy the PCA since a shotgun was not an automatic weapon and ordinary citizens could legally possess it. Harris floated the idea to Shurlock. "I would like to confirm the acceptability of altering the wooden stock of a Remington repeating shotgun, providing the barrel length remains a minimum of twenty inches. Specifically, what we have in mind is to saw off part of the shoulder stock and add a front hand grip."[57]

Shurlock replied by pointing out the obvious: that if a shotgun were disguised so that viewers, or other characters in the scene, mistook it for a sub-machine-gun, then it might as well be one and would thereby incur a violation of the Special Regulations. "We fear that what you have in mind would result in your re-constructing a Remington repeating rifle that, on the screen, would give the impression of a machine-gun or some other illegal weapon. This would . . . defeat the purpose of the Code, which requires that all illegal weapons be kept out of the hands of criminals. We therefore suggest that you drop this plan."[58]

The filmmakers remained unsatisfied with the PCA's policy and sought to prod the agency to their way of thinking. Kubrick now got involved in the

20. The unconventional design of this shotgun in *The Killing*—the front grip makes it look like an automatic weapon—prompted extensive negotiations between the PCA, director Stanley Kubrick, and producer James B. Harris. Kubrick and Harris wanted to suggest the look of a machine-gun, but the PCA resisted.

deliberations and, with a lawyerly approach, he asked whether an illegal weapon was truly equivalent to a legal one that merely *looked* like an illegal weapon. He wrote to Shurlock, "I respectfully ask whether the Code rule covering illegal weapons prohibits the use of illegal weapons, or a legal weapon which might give the impression of being an illegal weapon. Could you tell me specifically what the Code ruling regarding this matter is." With some impudence and his famous eye for technical detail, he pointed to the PCA's inconsistency in enforcing its own regulations. "By the way, I noticed what seemed to me to be an inconsistency in the ruling covering automatic weapons. In Twentieth Century Fox's film the *House of Bamboo*, Robert Ryan uses a German P38 pistol which is, as far as I know, a fully automatic weapon."[59] Indeed, in that film Ryan and his gang use automatic weapons to rob government supply trains and sell the goods on the black market.

Because of the filmmakers' persistence in pursuing their goal of showing, or at least suggesting, an automatic weapon in the robbery scene, Shurlock traveled to New York and met with Harris and Kubrick. At the meeting, they agreed that Harris and Kubrick would not give the impression that the weapon used in the robbery was a machine-gun or other illegal weapon. Since the PCA had not yet reviewed the script, everyone agreed that preparation for the production could continue and that the matter would be resolved in connection with the agency's script evaluation. Shurlock noted in a memo, "They are coming to Hollywood to produce the picture, so it will be quite feasible to go into this question in more detail when they arrive here."[60]

But the script that Harris and Kubrick submitted for evaluation did not seem to reflect the agreement that had prevailed in the New York meeting, since it described a machine-gun being used in the robbery. Writing the PCA's script response letter, Shurlock reiterated the agency's opposition to a machine-gun. Regarding page 154 of the script, he wrote, "we assume that the several mentions of 'machine-gun' in this sequence are in error and that you have reference to the trick shotgun already discussed. For the record, the use of a machine-gun in these circumstances would be unacceptable." A later scene in the script (and film) involves a shootout between a pair of thugs and the racetrack robbers. Shurlock cautioned about this scene, "Val and Tiny should not be armed with sawed-off shotguns, which are rated as illegal weapons."[61]

Later that month, in the last piece of correspondence addressing the machine-gun issue, Kubrick summarized their agreement with the PCA. "We agreed that a sawed-off shotgun of the minimum legal length mounted on a special stock with a front hand grip similar to the type used on sub-machine-guns would be acceptable by the Production Code as long as it was clearly not a sub-machine-gun and was not referred to as such."[62]

This is how the weapon appears in the film, used by Johnny Clay (Sterling Hayden) to take control of a room full of racetrack cashiers. The gun is clearly a pump- action shotgun with the eccentric feature of a front hand grip that enables Clay to swing it in a quicker and tighter arc as he herds the track employees together into a back room. Together with a grotesque facemask that he wears, the gun's odd appearance gives Clay a sinister, deviant menace and adds to the psychological power he wields over the employees. But the gun only appears briefly, and it is never fired, and one thus wonders whether its appearance on-screen, especially in this compromised form—shotgun rather than machine gun—merited the lengthy negotiations with the PCA that it took to get the weapon on-screen in a format that fell short of the filmmakers' intentions. Although the agency allowed Harris and Kubrick to use a trick shotgun on-screen, it took a rather firm line regarding the no-machine-guns-for-gangsters rule.

The irony in this is that while the PCA was enforcing its decades old ruling on automatic weapons, and while Kubrick and Harris were unable to realize their original intentions for the scene despite protracted negotiations, all of this was going to change very soon. Machine guns were going to reappear in the hands of gangsters. In 1958, Nicholas Ray's *Party Girl* returned to the *Scarface* era of blazing Tommy gun assaults and gangland hyperviolence. That same year, a relatively unknown actor named Charles Bronson starred in Roger Corman's *Machine-Gun Kelly*, playing the title character. Kelly's gun furnishes him with his sexual identity, and he cradles it in his arms lovingly and obsessively. Moreover, the camerawork frames the gun with close attention, giving it a visual prominence and sexualized aura that anticipates the kind of visual fetish that high-tech weaponry has become in cinema today. Kelly's machine gun is promiscuously flourished on-screen.

The film, though, shows its transitional status, as a work that followed the PCA's 1956 Code revision removing the prohibitions on most content areas. For all of the fetishized visual attention given the machine gun by the camera, owner Kelly doesn't use his gun very much. The film's title suggests that the viewer will get to see a lurid rampage of violent crime when, in fact, the machine-gun shootings are infrequent. Moreover, instead of the sustained firing of Tony Camonte or Loretta in *Show Them No Mercy*, Kelly's shooting is rather demure and inhibited. He lets off only a few, brief blasts instead of keeping his trigger taut with the determination of Camonte or Loretta, who are hypnotized by the power of their guns. When Roger Corman returned again to the genre in *The St. Valentine's Day Massacre* (1967), all inhibition was gone, and the machine-gun massacres and drive-by shootings are shown with a ferocity suitable for the year in which *Bonnie and Clyde* burst the representational barriers of screen violence and led to the new film ratings system the following year.

The PCA, then, was waging an ultimately losing battle—and not only because the exercise of prior restraint was on the wrong side of the direction in which society was moving by the late 1950s. The PCA's mission was antithetical to the ongoing interest of filmmakers to expand the restrictions on filmic representation and take cinema toward a violence harder than what the PCA, at the height of its power, would countenance. I explore this push toward more explicit violence in the next chapter. Since that chapter, in essence, deals with the limits of PCA power and its willingness to compromise in the interests of keeping itself viable and to serve production, it will be appropriate to end the present chapter by discussing how the agency responded with vigor to a picture that it regarded as truly dangerous and "very worrisome."

Gun Crazy (1949) is today a cult item, rather highly regarded as a stylish and subversive outlaw-couple-on-the-run picture directed by Joseph H. Lewis. Lewis was a talented filmmaker who worked on low-budget crime films such as *Detour* (1945) and *The Big Combo* (1955), stories peopled by obsessive and violent characters. *Gun Crazy* is about a young man, Bart Tare (John Dall), who has a lifelong infatuation with guns. As a boy, he steals a pistol and is sent to reform school. As an adult, he drifts around with a suitcase of expensive weaponry until he meets a circus performer, Annie (Peggy Cummins), who is even more gun crazed than he. Together, they embark on a spree of armed robberies until the police corner them. Bart kills Annie to prevent her from shooting the cops, one of whom is a childhood buddy. Bart is then shot and killed by the police.

Without question this is an atypical film, which sexualizes to an unusual degree Bart and Annie's attraction to guns, speed, and violence. At the same time, however, it is a highly bowdlerized picture, whose pre-production alteration of the original story synopsis and script considerably weakened its transgressive elements. The film's cult reputation tends to overstate its subversive qualities and to minimize the extent to which the PCA was able to gut the film of its scripted violence. The PCA was extremely concerned about the film's potential to glamorize its outlaw couple and about the likely effects upon young people of seeing a film that had a lurid fascination for weaponry and no voice for conventional morality within the story. Its handling of this picture belies the conventional notion that "B" films escaped the close regulatory and censor attention that "A" pictures invariably attracted.

In the original story synopsis and script, Nelly (as Bart was then named) shows no remorse over his life of crime with Toni (as Annie was then called), nor does he kill her at the end in protest over her murderous impulses. That ending was one the PCA required, as was the big change in Nelly/Bart, turning him from a rebellious kid with a violent streak into a weak-willed character pulled into crime by Annie and who responds by whining and nagging at her that their crimes are wrong. This change of heart enabled the filmmakers, as per the PCA, to inject a voice for morality within the film "which will point up and emphasize at all times the wrongness of Nelly's obsession for guns and his career of crime."[63] In the film, shortly after he meets Annie, Bart loses his passion for guns and turns into a chronic nag, worrying about the robberies they are pulling and about Annie's tendency to want to kill people. This revision to the character turned the film into something very different than what had been scripted.

The agency was especially worried about two scenes in the script that show Nelly, as a boy, pulling a gun on adults. The adults—one is a schoolteacher and the other is Nelly's stepfather—were both depicted as mean and oppressive,

21. *Gun Crazy*—but only a little. The PCA took a hard line with this picture and its violence, compelling the filmmakers to soften key elements.

which, the agency feared, would enlist viewer sympathy for Nelly's actions. The original story synopsis described the scenes.

> Sometime later an unsympathetic teacher, Miss Bressner, thinks Nelly has shot some popcorn at her and is about to whip Nelly when Nelly (by suggestion) draws a gun on her and flees. . . . At dusk Nelly takes his .22 rifle and goes to the barn. At dusk Tare [the stepfather] takes a lantern and whip with the intention of giving Nelly a beating. As Tare approaches the barn, Nelly shoots the globe out of the lantern and tells Tare he will never submit to any more whippings.[64]

The PCA rejected these scenes as manifesting a dangerous antisocial philosophy and an irresponsible appeal to juvenile viewers that might instill a desire to imitate Nelly. In its letter rejecting the scenes, and the entire script as written, the agency said

> These two criminal acts by Nelly are made to seem not only right and proper, as evidenced by the dangerous antisocial philosophy enunciated in

the story that "if you got a thing like this (a gun) no one could ever bother you—they'd be afraid to," but are justified by reason of the fact that the school teacher and the stepfather play the role of unsympathetic heavies in the first half of your story. This justification, we are convinced, could not do other than elicit audience sympathy for the boy's wrong-doing.[65]

Indeed, the agency concluded that "the entire story as presently written" inspires sympathy for the criminal. "This sympathy on the side of evil seems to us to be inescapable."[66] The scenes with the schoolteacher and stepfather did not survive the script draft process and are thus not in the finished film. These deletions, and changes in the second half of the story, which included changing the character of Nelly/Bart—"Nelly will be shown more as an unwilling victim of Toni's desire for wealth"—and minimizing the details of their robberies (as had been done with the crime spree in *G-Men*), served to make the film into a more conventional picture and one which never lives up to the promise of lurid violence contained in the title.

CONCLUSION

It would be easy to condemn the PCA's handling of this production. It did gut the filmmakers' original vision for the story and pass the project only on condition that its depiction of crime and violence was substantially altered. On the other hand, the agency was thinking about the kinds of values that the film would portray and to which viewers would be exposed. The fetishistic attention to weapons promised by the filmmakers' original vision, and the amorality of its two characters, had to give way to a story structure that incorporated a point of view condemning criminal activity and a promiscuous use of guns.

When one reflects upon the unceasing visual fascination with high-power weaponry in today's films, and the scenes that lovingly depict their destructive effects on people and property, and when one reflects upon the many instances of copycat crimes apparently inspired by movie scenes of flamboyant violence, the PCA's concerns about a film like *Gun Crazy* and its subsequent action may come to seem less indefensible. Moreover, the agency's spirited willingness to grapple with the depiction of guns on-screen, beginning with the cycle of gangster films in the early thirties, manifested clear pro-social impulses. Those impulses turn out to have had a significant degree of wisdom. Empirical studies indicate that the mere display of weapons—irrespective of considerations about their use—on-screen or in pictures can be sufficient to increase aggression among some viewers.[67] This outcome was a key concern of the PCA throughout the history of its negotiations with filmmakers over the depiction of gun violence.

Though the PCA's mission was ultimately a losing one, the agency implicitly confronted and grappled with the enduring questions about the social influence of movies that depict gun violence—questions that continue to plague us. These questions about the antisocial effects of films lay behind its efforts to negotiate the depiction of guns on-screen. In its day, the PCA had a workable means for addressing those questions, and it believed that there were serious issues inherent in the manner with which guns were displayed in film. As we have seen in this chapter, those policies and that philosophy guided its negotiations with filmmakers. True, it remained unaware how important the stylistic components of screen violence are, and it believed that control of referential components would be sufficient to keep violence within safe boundaries and minimize its antisocial content and appeals. But, by contrast, the industry today seems not to think of these issues at all. In the PCA, the film community had an institutional means for examining and reflecting upon these questions and engaging filmmakers over them. Today, there is no such mechanism for this kind of work. One wonders how this present indifference can be deemed preferable to the PCA's belief in the power of film to shape emotions, help instill values, and guide other elements of the viewer's response. By abdicating an engagement with these questions today, the industry surely takes the questionable position that vividly stylized film violence leaves viewers untouched. Perhaps a longer span of time will show which position is the naïve one.

4

Throwing the
Extra Punch

In its efforts to keep the violence in American cinema to a safe level, one that would not incite action by regional censor boards, the Production Code Administration (PCA) focused much of its energy on what may be termed a quantitative initiative. It tried to lower the number of violent acts that were proposed for filming in the screenplays that it reviewed. The agency regularly advised filmmakers and studio liaisons to reduce the incidence of shootings or beatings, or to lessen their severity, and it was typically quite exacting in its recommendations. The script for Nicholas Ray's *Party Girl* (1958), for example, contained a scene in which a gang boss clubs to death one of his underlings. The agency objected to the number of blows administered during the beating. "Salvi should be struck no more than two blows, preferably out of frame. The business of Sanangelo swinging again and again is absolutely unnecessary and unacceptable."[1]

The script for *The Man from Laramie* (1955), a Western by Anthony Mann, dispatched the villain, Vic (Arthur Kennedy), under a hail of Indian arrows. The PCA rejected the action as being too brutal. "Please avoid undue gruesomeness in scene 186, where the flurry of arrows strike Vic."[2] In the finished film, only one arrow strikes him. The agency objected to the "flurry of arrows" because it felt that the penetration of the body by a sharp implement such as a knife, sword, spear, or arrow represented a more brutal and gruesome type of violence than a shooting. Its judgment in this respect was influenced by a conviction that regional censor boards were especially prone to delete such details. As we saw in chapter one, censor boards as early as the 1920s were removing knife violence from films. Furthermore, there is evidence indicating that viewers generally construe stabbing violence to be more disturbing than gun violence.

As we have seen, the only deletions the PCA requested in the extremely violent wartime picture *Bataan* (1943) were close-ups of the bayoneting of soldiers. Regarding the first draft script for the Anthony Mann Western *Winchester '73* (1950), the PCA cautioned, "some political censor boards still delete scenes in which knives are shown sticking in people. With this in mind, you may want to take some protection shots in scene 152."[3] A decade earlier, the PCA had been especially concerned about some graphically depicted violence in the Errol Flynn action film *The Charge of the Light Brigade* (1936). In the climax of the film, the Surat Khan, the picture's villain, is speared by a number of British lancers. The PCA found the scripted action, as proposed for filming in close-up and wider framings, to be objectionable, and it included a quote from the scripted action in its reply: " 'Lance after lance plows into his (Surat Khan) weakly squirming body. He makes one horrible effort to live, but it is not his choice, and a moment later he is dead.' This is a particularly gruesome scene, about which we have written you before, and should not appear in the completed picture."[4] In the finished film, the visual design of the sequence places the victim off-screen for much of the spearing action. Khan is speared on-camera by the hero, Flynn, and then three other Lancers ride past his body and hurl their lances. As they do so, however, Khan is off-camera. The reverse-angle shot showing Khan reveals that several of these spears have missed, but we then see a spear striking his chest. To reduce the level of brutality in the action, however, Khan is depicted as being clearly dead when this last spear strikes him. There is no sign that he is reacting, as he does in the script, to the flurry of lances.

Earlier in the film, Flynn saves a woman from an Indian attacker during a large-scale massacre of civilians. The PCA objected, "your directions call for 'A close shot of Flynn killing the Suristani that was attacking Elsa. He runs him through with his sword.' This sort of shot will almost invariably be deleted everywhere by the censors. We suggest that you keep this in mind."[5] Flynn does use his sword on the man, but as filmed in a medium long shot, the blocking of the action obscures a clear view of the blade going into the victim's body. By minimizing the clarity with which the stabbing is depicted, the framing effectively reduces the amplitude of the violence transpiring on-screen.

With regard to gun violence, a wounding might be preferable to an actual killing. As an example of this, the PCA complained to Universal Pictures that its script for *Winchester '73* had too many killings. To reduce the number of murders, the PCA wrote Universal, "we must earnestly recommend that, whenever possible, you indicate that your secondary characters are wounded rather than actually killed. We particularly have in mind, on page 118, the killing of Dutch's two henchmen. Particularly in view of the fact that the Sheriff is present, we think these two men, in particular, could be disabled rather than killed."[6] In its review of another Mann Western, *Bend of the River* (1952), the PCA wrote, "we suggest that the man Cole shoots be wounded rather than killed."[7]

In cases where a script indicated that the victim of a killing was to be shot numerous times, the PCA typically requested that the murder be depicted with fewer shots being fired. The agency felt that reducing the number of shots fired would help to lessen the overall level of brutality. An example was this recommendation on the script for *The Case against Brooklyn* (1958): "We suggest having Bonney fire only once in scene 127."[8] The PCA had numerous recommendations of this type in its review of the script for *Bend of the River.* "It would be well if some of the killings committed by Cole could be eliminated. In any event, those retained should be committed with one shot and not three. . . . The killing of Wasco [for example] should be accomplished with one shot and not three."[9]

In Stanley Kubrick's *The Killing* (1956), George Peatty (Elisha Cook, Jr.) kills his wife, Sherry (Marie Windsor), when he learns that she has betrayed him with another man. The script called for him to shoot her repeatedly, and the PCA rejected this. "This scene of the murder of Sherry is unduly prolonged, due to the fact that he fires at her three individual times. It should be rewritten so as to avoid this excessively brutal flavor."[10] Kubrick acknowledged in response that "Sherry will not be shot three times."[11]

In the finished film George shoots Sherry only once, but Kubrick and his producer James B. Harris still managed to inject a substantial amount of gruesomeness into the scene. They filmed George with blood streaming down his face (George is the sole survivor of a gangland shootout), lit him with hard, hot light at a side angle that silhouettes the opposite side of his face, and had him lurch into frame on a crazy diagonal. He hangs unsteadily on a birdcage, the shadows of its bars splayed across his face, the parrot inside chattering manically throughout the violence in the scene. After George shoots his wife, she takes a while to die. When she is gone, George topples forward into the camera, pulling the birdcage with him. Kubrick then cuts to a tight close-up of George's bloodied and lifeless face, eyes open, still lit in hard light and at an unnatural angle.

In persuading the filmmakers to redesign the action of this scene, the PCA succeeded in its quantitative initiative. It did reduce the number of gunshots and thereby unquestionably reduced the level of sadism and rage that George expresses toward his wife. But in other respects, the scene's violence eluded the PCA's efforts. Sherry's death is still prolonged—not because she is being shot numerous times, but because the single bullet doesn't kill her right away.

She lingers long enough to vent a lifetime of anger and frustration at George for being such an inadequate husband. In addition, the scene's visual design helps to give the violence a lurid edge. The hard, violent angles of the lighting make George's bloody face look quite grotesque, and the mindless chattering of the parrot in its cage underscores the brutal nature of George and Sherry's confrontation.

Thus, it is questionable whether the PCA really succeeded in defanging the scene's violence. It is entirely possible that the agency's actions led the filmmakers to explore other ways of accentuating the killing. Having agreed to eliminate two-thirds of the proposed gunplay in the scene, the filmmakers augmented its other elements by letting the suppressed violence bleed into the lighting, framing, and sound design in ways that were not quantitative but qualitative. The institutional mission of the PCA, realized through its practice of script review, left the agency vulnerable to such maneuvers by filmmakers.

Because the PCA did not oversee production, filmmakers had a back door exit that they could use, if they were shrewd enough, to evade or to neutralize those recommendations of the agency that were the most unwelcome. If the visual design of a scene of violence was carefully conceived—as this one in *The Killing* is, such that all of its components work to create a lurid, harsh, or brutal tone—the agency would find it difficult to suggest alterations other than major deletions in the finished picture as screened for clearance. This it was loathe to do. Moreover, the agency would not wish to find itself in a situation where it felt compelled to recommend deletion of an entire scene. This outcome would call into question the rationality of its operating methods, which aimed to solve problems of representation before a picture went into production, after which alterations became very costly.

For the PCA, film style was the great unknown in the complex series of deals that it undertook with filmmakers, studios, and regional censor boards. In the most general terms, of course, style was predictable. The classical Hollywood system of filmmaking was rationalized according to standard shooting methods and editing patterns.[12] Nevertheless, the PCA's lack of control over film production, except indirectly through its vetting of scripts and screening of a finished film for Code certification, was the great lacunae in the system of regulation that the industry had devised as the antidote to regional censorship. Filmmakers found myriad stylistic ways to evade the agency's dictates and, more importantly, to press for expanding levels of screen violence in terms of its explicitness, intensity, and duration.

In the initial years of its operation, the PCA effectively rolled back the explicit brutality of horror and gangster films, and, as we will see, it made exceptions during wartime to permit greater levels of carnage in the industry's pictures about World War II. By the mid- and late-1940s, however, the agency found its authority under a relatively sustained assault by filmmakers eager to push the acceptable boundaries of screen violence. American films became more strikingly brutal in those years, and this trend carried over into the next decade. As a result, the movement toward graphic violence appears in American film *well before* the years 1966–1968, when the Production Code was scrapped and the Code and Rating Administration (CARA) system was implemented. American film unquestionably became more explicitly violent after these changes, as pictures like *Bonnie and Clyde* (1967) and *The Wild Bunch* (1968) demonstrate. But the pressure toward this outcome had been building for a long time. The system was like a pressure cooker. It finally blew in the late 1960s—but only because the internal pressure, the drive toward explicit violence, had been increasing for many years.

INDUSTRY CHANGES THAT ERODED PCA AUTHORITY

This escalation occurred at a time when the film industry was hit by a confluence of factors that changed its mode of operation and its audience and collectively undermined the operation and authority of the Production Code Administration. In order to set the institutional context in which filmmakers were able to push for harder violence as the PCA weakened, it will be helpful to briefly recount these factors here. In the late 1940s, the studios lost their theater operations at the very time they faced a new competitor for the audience. The Supreme Court's Paramount decision in 1948 (*United States v. Paramount Pictures*, 334 U.S.131) enjoined the Hollywood studios from engaging in restrictive trade practices and found that the industry's vertical integration—studios engaging in film production, distribution, and exhibition—was a key means of implementing these practices.[13] Accordingly, in a series of consent decrees, Paramount, RKO, Warner Bros., Twentieth Century Fox, and MGM agreed to relinquish their ownership of theater chains. As numerous scholars have pointed out, the severing of exhibition from production–distribution operations created an opening for independent producers to bypass the chokehold of the majors on exhibition.[14] Antitrust scholar Michael Conant suggests that this increase in the number of independent producers was the most important effect of the Paramount decrees.[15] Bypassing the majors in this way also entailed bypassing the PCA.

The majors' agreement not to exhibit films lacking a Code seal of approval had been a vital source of the PCA's authority, but it was enforceable only when the majors owned the majority of the nation's first-run theaters. The agreement effectively denied access to first-run theaters by independent producers and curtailed their ability to put films into national release that were not certified by the PCA. With the loss of theaters by the majors, this choke-hold on exhibition relaxed. United Artists, for example, bypassed the Code by taking Otto Preminger's *The Moon Is Blue* (1953) and *The Man with the Golden Arm* (1955) to theaters without a Code seal of approval. These pictures had been denied a seal because of their treatment of taboo subjects like adultery and drug addiction. The distribution of foreign films also expanded through-out the 1950s and early 1960s, and placed more films into distribution that lacked a Code seal of approval, such as *Room at the Top* (1959) and *Never on Sunday* (1960).

In the wake of the Paramount decision, the industry faced a new threat from television, which eroded the movie-going audience and box-office rev-enue. Film output diminished, with features in release dropping from 654 in 1951 to 392 in 1955.[16] Of greatest significance, however, was the change that television wrought in the nature of the movie-going audience. The Production Code was vested in the idea of a mass, national movie-going public. Televi-sion had changed the mass audience to a niche audience, one stratified by age. Young adult viewers, ages 15–29, comprised 41 percent of the movie-going public in 1957.[17] PCA staff member Albert Van Schmus said that the ideal of a *mass* audience had sustained the industry's commitment to the Production Code in the era before television—especially from the exhibition sector, which wanted inoffensive films that would appeal to as many people as possible. In the eyes of exhibitors, this was a strategy that would fill theaters, but only when motion pictures were the unchallenged medium of popular visual en-tertainment. "We were the one country in the world that was trying to put that *one* stamp of approval on all movies," Van Schmus recalled. "We were trying to make everything for everybody, which in a way is really impossible. But for years that was the idea, in order to make *money*. . . . And when television . . . took over that mass appeal, we were destined, we just simply had to face changes. The creative people weren't going to be stopped. They had to go into areas that would offer something that was *not* on television."[18] The col-lective and incremental push toward harder violence was one means of taking film to places television could not go.

As Hollywood struggled with the changes to its operation entailed by the Paramount decision and the competition from television, a series of court challenges began to erode the authority of the state and municipal censor boards, whose operations had posed an ongoing threat to creative expression in cinema and had prodded the industry to create the Production Code in 1930. As noted in chapter one, the Supreme Court's Burstyn decision in 1952 extended First Amendment protection to motion pictures, a freedom that the

Mutual decision of 1916 had denied. In *Burstyn,* however, the Court left the door open for censorship because it did not prohibit a state from censoring films based on a clearly drawn statute.

But other court challenges, from the mid-1950s to the late 1960s, began to erode and strike down the laws empowering state and municipal censor boards. *Commercial Pictures v. Board of Regents* (1953), *Superior Films v. Board of Education* (1954), *Times Film Corp. v. Chicago* (1957), *Embassy Pictures v. Hudson* (1965), *Cambist Films v. Board of Regents* (1965), and *Trans-Lux v. Board of Regents* (1965) struck down censor laws in New York, Ohio, Memphis, and Chicago.[19] In addition, *Gelling v. Texas* (1952), *Holmby Productions v. Vaughn* (1955), and *Londerholm v. Columbia Pictures* (1966) targeted censor laws in Texas and Kansas. *Freedman v. Maryland* (1965) placed the burden on the censor of proving that a film is obscene and found Maryland's censorship operations deficient because they failed to provide for prompt judicial review of censor rulings and placed the burden of proof on the exhibitor or distributor.[20]

In the wake of Freedman, the film licensing systems in New York, Virginia, and Kansas were declared unconstitutional, and by 1967 the only state censor board still in operation was Maryland's.[21] Summarizing the impact of the post-Burstyn rulings, some legal critics have concluded, "the demise of the whole procedure of prior restraint of movies, which began in 1952, was complete by the mid-1960s, when all but a handful of the boards had been invalidated because of their unconstitutional standards or effectively destroyed."[22]

In his classic study of motion picture censorship, Richard Randall ties the erosion of the PCA's authority to the constellation of factors that we have just reviewed. Randall writes, "the antitrust decision . . . was only one factor in the erosion of the code's authority. Changes in the constitutional status of movies and a narrowing of the legal concept of obscenity, one the one hand, and stiff competition from television and foreign films, on the other, all added to the decline of formal self-regulation."[23] Changes in film content and visual representation during this period provide measures of this decline. Existing discussions have tended to center on changes in the areas of language and depictions of sexuality in benchmark films like *Anatomy of a Murder* (1959) and *The Pawnbroker* (1965).

The escalation of film violence furnishes a significant measure of the PCA's decline. In this chapter I examine a series of key films on which the agency tried to negotiate with filmmakers who were intent on pushing the existing boundaries. In most of these cases, the PCA was on the losing end of the negotiations. This cumulative record acquired accelerating force during this period, until the agency eventually reached a point by the early 1960s where it ceased commenting on violence altogether.

While the PCA successfully made its case and had its way with many films during the 1940s and 1950s, the significant countertrend examined in this chapter inflicted long-term damage on the agency and helped lead to its weakened condition by the 1960s. In his study of the motion picture industry during the 1940s, Thomas Schatz points to ongoing tensions between filmmakers and the PCA and writes, "there were a number of serious internal Code challenges, particularly from leading independent producers on high-stakes, first-run productions."[24] His examples include *Gone With the Wind, Rebecca, The Outlaw,* and *Two-Faced Woman.* He concludes, "there was growing resistance within Hollywood to the strictures of the Code . . . resistance was more likely to come from major independent producers and in pictures geared to more sophisticated urban audiences."[25] While Schatz places this growing resistance early in the 1940s, I will be concerned with pictures mainly from the latter half of the decade and onward, when the growth of harsh violence becomes clearly evident. As the discussion that follows will suggest, I differ with his conclusion that conflict with the Code occurred mainly in high-profile productions aimed at sophisticated audiences. The conflict was more widespread than that. The films I study in this chapter are a mix of prestige productions and low-budget pictures, ones originating from the major studios as well as minors and independents. In each case, however, the documents in the PCA files reveal that the filmmakers were pressuring the agency to accept more and harder violence than it wanted to; the files also reveal the agency's ongoing difficulties, and sometimes outright failures, to keep the violence within the limits it preferred.

SADISM AND TORTURE IN *THE GLASS KEY*

Although the trend toward harder violence accelerated later in the 1940s, significant instances of this development appeared early in the decade, consistent with Schatz's description of the emerging tensions within Hollywood. *The Glass Key* (1943) was a tight, no-nonsense adaptation of Dashiell Hammett's novel about organized crime and political corruption and featured the star team of Alan Ladd and Veronica Lake, whose pairing together in *This Gun for Hire* (1942) had been very successful. Ladd plays Ed Beaumont, the loyal fixer of a corrupt politician, who tries to clear his boss of a murder charge. Doing so, Ed crosses paths with a psychopathic sadist, Jeff (William Bendix), who inflicts a terrible beating on him at the behest of a gang boss. The violence is uncommonly vicious, and its impact on Ed's face is portrayed in close visual detail. It is a lengthy scene of assault and torture, and several elements combine to heighten its violence. One is Jeff's cheerfully sadistic enjoyment of the pain he inflicts upon Ed, his sadism mixing with a clearly suggested sexual pleasure. He calls Ed "sweetheart" and "sweetie pie" and, when an associate objects that he might kill Ed after a couple of vicious punches, Jeff replies, in the tender tones of a lover, "you can't croak him—he's tough. He likes this. Don't you, baby?"

The grim surroundings help to make the beatings more savage. Jeff holds Ed prisoner in a bleak warehouse apartment, with filthy doors and walls and broken down furniture. Ed rests between beatings on a rumpled bed with a bent metal frame. As the scene opens he lays on the bed, barely conscious and moaning in pain—the kind of vocalized distress rarely heard in American film since the early thirties. The lighting is hard and low-key, emphasizing the room's angular shadows and sharp-edged furnishings: the general bleakness conveys the hopelessness of Ed's predicament and, in that context, the ruthlessness of the torture being visited upon him.

Jeff's beatings inflict considerable damage on Ed's face. Despite the hard, cynical character he plays here (and in *This Gun for Hire*), Alan Ladd was a

---

22. Ed Beaumont surveys his ruined face in *The Glass Key*. The beating scene prompted letters of protest from viewers and an admission by the PCA that it was in violation of the Production Code.

star whose features conveyed a softness and glamour that was relatively ill-suited for these roles and contrasted with his gravel voice and clipped, tight delivery of dialogue. The disfigurement of Ladd's pretty face furnishes a vivid register of the scene's brutality, and the camerawork emphasizes the damage with close-up framings. He has bloody lacerations, one eye is swollen almost closed, and his upper lip is distended. The swelling of eye and lip is so severe that it changes the contours of Ladd's face and makes him look like another person. This alienation from his former handsome self is nicely conveyed when he drags himself to a mirror and gazes into it, the camera framing him over his shoulder so as to reveal only the mirrored face. A monstrous-looking individual peers back at him from the mirror.

Such close attention to the visible signs of physical trauma is quite rare in Hollywood film of this period. As I pointed out in a previous chapter, most Hollywood films presented the human body as being generally inviolate and immune to destruction or disfigurement as the result of violence. Sustained cries of pain, for example, were suppressed from film because they pointed to extended physical trauma. This aesthetic of inviolability is related to the PCA's disdain for knives as weapons of violence. A knife or other sharp-bladed instrument rends, tears, or otherwise pierces the body, and this kind of violence was more amenable to explicit visualization than gun violence. The viewer's eye and the camera can more easily track the sword that runs through a movie villain than the high-speed path of a bullet. Squibs, of course, could visualize bullet hits, but these were rarely as flamboyantly obvious as the knife or arrow that impales the back of a movie cowboy and remains visibly protruding after the character has pitched to the ground. Conventional movie violence was sanitized; the body was not severely harmed. Movie characters might bleed a little, or show a visible cut, but these were discrete. The grotesque swelling of Ladd's face in this scene is not discrete. It is a vivid detail that explicitly marks the body in terms of the violence that has been visited upon it. Ed's disfigured face is beyond the norms of the period. Altogether, this scene is an extended passage of sadism and torture, twisted sexuality, and bleak hopelessness.

The agency worried about the scene because it exemplified the kind of graphically detailed violence that it routinely labeled with its favorite descriptors, "brutal" and "gruesome." It was one of the elements in the picture that led the PCA to veto the initial script, judging it to be full of "numerous scenes involving unacceptable brutality."[26] The agency directed that the beating scene be rewritten to address this problem. "These scenes where Jeff slugs Ed repeatedly are unacceptable because of their undue brutality. They must be rewritten in such a way as to avoid such brutality. Otherwise, they could not be approved in the finished picture."[27] While many of Jeff's punches are filmed so that they occur off-screen, with cutaways to the reaction of a queasy on-looker as the punch lands, this device hardly addresses the substance of the PCA's concerns that the action contains a great deal of brutality. Much of this made it to the screen, despite the PCA's verdict that the material as written could not be approved.

The agency worried about another scene of violence involving Jeff. Recovered from his wounds, Ed confronts Jeff and intends to forcibly extract some information from him. But to get the bigger man alone, Ed has to pretend that he's a homoerotic masochist who wants another beating. Aquiver with sexual anticipation, Jeff promises to give one to Ed. Upstairs at the gang hideout, however, Ed maneuvers Jeff into attacking and strangling his boss, Nick. The scripted action included a detail that the filmmakers had to know the PCA would not allow on-screen. Its inclusion in the script suggests a desire by the filmmakers to push the existing boundaries. That detail was the sound of Nick's neck snapping as Jeff strangles him. The PCA rejected this detail and wrote, "we must likewise insist that there be no undue gruesomeness attendant on the choking of Nick by Jeff, particularly with regard to the snapping noise, as Nick's neck breaks. It would be well to substitute some other sound, such as choking or gasping to get away from any undue gruesomeness."[28]

The sound of the snapping neck does not appear in the film. The PCA wanted another alteration in the scene to lessen the suggestion that Ed, who watches Jeff strangle Nick, is allowing the murder to take place. "We must insist that some line or business be inserted in scene E-56 to the effect: 'Take it easy, Jeff,' in order to get away from the present unacceptable flavor that Ed is allowing Jeff to murder Nick, which could not be approved in the finished picture."[29] The PCA granted the film a Code certification on condition that this line is inserted. Although the line was added, the filmmakers obviated its effect, using style—in this case, the actor's performance—to subvert the agency's intentions. Watching the strangling that is in progress, Ed tells Jeff to take it easy, but Ladd delivers the line cynically and sarcastically, with a grin on his face. The words are there but Ed's tone and facial expression negate them, and, in any event, Jeff doesn't stop choking Nick. Smiling, Ed—the picture's nominal hero—watches him die.

When the picture was released, the PCA received complaints from viewers about its violence. Seeking to disassociate itself from the film, the agency placed itself in an awkward position by acknowledging that *The Glass Key* should not have been released in its present form—that the picture, in fact, was in violation of the Production Code. One viewer denounced the picture as containing "disgusting brutality [that] is presented in its lowest form" and said that the film's violence made the blood freeze in his veins.[30] In his reply, Breen acknowledged that the agency had made an error and that the picture really should not have been approved. "It went through our machinery here before my return to this office last June. Upon inquiry, however, I find that our staff members here pretty much agree that the story was shockingly brutal."[31]

To assuage the viewer, Breen assured him that the agency had actually cut most of the violence out of the film. "That which gave you serious offense was what was kept after long and drastic cutting." So, according to Breen, the film was *even more* violent before the PCA went to work on it. This, of course, begged the original question: how did such a violent picture come to be approved under the Production Code? There are two possible answers. One, as Breen claimed, is that the agency had made a mistake—that it didn't scrutinize the film's violence closely enough. An alternate explanation, however, is that the agency did what it could to tone down the brutality but that its efforts were simply inadequate to the task, given the investment of the filmmakers in depicting hard violence. With the problem viewed this way, *The Glass Key* becomes an early example of the trend that accelerated after the war in which the appeal of violence for filmmakers was outpacing the PCA's ability to manage it. The agency was able to excise some of the script's nastier elements, such as the snapping neck, but the filmmakers successfully evaded the agency's concerns using a clever deployment of style—by choreographing the violence to accent its physicality, by using lighting and production design to create a patina of ugliness, and by calibrating Ladd's performance to undercut the meaning of dialogue whose inclusion the agency had mandated.

Breen was more candid about the agency's "error" when he wrote to Luigi Luraschi, the Paramount Pictures studio liaison. Luraschi had complained that the film was banned in Trinidad. Breen replied,

> It is no surprise to us that the censors in Trinidad banned your picture "The Glass Key" on the grounds of excessive cruelty, torture and violence. We, in this office, have received numberless complaints about this picture from patrons here in the United States. It would appear that both studio and the Production Code Administration may have been in error in approving the picture in the fashion in which it went out.[32]

The Glass Key was released in 1943, in the midst of World War II, when the PCA was loosening its restraint on violence in the period's combat films. The agency had always varied its regulatory impulses by genre, allowing some genres greater latitude. Everyone seemed to accept that war films, for example, needed to carry a somewhat larger and stronger dose of violence than other kinds of pictures, and this was especially true now that the country was engaged in a protracted and difficult conflict.

During the war years, the PCA operated in cooperation with the federal Office of War Information (OWI), whose Bureau of Motion Pictures monitored the content of Hollywood film to make sure that it would aid the war effort. The BMP's "Manual for the Motion Picture Industry," published in 1942, outlined the kinds of political views that wartime pictures were to espouse, how fascism was to be explained, and how the enemy was to be depicted. Thus, the industry really had two kinds of production codes to follow: one for moral content, the other for political content. As Koppes and Black write in their study of Hollywood's wartime productions, "the two codes coexisted uneasily, for they had different purposes. Both codes were designed to ensure that the movies reflected their sponsors' point of view, to be sure; but the challenge for the PCA code was more to remove material, that of the OWI to insert it."[33]

Scholars of wartime Hollywood have been somewhat divided about the amount of violence the PCA and the industry permitted in the combat films. Gregory Black, for example, has argued that the PCA and OWI wanted "battlefield violence to be carefully contained. The PCA strictly enforced the Code's warnings against gruesomeness. The OWI encouraged a modicum of battlefield realism . . . but within rather antiseptic limits."[34] By contrast, Clayton Koppes has suggested that the PCA recognized that the war would bring more violence to the screen.[35] Thomas Doherty also suggests that violence "inspired the more substantive and visible shift in standards," especially under the impact of the era's documentary coverage of battlefield violence in newsreels and in the photography of *Life* magazine.[36] Although Hollywood films would never show war's full fury, Doherty suggests that the OWI eventually gave the industry greater latitude in portraying enemy atrocities.[37]

Although many films, like *Wake Island* (1942), portrayed combat as action–adventure, a new level of graphic detailing nevertheless began to appear in the era's combat films. This detailing is significantly harsher than what had been permitted in the industry's films before the war. As a result, filmmakers learned new ways of staging and visualizing the experiences of wounding and death by gunfire, artillery, or knife blade. These films represent a significant stage in the movement of American film toward more intensive depictions of physical assaults on the body. Alan Ladd's deformed, pulpy face in *The Glass Key* is a striking instance of such depictions outside the combat films. Since the history of American screen violence forms a trajectory toward ever more intimate and finely observed depictions of bodily trauma, we need to explore some of the significant instances of this process in the World War II films.

THE NORMATIVE CONVENTIONS OF SCREEN VIOLENCE

Before we explore this group of pictures, a caveat is necessary. The conventions of representing violence within any period are not rigid or monolithic, and they coexist with countertraditions and alternative styles. We need to consider the relatively explicit violence in some of the combat films as a stylistic variation upon other modes of representation. With this logic, we should view Ladd's disfigured face in *The Glass Key* as a variation from the normative mode for depicting beatings, whereby they are shown as resulting in little physical damage beyond superficial cuts or bruises. To appreciate the way in which imagery of explicit violence stands out from other films of the period, we first need to characterize the normative mode for rendering gun violence or other assaults on the body. By normative mode, I mean the convention of representation that was generally observed throughout the bulk of Hollywood films during the industry's classical period.

In terms of cutting implements such as knives, axes, spears, or bayonets, conventional staging for the camera obscures the weapon's point of entry into the body. Typically the victim is clothed, so that the blade does not touch and penetrate bare flesh, and the camera is positioned to view the action from an oblique angle in which one or both bodies of the combatants, or some other physical object, prevents actual sight of the blade entering a victim's body. As we saw earlier in this chapter, the PCA was very concerned about this kind of violence because it represented a heightened kind of aggression relative to a shooting and because it threatened the aesthetic and ideological notions of the body's inviolability.

Shootings typically occur at a distance, whereas stabbing or slashing is a more personal assault requiring a greater level of savagery, in which the killer needs to get close to the victim and may literally have blood on his hands afterward. By contrast, a shooting may be depicted as inherently cleaner, more controlled, and more distanced emotionally. Thus, the conventional mode for depicting violence done with bladed instruments generally worked to conceal and reduce the intimacy and savagery of the act. Errol Flynn's sword is barely visible going into the body of the Suristani in *The Charge of the Light Brigade*. When John Wayne stabs an Indian enemy in *Red River* (1948), he holds his victim underwater, and the camera sees only Wayne's arm with the knife rising above the water, then plunging down and disappearing into the river and, by implication, into the body of his foe. The staging of the action obscures the penetration of knife into flesh, which is especially critical since the Indian character is bare-chested.

In terms of shooting, the same general obfuscation of physical damage prevails. Since the beginning of the sound era, filmmakers commonly used squibs to visualize bullet strikes on property such as masonry-fronted buildings, wooden furniture, mirrors and glass fixtures. The machine-gun violence in the early gangster films gets its ferocity from the exploding walls, tables, and windshields riddled by drive-by shooters. By contrast, bullet strikes on the body were rarely depicted, and this disavowal acquired the force of a major prohibition although it was never actually written into the Production Code. One of the reasons that *Bonnie and Clyde* was so stunning in 1967 was that audiences had not often seen actors squibbed and certainly never so extensively.

Squibs were used on occasion in earlier years. As we shall see, some squibbing can be found in the World War II films. Moreover, other means for depicting bullet strikes on the body can be found in films before 1967—as in, for example, the startling machine-gunning of Bruce Cabot at the end of *Show Them No Mercy*. In this case, colored pellets were fired at a transparent screen in front of Cabot's body.

Despite these instances, the normative mode for depicting gun violence was similar to that prevailing for bladed instruments and entailed showing little or no trauma to the body. I call this normative mode for gun violence *clutch-and-fall*. This mode has a number of components, and some or all may be present in any given instance. The defining feature of this mode lies in the victim's response. The victim takes the bullet with little to no physical reaction, even if the shot is fired at close range. Rather than responding with pain or distress, or with an involuntary physical reaction such as the spasms that wrack Scarface when the police machine-gun him, the clutch-and-fall victim falls into a trance, or seems to fall asleep, and then sinks gracefully and slowly out of the frame.

The most striking anomaly of this mode is the bizarre nature of the victim's response. Victims die in increments, sequentially and from the ground up. Their feet and legs are the first to go, with their torso and head, unmarked by gunfire, the last to expire. As a result, their legs may buckle while their upper bodies show no loss of faculty until they topple or sink out of the frame. No bullet strike is visualized—even in cases where one should be plainly evident, as when the victim wears a white shirt and is shot in the chest, or when, as in *The Big Heat* (1953), a suicide shoots himself in the head and slumps quite bloodlessly onto the top of his desk. Significant examples of clutch-and-fall occur in *Casablanca* (1942), *Double Indemnity* (1944), and *The Strange Love of Martha Ivers* (1946). At the conclusion of *Casablanca*, the venomous Major Strasser takes a shot in the chest at close range while holding a telephone. Strasser's legs are the first part of him to die because he sinks slowly below frame level while still holding the telephone. In the other two films, Barbara

23. Clutch-and-fall sanitized violence by presenting violent death as the onset of sleep. Martha Ivers (Barbara Stanwyck) has just been gut-shot at close range, and she reacts by going into a dreamy trance and sinking out of the frame.

Stanwyck's lover (*Double Indemnity*) and husband (*Strange Love*) shoot her while she hugs them in an intimate embrace. Gut-shot, her only response is to succumb to a sudden and general lassitude as, swooning, she is lowered out of the frame.

The coexistence of alternate styles for rendering violence in classical Hollywood cinema is evident in the co-presence in many films of clutch-and-fall with more explicit depictions. In *Scarface,* for example, when Tony Camonte shoots his buddy Guino (George Raft), Guino does a clutch-and-fall that is nothing like the later spasmodic response of Camonte to the police bullets. Although graphic violence may be found more widely in the World War II films than in other genres of that period, clutch-and-fall deaths are also pervasive in these films. The battlefield violence in *The Fighting Seebees* (1944) and *Objective, Burma!* (1945), for example, is replete with clutch-and-fall as hundreds of Japanese enemy and scores of American soldiers are shot down with no visible effect or response beyond falling to the ground. Even when they die from grenade or artillery explosion, the actors stay at a safe distance from the special effect, and, after the explosion and shower of dirt or sand, they clutch and fall. This mode precludes them from being caught *in* the explosion, hurled into the air or into pieces.

The sanctity of the body is the ideological premise of clutch-and-fall, and it is this idea which the style works to visualize and to safeguard. Clutch-and-fall ensured that death, overall, would be sanitized in Hollywood films; the application of this mode in the combat films helped to make many into action–adventure spectacle. Violent death might occur but the body would not be torn asunder, nor would wounding or dying be made to carry crippling pain and dehumanizing agony. Indeed, there is nothing dehumanizing about violent death in clutch-and-fall. The aesthetic expresses an epistemology about the passage between life and death and about the physical experience of mortality. The passage is an easy one, to be made with grace and calm, with death merely the onset of sleep. Director Sam Peckinpah's effort to put the sting back into violent death by showing the pain and dehumanizing brutality that often accompany it was an attempt to overcome the ideological legacy of this aesthetic in American cinema.[38] Similarly, Steven Spielberg's depiction of graphic carnage in *Saving Private Ryan* (1998) was a conscious attempt to negate the action-adventure terms of many of Hollywood's World War II movies.

HARD VIOLENCE IN WORLD WAR II COMBAT FILMS

Clutch-and-fall, then, provides the stylistic background or horizon against which the more graphic renderings that we now consider stand out in relief. Like the beating scene in *The Glass Key,* these scenes question the ideological premise of clutch-and-fall by showing that the body is not impregnable—that bullets strike with force, and that physical violence wrenches the body into ugly spasms and damages or destroys the being that inhabits the body. *Pride of the Marines* (1945) portrays the emotional recovery of Al (John Garfield), who is blinded by a hand grenade during a fierce battle against the Japanese on Guadalcanal. Al and two Marine buddies, Johnny and Lee, are dug in with a machine gun, trying to halt the Japanese advance on the island. The Japanese kill Johnny and wound Lee before Al is blinded. The film shows Al's great fear and anxiety during the long night during which he faces the enemy, and it subsequently portrays the bitterness that seizes him after he is blinded. These depictions of an all-too-human response make for a notable departure from the stock heroics of many World War II films. Moreover, the violence is unusually detailed, particularly the shootings of Johnny and Lee. Al's blinding is also portrayed in horrific terms, first as Al's subjective view of the exploding grenade and then in the grimly stoic response of Lee when he sees Al's face (a

24. This close-up view of the dead Johnny in *Pride of the Marines* is grim and de-romanticized. The visual presentation derives from the realism of documentary and news photography.

view of Al that the oblique camera framings do not allow the viewer). Along with the accounts of returning soldiers, by 1945 documentary films and photographs had informed viewers of the terrible terms of the fighting in the Pacific. The film's carefully detailed violence is responsive to this context and provides a realistic foundation for Al's difficulties adjusting to civilian life without sight.

The shootings of Johnny and Lee occur suddenly and without warning, as Japanese snipers pick off the Marines. The shootings contain several notably graphic elements. Johnny is shot in the head, quite rare in this period. Normative, sanitized shootings almost always involved chest shots, or a winged arm or shoulder. Head shots are more gruesome than chest shots, and the PCA was always vigilant about details that it deemed excessively gruesome or brutal. A bullet in the head would be a prime example of such unseemly brutality. To the extent that one might attach epistemological issues to gun violence, a head shot can be said to represent a more personal and powerful affront to the integrity and dignity of a victim's being than a body shot. The head contains the brain—the seat of reason and the locus of personality—and the face is the gateway to one's being and the public token of its uniqueness. Violence done to the head or face, therefore, entails a serious violation of the victim's dignity and integrity of self, especially when that violence carries the stigmata of visible wounding. Thus, Hollywood film generally avoided head shots, and when they did occur, as in *The Big Heat* or *Machine-Gun Kelly*, they produced no blood or visible damage.

Given the exclusion by the clutch-and-fall aesthetic of head shots, Johnny's death is especially deviant. Not only is he shot in the head, but the bullet strike is visualized. The shot penetrates his helmet, and the viewer sees and hears this quite clearly. The soundtrack carries the thud of the bullet's impact. The helmet bends inward where the bullet hits, and a puff of smoke rises from it. Johnny's physical response then becomes a clutch-and-fall: his legs gradually weaken and he sinks down. But a subsequent close-up of his face, after Al and Lee lay him on the ground, provides a significantly de-romanticized view of death—one that almost certainly derives from the iconography of death that documentary films and photographs were providing in the period. His head lolls back at an unnatural angle, his eyes are partly open and stare sightlessly at his comrades, and his mouth hangs slack-jawed, the strap of his helmet holding it semi-closed. In most clutch-and-fall deaths the body merely "goes to sleep" with no trauma, while retaining its dignity and uniqueness of self. Johnny's lifeless face, by contrast, is one from which all personality has gone. It shows no emotional tone, no muscle control. It is unmistakably a body done to death by violence, without the cosmetic gloss that typically surrounds violent death in the movies. The camera angle and detailing of Johnny's face emphasize the ungainliness of death, with the awkward posture rendering him less than fully human. This visual insight anticipates the greater elaboration in the montage slow-motion style used in films after 1967 to visualize the loss of volition in bodies subjected to sustained weapons fire.

Shortly after Johnny's death, Lee is hit in the arm. Once again, the bullet strike is visualized, this time with an exploding squib that blows out a portion of Lee's uniform, sends up a spray of smoke, and reveals a bloody wound where the bullet has entered. When Lee is hit his body jerks convulsively, his head snaps back, and his helmet flies off. These involuntary physical reactions compliment the visible detailing provided by the squib and convincingly suggest the velocity and force with which the bullet strikes his body. The clutch-and-fall aesthetic excludes squibbing from its depictions of death, and it excludes these involuntary physical reactions.

Furthermore, the filmmakers wanted to make sure that the audience saw the exploding bullet wound, and they arranged the lighting of the camera shot to facilitate this. Just before Lee is hit, he is framed by a new camera position with a bright key light directed at the spot on his arm where the bullet will hit. The light draws the viewer's eye to the precise spot where, and at the moment when, the squib is detonated. This use of lighting to augment the violence is clever, subtle and effective, and it demonstrates that the filmmakers are not merely staging violence for the camera but are searching for ways to make it vivid and drive home its impact for the viewer. After Lee is shot, Al places him on the ground and continues to man the machine gun. Subsequent cutaways to Lee reveal blood pooling in his wound.

Other World War II films offer imagery contravening the clutch-and-fall aesthetic. In *Back to Bataan* (1945), John Wayne machine-guns a wounded Japanese soldier, and the victim's legs jerk and thrash spasmodically as the bullets hammer into his body. Gun violence in prewar films does not evoke this reaction from victims. *Objective, Burma!* includes audio information about a bullet strike. During one of that film's many battles against the Japanese, the viewer hears an Allied bullet hit the enemy. No squib is employed to visualize the strike, but the audio—a distinct thud—provides a kind of aural equivalent.

Elsewhere in *Back to Bataan* a Japanese soldier is dispatched with a bayonet—not just in the throat, but all the way through it and out the other side. In the context of my earlier remarks about the PCA's attitude toward violence done with bladed instruments, this scene is especially flamboyant. As with the shooting of Lee in *Pride of the Marines*, the action is staged to accentuate its clarity and impact. The sound of a bayonet slicing through the air and striking a soft object precedes the cut to a close-up of the victim with the knife penetrating his throat and sticking out the other side. The close-up shows the character in profile, the better to see the knife in his neck. He lingers a moment before falling, to give viewers a lasting impression of the violence.

In this case the uncommonly graphic violence furnishes an index of the impassioned wartime feelings against the Japanese, as it does also in *Flying Tigers* (1942), which portrays aerial combat against the Japanese by volunteer fliers based in China. In Hollywood's wartime productions the Japanese were often caricatured in dehumanizing ways that the German and Italian enemy was not. Thus, it seems likely that the racist components of anti-Japanese sentiment may help provide a motivation for some of the styling of violence done to Japanese characters. In *Flying Tigers,* for example, when they are hit during the film's many aerial dogfights, the Japanese fliers bleed profusely from head and chest shots. They either vomit blood at the camera or put their hands to their face while blood thickly streams between their fingers. Only the Japanese characters bleed like this. The Allied fliers who die do so in a cleaner and more sanitary fashion. Perhaps anti-Japanese sentiment played some role in the PCA's willingness to countenance headshots and hemorrhages from America's wartime enemy. One must be careful, however, not to oversimplify the complex forces at work in the combat films. As Doherty and other scholars have pointed out, the OWI was opposed to the caricaturing of Japanese characters in Hollywood films, fearing that it could lead to reprisals against Americans held in captivity. Furthermore, the knife-in-the-throat of a Japanese soldier in *Back to Bataan* is matched, in its visual hyperbole, by the sword-in-the-neck of an American soldier in *Bataan*.

THE HORRORS OF WAR IN *BATAAN*

In other words, American and Allied soldiers might also be depicted as the victims of graphic violence, especially when that could help dramatize the difficulty and the importance of wartime effort and sacrifice. *Bataan* (1943) opens with a savage evocation of a Japanese bomber attack on a military installation in the Philippines. The sequence graphically shows violence against civilians and war wounded as well as soldiers. As the attack begins, a blind soldier, with his head and face wrapped in bandages, cannot see to reach safety. He stands helplessly as the bombs fall and, after a few cutaways to other action, is seen crawling for shelter. As he crawls beneath a porch the house is bombed, and a burning piece of rubble falls across his back, trapping him, as he screams in pain.

A jeep of soldiers driving through the village is blown to pieces, and the staging of this action takes the unusual and highly effective step of indicating what an explosion of such force can do. Typically, in films of the period such scenes are staged so that grenade and artillery victims stay well clear of the special effects explosions. They are then showered with dirt, and they fall after the explosion has detonated. This mode of staging the action fails utterly to suggest that the blast unleashes substantial power. In this scene, however, the explosion obliterates the screen image momentarily, as an interval of black frames separates the explosion and the view of its effects. After the interval of black frames, when the image returns, pieces of the jeep and a body part fall out of the air to the ground. A close-up shows a severed hand and forearm lying in a pile of smoking debris.

This opening scene tells the viewer that the carnage to come will be uncommonly detailed and unsparing. The story portrays the efforts of a small group of Americans to hold the island against the Japanese until a larger contingent of Allies can engage the enemy in the Pacific. It is a 'nobility of failure' story in that all of the Americans die trying to hold the island, but their sacrifice itself becomes the measure of their heroism and an inspiring example. Japanese snipers pick off many of the men. The unit's captain is one of the first to die, and the film's evocation of his physical response to the bullet is especially impressive. No easy clutch-and-fall death this: he suffers a convincing loss of muscle and joint control when the bullet hits. Its force nearly knocks him off his feet, and he stumbles, trying to stay upright, but his body no longer works properly and he cannot coordinate his limbs sufficiently to remain standing. He wobbles as if drunk and is caught by his men as he finally falls to the ground. The choreography of his reaction shows the viewer the process whereby a life leaves the body, and evokes this as a gradual event accompanied by the progressive dehumanization that occurs as the linkages between mind and body are severed.

The sniping death of another soldier, who has climbed a tree to try and scout the enemy, is visualized as a head shot with a squib on the helmet that sends out a puff of smoke to accompany the audio of the bullet slamming into his head.[39] A Japanese flier machine-guns another American, and, while this happens off-camera, a cut back to the victim before he falls shows his chest riddled with bleeding wounds. When Sergeant Bill Dane (Robert Taylor) grenades a machine-gun nest, the force of the explosion blows the enemy into the air, and, as in the film's opening scene, the viewer sees bodies fall to earth.

The film contains some absolutely ferocious and savage scenes of hand-to-hand combat that include action in which a soldier slams the butt end of a rifle into an opponent's face, and several point-blank shootings in which killer and victim are both in the frame. The longest of these scenes is a large-scale slaughter sequence—truly an orgy of killing—played effectively without music, in which the Americans slash, stab, bayonet, grenade, and shoot their Japanese enemies, all at close range, and suffer the same fate at their hands. In other films, crime films and Westerns in particular, the PCA vigilantly rejected scripted instances of kneeing and kicking during fights, but here we see this kind of action in addition to clubbing with the barrel and stocks of rifles. The sustained strangulation of a Japanese soldier is followed by action (discretely hidden behind a rock) of his American antagonist hacking and slashing at the body with a machete. A machine-gun nest hidden in a group of trees cuts down Feingold (Thomas Mitchell), and while the squibs on his chest do not explode on-camera, they do begin to smoke while the shot runs. Todd (Lloyd Nolan) loses his rifle in the fighting and uses his fists to beat the face of a Japanese until the man loses consciousness and falls to the ground, whereupon Nolan draws his .45 and shoots the unconscious soldier at point-blank range. The climactic horror of the sequence occurs with the death of Eeps (Kenneth Spencer), the unit's only African American soldier. A Japanese swings his bayonet with such force at the man's neck that its blade nearly decapitates him, lodging in the back of his neck and shown in a close-up of Eeps's screaming

25. This close-up depiction of a partial decapitation in *Bataan* is an extreme example of the rising tide of violence that the World War II combat film helped bring to American cinema.

face. As Jeanine Basinger points out, "the blade enters halfway through his neck. Although we do not actually see the head fall, or blood spurt out, this is one of the most graphic and violent killings of the pre-sixties period of film history."[40]

But it isn't only this one killing that is depicted in such extreme terms. The entire sequence of close-quarter combat is one of the most sustained, brutal, and vividly depicted episodes of violence in all of Hollywood film prior to the late 1960s and the gun battles that Sam Peckinpah filmed for *The Wild Bunch.* When the film was released, the reviewer for *Variety* remarked that it contains "scenes seldom seen in commercial features and, as uncomfortable as they make audiences, bear the imprint of stark reality."[41] The cruelty and savagery of the violence easily surpass anything that gangster or horror movies had shown audiences, even in the so-called pre-Code period prior to 1934.

To modern viewers, however, some aspects of the sequence may look relatively antiquated. While the violence is intense and unremitting, most of it is filmed in full- figure shots that are extended in time. In other words, whereas a

161

modern film would use many camera set-ups edited into a montage of violence, the close-quarter fighting in *Bataan* does not. A single fight is typically shown in a single camera set-up, with the actors framed in full-figure style. The dramatic action of an individual fight scene often unfolds as a complete unit within a single frame. Moreover, the camera is undercranked to make the action look slightly speeded up. While the undercranking is obvious and might strike a modern viewer as a somewhat anachronistic device, it works to produce the same intensification of violence that montage does today and therefore could be taken as an equivalent of this more contemporary way of styling violence. The absence of complex montage—despite the fact that the scene is built using cross-cutting—reveals one of the limits of its stylistic amplitude.

The extraordinary amount of carnage in the scene shows how wide-open the PCA held the door for some films during the war years to depict battlefield violence. Of all the arenas in which World War II was fought, the battles for the Pacific islands were some of the hardest and bloodiest contests. In this respect, the real-world violence of wartime drove its awful lessons deep into American film, and it has done so more than once. It was the Vietnam War that pushed Arthur Penn and Sam Peckinpah to the graphic heights of bloodshed in *Bonnie and Clyde* and *The Wild Bunch,* and, as we are seeing in this chapter, World War II brought a new degree of explicitness to the screen violence in pictures like *Bataan, Pride of the Marines,* and *Flying Tigers.*

At the same time, however, the PCA did not turn a blind eye to screen violence. It couldn't, because it still had to anticipate the reactions of regional censors. As we saw in an earlier chapter, the agency required some of the close-quarter bayonet fighting to be excised in order for *Bataan* to be given clearance for release. Once released, the picture was subject to a high number of eliminations from regional and overseas censors—unusual for a film not of the horror or crime genres. Pennsylvania, for example, eliminated all views of the blind soldier crawling on the ground and being hit by the burning rubble, the dismembered hand, the sniping of the American soldier in the tree, the sound of the black soldier screaming after the bayonet hits him in the neck, and all views of the body of an American hung by the Japanese from a tree. Ontario also ordered the elimination of the black soldier's screams. England ordered that the "gruesome details of individual bayonet fighting" be reduced. Sweden likewise excised some of these shots, as well as the opening action of the Japanese plane strafing an ambulance, the wounded, and civilians.

In *Objective, Burma!*, the Japanese capture several Allied paratroopers, torture and kill them, and then leave their bodies where they will be found by their comrades. The PCA strongly cautioned the filmmakers about this scene. "Great care will be needed with the shooting of scene 253. We call your atten-

tion specifically to the stage direction 'his face has been mutilated beyond recognition.' We assume there will be no attempt to show any such unacceptable gruesomeness, and that all these tortures and mutilations will be gotten over by means of suggestion, with no attempt to photograph them directly."[42] Indeed, the capture and torture is not portrayed; it happens offscreen. When the bodies are found, they are discretely positioned to be either off-frame or concealed from view by some object on-camera. The reactions of distress and disgust by hero Errol Flynn and his men suggest the terrible character of the mutilations.

Why would the PCA allow the extreme violence of *Bataan* while restricting the torture and mutilation of *Objective, Burma!*? The schematic answer to this question is that the Office of War Information frowned on atrocity scenes, fearing that they might lead to real harm to U.S. soldiers held in captivity.[43] The film, though, does include the atrocity episode, with a surviving but mutilated paratrooper gasping out his last seconds of life and an angry reporter saying that the Japanese are animals and ought to be annihilated.

The horrific violence depicted in *Bataan,* or the mutilations just off-camera in *Objective, Burma!,* or the tortures inflicted on captured Americans by the Japanese in *The Purple Heart* (1944) are unquestionably brutal and gruesome—two qualities that the PCA consistently sought to minimize or eliminate. While the Code itself was systematic in detailing prohibited content, the PCA dealt with production on a film-by-film basis. Each film presented its own somewhat unique set of circumstances and considerations: this accounts for some of the variation in the degree of explicitness found in the violence of the war films, ranging from the graphic on-camera brutality of *Bataan* to the more obliquely treated atrocities of *Objective, Burma!*

Moreover, as we have seen, referential considerations continually inflected the agency's regulation of violence. In this regard, the PCA might permit a higher degree of brutality in wartime pictures because it provided for greater realism and authenticity (as we saw, *Variety*'s reviewer excused *Bataan* on this basis), whereas a similar degree of brutality in the gangster film would be seen as exploitative and in bad taste. To put it baldly, in the mid-1940s a gangster could not machine-gun a cop, but Robert Taylor could gratuitously machine-gun the bodies of already-dead Japanese soldiers, as he does near the end of *Bataan.* In terms of how much brutality to permit in wartime pictures, the PCA evidently believed that a higher threshold was warranted for battlefield violence than for behavior that is illegal even in times of war. Moreover, a high threshold for battlefield violence might be acceptable if the real circumstances depicted by a film—such as the fighting on the Pacific islands—were unquestionably horrific.

These considerations show that for all of the Code's schematic wording, the PCA handled screen violence in the wartime pictures in a flexible manner, allowing filmmakers greater freedom to depict events that were in the headlines—as the Pacific fighting was—while continuing to restrict forms of violence regarded as illegitimate or immoral. The wartime context complicated the regulation of violence. Though it worked relatively well in regard to crime and horror films, simply prohibiting brutality or gruesomeness in the war films would be an undesirable and ineffective strategy. It would falsify historical realities that Americans knew too well, and it would undercut the patriotic appeals that such films needed to make. Thus, the PCA countenanced an expansion in the detailing and duration of screen violence in some of these films. Bodies bled profusely; they were blown to pieces and otherwise violated in sometimes-explicit detail. At a minimum, even when clutch-and-fall was employed, film characters were slaughtered on-screen by the hundreds. But while this made for rousing or sobering patriotic fare, the genie of violence was now out of the bottle, and the PCA was never able to get it back in.

THE POSTWAR PERIOD: APOCALYPTIC VIOLENCE IN *BRUTE FORCE*

After the war a progressively harder violence began to appear on American screens, and the PCA found itself in frequently losing battles with filmmakers determined to take film in this direction and with studios willing to back them. To an extent, perhaps, the expansion of screen violence can be attributed to the effects of the war, which had made horrific real-world violence an inescapable reality. But this provides only a partial explanation. Film did not just suddenly grow more violent in the postwar years. The impetus in that direction was already rooted in American screen history and in the creative inclinations of Hollywood filmmakers. From their work in crime and horror pictures, filmmakers learned that it is the stylistic amplitude given to behavioral acts of violence that makes them interesting and viable as cinema. They inflected these behavioral acts with lighting and production design, with editing and camera movement and the dynamic choreography of action in the frame. Using these tools, they increased the duration and the insistence of acts of screen violence. While the PCA and regional censors consistently failed to perceive the importance of this acceleration in stylistic amplitude, filmmakers were busy at work creating a formal language and legacy for subsequent directors. The historical trajectory was established. The realities of the war years, along with the PCA's willingness to allow films to embody this violence, helped to accelerate the pre-existing tendency to embrace more elaborate and intense depictions.

And there would be no going back. There never is. Once new thresholds of permissibility were established, the agency could not thereafter return film-making to prior norms. The Mark Hellinger production *Brute Force* (1947) exemplifies these trends. Hellinger was a key figure in postwar crime films, producing some of the best and darkest work of the period including *The Killers* (1946), *Naked City* (1948), and *Criss Cross* (1949). *Brute Force* portrays the harsh and despairing lives of men in prison, who are subjected to the rule of the brutal and tyrannical Captain Munsey (Hume Cronyn).

The film climaxes with an astonishing orgy of slaughter as a group of inmates, led by Joe Collins (Burt Lancaster), puts into play a violent escape plan. Munsey knows the break is coming and has stationed guards with machine-guns along the escape path. In the frenzy of violence that follows, the escaping inmates are slaughtered, the enraged population of prisoners torches the guard tower, and Collins, dying from a gun wound, confronts Munsey and throws him from the burning tower. The rioting prisoners swarm over the body of the hateful captain, and the remaining guards resort to tear gas to dispel the crowd.

This climax prefigures modern screen violence in so many ways—chief among them the high rate of killing in the sequence, the baroque forms that it assumes, and the nastiness with which it is executed. Director Jules Dassin imbues the violence with rage, pain, and a sadistic frenzy, so that it is not just the high body count that takes the carnage to an impressive level but the extreme brutality with which it is inflicted. Prison guards coldly machine-gun unarmed prisoners. An enraged Collins machine-guns a pair of guards who are prone on the ground, either stunned or already dead. Earlier in the film, the cons use blowtorches to burn the face and hand of a stool pigeon and force him into heavy machinery that crushes him. In a scene of extended sadism Munsey tortures and beats a handcuffed prisoner with a rubber truncheon while a classical recording plays on his phonograph.

This carnage is significant for containing numerous violations of the Production Code and of general PCA policy. The agency strongly urged that the picture's mayhem be handled through suggestion rather than be shown explicitly. "We wish to stress again the importance of avoiding any undue emphasis on brutality and gruesomeness throughout the picture. Whenever scenes of this nature are indicated, we urge that they be done largely by suggestion, and not in any detail which might prove offensive."[44] The recommendation met with partial success, at best.

In terms of specifics the agency wanted several details omitted, or only suggested, in the scene with the blowtorches and the stool pigeon. "The action . . . where Coy directs the blow torch at the hands of Wilson should be done by suggestion and not in detail. Also, the later scene of Wilson falling to his

165

26. In the hyperbolic violence that caps *Brute Force,* the stoolie, strapped to the front of a coal cart, is blasted by machine-gun fire. Hard violence was increasing by the late 1940s.

death in the stamping machine should be done by suggestion."[45] Despite this unambiguous warning, the scene clearly shows a prisoner burn Wilson's hand with the torch. Later, when Wilson is backed against the stamping machine, the sequence is designed to show the viewer clearly how it operates and how it is going to kill the victim. Thrusting with great force, a huge, corrugated press stamps downward into a recessed chamber. As Wilson stands in front of it, the cons surround him and thrust their blowtorches into his face in order to drive him into the machinery. When his face is burned, Wilson lurches backward into the chamber and vanishes from view just as the press smashes downward. The camera stays on the machinery and does not cut away to a reaction shot of an onlooker or to some other object. There is no visual evasiveness. Though the viewer does not see his body being crushed, there is no ambiguity about what is happening. Nor is there much occurring in the scene that would count as "suggestion." Everything is shown, except for the body actually being mangled. Moreover, beyond the violence directly depicted, the threat of unspeakable violence is keenly apparent. The blowtorches threaten terrible pain and disfigurement. As instruments of violence they are sadistic in the extreme, and none of the prisoners hesitate to use them.

The PCA was relatively more successful with the torture scene in Munsey's office. It urged that the filmmakers avoid undue brutality and portray the beating by suggestion, and it also urged that the reaction of guards who hear the beating "will be one of disgust with what is going on in the other room."[46] Accordingly, the viewer never actually sees the truncheon strike the prisoner. The blows occur offscreen, though their sound is heard. Cutaways to other objects, or to the guards outside, substitute for direct shots of the blows. And, as the PCA directed, the guards outside are visibly upset, thus providing, according to the agency, a voice for morality in the scene.

In these ways, then, the filmmakers seemingly heeded the agency's directives about the scene. However, the filmmakers managed to create such an aura of sadism that the violence not explicitly shown is nevertheless felt as palpable and toxic. Before the beating begins Munsey carefully washes his hands, suggesting that the torture has a ritual quality for him and that this is not the first such interrogation that he has held in his office. He strips off his uniform coat and shirt, revealing a muscle t-shirt underneath. His partial nudity eroticizes the encounter and changes the nature of the scene. It is not to be simply a beating. For Munsey, the infliction of pain is bound up with darker currents of twisted sexuality. He will find a perverse pleasure in marking the skin of his victim. While the undressing could have a practical motive—he may not wish to get blood spatters on his uniform—it also points to the motive of sexual sadism as a prime force driving his behavior. As a sexual sadist he feels a kind of love for his prey. Munsey closes the blinds and turns down the lights, creating an ambience of intimacy, and he speaks softly to his victim, as to a lover, caressingly and without anger. When the beating is over so, too, is this moment of intimacy. He raises the lights and washes the blood off of his hands.

The scene's depiction of eroticized violence, of a powerful man violating a weaker one, is sufficiently unpleasant as to compensate for the visually elided beating. The filmmakers' success taking the scene in this direction shows how elusive violence is for those who would regulate it. The PCA succeeded in minimizing its overt manifestations: the beating itself is not shown, at least not in terms of seeing the truncheon strike the prisoner. But the emotional and psychological tone of the scene, its aura, retains all of the violence that the camerawork elides—and, arguably, the twisted behavior it suggests is worse and more depraved, is more sinister in conception, than any beating itself could be, conceived as the PCA did in terms of visible blows on-camera. What is suggested is often more powerful than what can be shown, a principle exemplified in this scene. It is one that undermines regulatory efforts, especially when those efforts require that specific instances of content be identified for suppression or excision.

The paroxysm of violence at the film's climax is impressive not just for its epic scale but for its baroque conception and staging. The prisoners intend to commandeer a coal car that runs on a rail line going outside the prison walls and to the main gate. Once there, they intend to take over the guard tower and open the gate so every con in the joint can escape. One among them, however, has alerted Munsey to the break. Aware of this, Collins and his men lash the hapless stool pigeon to the front of the coal car and send it down the tracks, where a pair of guards with a machine-gun blasts the shrieking stoolie. The imagery that precedes this shooting—the screaming stoolie bound to the front of the cart, like a cow chaser on a locomotive, barreling down the tracks toward his inevitable doom—is a conception of startling flamboyance. It takes violence to the level of high baroque. Astonishing and outlandish, the design is also revelatory, pointing to the deep investment of the filmmakers in creating novel and memorable images of violence. This, too, is a very modern attribute. Elaborately choreographed violence typically reveals the aesthetic pleasures taken by the filmmaker in its design. This is true of the slow-motion ballets in *Bonnie and Clyde* and *The Wild Bunch,* and it is true of the holocaust that concludes *Brute Force.*

The ensuing action contains several significant Code violations, one of which I briefly mentioned in a previous chapter. As scripted, the climax was to show ten guards dying at the hands of the prisoners, but the PCA properly flagged this action as a Code violation that "could not be approved in the finished picture."[47] The Special Regulations on Crime forbade depictions of law officers dying at the hands of criminals. Nevertheless, in one of the most striking instances of the agency's limited powers to regulate violence, the finished film shows five guards dying in the prison riot. That amounts to a 50 percent enforcement rate on this issue by the PCA.

Collins and two other cons, Coy and Soldier, ride the doomed coal cart behind the helpless and shrieking stool pigeon. When the guards open fire, they kill the stoolie and wound Coy. Soldier and Collins leap from the cart. Shot in the face and bleeding heavily, Coy climbs atop the cart and makes a suicide leap over the lashed body of the stoolie and onto the two guards wielding the machine-gun. The continuity of the action now becomes jagged—almost certainly because material has been deleted, probably at the PCA's instigation following a screening for clearance, though only limited documentation about this exists in the case file. The file indicates that the film was screened more than once for approval and certification, and that it was accepted for release in

27. Late-in-the-game re-editing removed the action of Collins machine-gunning the prone prison guards, but some traces of this action, a Production Code violation, remain in the film.

a subsequently revised version that was re-screened by the agency.[48] This sequence of events suggests that there were post-production trims, and the jagged continuity of the action following Coy's leap from the cart suggests what some of those trims were.

When Coy throws himself into the machine-gun nest he topples the two guards, and they all sink below the frame line while in the background of the shot Collins and Soldier run alongside the tracks toward the gun emplacement. The action then cuts to a close view of Collins and Soldier, with the camera racing beside them. When they reach the emplacement Coy, who vanished below the frame line when he jumped onto the guards, now reappears in the frame. He is clearly dead and the two guards are either dead or stunned. Perhaps the force of Coy's impact killed them or has only knocked them out. Perhaps Coy has murdered them. The continuity is unsatisfactory because it cannot resolve the ambiguity about the fates of Coy and the guards. What happened in the machine-gun nest after he jumped? The continuity of the action as edited does not provide an answer to this question.

Collins's next act is a violation of the Production Code. Although it was excised from the scene, it left unambiguous markings of its identity, traces that reveal its former presence. The deleted action is Collins machine-gunning the two prone guards. In the film as it now exists, he stands with a Tommy gun pointed down at them. An insert of Soldier shows him cradling the dead Coy, and the action cuts back to Collins. The cutback is a very quick shot, only a few frames long, that shows his face contort with rage as he begins to lift his gun. It's evidently just the surviving fragment of a more lengthy shot that showed him blasting the guards. With that action now deleted, the film cuts to Munsey, who is up in the guard tower, but viewers with keen ears can hear two bursts of automatic weapons fire coming from Collins's location offscreen. That is the surviving sound of Collins' deleted action. In the original edit of the film, it was part of a sound bridge that connected the shooting to the next scene—the adjacent locale of the guard tower, where Munsey hears the shots. All that remains of that bridge now is the piece of sound that opens the guard tower scene.

Munsey hears the gunfire, and he sends two guards down to investigate. The action then cuts back to Collins and Soldier, and the gunsmoke from Collins's weapon can clearly be seen rising in the frame. The shooting was gone but not its traces. The surviving fragments of the deleted material—the glimpse of Collins raising his weapon, the little piece of sound, and the gunsmoke—show how deferential the PCA could be toward filmmakers when requesting post-production trims. As in the example from *Party Girl* cited earlier, problematic sequences were fixed by making trims, preferably the ones that were easiest to make. Thus, the frames that showed Collins shooting the guards were simply cut out, but the re-editing did not extend to the removal of sound information from the beginning of an adjacent scene or to the removal of additional frames from subsequent views of Collins that contained the gunsmoke.

One of the guards sent by Munsey shoots Soldier (an on-camera shooting showing killer and victim in the same frame), and Collins then machine-guns both guards. One, however, manages to shoot him in the back, and Collins reacts with an astonishing scream of rage, pain and despair. This cry of pain and existential anguish—Collins now knows their break is doomed—is possibly the most extraordinary moment in the film's extensively detailed violence. Collins's cry is all-consuming. It takes possession of him, and his surrender to rage and pain is a berserk loss of self-control that is almost never seen in commercial film of this period. Moreover, as the response to a shooting, it conveys the violence of the bullet strike in terms that are more vivid and overpowering than what any squib could suggest. Squibs provide exterior signs of the results

28. Collins's cry of rage, pain, and existential anguish was the kind of vocalized suffering that the PCA had worked to suppress from American film since the early sound era. But though his scream passed the PCA, it was targeted by local censors.

of violence. Collins's scream shows its interior components. His cry is also the kind of vocalized pain that the PCA had virtually expunged from Hollywood film after the pre-Code years. The bullet hole in the back of Collins's shirt and his profuse bleeding, which a viewer sees in the subsequent action when Collins attacks Munsey, seem anti-climactic after the sheer force of this scream. Censors in Alberta directed that Collins's "scream of rage and agony" be excised from the film and its trailer.

At the film's climax, Collins machine-guns four guards. The first two guards that he guns down may already be dead, making his action a gratuitous expression of sheer rage. It was possibly for this reason that the PCA ordered the material deleted, but viewers see the killing of the other pair of guards (those sent by Munsey). The larger point in all of this is that any shooting of a guard whatsoever by Collins was a Code violation. Collins should not have been depicted handling a machine-gun, much less killing four guards with it.

None of the correspondence in the case file addresses this issue; there is no indication that the PCA evaluated and responded to the manner in which the film would show automatic weapons in the hands of criminals. This is an interesting oversight because the agency did take a tight line with another film in production that year, *Kiss of Death,* instructing the studio that the film's hoodlums could not be shown with a Tommy gun.[49] As we saw when examining *The Killing* in the previous chapter, the PCA remained attentive to the weapons issue in films as late as the mid-1950s, but apparently the attention was not systematic. *Brute Force* escaped its scrutiny in this regard, and the film stands as a landmark in the expansion of violence in postwar American cinema. The film's myriad acts of violence are depicted with a level of brutality that the PCA could not restrain, and the fiery climax explodes with a degree of rage and nihilism that the crime film in general had not yet begun to tap.

DIRECTOR ANTHONY MANN AND *RAW DEAL*

It was, however, already moving in that direction. Anthony Mann brought concentrated doses of brutality to a series of low-budget crime films (often with John C. Higgins as screenwriter and John Alton as cinematographer) in the late 1940s, and he would do something similar with Westerns in the 1950s. Mann is best known for his fifties Westerns starring James Stewart—films in which Stewart's character must undergo some experience of intense physical brutality. In *The Man from Laramie,* for example, a villain shoots a hole in Stewart's hand at point-blank range.

Mann's flair for staging violence was first showcased in the late forties crime films, where his penchant for wide-angle filming and deep-focus staging combined with Alton's classic low-key lighting to punch the scripted violence forcefully across the screen. In *Railroaded* (1947), when a cop shoots a robber, it would be too easy and cinematically unremarkable for the bullet merely to harm him in some nondescript way. Instead, it hits the victim in the throat, shatters his jaw, and travels upward, lodging at the base of his brain. He clutches at his throat and doubles over, and when we next see him in the getaway car he has a scarf wrapped around his jaw and mouth. The strangled sounds he makes when speaking point to the damage he has suffered. Instead of putting its victim gently to sleep, as clutch-and-fall does, Mann's bullet causes pain and disfigurement.

Another Mann film the following year, *Raw Deal* (1948), was deemed so unacceptable in script form that the PCA took the unusual step of trying to discourage the studio from pursuing the property. The agency condemned the script as "a sordid story of crime, immorality, brutality, gruesomeness, illicit sex and sex perversion, without the slightest suggestion of any compensating moral values whatsoever."[50] Even unfavorable script evaluation letters typically contained some qualifier that the judgment was rendered on the material as written. In this case, however, the agency wrote that the story is "fraught with so many major problems, we earnestly suggest that you dismiss considering developing this present material into a motion picture to be submitted for our approval."[51] This conclusion was a highly unusual one for the agency to reach and indicates the distaste and disapproval it felt for the project.

Nevertheless, negotiation remained the PCA's mode of operation and doors to production were never closed in any final, absolute sense. Two days after this letter, Harry Zehner and Eugene Dougherty of the PCA met with director Mann and two executives from Eagle-Lion Films. Wanting to proceed with the project, the studio agreed to eliminate the villain's homosexuality from the script, beef up the roles of the police, and add a character that would supply a voice for morality. In addition, one of the scripted scenes had the police gunning down a criminal who was trying to surrender. The PCA felt this amounted to cold-blooded murder and wanted the police merely to arrest him. The filmmakers were semi-compliant with this advice. In the finished film the cops still shoot him down, but only after he fires first.

The most troubling and vicious act of violence in the script prefigures and probably inspired the more famous scene in Fritz Lang's subsequent *The Big Heat* (1953). *Raw Deal*'s villain, Rick (Raymond Burr), throws a flaming fondue into a woman's face (in the Lang film, it's a pot of coffee). The PCA was adamant that this action was too brutal and that the filmmakers must completely avoid it. The agency rendered its verdict against the fondue scene without equivocation, basically telling the filmmakers they couldn't do it. "The action of Rick hurling the flaming casserole on the cigarette girl is completely unacceptable and could not be approved in any circumstances."[52] This language seems unambiguous, and yet the filmmakers were stubbornly persistent. They continued to include the scene in subsequent script drafts, and the PCA continued to condemn it. A month later, for example, as it continued to review script changes, the agency wrote the studio, "we still remain of the opinion that the action of him throwing the flaming casserole at the girl and the horrible reaction of screaming and groaning on her part is unacceptably gruesome and could not be approved."[53]

If the PCA operated as current folklore has it doing, as an office of censorship, its rejection of the scene would have been the last word in the matter. The scene would be dead, and the agency would have imposed its norms and vision of morality upon the filmmakers. But the folklore about the agency being a censor and a bluenose is wrong, at least in terms of screen violence. The matter was not dead and the filmmakers continued to pursue it, defying the agency's evaluation that the scene was unacceptable. Joseph Breen, Jr., who

29. The subjective view in *Raw Deal,* from the victim's point of view, of Rick (Raymond Burr) as he hurls the flaming fondue at her (and into the face of the camera). The wide-angle composition enhances the impact of his action.

worked in the story department at Eagle-Lion Studios, wrote Dougherty and Zehner to inform them that the filmmakers were going to shoot the scene. In deference to the PCA, however, the action would be shown indirectly, as much as possible, in order to lessen its brutality. "We will not show the flaming dish hitting Marcy. We will show Rick throwing it and then cut to the reactions of the crowd; or we will show Rick throwing it and then go to a close-up of Marcy and show her reaction, without showing the flaming dish hitting her. We feel this can be done without being excessively brutal."[54] Despite the PCA's strong opposition to the scene the filmmakers went ahead and shot it, and the agency declined to have it removed from the finished film. The filmmakers were determined to put a savage act of violence on the screen, and the agency did not overrule them.

As the scene appears in the finished film, the staging shows some of the concessions to the PCA that Joe Breen, Jr. outlined in his letter. The victim is off-camera when the fondue hits her, and after her initial scream, which is loud, the sound mix mutes her subsequent cries and then fades them out altogether. As a result, except for that first cry, the audio contains little evidence of her pain. The sound mix abbreviates it as a way of lessening the scene's brutality and in a manner that conforms to the general prohibition on extended cries of pain or terror. In terms of the imagery, Marcy is never seen after the casserole hits her. Rick tells his men to take her away, and she is escorted out of the room but the blocking of the actors keeps her out of the camera's line of sight.

In these ways, the filmmakers adopted an oblique presentation of the action. At the same time, however, they went in the other direction: toward an increase of stylistic amplitude, intensifying the brutality by using a subjective shot from Marcy's point of view, to show Rick throwing the fondue and the flaming mess hitting her face. We see it from Marcy's perspective. He literally throws it in her (the camera's) face. Everything about the design of the shot serves to exaggerate the viciousness of Rick's action. Because it is a subjective composition, he flings the flaming casserole into the eye of the camera. Mann and Alton use their widest angle lens to capture this action. The camera is at a low angle, increasing Rick's looming presence in the frame, and the wide-angle lens distortion enlarges the size of the burning dish as Rick swings it toward the camera. The size change is faster and bigger than what a normal focal-length lens would produce, and this dynamic change adds considerable force to the action.

Furthermore, the editing of the action is shrewdly considered when the dish hits the camera. Most filmmakers would cut immediately to the next shot, but Mann and his editor allow the take to continue for several more frames, as the flaming liquid covers the lens and streams down it, obliterating a clear view of the Rick and the room. The camera burns and is blinded by the liquid in its face. Because we are in a subjective shot, this is Marcy's face that we now see, from the inside, as she sees it and feels it. It turns out that she is not off-camera at all. The impact of the violence against her *is* shown—it is visible in those seconds when the camera sees the fire splash across its eye. The action then cuts to a new framing of Rick, no longer a subjective view, with Marcy now unambiguously off-camera.

Again, we are seeing how slippery style can be for those who would regulate media content. By making careful stylistic choices, filmmakers could evade the letter of the PCA's wishes even as they claimed to be working via suggestion to lessen a scene's brutality. Because the system of PCA supervision was front-loaded at the scripting stage and because the agency did not supervise actual production, it was vulnerable to a director's use of style to reorganize the set of negotiated agreements about the material a script contained. In the case of *Raw Deal*, the filmmakers pressed ahead to film a disputed scene and then carefully designed its violence to counteract the oblique presentation they claimed they would adopt.

Raw Deal was a low-budget film released by a minor studio. Film scholars sometimes suggest that filmmakers working for second-tier studios and on low-budget productions, without prestigious stars, had more freedom to push subversive topics like sex and violence. The case of *Gun Crazy,* reviewed earlier, offers a counter-example to this idea. Moreover, the idea is not sufficient to account for the ability of the *Raw Deal* filmmakers to film a scene that the PCA had rejected in the script. More relevant as an explanation is the factor that we have already considered: that the agency did not function simply as a censor of motion picture violence. It negotiated content with filmmakers. Sometimes it lost the negotiations, and it then faced a choice about which of its objectives to honor—avoiding action by the regional censors or assisting production. It frequently chose to serve production rather than the censors.

KILLING THE HANDICAPPED IN *KISS OF DEATH*

A striking instance of this trade-off, and a significant example of the agency's failure to keep a scene of notorious violence off the screen, is provided by *Kiss of Death* (1947), which, unlike *Raw Deal,* was a major studio production, the studio in this case being Twentieth Century Fox. The film is famous today, and made a tremendous impression on viewers when first released, for the scene in which the psychopathic hood Johnny Udo (Richard Widmark) pushes an invalid woman in a wheelchair to her death down a flight of stairs and laughs while he does it. The scene was widely understood as representing a new high in screen violence, a sadistic, cold-blooded, and chilling assault on a character whose composite traits had generally been off-limits to movie villains. Mrs. Rizzo, the victim, is a woman and a mother, elderly and handicapped. Ordinarily, that's a quadruple level of protection against dastardly deeds. In a film that was less ruthless, any one of these traits would sanctify her against the villain's powers, but not here, not now—not when movie villains were reaching for new heights of meanness. The notoriety of this scene has unfairly overshadowed the film, which is a tight, tough story about a good-hearted jewel robber, Nick (Victor Mature), who is forced by the cops to turn informant, thereby incurring the enmity of the sinister Udo.

The PCA rejected the first draft of the script, judging it to be unacceptable under the Code because the opening jewel robbery was too detailed, a brutal cop was included among the characters, Nick's wife commits suicide, Udo was portrayed as a drug addict and living with a woman out of wedlock, and because of the "excessively brutal" murder of the invalid mother. In its rejection letter, the PCA told the studio that this murder could not be approved.[55] After the round of script conferences with the studio and the filmmakers that typically followed issuance of a rejection letter, and the submission of revised scripts, the PCA relented by consenting to the murder scene but only on condition that it be portrayed through suggestion and not be, under any circumstances, actually shown. "As previously discussed, we could not approve the scene of Mrs. Rizzo hurtling down the stairs. This murder must be no more than merely suggested."[56] The PCA wouldn't get its way.

Nothing about the scene in the finished picture works by "mere suggestion." The viewer sees it all, from the point where Udo gets the idea, prepares his victim by lashing her to her wheelchair with a lamp cord, and wheels her outside her apartment to the landing above the stairs. Mrs. Rizzo is terrified, and she cries and pleads with Udo not to harm her, finally screaming as she realizes what he is about to do. Udo laughs with sadistic pleasure as he binds her to the chair, and he smiles throughout the remainder of the killing.

---

30. The psychotic Johnny Udo tosses an old lady down the stairs in a notorious and legendary scene from *Kiss of Death*. The PCA had prohibited the scene, but the filmmakers ignored the agency's wishes.

There is a clear point in the sequence where the PCA could have intervened, even as late as the screening for review and certification, to have its way by moving the violence off-screen and handling it obliquely, via suggestion. When Udo pushes Mrs. Rizzo out of her apartment and onto the landing above the stairs, his intended action is fully clear. A fade, at that point, could have been used to take viewers out of the scene. This editing would have been a reasonably simple task to carry out and would have amounted to the type of low-level structural change that everyone in the system agreed the PCA could reasonably ask of a completed film. It would have made the scene conform to the agency's original specification, that the murder be no more than merely suggested.

But nothing of this sort occurs in the film as released. The agency typically was loathe to order recuts. Udo pushes the shrieking Mrs. Rizzo off of the landing, and a reverse-angle shot shows the wheelchair bouncing down the stairs. It is a long staircase, and the wheelchair tumbles all the way down and skitters some length along the floor below. Then and only then does the fade occur, taking the viewer out of the scene.

The placement of this fade occurs one shot too late. To honor the PCA's original directive that the murder not be shown, the fade should have come one shot earlier, when Mrs. Rizzo was still on the landing. The decision to keep the fade at the end of the scene incurred a significant amount of censor action. Censors in Ohio, Pennsylvania, Alberta, and Australia deleted the last two shots of the sequence—Udo pushing her off the landing, and the chair bouncing down the stairs—and Sweden deleted the entire sequence.

These eliminations illustrate how the PCA's dual obligations—to help the industry ward off action by regional and overseas censors and to negotiate with filmmakers in ways that would help them achieve their goals—could be contradictory and mutually exclusive objectives. Avoiding the censor action in Ohio, Pennsylvania, Alberta, and Australia would have been easy enough. It merely would have entailed shifting the location of the fade in the manner that I indicated. Doing so, however, evidently conflicted with the determination of the filmmakers to get this killing on-screen in as explicit and disturbing a form as they could. The PCA could not realize both objectives. Deferring to the filmmakers made censorship action inevitable. It is significant that the agency chose in this case to defer to the filmmakers—action that offers a telling indicator of where its ultimate loyalties lay.

The PCA was more successful at restraining the violence in RKO's *The Set-Up* (1948), a grim tale about a battered, weary, middle-aged boxer who earns the enmity of a local mobster when he doesn't take a pre-arranged dive. The script contained numerous details of violence that were too extreme and explicit for the period. For example, in one scene the script called for blood to spurt from a boxer's face. While the PCA might permit a small amount of blood, spurting was out of the question. It asked the RKO studio liaison to keep such details to a minimum. With respect to other scripted details it suggested, "the rubbing of the glove lacing over Stoker's eye ought not to be shown" and "Please omit the jabbing of the thumb into Stoker's eye."[57] About a subsequent script draft, it took exception to such descriptions as Stoker's face being "blood bespattered," "bleeding profusely from both eyes, nose and mouth," and "slashed to ribbons, with only a slit left for one eye."[58]

The presence of these details in the script illustrates the general process this chapter has been describing: the push by filmmakers for stronger violence. The screenwriter and the film's producer, of course, had to know that these details were beyond the boundaries of what was permissible and could not be shown on-screen, and yet the imagery was written into the script and retained during the initial phases of negotiation with the PCA.

The PCA also worried about a scene where the gangsters beat up Stoker and break his hand. Its letter on this issue took the unusual step of suggesting how the filming ought to proceed. The PCA rarely gave filmmakers advice on the specifics of actual filming, beyond such general parameters as being indirect rather than explicit. Here, though, the agency recommended that the filmmakers protect themselves by shooting enough footage to make it possible to re-edit the scene if necessary. Its advice reveals that the agency was concerned enough to be thinking downstream, to the screening for clearance, and anticipating that some recutting might be necessary. (As used in this citation from the letter, "scene" means "shot.") "We are still vastly concerned over the scenes indicating the breaking of Stoker's hand. We believe such a scene would be unduly horrifying to audiences generally and we recommend that the scenes leading up to . . . the breaking of his hand be photographed in such a way that, if on review the final scenes seem unacceptable, they can be deleted. This is important."[59] In the finished film, the hand breaking occurs off-camera, and the framing of subsequent action prevents the viewer from seeing Stoker's maimed hand.

After two months of script revisions and even as it okayed the final draft, the agency worried about the overall level of brutality in the boxing scenes. Stoker's match against a younger opponent is the central act in the film's drama, and it occupies a lot of screen time. The PCA worried about the scene's potential for explicitly visualizing unacceptable forms of violence. The agency again recommended to the filmmakers that they shoot the action so as to maximize its editing possibilities. "We are particularly apprehensive of a great many medium and close shots in the fight between Stoker and Nelson in

179

which we fear the showing of the terrible beating which Stoker takes may unavoidably come through in an excessive and brutal manner. We recommend that you take sufficient protection material so that if these scenes appear unacceptably brutal, you will have material to which you can cut away."[60]

In the finished film, close-ups of bleeding and cutting are rare, though Stoker's face does take a pounding. It looks swollen and suffers a number of cuts, though these do not bleed excessively. This seemed to make all the difference for the PCA. In the absence of spurting blood, it permitted a screen fight of uncommon duration and intensity to appear in the finished film. The fight is impressive mainly because of the pounding that Stoker and his opponent endure. The fight seems to go on forever, with seemingly hundreds of blows landing on their faces and bodies. The choice of camera set-ups, however, using longer shot framings in the editing, helped to minimize the overt detailing of physical damage to the fighters. The fight is filmed almost entirely in full-figure and medium-shot framings, with very few tight close-ups of their faces except during ring breaks when they are in their corners. As a result, the script's detailing of cutting and spurting does not appear on-screen. *The Set-Up* marked a partial victory for the PCA: It had taken an exceptionally violent script and significantly reduced its level of explicitness.

Sexual Sadism in *The Big Heat*

It was not as successful with *The Big Heat,* which took the face-burning scene from *Raw Deal* and placed it in a story that contained a lot more violence, brutality, and sadism than did Mann's film. Actually, the film doubles the face-burning scene. There are two of them in *The Big Heat*. Detective Dave Banyon (Glenn Ford) is investigating a cop's suicide when his queries lead him to one of the master criminals who frequently appear in director Fritz Lang's films. Laguna controls the city's politicians and the police department, and when Dave's questions threaten to expose his organization Laguna has his enforcer, Stone (Lee Marvin), who is a sexual sadist, plant a bomb in Dave's car. When the bomb kills his wife, Dave embarks on a bitter quest for revenge that leads to a shoot-out with Stone and, it is implied, the downfall of Laguna. Along the way, Stone and his men torture and kill one woman, Stone burns the hand of another with a cigar, and, in possibly the film's most famous scene of brutality, Stone hurls a pot of hot coffee into the face of his girlfriend.

We might pause here for a moment to consider the special qualities of the violence against women that appears in this film and also in pictures we've previously examined such as *Murders in the Rue Morgue* and *Raw Deal*—and those yet to come, such as *Kiss Me Deadly* and *The Killers*. On the one hand, bad as it is, these female victims do not suffer any forms of violence not meted out to male characters in films of the period. In pictures like *The Black Cat, Objective, Burma!* and *The Glass Key,* men are maimed and tortured to death or disfigured by severe beatings. (And in a great many other pictures, women characters have a kind of protected victim status that insulates them from physical violence.) And yet the violence in these scenes of women being tortured or beaten has a particularly disturbing quality that is not apparent in those scenes where men are the victims. This is because the violence is sexually charged. It expresses a sexual rage or contempt for the woman as victim that has no counterpart in scenes with male victims. The violence in the scenes seems to flow as much from this sexual anger as it does from the narrative situation. Because the sexualized rage adds an extra component to the violence it amplifies its ugliness and intensity, and this is what makes these scenes feel so uniquely different from the male-on-male violence that we've been examining.

The sexual rage is often an undercurrent of the scene, sometimes disconnected from the overt details of situation and character but nevertheless lending its special charge. This suggests that the attitudes and feelings may be coming from somewhere other than scene-specific material. In *The Big Heat,* Stone hates women, and that's why he torments them. In *Murders in the Rue Morgue,* however, Dr. Mirakle isn't a woman hater. Nevertheless, the violence in that film's torture scene becomes thoroughly sexualized in its bondage imagery.

While male characters suffered abundant and horrific violence in classical Hollywood films, when that violence came the way of female characters it sometimes carried the additional dimension of sexualized rage, making the violence feel more harsh and cruel. This could even knock the viewer off-balance, to the extent that a scene might feel covertly about something other than what the narrative situation called for. At the level of narrative the scene in *Murders in the Rue Morgue* is a medical experiment, but the imagery and sound make it one of sexual torture. While the PCA would typically object to the gross level of brutality found in a scene, it was much slower and less effective in dealing with the special qualities of this exceptional violence against women. In the Code files that I examined, there was no indication that the PCA recognized this category of scene and violence as being distinct from the more ordinary run of movie violence. It seemed to fall outside the regulatory parameters of the period.

Let us now return to discussion of *The Big Heat.* The PCA rejected early script drafts because they contained numerous Code violations. These included Dave's quest for revenge. The Code stipulated that stories with contemporary settings should not glorify revenge or portray it as a justifiable motive for character behavior. Revisions to the script softened Dave's character and removed some of the brutality from his pursuit of Stone and Laguna. In early drafts Dave used his influence essentially to murder one of the crooks by putting out the word that he was a snitch to the cops. Dave's intent is that he be killed, and he is. The PCA objected, "when Dave Bannion arranges to have the word passed throughout the underworld that Larry Smith has turned informer, he is deliberately setting up a murder, which appears to be completely justified."[61] The agency suggested that instead of Dave deliberately setting up Smith's destruction, he merely tell Smith that in all likelihood Laguna's men would learn that he had informed.

Early drafts also had Dave pistol-whipping Stone and stomping on his hand. The PCA regularly objected to this kind of cruelty, whatever the genre. Kicking, gouging, stomping, kneeing, and pistol-whipping always drew a sharp response. (It is in this context that the close-quarter savagery of the fighting in *Bataan* is so remarkable.) Accordingly, these details were dropped from the film, as was scripted action in which Stone crushes a woman's hand by smashing a heavy glass on it.

While the PCA managed to get these details removed, it only did so at a late point in the script review process—evidence that the filmmakers were pushing at the agency to get as much sadism into the picture as possible. The PCA had been reviewing script drafts for the film since January 1953 and cautioning the filmmakers about the "excessive amount of brutality and gruesomeness."[62] While the revisions addressed and fixed most of the problem areas—these included the vengeance motive, the story's implications of widespread civic corruption, and Dave's sexual involvement with Stone's girlfriend—the PCA complained that the amount of brutality in the scripts was actually increasing rather than diminishing. Two months after the start of the script review process, the agency wrote to the head of Columbia Pictures, Harry Cohn, to complain about this development.

> We note that in the several scripts that have been submitted for our consideration since our original discussions with the men of your studio concerning this story, an increased amount of violence and rather spectacular brutality has been injected into it, and the accumulative effect of this, we think, is definitely not good. We must, therefore, respectfully request that some of these acts of brutality be eliminated and the overall violence considerably reduced.[63]

In making this request, the PCA specifically cited the action where Stone presses the lighted cigar onto the hand of a woman in the Laguna gang's bar.

But its efforts were for naught: The action is in the film. In the scene, Stone sits at the bar next to one of the gang's women and berates her for picking up a pair of dice too quickly after she has rolled them. He hates women and enjoys abusing them.

The woman apologizes and offers to roll the dice again. The camera frames her and Stone in a two-shot, with their hands just below the bottom frame line. She rolls the dice. Seized with frenzy, Stone reaches over and pins her hand to the bar, then shoves his cigar down on it. In an extra jolt of sadism, he keeps the cigar on her hand. Debbie, Stone's girlfriend, pulls him off the victim, who is screaming with pain. All of this action, strictly speaking, is off-screen since it occurs below the bottom frame line, but just barely. The camera's area of view is mere inches from the action with the cigar. As a result, the viewer knows exactly what Stone is doing. Moreover, his victim stays on-camera while she is being burned. There is no cutaway or camera movement to take her out of frame. The viewer cannot see her hand, but her face, shoulders and upper arms clearly convey her distress.

---

31.   PCA restrictions often led filmmakers to flirt with the frame line by placing objectionable violence off-camera, but just barely. In *The Big Heat,* Stone (Lee Marvin) burns a woman's hand with a cigar. In this teasing composition, the lower frame line almost fails to conceal the action.

There is little in the scene that works by way of "mere suggestion." In deference to the PCA, the filmmakers do use the frame line to conceal the burning, but they play it as close to visibility as they can. The staging flirts with the frame line as the demarcation between visibility and implication, just as the staging in *Kiss of Death* put Udo's gun just out of frame when he shoots Nick but so close that its sparks and smoke are on-camera. This kind of staging shows the filmmakers playing with the PCA, threatening to cross the line from implication to visibility and not actually doing so but coming as close to the demarcation as possible while honoring, in letter though not in spirit, the injunction to suggest but not display brutality.

Stone's cruelty in the bar is part of a pattern of sadistic behavior toward women. Earlier, he abducted a woman and tortured her with cigarette burns before killing her. (None of this action is portrayed. It is described after the fact.) Subsequently, he tosses the pot of coffee into Debby's face. The PCA was very specific about how the mutilation of Debby was to be presented. "This whole business will be handled merely by suggestion. It will not be photographed."[64] The agency was relatively more successful here in getting the filmmakers to abide by its wishes. Unlike the comparable scene in *Raw Deal*, there is no shot that actually shows the hot liquid being hurled at an off-camera victim. Stone is enraged to learn that Debby has been talking with Bannion. He twists her arm and calls her a lying pig. In a tight close-up, he then looks around the room for something to hurt her with. A close-up shows a pot of boiling coffee, and after a moment Stone's arm comes into frame, lifts the pot off the burner and thrusts it out of frame. As the camera continues to film the empty burner, the sound of splashing liquid is heard, followed by a long scream from Debby. She is then seen rushing into an adjoining room, covering her face, and crying. Stone's men escort her out of the apartment.

The referential action—Stone hurling coffee into Debby's face—is portrayed, but the burning itself is not photographed. Everything leading to it and from it is shown, but not the assault itself. In that regard there is no depiction of the actual moment of violence, but the act is evoked and Debby's response—crying and running from the room—is on-camera. Furthermore, its consequences—the ravaging of Debby's face—are vividly presented in a later scene when she removes her bandages to reveal extensive scarring.

She shows her disfigured face to Stone after she has her revenge by hurling coffee into his face. She is off-camera, but Stone is on-camera, so we see the coffee hit him. As he collapses in pain, she sits beside him and unmasks, revealing a patchwork of scarring over half of her face. Although the make-up effect is not very convincing, this is a rare instance of a film showing extensive physical and emotional consequences of violence. The victim reveals her trauma and it has changed her character, eroding Debby's naiveté and joie de vivre and substituting for them a new bitterness and brutality. Scarred, she is even capable of murder, coldly gunning down a woman associated with Laguna.

As sadistic as the coffee-burning episodes are, the killing of Dave Bannion's wife is perhaps a more brutally disturbing episode of violence because Dave's home life has been portrayed with conventional warmth and sentimentality and the violence against his wife comes abruptly and without warning. By contrast, the viewer already knows that Stone is a vicious sociopath when he assaults Debby. Dave's wife borrows his car keys to run an errand, and the car bomb explodes while Dave is tucking their little girl into bed for the night. He rushes outside and finds the car crumpled and in flames. Frantically pounding on the splintered windows, he tries to get to his wife. The door is jammed shut, but finally he opens it and drags out her lifeless body.

She is cosmetically untouched, with no bruises, cuts or visible damage, but this does not overly compromise the power of the scene. Its brutality lies not in its visualization of trauma to her body (there is none) but in the sudden evocation of savage violence within the storybook context of domestic family bliss—a setting that 1950s culture and cinema invested with tremendous ideological sanctity. Violence occurring in this context can seem worse, especially since it involves an attack on a woman who is both wife and mother. The car bomb shatters the idyllic suburban life of the Bannion family, destroying the wife and mother in an inferno.

In contrast to the coffee burning and the scripted instances of pistol-whipping and hand crushing, the PCA had nothing to say about the murder of Dave's wife. The script evaluation letters and internal memos do not mention the car bombing. Considering the magnitude of this violence and the nature of the victim it claims, this omission is significant, and it's an early manifestation of a development that would accelerate over the next ten years. As the PCA lost ground to filmmakers in their drive to push screen violence, it began to lodge fewer objections. This tendency greatly accelerated in the early 1960s, when the agency was largely rubber-stamping the violence in scripts. The lack of documentation in the case file about the car bomb and the wife killing presages this emerging trend.

ULTRAVIOLENCE IN *KISS ME DEADLY*

The exceptional brutality and sadism in *The Big Heat* embodies the direction in which American screen violence was now headed. Robert Aldrich's *Kiss Me Deadly* (1955) amplifies these elements to a pitch of near-hysteria. The film contains shootings, beatings, a knifing, two torture scenes, an attempted bombing, and a character burning to death on-camera. With wit and gusto, the movie hurtles from one violent episode to another, all pitched at exceedingly high levels of stylistic amplitude.

The PCA told director Robert Aldrich that a script based on Mickey Spillane's novel about drug dealing and featuring Spillane's brutal hero, Mike Hammer, would be a "complete violation of the Code."[65] Hammer was a hard-punching, promiscuous private eye whose tactics were far removed from the finesse and nobility of his literary antecedents, such as Raymond Chandler's Philip Marlowe. But the door to production was not closed. Aldrich tailored the script to avoid what he called the novel's "narcotics complication" and to add a voice of morality to the abundant brutalities of the story.[66] Aldrich told the PCA that he aimed "to successfully marry the commercial values of the Spillane properties with a morality that states justice is not to be found in a self-appointed one-man vigilante."[67] Aldrich reiterated this goal when the Legion of Decency threatened to give the picture a Condemned rating unless more than thirty changes, cuts, and deletions were made. The picture was about to go into release with a Code certification, and Aldrich, in a panic, beseeched the PCA to intercede. The Legion's action, he wrote, "comes as a most rude and expensive surprise since it was my belief and understanding that there certainly could not be this wide a divergence between the opinions of the Legion and those of the Code administration." He reminded the PCA about the "voice of moral righteousness" in the film, "since so much time and effort was spent in finding and properly developing such a voice in this film and it was my understanding that the Code administrators both knew and appreciated this fact."[68]

We should not assume that Aldrich is being disingenuous. Numerous characters in the film tell Hammer (Ralph Meeker) that he is scum, wrong-headed, and responsible for the death of innocent people. But *Kiss Me Deadly* is an example of style trumping content. Ralph Meeker's jazzy performance is so cocky and full of testosterone that it becomes endearing in a way the filmmakers may not have fully intended. Hammer is a low-life, but he's got panache, and viewers happily climb aboard for the violent ride he takes them on. Discussing the power of charismatic performers to overwhelm a film's nominative point of view, Leo Braudy points out that "a director can easily make mistakes that destroy the unity of his film." Braudy was writing about *The Battle of Algiers* (1966), but his point goes directly to one of the problems with *Kiss Me Deadly*. In that classic political film, Braudy noted that "the actor playing the paratrooper Colonel Matthieu [who is sent by France to crush the Algerian revolution] does such a good job that he confuses our understanding of the political point of the film. In films one well-acted fascist easily overbalances mobs of politically correct people."[69]

In the same way, one lovingly played and appealing thug easily overbalances the moralistic verdicts other people render about him. More to the point, in terms of the film's violence Ralph Meeker's Hammer is the viewer's charismatic guide into a nightmare world of abduction, torture and murder, perpetrated for much of the film by shadowy, dimly understood emissaries of evil. Hammer's righteous quest for answers to the savage killing of a young woman whom he had picked up hitchhiking, and his need to avenge the murder of his friend Nick, are motives a viewer can heartily endorse, especially in a film world filled with the kind of predators who lurk there. Not surprisingly, therefore, the Legion of Decency apparently missed the film's "voice of moral righteousness," as did the PCA, which originally was not going to pass the film for certification. The voice of righteousness can be found in the condemnation of Hammer by the other characters, but it's not very loud and Meeker's swagger easily negates it.

What most impresses a viewer today about *Kiss Me Deadly* is not its voice for morality but the pitch of its violence, at a level of sustained cruelty and vindictiveness. The film opens with the abduction and torturing of a woman. Hammer has just picked up the hitchhiker, Christina, who is distraught, naked but for a trench coat, and fleeing in terror from unnamed pursuers. The onset of violence is sudden and abrupt, and its detailing—the naked Christina will be tortured with a pair of pliers—is far more horrific than the viewer expects. A car forces Hammer off the road, and three men abduct him and his passenger. Aldrich shoots the action in a very disorienting style. We only see the feet and lower legs of the killers, and an audio transition to the torture scene precedes the visual one. As the killers walk toward Hammer's car, framed so that only their legs are visible, the sound of Christina shrieking under torture, from the next scene, starts here and then continues across the shot transition to the torture scene proper and a new framing that shows her naked lower legs hanging off the end of a table and jerking with pain while she screams.

Her cries are sharp, sustained and intense—the sort that had been largely off-limits to Hollywood film since the early 1930s—but now here they are, a prolonged cacophony of suffering that ends only when the victim dies. Christina expires under torture far more horribly than had Dr. Mirakle's victim in *Murders in the Rue Morgue,* the scene that helped initiate a crackdown on screen sadism and set a limit defining the forbidden zone for depictions of the body in distress. Christina's assailants have removed her trench coat and are using the pliers to inflict exquisitely crude torments upon her naked body. These cruelties are enacted out of frame. The viewer sees only her legs jerking convulsively. But when she dies and one of the killers enters the frame holding the pliers, the nature of her torment becomes clear enough.

187

What did the PCA have to say about this amazingly brutal scene? As an index of changing times and relaxing standards, the agency said nothing in the case file about the torture itself. By contrast, it worried about nudity. It cautioned the filmmakers not to suggest that she is naked while being tortured. The agency wrote in its script evaluation letter, "it is our opinion that the shot of the girl's legs should still indicate that she is wearing the coat. We ask that you do not suggest that she is lying on the table nude and being tortured by the killers."[70] In regards to this advice, it would appear that nakedness was deemed to be of greater offense than being tortured to death. In any event, the filmmakers ignored the suggestion. In the shot of Christina's bare legs dangling from the torture table, the trench coat is plainly visible on the floor beneath them.

It would have been a simple matter to comply with the PCA's wish. In fact, to comply the filmmakers needed do absolutely nothing. The scene could have been staged and shot exactly as it now appears with the exception of the coat visible on the floor; the filmmakers could have claimed that Christina was still wearing it. Her legs even could have remained bare since the coat did not completely cover them. The ambiguity about its whereabouts would have permitted the filmmakers to claim that they were complying with the PCA's wishes while still suggesting, to viewers whose minds were so inclined, that

---

32. The torture of Christina in *Kiss Me Deadly* is notable for the extent of her vocalized pain. Notice also the strategically placed trench coat, plainly visible on-camera.

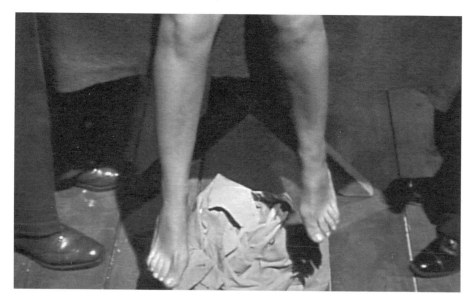

perhaps she was naked. But instead of this approach, which would enable all parties to claim victory, Aldrich placed the coat on-camera so as to establish that Christina was indeed naked while being tortured. It unquestionably makes her violation more appalling, which, in turn, makes the PCA's failure to address the torture itself more significant.

In its dealings with Aldrich, the PCA conceded that the story "has valid requirements for a considerable amount of violence," but it wanted specific instances of detailed brutality kept to a minimum.[71] One episode of violence that concerned the agency was Hammer's fight with a thug who is tailing him on the street. The fight as scripted contained the kind of behaviors that the agency traditionally warned filmmakers about. The PCA wrote Aldrich, "Mike's attack on the potential killer includes certain items of excessive brutality, and we ask that they be eliminated. Specifically, we refer to kneeing and kicking, as well as the deliberate head-banging and slugging after the man is hanging limp."[72] The kneeing and kicking went out, but the head-banging stayed. It is one of the scene's most startling and vicious ingredients, applied by Hammer with sadistic glee. He has already punched the man nearly senseless when he grabs his chest and slams his head against a concrete wall not once, but five times. Only one of these blows is on-camera. Most shots show Hammer's face—he's grinning with delight—with the other man out of frame, but the audio contains the sound of the five head smashes on the wall.

The head bashing is flamboyant, and Aldrich goes on to top it with a gratuitous and baroque coda. After smashing the guy's head, Hammer walks away, but his insensate victim improbably gets back to his feet and comes after him. This enables Hammer to knock him spectacularly down a huge, three-tiered stone stairway. Aldrich uses wide-angle framings to accentuate the size of the stairway, and he gives us a shot from the top of the stairs of Hammer knocking the man down the steps, and then a shot from below of the victim tumbling toward the camera, legs akimbo and arms flailing.

The violence of the fight is lavishly choreographed; the camera style is in love with the sensuousness of the carnage. In this respect, the style overwhelms the "moral voice" that Aldrich claims he wanted to place in the film. More significantly, the manner in which Aldrich's filmmaking instincts short-circuit his intentions darkly portends what is coming in the history of American film violence: its terrific expansion in stylistic amplitude. Taken to this degree, style begins to subvert the ability of a filmmaker to create a perspective on violence that is other than celebratory. Whatever a filmmaker might want to claim for a movie, the elaborate styling of violence overwhelms it; it neutralizes it and makes it for the viewer what it is for the filmmaker, an exciting and pleasurable enterprise.

The stylistics of film violence today tend, in almost every case, to be cele-bratory. They enhance, embellish, and flaunt violence before the viewer, and reveal filmmakers' tremendous satisfaction in doing death for the camera. Very few films show violence as ugly and *unpleasurable.* The history of film vio-lence shows us that cinema is complicit in these pleasures. It honors them, and its filmmakers are forever transacting them. A stylistic inquiry into the his-tory of American screen violence shows us this truth very clearly, whereas the social history approach tends to minimize it. This is because framed by its template, screen violence seems to be constantly mutating so as to express the ideological or social power dynamics in a given period. The enduring param-eters of screen violence, however, are found in the stylistic domain and its consistent orientation toward providing a pleasurable entertainment for the viewer that in practice renders almost all screen violence, of whatever appar-ent ideological inflection, into an easily consumed commodity. Aldrich's joy in filming Hammer's fight is lethal to his objective of portraying Hammer as a vig-ilante. As such, the scene is consistent with the stylistic history of American screen violence and furnishes a template for the future. Because screen vio-lence a decade hence would be freed from censorship, the scene anticipates the powers of cinema that were soon to be fully unleashed.

Extended Sadism in *One-Eyed Jacks*

Even the Western, a genre long regarded by the PCA as being relatively safe and nontroublesome, was showing the new cruelty surfacing in American film. As I have previously mentioned, Anthony Mann brought the hard vio-lence he had elaborated in his low-budget crime films to the Western during the 1950s, with the hand-shooting in *The Man from Laramie* as a particular high point. Sam Peckinpah's work would be at forefront of the graphic vio-lence of late sixties cinema, and in the 1950s he was a screenwriter scratching around for work. One of his scripts went into production with Marlon Brando, and, after extensive revisions by six other writers, it became *One-Eyed Jacks* (1961). The production was a troubled and difficult one, and Peckinpah later claimed that only two sequences from his script made it into the finished film. The picture changed directors, passing from Stanley Kubrick to Brando, and the final result bears the imprint of numerous authors. Possibly due to Peckin-pah's involvement, the script and its revisions contain numerous instances of strong violence that the PCA identified as serious problems with the project.

For decades, screenwriters had been writing action they knew could not be filmed under the Production Code. In *Objective, Burma!* the description "his face has been mutilated beyond recognition" was unfilmable. No image conveying this level of information would be shot or included in a finished film. The script for *The Set-Up* contained numerous instances of violence that would be off-limits to the filmmakers. In a similar fashion, much of the violence in the *One-Eyed Jacks* script was beyond the pale of what could then be shown. The victim of a barroom beating, for example, is described thusly: "He is battered and bloody. Several teeth have been knocked out, and now half-conscious he spits them out. One eye is swollen, already half-shut, blood pours in twin streams from his nose, his chin and cheekbones are bruised purple."[73] Bullet damage is visualized with a level of detail that could not be portrayed for another decade: "One of the shots has shattered the bridge of his nose, spraying his face and eyes with blood."[74] Enraged townspeople hang and set fire to the corpse of a freshly dead outlaw: "The crowd hauls on a rope, which is attached to Bob's right ankle. He is pulled up into the air and his dead body dangles head downward, the other leg flopped awkwardly over at an angle. . . . The barber douses Bob's body with the kerosene and then holds a lighted match to it."[75]

None of this material—the facial disfigurement, the gun wound, the corpse burning—made it into the film. About the corpse burning, the PCA told the studio liaison, "the manner in which Bob is destroyed by setting him afire, would be unacceptably gruesome."[76] In addition to these instances, the agency had to contend with other forms of violence which it preferred the film not to contain but which the filmmakers wanted. One of these is the shooting death of a female bystander during a bank robbery. It's the kind of civilian death—an innocent person caught in the cross-fire of a shootout—that Peckinpah would portray so vividly in *The Wild Bunch*. In the *One-Eyed Jacks* script a little girl comes into the bank during the holdup and runs in terror when she sees the outlaw's gun. Crossing the line of fire, she is hit by a wild bullet and goes down. This action violates the protected victim status of the era's movie characters in several ways. The victim is female, a child, and she is in a state of terror when she's killed. With superb understatement, the PCA registered its distaste over this killing: "To avoid excessive cruelty, we earnestly suggest you reconsider the killing of the little child."[77] The filmmakers reconsidered it but only in terms of making the character a few years older. The bank robber still calls her a "little girl," but she's evidently a teenager and is played by a mature-looking actress, which makes the character's age ambiguous. The killing remained, but the PCA got some of what it wanted via the age change.

The agency lost the battle, however, over the film's most extended and significant episode of violence: the whipping of the outlaw hero, Rio (Brando), by his former friend and now town marshal, Dad Longworth (Karl Malden). Rio is tied to a post, and Dad flogs him at length, capping the cruelty by bashing Rio's hand with the butt of a shotgun. The PCA did not like this scene and felt that its level of cruelty was excessive. As a form of violence, whipping fell into that broad category of censured acts that we have already noted.

The agency thus advised Paramount Pictures that the whipping, followed by the hand bashing, was inherently too gruesome and that if it were to be featured in the film, it would have to be handled discretely. The agency repeatedly conveyed these instructions to the studio, only to have them disregarded or ignored. The case file contains a series of letters spanning nearly six months, during which time the agency tried to persuade the filmmakers not to portray the whipping at length and not openly on-camera. Throughout this long interval the agency reiterated this advice as it responded to script revisions, but the script revisions consistently failed to conform with the agency's recommendations.

At the beginning of December 1958, the agency informed the studio, "the scourging of Johnny [Rio] is unacceptably brutal and gruesome as written. This scene will have to be gotten over by suggestion." It added that "the business of crushing Johnny's hand with the shotgun would have to be gotten over with suggestion. The elements of violence and brutality are one of the serious problems latent in this material."[78]

By early March 1959, little had changed. The agency wrote, "we have in mind, first of all, the sadistic whipping which Dad administers to Rio. As described, it would appear to be both too prolonged and too savage. In addition, there is the shocking brutality of crushing Rio's hand with a shotgun."[79] Several days later, after another set of revised script pages were submitted, the PCA wrote, "inasmuch as we have already commented on the whipping scene contained in these pages, there seems little point to simply repeating the various cautions and admonitions once more."[80] The following month the agency felt compelled to again write, "we have already commented on the sequence contained in the first series of pages and still feel that they are sadistic."[81] A week later, the PCA still condemned the scene but now conceded that the hand maiming might be permissible (though a new element, kicking, now had to be contended with). "The extreme violence indicated on page 144A would not be acceptable under the Code. The business of 'bayoneting' Rio with the rifle butt would be acceptable only if it were done moderately and without extreme cruelty. The business of Rio swinging around and kicking at Lon would not be acceptable under the Code."[82] Five weeks later, the remarkably patient Geoffrey Shurlock wrote again, "with regards to the whipping scene beginning on page 109, may we please refer you to our previous correspondence regarding the unacceptability of this episode."[83]

The agency could not keep the whipping and hand-maiming out of the film, nor could it persuade the filmmakers to convey these by suggestion, except in one notable instance. In the finished film, Dad whips Johnny for a long time, administering twelve lashes, each of which is given prominence in the sound mix. The action begins with a deep-focus shot, framing Rio in the center foreground, bound to the post and facing the camera, with Dad in the background, whip in hand. The first two lashes are administered in this camera set-up, which enables the viewer to concentrate on Rio's response and also to see Dad wielding the whip. Other films have shown whippings, but the framing here is unusual because it shows both victim and victimizer within the same shot and in a way that shows their contrasting responses, the pain of the one and the sadistic glee of the other. Moreover, the deep-focus framing shows the effort Dad puts into each stroke, coiling his entire body and throwing with speed and force to deliver the lash.

The film then cuts to a medium close-up of Rio that shows him flinch as he takes another stroke. This is the first conventional framing of the violence. It excludes Dad and the views of the whip and shows only Rio's face and torso, discretely from the front so as to place the actual violence off-camera. This set-up is the kind of framing that would count as suggestion for the PCA, and it's the kind of framing that Hollywood traditionally used to depict whippings. This shot is brief, however, and the scene then cuts away from the immediate space of the flogging to an upstairs room in a building well down the street from the beating. Johnny's partners (the gang has planned to rob the town bank) are watching from the window. As they deliberate over what to do, the ongoing beating can be heard through their conversation. What the script expressed is in the film: "The sound of the blows of the whip can be heard from this distance." As they talk, the sound mix gives prominence to three lash strokes, occurring offscreen. A reverse-angle shot then shows their view of the street, during which Dad can be seen administering a fourth lash to Rio.

The action then cuts back to the street-level framings of Dad and Rio for three more strokes of the whip. The first one frames Dad in medium close-up, with his sadistic grin prominently visible. The second lashing shows Rio in close-up. The whipping has knocked him to his knees, and he's trembling. For the third and final stroke, the framing returns to the deep-focus set-up of Rio and Dad, both in the frame, though this time from a lower angle because Rio is now on his knees.

During filming, this set-up was evidently a long take that was subsequently cut apart in the editing. In the action in this framing, once Dad is finished flogging Rio he walks over to him, taunts him a little, and then reaches for a shotgun. He raises it up, butt end forward, but as he brings it down the film cuts to a more discrete framing, showing Dad in a medium close-up that excludes from sight the impact of the blow on Rio's hand. This framing is clearly a concession to the PCA because it occludes the hand-maiming at the moment of violence. The editing then returns to the previous wide-angle, deep-focus framing of Rio and Dad. From a cinematography standpoint this take was a continuous one, and included all of the action beginning with Dad's final two lashes with the whip, his walking over to Rio, taunting him, reaching for the gun, bashing the hand, telling Rio his gun days are over, telling his men to untie Rio, and their coming forward and beginning to do that. Imbedding the hand-bashing within all of the business of this long take, as the design of the shot during filming evidently did, worked to give the violence even more force by placing it within a continuum of real-time brutality (the real time of the unedited long take), as one moment in a continuing process of brutalization.

The cutaway to the medium-shot of Dad delivering the blow is an example of coverage—shots taken during filming to increase the number of ways a scene can be edited. Coverage enables editors to finesse problems by cutting away to something else. Typically, these problems involve issues of continuity, but they can also involve disputed areas of content such as sex and violence. Cutting to coverage is one way of eliding such trouble areas, and whenever the PCA advised a filmmaker to handle something by suggestion it invariably meant to place it off-screen, either by cutting to coverage at the damning moment or by writing scenes so that they leapt over the offending incident. In the case here, the insert of Dad enables the filmmakers to handle the hand-bashing by suggestion, in that it is not directly shown. But we have seen numerous examples of filmmakers using elements of style to minimize the extent to which the visual euphemisms, created by coverage, take the viewer away from a more direct presentation.

This scene includes one of these compensatory stylistic designs. During the cutaway to Dad as he brings the gun down, the audio works to magnify the impact of the weapon and the savagery of the act. A large group of townspeople has been watching the whipping. As Dad thrusts the gun downward, the viewer hears it thud against Rio's hand but also hears the high-pitched wail of a woman offscreen, shocked at what she sees, followed by the distraught cries and murmuring of the crowd. It's that high-pitched wail that especially captures the violence and conveys its magnitude. It's almost a shriek of pain, standing in for Rio's off-camera response, and it conveys the horror, outrage, and suffering that the cutaway itself has worked to conceal. The audio design works in opposition to the cutaway, giving back to the violence some of the harshness that the editing and framing have occluded.

33–34. The master-shot framing in which much of the whipping occurs in *One-Eyed Jacks*. The hand-smashing, though, plays in this tighter shot, which serves to make the mutilation more oblique.

THE ERA OF THE PRODUCTION CODE ENDS

One-Eyed Jacks was released in 1961, and, in just a few more years, the ability of the PCA to restrain expressions of violence—and its inclination even to do so—had completely collapsed. The escalation of hard violence in American cinema helped to undermine the agency's authority, and this trend was conjoined with the larger, structural changes that the industry was undergoing and that we examined earlier in the chapter.

Moreover, the industry itself was actively working to undercut the legitimacy of the PCA, and the agency's staff members could see the writing on the wall. For reasons of sexual content and language, the PCA declined to grant seals of approval *for The Pawnbroker* (1964), *Who's Afraid of Virginia Woolf* (1966), and *Alfie* (1966)—only to have its decisions overturned by the Production Code Review Board, which granted special exemptions for these films. PCA head Geoffrey Shurlock claimed to have been pleased that the agency lost these cases. Interviewed in 1970, he stated that the PCA's rejection of these films had been deliberately heavy-handed in order to demonstrate how outmoded the Code was and to ease the way for its replacement by an age-classification system.[84] Shurlock said that he had favored such a system since returning from a trip to Europe in 1956, when officials in England, Ireland, France and Germany had all asked him how a picture like *The Blackboard Jungle* (1955) could be approved and released in the United States for all audiences. In Shurlock's view, the release of such films as *Anatomy of a Murder* (1959) and *The Pawnbroker* was really a transition toward age-classification. He described the rhetorical strategy that he employed to ease the transition. Of *The Pawnbroker* he said, "in no case did I ever attack the picture or report on it in any but the most glowing terms. 'This is a great picture, a fine picture, a great piece of work, you know, but the Code.' We blamed it on the Code."[85]

As a first step, the industry scrapped the Code's existing provisions in 1966 and replaced them with a few general principles that were to guide filmmaking. These were broadly phrased and included such objectives as, "restraint shall be exercised in portraying the taking of life." In publicizing this revision, the MPAA stressed that it would help to bring filmmaking into line with contemporary mores. The Production Code had been written almost forty years ago, and American society had grown more liberal and tolerant about sexual and religious matters. This trend was especially apparent among young viewers—to whose tastes the industry, then as now, wished to cater. Accordingly, the MPAA declared, "this revised code is designed to keep in closer harmony with the mores, the culture, the moral sense, and the expectations of our society."[86]

The most significant feature of the revision was its provision for designating certain films SMA (Suggested for Mature Audiences), a labeling for frank content that was intended to help expand the creative license of filmmakers. Two years later, in *Interstate v. Dallas* (1968), the Supreme Court struck down a Dallas ordinance restricting viewers under sixteen years of age from viewing films "not suitable for young persons." The Court, however, indicated that it was not averse to better-drafted legislation applying an age-based approach, and, in another case that year, *Ginsberg v. New York,* it held that minors might be prohibited from purchasing materials (in this case, erotic literature) that adults could freely possess. *Variety*, the film industry's trade paper, assessed the fallout: "Rather than killing the idea, the Court is seen as having opened the door, finally, to classification throughout the United States . . . few doubt that the floodgates have now been opened for thousands of local communities to pass [age-based] classification statutes, as long as they meet the constitutional test."[87]

The creation in 1968 of the MPAA's Code and Rating Administration, with its G-M-R-X classification scheme, has been tied to the perceived effects of the Interstate and Ginsberg rulings—effects construed as *Variety* had described them. The Court issued its Dallas ruling in April. MPAA President Jack] Valenti, "at least by mid-May and probably within two weeks after *Dallas,* saw that some voluntary classification scheme was necessary to fend off governmental classification."[88] With its age-based approach to film viewing, the CARA system represented the same kind of industry-wide voluntary reform, in response to specific outside pressure, that the Production Code had embodied in 1930. The CARA system, however, instituted new freedoms for filmmakers at the same time that it restricted children, without accompanying parents or guardians, from seeing the results of those new freedoms.

The system enabled filmmakers, for the first time, to shoot and edit films with adult content for an adult audience. In *Savage Cinema: Sam Peckinpah and the Rise of Ultraviolent Movies,* I discussed the connections between CARA and the efflorescence of graphic violence in Peckinpah's *The Wild Bunch* and the films that it, and his work generally, helped to inspire. *The Wild Bunch* went into production under the 1966 Code revision, and the PCA had rejected the script. It went into post-production (editing of picture and sound) and theatrical release under the CARA system as an R-rated film. Peckinpah was able to shoot, edit, and exhibit a newly graphic dimension of violence that would simply have been impossible to achieve in the system prevailing before 1968.

The SMA designation, and then the CARA classification system, put an end to the Production Code Administration. As noted, however, the Code system had essentially collapsed by the mid-1960s. The case files of violent films grow very thin, and the script evaluation letters contained within them have nothing to say about the presentation of what, in the old days, the agency would have called unacceptable levels of gruesomeness and brutality.

Several examples will help to clarify this. Released in 1964, Don Siegel's *The Killers* is an amazingly violent film, especially when one considers that the project was initially planned as a television movie. Loosely based on a short story by Ernest Hemingway that was previously filmed in 1948 with Burt Lancaster, the film depicts two hired killers who become curious about why their latest victim chose not to run from them but submit to his death instead. The victim, Johnny North, is working in a school for the handicapped, and the picture opens with the killers arriving at the school. In the first scene, they terrorize a blind receptionist. In a previous era, this character—who is not only blind but a woman—would almost certainly have had protected victim status, ensuring that she would be spared such harsh treatment. Nevertheless, Charlie (Lee Marvin) frightens her by playing on her inability to see and then, off-camera, beats her unconscious.

When North is cornered, the killers shoot him many times over with silenced pistols. The multiple shooting—the overkill—escalates the intensity and duration of the murder and would never have been permitted in previous decades. As we saw, the PCA often requested that filmmakers reduce the number of shots fired or punches thrown. Here, though, Charlie and his partner indulge in an orgy of shooting, blasting away at North with abandon.

The murder is interesting from a stylistic angle, as well. Director Don Siegel was a very fine editor and created, in such films as *Madigan* (1968) and *Dirty Harry* (1971), outstanding montages of gun violence. Here, though, he eschews montage in favor of varying camera speeds. North takes the first slugs in slow-motion. The camera's operating speed is then brought back to twenty-four frames per second, so that the action changes from slow-motion to normal speed within the duration of a single take. Well before *Bonnie and Clyde* popularized slow-motion, the scene manifests an early usage of the device. Unlike *Bonnie and Clyde* and the films that it inspired, however, where slow-motion shots alternate with normal speed shots in a montage, the change in camera speed occurs here within one shot. The scene thus prefigures the efflorescence of slow-motion violence in late sixties cinema, as well as being a deviant example of it.

After killing North, the hit men look into the reasons someone wanted him dead, and they follow the trail of stolen money to the ringleaders of an armored car heist. In a scene of intense brutality they question North's girlfriend, Sheila (Angie Dickenson), about the whereabouts of the money. Without warning one of the killers punches her in the face. This is not the kind of light slap that a man might occasionally administer to a woman in older pictures. It

35.   The extremely harsh and sadistic violence in *The Killers* elicited no reaction by the PCA. This wide-angle composition exaggerates the prominence of Lee Marvin's silencer. It amounts to a flamboyant brandishing of a weapon, unacceptable in earlier decades.

is a clenched-fist blow, delivered with downward force at a seated victim by a man who is standing and thereby able to put his body weight into the punch. It knocks her out of her chair and quickly raises an ugly bruise on the side of her face.

Men in movies have been punched for decades, but not women, and not in this manner. Seeing that she is insufficiently persuaded, the killers then terror-ize her by dangling her outside a high window. They hang her upside down by the feet, and threaten to drop her to the street below. But our killers are not through with her yet. In the last act of the film, Charlie shoots her at close range, as well as her lover, Jack Browning (Ronald Reagan, looking very un-Presidential as this villain), the character who masterminded the heist and hired North's killing. Filming these murders, Siegel uses a wide-angle lens to produce exaggerated images of the gun. Charlie points his pistol at the cam-era, and the silencer at the end of its barrel looms hugely in the frame, its size magnified by the short lens. These compositions are definite examples of what the Production Code had forbidden as an undue visual attention to firearms. Like the use of slow-motion earlier, during North's killing, these compositions anticipate a future line of development in American cinema, in this case the exaggerated display of firearms.

The Killers thus brings the looming shape of American cinema closer to the foreground. It contains an abundance of savagery and brutality and little of what the PCA would call a redeeming voice for morality. Much of the film is conventional and unremarkable in its audiovisual design, but these are narrative sections in which Charlie and his assistant do not appear. By contrast, when they are on-screen, the film comes alive with the energy of lovingly depicted violence. This aestheticization is where the film's true level of energy resides. Their scenes showcase the superviolence—vicious, ruthless, without limits—that became an enduring feature of post-Code cinema. Despite this, the film's case file is very thin and contains nothing on the picture's violence.

The silencing of the PCA's voice helps to erase the distinctions between Hollywood at the end of its classical era and the onset of the CARA system. Arthur Penn, of course, helped to initiate the post-Code explosion of graphic violence with *Bonnie and Clyde* in 1967. Like Aldrich, Peckinpah and Siegel, each of whom would make key films of superviolence in the post-classical period (*The Dirty Dozen, The Wild Bunch, Dirty Harry*), Penn's interests in violence pre-date that period and helped to propel American cinema toward its inception. In *The Left-Handed Gun* (1958), he showed a deputy literally blown out of his boot by the force of a shotgun blast and employed slow-motion to do so. He moved on to a greater level of lurid and explicitly detailed violence in *The Chase* (1966), a melodrama about a convict, Bubba (Robert Redford), who returns to his small hometown where his presence instigates an outbreak of vigilante violence. In the climax of the film, town thugs severely beat the sheriff, Caulder (Marlon Brando), and one of them guns Bubba down on the steps of the courthouse.

Penn visualizes both scenes with exceptional intensity, and each contains specific types of violence that in earlier times the PCA would have worked to keep off the screen. During the beating of Caulder, for example, one of the gang goes downstairs to get information from a prisoner in the jail cell. He pistol-whips the defenseless man. Like kicking and kneeing, pistol whipping had been a relatively prohibited form of violence in classical Hollywood. No longer.

Upstairs, the beating of Caulder goes on past any point the PCA would have tolerated before. The thugs beat him to the ground several times, kidney-punch him, and, with Caulder sprawled atop a desk, one thug climbs on top of the sheriff and pummels his face at length. Despite the extraordinary viciousness of the beating, however, Penn is working in a transitional era and isn't yet in the period where he can show the kind of relentless and unrestrained carnage that he depicts in *Bonnie and Clyde*. Accordingly, the scene contains one of those "stop-you'll-kill-him" moments when one of the thugs restrains another, and this brings the assault on Caulder to an end. Except for this limitation, a vestige of the classical period, the violence is vicious and excessive.

Aside from the duration of the beating, the most disturbing part of the scene is the way Penn visualizes its consequences for Caulder. Following the beating, Caulder cannot get his body to work properly. His arms and legs are uncoordinated and will not move with the synchronization necessary for standing and walking. The portrayal of this goes beyond the kind of general, nonspecific lassitude that beating victims exhibited in earlier decades. In an offshoot of the clutch-and-fall aesthetic, beating victims in classical Hollywood showed mostly fatigue during their recovery. But Penn's depiction here follows the countertradition exemplified by scenes like the beating of Ed Beaumont in *The Glass Key* and the beating that Brando sustains at the climax of *On the Waterfront* (1953), where he is bloodied, hobbled, and nearly blinded in a fight with crime boss Johnny Friendly (Lee J. Cobb).

In *The Chase,* Penn and Brando suggest that Caulder suffers a neuromuscular breakdown, which, though temporary, is thoroughly debilitating. He can barely stand, and when he moves, he does so in a grotesque and disjointed fashion. Caulder cannot even put his gunbelt on and buckle it. He staggers out of the sheriff's office and tumbles down the front steps outside the building. His face is bloody and swollen beyond recognition, and Penn includes subjective point-of-view shots indicating that Caulder can barely see. His shirt is covered with blood in an amount much greater than the relatively small quantities countenanced by the industry in earlier decades.

Later, when Caulder, one eye now closed by swelling, returns to the jail with Bubba, one of the town vigilantes shoots Bubba in the kind of sudden, unannounced attack that Jack Ruby used to kill Lee Harvey Oswald (Penn intends the comparison). The quantity of shots—five in all—is excessive, and the visualization of their impact stresses the force of the killing. No squibbing is used, but the punch of the initial shot knocks Bubba backwards off his feet. As he tries to rise, more shots hammer him down. Bubba's death does not occur quickly. It takes all five shots to kill him, and he is shown looking at the killer as the bullets go in.

With his prisoner murdered, Caulder flies into a rage and unleashes a savage beating on the assailant. The beating is unrelenting, even as Caulder's deputies try to restrain him. When they pull him away, Caulder shakes them off and continues his attack. When Caulder finishes with him, the killer is insensate and moves with the same spacticity that Caulder showed earlier. (This is the very quality that Penn aimed to evoke in the montage showing the deaths of Bonnie and Clyde. The action achieved in the actors' performances in *The Chase* prefigures what the editing and different camera speeds accomplished in that more famous murder scene.) Penn gets every detail right, even the small observations that show how a body suffering violence loses its dignity. When the deputies drag the shooter, stunned by Caulder's pummeling, up the steps and into the jail, his shirt pulls loose from his pants on one side, exposing his fleshy belly. It is a small but authentic and vivid detail. It's an awkward and unflattering sight, but it suggests how far beyond the bounds of propriety the escalating violence has taken everyone.

The carnage in the last act of *The Chase* is visually grotesque, and yet the PCA's case file on the film shows no response to this. Judging from the case file, the agency had no qualms about the proposed project.

Also released in 1966, *Duel at Diablo* was a cavalry-vs.-Indians picture

---

36. *Duel at Diablo* showed the kind of torture by burning that earlier Westerns had discretely omitted, as well as more abundant and graphic arrow strikes. The PCA made no response.

that added doses of hard brutality to the familiar story. Two characters in the film are roasted over open fires—one of them on-camera, screaming in pain. In each case their charred, ash-covered limbs are prominently shown, a detailing that earlier Westerns had omitted. Elsewhere in the film the hero, James Garner, puts a knife to a man's throat and draws blood. The most vividly depicted violence involves the kind of wounding and killing by sharp bladed instruments that the PCA was keen to avoid in previous decades. The Indians shoot arrows into the legs, arms, hands, backs, and chests of the soldiers in greater quantities, and with more convincing penetration, than earlier Westerns had depicted. As documented in the case file, the PCA had nothing to say about any of this. Its only response to the project's proposed violence was the recommendation that the filmmakers consult with the American Humane Association in regards to the handling of horses. (Since *The Charge of the Light Brigade* in 1936, the filming of which injured and killed numerous horses, the PCA had been careful to refer filmmakers with new projects to the AHA.)

The carnage in Robert Aldrich's *The Dirty Dozen* helped to make it one of the most controversial pictures of 1967. The army recruits twelve felons for a commando raid on a German chateau, where they are to kill as many German officers as they can. This they do, along with numerous women, by dousing them with gasoline and setting them afire. The picture also contains abundant shootings and stabbings, and yet the PCA case file shows that the agency's concerns about the project lay exclusively with the script's profanity and with a scene where a group of hookers visit the dozen, a scene that the agency deemed to be "totally unacceptable."[89] The script evaluation letters contain no reaction to the film's remarkable level of violence, and material in the Robert Aldrich collection at the American Film Institute confirms that the major problem area on which script negotiations focused was the abundance of profanity.

CONCLUSION

The appearance of *The Dirty Dozen* and *Bonnie and Clyde* in 1967 helped to make that year the major signpost of the changes in American cinema in respect to screen violence. And yet the fundamental rule of film history is that nothing ever happens for the first time. As this chapter and the preceding ones have shown, the investment by filmmakers in depicting strong violence goes back decades—and it was the forces of regional censorship, coupled with the industry's voluntary system of compliance with PCA directives, that kept the level and intensity of violence under relative control during the period of classical Hollywood. I say relative control because, as we have seen, the PCA's word was not final and filmmakers could find stylistic ways of evading the agency. The human torches in *The Dirty Dozen* and the machine-gun mangling of Bonnie and Clyde represented the outcome of forces that had been building for decades. But in the imaginations of filmmakers, those characters had been dying in that fashion for a long, long time.

5

The Poetics of
Screen Violence

The ongoing tensions between filmmakers, the Production Code Administration (PCA), and the nation's regional censor boards left a long-term legacy to American film. That legacy was the creation of a visual approach for representing violence that avoided the simple dynamic of transgression/suppression—filmmakers doing something naughty, censors cutting it out—that typified the industry's relation with the regional boards. This visual approach was based on the logic of a substitutional poetics, whereby unacceptable types of violence could be depicted not directly, but through various kinds of image substitution. By replacing the offensive or impermissible image or action with a less offensive substitute, the substitute could be used to evoke the more problematic, and censorable, representation.

As Ruth Vasey has pointed out, "the general effect of industry regulation was to encourage the elision, or effacement of sensitive subjects."[1] The forms of visual rhetoric that I analyze in this chapter are examples of such elision. Using them helped filmmakers and the industry to solve the problem of how to depict actions on-screen that were essential to a story but involved some category of prohibited content. Thus, the evolution of a taxonomy of substitutional types proved to be an excellent means of avoiding the many problems that were inherent in the tangle of regulatory action that governed filmmaking until the fall of censorship in the 1960s. By deflecting problematic content into safer modes of expression, filmmakers were able, to an extent, to bypass the vagaries of individual censor boards.

Moreover, elaborating the codes of substitutional poetics helped to expand the creative possibilities of expression in American cinema. This poetics gave filmmakers a wider range of visual devices for portraying violence, and this range was especially important at a time when regional censorship operated to constrict the depiction of violence. As these codes became established and familiar through usage they acquired a degree of legitimization, both for filmmakers and the PCA, which was useful for resolving questions about how much and what kind of violence to show in a given production. When the PCA deemed a particular kind of violence to be unacceptable, either because it was too gruesome or because it contravened a specific section of the Code—a cop killing, for example—the use of substitutional poetics could provide a compromise solution to the problem.

This chapter examines the basic codes of this visual system. They are, in a sense, filmmaking "norms" in the manner that David Bordwell discussed in *The Classical Hollywood Cinema*—except that, rather than originating in response to the demands of production or technology, they arose primarily from regulatory pressures and as a solution to those pressures. Bordwell pointed out that any given film was likely to contain an aberrant and less than ideal mixture of the classical norms of time, space, and narrative. "The idea of multiple norms impinging upon the same work helps us see that it is unlikely that any Hollywood film will perfectly embody all norms . . . No Hollywood film *is* the classical system; each is an 'unstable equilibrium' of classical norms."[2]

In the same way, Hollywood films may exhibit one or more of the codes of substitutional poetics *and* more graphic and transgressive depictions of violence. Filmmakers might resort to substitutional poetics in one sequence and, in another, to a provocatively explicit depiction of violence. The presence of one or more substitutional codes in a film, then, should not be taken as implying that the film overall is necessarily discreet in its depiction of violence.

One more caveat is necessary. The devices that I will identify and analyze are not violence-specific—that is, filmmakers are not bound to use them only with reference to violent material. Because the logic of these codes is one of elision and substitution, they are excellent devices for handling many kinds of prohibited content areas. Depictions of sex, for example, may employ these codes. The train entering a tunnel at the end of *North by Northwest* (1959), which substitutes for the lovemaking of Roger Thornhill and Eve Kendall, is an example of the device that I call metonymic displacement. While I examine this and other devices in terms of they way they facilitated the expression of violent content, their usage was not bound only to that category of content. At a time when the regional censors were the ultimate arbiters of motion picture content, the codes of substitutional poetics aimed to allay the reaction of these boards and might be used by filmmakers with reference to a variety of content areas.

These codes were especially useful when the cameras turned on scenes of violence, and they became basic components of Hollywood filmmaking. Understood as norms of the system, they are trans-director and trans-genre. They supersede the style of Hollywood's auteurs, and they supersede genre. They operated in Westerns, war films, gangster films, swashbuckling adventure pictures, Biblical spectacles, spy films—in virtually any genre where the depicted violence entailed serious consequences to the human body. In terms of auteur considerations, they seem not to be the invention of any particular filmmaker but became a kind of visual Esperanto, available to all. Thus, auteurs like Alfred Hitchcock and Stanley Kubrick employ these codes as well as Hollywood filmmakers who have a less distinctive stylistic personality.

But there is another sense in which the codes of substitutional poetics furnished American film with a supra-system of visual rhetoric. If these codes subsume issues of genre and directorial style, as a master set that contains these areas as smaller sets within, they also transcend time periods. While I will discuss them within the time frame of classical Hollywood, where they had their greatest utility as a means of evading censorship, they have become so embedded within the creative language of American cinema that filmmakers today continue to employ them at a time when there is virtually nothing in the way of screen violence that cannot be shown. From a strictly regulatory standpoint, there is no reason to employ them any longer. Because filmmakers today can freely depict any sort of violence, they would seem no longer to need a rhetoric of visual evasion.

The continued usage of these codes points to the great paradox of movie censorship: that there are times when indirection is powerful and is to be prized. While censorship restricted expression, it also encouraged the operation of the imagination in viewers who had to picture for themselves what otherwise was not shown, and for filmmakers who had to devise ways of suggesting what they couldn't depict openly. Restrictions on the image, paradoxically, open onto plenitude—the rich and fertile area of the imagination—which requires very little data to perform prodigious feats of creation. The oblique image, violence hinted but not displayed, can arouse the viewer's imaginings with great ferocity. Thus, even in otherwise graphic works, filmmakers today employ the old system of substitutional rhetoric as a way of returning visual poetry to depictions of carnage that have become mundane with a level of explicitness that is no longer remarkable. This poetry of the indirect accompanies the more graphic imagery of today's films in a state of "unstable equilibrium." Used in place of graphic imagery in contemporary film, it restores an eloquence of expression that splatter effects often degrade. As I discuss the codes of the system, I will mention some of the contemporary filmmaking in which their usage persists.

Five visual codes provide the foundation for the poetics of violence in classical Hollywood cinema. They are: *spatial displacement, metonymic displacement, indexical pointing, substitutional emblematics,* and *emotional bracketing.*

SPATIAL DISPLACEMENT

This is the master code whose logic and function organize the *metonymic* and *indexical* variants. Spatial displacement operates to remove instances of egregious violence from the eye of the camera and spectator. Editing or moving the camera away from the main line of action activates the code. Rather than directly showing a beating, stabbing, shooting, or the bloody results of these acts, a filmmaker using spatial displacement will cut away, either to a new scene or to some other object or character in the vicinity of the violence that has been suppressed. The cutaways act as covers for the violence that is not directly shown. An alternative means of creating spatial displacement involves methods of framing the action so that those portions of the frame holding violence are occluded from view. This is a form of intra-shot displacement, in contrast to the inter-shot displacements achieved by editing cutaways. It can be achieved using camera movement or changes in the blocking of actors.

Spatial displacement removes the viewer from a vantage point where violence may be directly witnessed. It offers an oblique approach. The viewer typically knows the kind of violence that has been (or is about to be) perpetrated, but the scene is structured so as to transport the viewer out of the immediate time and space of the act. In *The Set-Up* (1949), for example, when the mobsters corner Robert Ryan, playing a washed-up boxer, the dialogue establishes that they are going to break his hand, and when the cutaway occurs— to a crashing cymbal in a jazz band—it introduces no ambiguity about the action that is occurring out of sight. The viewer knows that Ryan is getting his hand broken. It does, however, create ambiguity about what the action—the hand breaking—*looks* like, and this goes to the heart of the matter. The politics of the period placed some kinds of violence off-limits to visual representation. By creating an ambiguity around that very issue—the appearance of censured forms of violence—spatial displacement provided filmmakers with a means for indirectly depicting things that could otherwise not be shown.

In most instances, spatial displacement does not create serious narrative ambiguities. The code, though, does foreground itself as a rhetorical form governing the presentation of extreme violence. Seeing the code, the viewer understands its operation and those things that it implicitly references. These are not just the details of the violence that has been occluded from view; it is also the presence of the system of film censorship and regulation governing screen content in this period. The code points to the operation of that system within the film. Seeing the code, a viewer knows that it is working to conceal violence from the camera. The code marks that violence as being beyond the bounds of what is acceptable. Doing so, it necessarily reminds viewers of the act of suppression that has called it into existence.

I'm not suggesting by this that the viewer's awareness of spatial displacement works in any kind of intellectualized Brechtian sense. The code doesn't break the illusion of the film narrative or even remind viewers that they are watching a movie. Conventional film theory has grossly overstated and mystified the mental conditions that accompany film viewing. Movie viewers in the 1940s, seeing spatial displacement, simply understood what it was and what it signified: that there was violence in the story they were not permitted to see. In this sense, the assumptions they would make as viewers differ significantly from what a contemporary film viewer might infer. In a period when censorship and regulation of screen content were an everyday reality, viewers understood the moments of discretion created by spatial displacement as instances of that regulation. The screen did not show everything. Visual discretion was an anticipated, expected, natural, and normal part of the screen experience. In this way, far from constituting a threat to continuity or to the norms of classical filmmaking, editing that deflected visual attention away from the main line of the narrative was thoroughly rationalized as one of the norms of that system, even though it might require the use of non-normative camera set-ups and editing methods.

In *Objective, Burma!* (1945), Captain Nelson (Errol Flynn) leads a group of Allied paratroopers into Japanese-occupied Burma during World War II to blow up a radar installation. The Japanese capture several of Nelson's men, torture them to death, and leave the bodies for their comrades to find. As I discussed in an earlier chapter, the PCA felt that this violence constituted excessive brutality and gruesomeness and stipulated to Warner Bros. that the mutilations would have to be conveyed by suggestion and "with no attempt to photograph them directly."[3]

The action in the film jumps over the capturing and torture deaths. These occur off screen. When Nelson and the others come upon the bodies, spatial displacement prevents us from seeing the details. The horror-struck faces of the soldiers convey the extreme nature of the disfigurements. Several levels of displacement operate in the scene. Nelson and his men catch up to an advance patrol that has stopped in a village, and Prescott, one of the scouts, tells Nelson that the patrol has found his boys. Prescott says that he wishes he hadn't found them, that they're all cut to pieces. This dialogue serves to remove ambiguity about the nature of the details that will not be shown to the camera, and it serves to cue a cut to a close-up of Nelson's face. As Prescott continues off-camera, saying, "they're too awful to look at," the dialogue explains the rationale for the scene's visual displacement and we see Nelson in close-up absorbing this news. His jaw drops, and his eyes wander off-frame and finally settle on a point beyond the lower right border of the screen. He stares at this area with fixed intensity as a musical cue plays his emotional response.

After a moment, he crosses to a new location where he will be able to see the bodies. A brief point of view shot—only two seconds in duration—shows the legs of the dead men protruding from a copse of trees. The cut that follows shows a reaction shot of Nelson and his men, turning their faces away in disgust and nausea from what they—but not the film's viewer—can see.

Intra-frame and inter-frame displacement operate here. Most immediately, when the camera provided a shot of the bodies, it was only a partial view, concealing the mutilations. We see only the lower legs of the dead men. The trees and the frame line block our access to what Nelson and his men can clearly see. The camera's positioning relative to the trees occludes our line of sight, but not theirs. The characters in the scene have an unrestricted visual access to the bodies; we, the film viewer, do not.

The reaction shots depicting Nelson and his men responding to what they see operate as a secondary level of displacement. These are medium shots and close-ups of their facial reactions. In these shots the bodies are off-camera, and the details of the violence are implicitly referenced through the reactions of the characters. Nelson scans the bodies (i.e., he looks off-camera), but he can't recognize anyone. "That's Harris, isn't it?" he murmurs. "But who are the others?" The soldier next to him cries out that he wouldn't know them even if they were his own brothers. This action and dialogue convey the scripted information that the PCA had censured the studio from filming—namely, that the faces of the dead are mutilated beyond recognition. Nelson says, "take it easy. They can't feel anything [pause] now." The pause tells the viewer about the horror of what the men did feel as they died under torture. This and other dialogue spoken in the reaction shots gives the viewer more information about that which the camera cannot show. Thus, the mutilations, which were not to be photographed, are indirectly depicted by (a) shots that block the action in a manner that impedes a full view of the bodies and (b) reaction shots of the witnesses in which the bodies are off-camera. The reaction shots convey information about the mutilations visually through the facial responses of the witnesses, and verbally in the things they say about what they see.

Lieutenant Jacobs, however, is not among this group of dead. Nelson finds him still alive, sprawled inside the village temple. He, too, has been tortured and mutilated. As in the previous scene, a masking device within the frame prevents us from seeing his condition. He lies in a doorway, with the camera positioned outside so that only his lower legs are visible, protruding beyond the doorframe. Nelson stoops down to help him, but stays outside the room so the camera can frame him with the lower portion of Jacobs's legs that protrude beyond the doorframe. Jacobs will remain off-camera throughout the scene, except for this view of his legs. The explicit masking created by the doorframe emphasizes the off-limits character of the atrocity—off-limits to pictorial representation. The occlusion provided by the doorframe instantiates the operation of censorship, making it tangible and inescapably apparent in the visual design of the scene. Viewers in 1944 would not fail to notice this, but neither would they make much of it. It is simply the "what is" of screen violence in the period.

The scene's sound design shows the industry's continuing suppression of explicit audio depictions of extreme pain. When Jacobs speaks, his voice conveys no anguish or suffering. There are no shrieks, no cries, no sustained moans of the sort that we found in *Murders in the Rue Morgue* (1932) and *Island of Lost Souls* (1933). He is simply fatigued. He speaks very softly and with great weariness, the fatigue being a cover for, and a trope to suggest, the pain and disfigurement that have been inflicted upon him. An organ softly plays the musical score for the scene, linking the action to a religious context and transubstantiating the pain of the flesh into the transcendence of the spirit.

When Jacobs quietly asks Nelson to kill him, the action cuts to a camera set-up inside the room where he lies, framing Nelson in a frontal, head-on fashion. We see Nelson from Jacobs' point of view. By its nature, this subjective framing excludes the disfigured man from the field of view. The subjective framing provides another means of concealing Jacobs from the camera. In this framing Nelson's face is dimly lit and the wall inside the doorframe to his right is unlit, creating a wide, black column that runs along the edge of the screen from top to bottom. The low-level lighting and the black border tell us that the room contains things that should not be revealed to the eye or to the light of day—except through Nelson, who will be our mediator between the zones of vision and the zones of occlusion established by the lighting, framing, and blocking of the action.

In the end, of course, Nelson is spared the necessity of putting Jacobs out of his misery. The poor man dies without his assistance and without the camera ever filming the room from Nelson's point of view. The standard Hollywood method for filming dialogue scenes—shot–reverse-shot cutting—is not employed here because each shot change would reveal the reciprocal views of the speakers, and Nelson's view (of Jacobs) must be suppressed. Jacobs's view of Nelson can be shown and is, in the subjective shots. But subjective

37–38. Spatial displacement in *Objective, Burma!* A doorway that blocks the camera's line of sight and a nonreciprocal point-of-view shot serve to hide a horribly mutilated soldier from view.

framings are not part of standard shot–reverse-shot framings. The requirement for spatial displacement means that the editing of the scene must build the action using some method other than shot–reverse-shot cutting. That alternative is provided by editing between two non-normative camera set-ups, at approximately ninety-degree angles to one another. One set-up is the subjective framing from inside the room, showing Jacobs's view of Nelson. The other set-up frames Nelson outside the room and the lower portion of Jacobs's legs, but occludes Nelson's field of view. Whereas shot–reverse-shot cutting shows both speakers and their fields of view, the set-ups here show nonreciprocal fields of view.

This approach does not subvert the norms of classical cinema, nor should it be interpreted as instancing any ambiguities of space or point of view. The oblique visual approach poses no problems of this kind. It is clearly motivated by events in the narrative that cannot be shown directly, and it creates no ambiguities about the narrative situation, action, or point of view. A 1940s viewer would experience no problems in contextualizing the relatively unconventional camerawork and editing. They point to the boundaries on representational content beyond which films in the period would not go.

The branding scene in *Captain Blood* (1935), the swashbuckling adventure picture that made Errol Flynn a star, provides another example of non-normative editing in the service of spatial displacement. The evil manager of an island plantation tells his underlings to brand the face of a slave who has tried to escape. The victim is bound to a wooden cross. He stands with one cheek against the cross, the other exposed to the brand. The iron is heated in a fire until it glows, and the branding is shown on-screen, with no cutaways to displace the action. Instead, the camera set-ups block a clear view of the branding. One set-up frames the victim from the side of his face opposite the one being branded. The other set-up places the edge of the wooden cross between the camera and the victim's face. Editing between the two set-ups entails crossing the line of action. The editing breaks the 180-degree rule that provides for continuity of screen direction. It occasions no loss of coherence in the action; the branding remains clear enough. But it's an irregularity in the conventional approach to filming continuity and suggests that the need to block the action and shoot for visual displacement might lead a filmmaker to some atypical choices about camera set-ups and how to edit among them. As such, the construction of visual displacement would occasionally produce shot structures alternative to traditional Hollywood decoupage.

The blocking of the action in this scene from *Captain Blood* creates framing devices internal to the shots, which serve to occlude the violence. This is a standard and common method for creating visual displacement, and we noted its use as well in *Objective, Burma!* Props, doorways, the edges of walls, foliage, other characters—numerous objects on-screen can serve as shields to cover violence, intervening between the camera and its line of sight. When James Cagney guns Humphrey Bogart at the end of *The Roaring Twenties* (1939), Bogie falls behind a chair, which shields him from the view of the camera when Cagney shoots him. The possibilities for providing visual displacement in this manner are limited only by the range of materials and locations contained in a scene.

In *This Gun for Hire* (1943), a professional assassin named Raven (Alan Ladd) takes down a hit, a blackmailer who's trying to extort money from Raven's boss. Raven expected the man to be alone, but his secretary is lounging around the apartment. Apparently, they are having an affair. Raven pulls a pistol and shoots the man. He turns the gun on the secretary and pulls the trigger, but it misfires. That gives her time to run into the kitchen and the filmmakers time to put together a splendid displacement. It wasn't kosher in 1943 to shoot a woman on-screen in cold-blooded murder, but you might do it through a door. She runs into the kitchen and slams the door shut. Raven walks over and drills her through the door. We can't see her, of course, because the camera stays with Raven outside the closed door, but we hear her body hit the floor. To make sure he's got her, Raven tries to open the door but has trouble because she has fallen against it. With some effort he shoves it part way open and looks inside. Now he sees what the camera does not, framing the action from its position in the adjoining room. The edge of the opened door becomes another frame, shielding our view from the results of Raven's handiwork, which he is in the process of approving. He is not looking off-frame but at an occluded area within the frame, the occlusion serving to conceal a degree of violence best referenced through indirection.

The murder of the Indian agent, played by John McIntire, in *Winchester '73* (1950) is signaled by a sudden occlusion of the entire frame and a burst of music. McIntire has brought a pack of old, shoddy rifles to a band of Indians who are led by Rock Hudson in warpaint. Young Bull (Hudson) spies the fancy, titular Winchester in McIntire's saddle and tells him he wants it. McIntire refuses, and Young Bull leaps between the camera and McIntire. His broad back fills the frame, blocking our view. With a burst of music, a dissolve takes us out of the scene. Young Bull's occlusion of the frame, and the dissolve that follows, provide for a complete displacement of the ensuing violence. In order to let the viewer know what has happened to McIntire, the film shows a band of outlaws finding his body in the next scene. His body stays off-camera, but the dialogue makes it clear that he has been scalped.

In *The Naked Prey* (1966), a village of Zulu warriors set out on a ritual hunt.

Their quarry is a white man (Cornel Wilde), whom they have given a head start. One by one the warriors close in for the kill. After a fight with spears and then knives, Wilde severs the carotid artery of one. A tree trunk occludes this action. Up to this point the fight has been filmed in the full openness of the Panavision frame. But when Wilde slashes his victim's throat, the camera films them from behind a tree so that the victim is blocked from view. A blood spurt hits Wilde in the chest and shoulder, but the knife slash is hidden from view.

In contrast to intra-shot displacement, more elaborate designs use editing to move the optical focus away from the open display of violence. In its most straightforward form, inter-frame spatial displacement involves the use of editing to drop in a series of "extra" shots that shift the optical focus of the scene to an area outside of the violent action. Often, this area may be adjacent to the space in which the violence is occurring or, alternatively, it may be more distant from it. During the beating scene in *Brute Force* (1947), when Captain Munsey interrogates one of the prison inmates and beats him with a rubber truncheon, most of the violence is elided by edits that provide framings from which Munsey and his victim are excluded. The first of these occurs just after Munsey strikes the first blow. When he prepares to strike his victim, he stands up and the camera dollies forward to him. It had been framing both characters in a medium-shot, and the move to a tight framing of Munsey places his victim off-camera when the first blow falls.

Obviously, the camera move provides a degree of intra-shot displacement, but the significant inter-shot displacements now occur. The editing cuts outside Munsey's office for three shots, to a room where a group of prison guards are playing cards. They can hear the beating, as does the viewer—five distinct blows. We first see the guards in a group framing, then a close-up of a single guard, then a repeat of the group framing. The men look uncomfortable and disgusted. One stands up and slams his cards to the table, providing the implicit condemnation of the beating that the PCA had asked for (see chapter four).

After this three-shot displacement we return to Munsey's office, and the action resumes in the same framing where we left it. In low-angle, Munsey reaches forward and pulls his bloody, semiconscious victim into the frame. He repeats his questioning but still gets no answer, and this prompts another round of beating, cuing a second intervention by the editing to displace the violence from the camera's view. This time, the displaced framings remain within the office. Before he resumes his attack, Munsey goes to his phonograph and turns up the volume. The implication is that this beating will be even more savage, and he needs the music to cover it. The camera frames him by the phonograph, his victim off-screen. As he walks back to his victim the

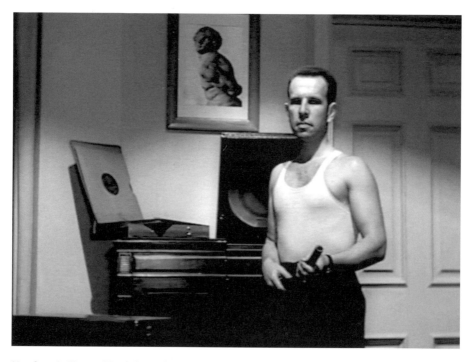

39. Captain Munsey (Hume Cronyn) turns up the volume on his phonograph to cover the cries of his victim. But when he resumes the beating, the editing displaces the violence with shots of neutral objects in the office.

camera begins to dolly with him, and then the edited displacement begins: three shots showing various objects inside the office (the phonograph, a line of potted plants along the window, and a portrait of Munsey on the wall). Except for the phonograph, these inserts have no connection to the narrative. The objects they show are relatively random, and their appearance is somewhat reminiscent of the way Japanese director Yasujiro Ozu uses object inserts as a means of leaping over narrative time and space. As in Ozu's films, there is a degree of temporal ambiguity. After the three inserts, the editing cuts to a shot of Munsey shaking his victim, and the viewer cannot say how much time has elapsed or how severe the beating, or whether an additional beating has occurred. The raised volume on the phonograph and the three inserts imply that it has: yet unlike what accompanied the shots with the guards outside the office, there have been no sounds of beating. This lack of fit between the visual and audio information creates an interesting evasiveness, enabling the film to be relatively nonspecific about the extent of the violence in the scene.

Using spatial displacement to create ambiguity provided a useful means for getting around prohibited forms of violence. *13 Rue Madeleine* (1947) climaxes with an extended torture scene. Office of Secret Service agent James Cagney suffers what one character describes as "the cruelest tortures the Nazis can devise." That he will talk is inevitable, given the magnitude of the torture. The OSS chief explains that no human body can withstand such abuse. Not surprisingly for the period, this torture is not depicted. Camera set-ups stay outside the room where it is occurring. A group of Nazis waits there, listening to the off-screen whipping. Their leader waits for Cagney to crack, and shots of his anxious face are intercut with framings of the torture room door, which is closed, sealing the room from view. Even when the door is opened Cagney remains off-frame, hidden from view until the penultimate shot of the film when his bloody body is revealed just before the Allied bombs fall and obliterate the house. Because of these framings, the "cruelest tortures" that can be devised are left to the viewer's imagination. Those that are conveyed through the audio information are quite mundane. Whipping, however nasty, is hardly what the dialogue and the visual displacement have invited us to conjure.

These ambiguities in *Brute Force* and *13 Rue Madeleine* are strategic and serve the regulatory policies of the PCA and the regional censor boards. If, however, the spatial displacements are awkwardly handled—if they are too abrupt or the cutaways are too brief to cover the amount of narrative action they are meant to conceal—then instead of creating a strategic ambiguity the displacements may cause confusion about what is happening in the scene. In *Back to Bataan* (1945) the Japanese, occupying the Philippines in World War II, try to force a school principal to take down the American flag. He refuses, and the Japanese commander tells him that unless he takes it down, he will hang with the flag from the pole. The commander wraps cord from the flagpole around the principal's neck, and when the man again refuses, the commander tugs on the cord.

As soon as he does this, the scene launches into a displacement of the hanging. At the moment the cord is tugged, the action cuts from a close-up of the principal to shots of horrified onlookers averting their faces and a priest performing the last rites. These reactions imply that the poor man is already aloft and swinging from the flagpole, and all of this has occurred within an instant of screen time. Even allowing for the ambiguities of time and space that displacement can create, there is too much discrepancy here between the before and the after. The principal was standing beneath the flagpole, and the Japanese commander had no means of hoisting him up except through brute strength, and this would require at least a few moments to get him aloft.

Following the two cutaways to the onlookers, a shot shows two Japanese soldiers tugging on the flagpole cord to raise the victim up in the air. This shot, though, the only one of its kind, is not in the best position in the

217

sequence. For the sake of narrative clarity it would have been better to place it *before* the reaction shots of the onlookers. Doing so would have extended the duration between the commander's signal to hang the principal and the reactions of the onlookers that denote the man's death. As the editing is now, the execution has no duration; the killing occupies no screen time, which may have been a desirable effect from the standpoint of regulation. The principal is instantly dead the moment the commander signals for him to be hung.

After the shot of the soldiers tugging on the cord, another cutaway shows us a saddened young man in the crowd, and then the interval of displacement is marked as being formally closed with a shot that shows the hanging victim. He is framed discretely, his upper body covered by the American flag, only his lower legs visible below it.

The awkward editing of this scene creates a much less serviceable set of ambiguities than those in *Objective, Burma!*, *Brute Force*, and *13 Rue Madeleine*. The narrative action is confusingly portrayed, and the interval of displacement begins too soon, ends too quickly, and lacks the details that it needs to properly reference and clarify the action that is occurring off-camera.

In the examples from *Objective, Burma!*, *Back to Bataan*, and *Brute Force*, the interval of displaced space is clearly marked with a beginning and an end. The camera's discreet framing of the action is set with boundary points, defining its onset and conclusion and therefore its duration. Not all instances of the code, however, work like this. In some cases, the beginning or the end of the displaced shot series lacks a marker or the series itself is positioned in an unusual location in the overall sequence of violent action. In *The Roaring Twenties* (1939), for example, Bogart and Cagney are robbing a liquor warehouse when a security guard (who, coincidentally, had been their army sergeant during the World War) surprises them. Bogart clubs him with a gun, action that is displaced into a shadow-play silhouette. The camera then frames the guard, who has been knocked to the ground, in a medium-shot. He draws his gun but Bogart kicks it away. The camera then cuts away from the guard and stays on Bogart, in a close-up and then in a two-shot with Cagney, who is watching from a distance. The guard does not reappear in the framing. Cagney calls to Bogart that it's time to go, but Bogart, who is looking down and off-frame to the left, viciously shoots the unarmed guard, who is off-camera.

When he fires, it activates two levels of displacement. In one, the guard is off-frame. In the other, however, the camera cuts away from Bogart to a close-up of Cagney at the moment the shot is fired so that we are looking at Cagney, not Bogart, when this happens. Not only is the shooting victim off-frame, but the shooter is, too. After Bogart fires, the editing returns to a two-shot showing Cagney rushing over to Bogart. Cagney angrily tells him that he didn't have to do that. He pulls Bogart away, and they run to their getaway truck and speed away outside the warehouse, where they exchange fire with another guard and drive through the front gate. But in all of this action, the camera never returns to provide a view of the guard whom Bogart has shot—a composition that would serve to close the interval of spatial displacement. In this sense, the editing never takes the viewer out of that interval. The narrative proper simply resumes within it.

Unlike metonymic displacement or indexical pointing, which create categories of logical relationship between what is omitted and what is shown, spatial displacement simply involves a decentering of optical focus away from the line of narrative action containing violence. It is, therefore, a somewhat less inflected, less inventive, and expressive mode of displacement than these other categories. Like them, however, it provided filmmakers with a form of visual rhetoric tailored to the needs of regulation. This rhetoric has become an enduring part of the screen language of violence, persisting beyond the era to whose politics it was responsive and which made it necessary.

Sam Peckinpah, for example, employed it regularly. Peckinpah was the key filmmaker who popularized ultraviolence in the years following the onset of the Code and Rating Administration system in 1968. The bloody squibs, slow motion, and elaborate montages of violence in his films became synonymous with the newly graphic violence of modern cinema and established a stylistic template for filming and editing graphic gunbattles that filmmakers still employ today. Peckinpah also showed discretion in his presentation of violence, and one of the ways he did this was to employ visual displacement. In *Straw Dogs* (1971), he uses intra-shot displacement during a key moment of violence. When the protagonist, David Sumner (Dustin Hoffman) beats a man to death with an iron poker, his victim is hidden from view by a sofa which he has fallen behind. Similarly, in *Bring Me the Head of Alfredo Garcia* (1974), when Benny (Warren Oates) pumps some extra bullets into a man who has tried to ambush him, Peckinpah films the action from behind an open car door. As the sofa does in *Straw Dogs*, the open door blocks the victim from the camera's view and thereby hides the damage being done to his body. In *Alfredo Garcia*, Peckinpah also uses inter-shot displacement, employing editing to cut away from the scene where a ruthless rancher instructs his henchmen to break his daughter's arm. As they twist her arm inside a baroque, manorial room, Peckinpah cuts completely outside the space of the scene, going to a high-angle long shot outside of the hacienda just before the arm is broken.

In *Body Double* (1984), Brian De Palma plays with this code in order to fool the viewer into thinking that he will be relatively discrete in depicting a terrible drill murder. As the killer impales his victim with a huge power drill, De Palma films this with a sofa occluding the camera's view of the action and with shots of the ceiling of the room below, through which the end of the drill punches. So far, so good—the scene's design is consistent with the objectives of visual displacement. But at the end of the scene, he shows the horribly impaled victim. The strategies of occlusion lessen some of the graphicness of the scene, but since the picture was produced in the mid-1980s, when there were few restraints, De Palma can invoke the code and then go on, essentially, to ignore it. Nevertheless, though it is inflected somewhat differently in *Body Double,* the operation of visual displacement is a clear part of the scene's design.

In *Reservoir Dogs* (1992), Quentin Tarantino abbreviates the level of explicitness in the famous ear-cutting scene by moving the camera away from the bloody act at the moment it is being committed. The camera move serves to place the violence off-screen visually, though not aurally since the victim's shrieks continue in full force on the soundtrack. The camera move does not reveal or anticipate some new action or character, nor does it move to follow some other action. The move is purely self-referential, pulling the viewer's eye away from the violence by displacing it into an off-screen area of space.

These continuities across eras in the use of this code suggest that it has settled in and become part of the deep structure of cinema—just like point-of-view editing, the 180-degree rule, and the angled, three-quarter view of facial close-ups. It is trans-director, trans-genre, and trans-historical period.

METONYMIC DISPLACEMENT

This code is a form of spatial displacement in which the occlusive or evasive composition contains some object or action that stands in for the violence that is occurring out of view. Whereas spatial displacement involves various strategies for keeping violence out of sight, its metonymic variant adds elements that embody or symbolize the off-frame violence. These metonymic elements are typically quite explicit and denotative: The viewer has no trouble inferring the substitutional meaning that they propose. Too much subtlety in their design, in fact, will tend to nullify the purpose and utility of this code. If the metonyms are not subtle, however, they are often extremely creative, and they can sometimes surprise and startle viewers with their inventiveness. The metonym is a smart flourish that transforms spatial displacement into this rather more interesting code.

The killing of Gaffney (Boris Karloff) in *Scarface* (1932) occurs by way of a clever metonym. He belongs to a rival gang that has been at war with Tony Camonte's mob. Tony and his boys track Gaffney to a bowling alley, and they sneak in to ambush their quarry. Numerous members of Camonte's gang accompany him into the bowling alley, and the group watches as Gaffney rolls a strike. The camerawork emphasizes this action. We see Gaffney in a medium close-up as he rolls the ball. The action then cuts to a panning shot that follows the ball down the lane and shows it crashing into the pins. They all fall cleanly for a strike. Another cut shows Gaffney's scorecard being marked for a strike.

Gaffney's skill with the ball, and specifically the action of him rolling a strike, has been emphasized in order to provide a contrast with the subsequent metonymic imagery. This contrast will give that imagery greater articulation and emphasis. Gaffney tells his bowling partner to try his luck, and the camera cuts away to show several shots of Camonte and his men taking up various positions throughout the bowling alley. No guns are visible in any of these shots. When the camera returns to Gaffney, he is preparing to roll another ball. Just as he releases the ball, a short burst of machine-gun fire is heard off-screen, and Gaffney recoils and begins to fall. Before he hits the ground, however, the camera pans away from him to follow the ball down the lane. It hits the pins smartly, like before, but this time they all fall except for one. As another burst of machine-gun fire is heard off-frame, this pin rocks back and forth, spins around, and finally collapses. After a moment, the shot fades out.

The lack of subtlety that is a feature of metonymic displacement is quite apparent here. But the objective of the code cannot be achieved with excessive subtlety. Not only is the sole remaining pin a metonym for Gaffney; the duration of its fall is a displaced means for embodying the idea that Gaffney takes a few moments to die. In fact, it evidently takes a second round of machine-gun fire to finish him off, and this causal relationship is established by having the pin "react" to the gunfire. The shooting stops when it finally topples over.

Although we do briefly see Gaffney react to being shot before the camera pans away from him, his death plays off-frame, as does the shooting. There are no images of Camonte and his gang after the cutaways that showed them stationing themselves around the bowling alley prior to the shooting. Consequently, within the scene one cannot say who it was that shot Gaffney or at what distance or from where the shots came. The editing elides all of this narrative information.

Unlike spatial displacement, the metonymic variant adds poetic value to a scene, this poetry being located in the way that metonymy is concretized in an object or action. This added value often provided a sufficient means for a filmmaker to use the code. Although he is hit with two bursts of machine-gun fire, Gaffney's murder does not seem so brutal as to risk censorship action. The murder is displaced onto the action of the falling pins, and though they stand in with some specificity for the details of Gaffney's death the very action of standing in serves to blunt some of the brutality of the killing. The brutality has been sublimated poetically. This poetic sublimation serves to remove the graphic edge from the killing. Thus, its displacement into metonymy is motivated by this "added value" consideration, and in a film with an extraordinary level of violence like this one, that consideration could play a strategic function. By using metonymic displacement to offset the explicitness of some of the film's killings the filmmakers gained room to show harder violence elsewhere in the film, as in the montage of machine-gun deaths climaxing in the St. Valentine's Day massacre.

Doorway to Hell (1930) provides another example where metonymic displacement substitutes for a murder. In this splendid sequence no details of the murder are depicted on-camera, making its displacement even more thorough. On the basis of the metonyms in the scene the viewer must infer that the murder has occurred. In the story, gangland boss Louis Ricarno (Lew Ayres) forces the city's bootleg gangs to consolidate, but when he retires, they start warring against one another. Ricarno's kid brother is one of the casualties, killed by a character known as the Midget. In this scene, Ricarno gets his revenge.

We see him take a violin case—in gangster movies these always contain an automatic weapon—into a storefront cleaners. Inside, he draws the blinds. The Midget approaches on the street, having been told that a payoff he's expecting will take place in the cleaners. Cutaways show a policeman and other pedestrians nearby. Their presence complicates Ricarno's scheme and motivates the gangster's stratagem. The Midget enters the cleaners. As he does, the action cuts to one of Ricarno's hoods, stationed in a garage. He's been flipping a coin, which he now drops on the floor. At his signal, a gang of truckers gets into their vehicles and runs the engines to make them backfire. A brief montage of belching tailpipes accompanies backfire noises on the soundtrack. These sound like gunfire, and a cutaway shows two members of the Midget's gang, outside the cleaners, growing alarmed. Thinking that they're hearing gunfire, they run away. The action cuts to the cop glancing in the direction of the backfiring trucks, but a storeowner tells him that this racket starts every night before the trucks go out on delivery. The cop smiles and saunters off. As he passes the cleaners, someone inside raises the blinds. The next cut shows Ricarno in a restroom grimly washing his hands. The scene ends with a shot of the convoy of trucks rolling past the cleaners. Fade out.

The metonym of backfiring trucks substitutes not only for the sound of Ricarno's gun (he evidently shoots the Midget inside the cleaners), it stands in for the entirety of the murder, none of which is depicted on-camera. The narrative leaps over it by staging it off-screen and using the substitute imagery and sounds to convey its occurrence. Ricarno's action has to be inferred from the glimpse we have of him going into the cleaners, from the connection the editing invites us to make between backfire and gunfire, and from the hand-washing, which Ricarno does with solemn intensity. This is an especially clever example of the code, used to effect a total displacement of violent action from the eye of the camera.

This example from *Doorway to Hell* uses sound to create the metonymy, and many of the most striking instances of the code are achieved with sound as a dominant ingredient of the substitutional expression. In this regard, metonymic displacement should be understood as a device that can activate an aggressive use of sound, which is thrown forward into a dominant register and into denotative combination with pictorial elements—a status quite unlike the more subliminal ways that sound is typically used in films of the Holly-wood period.

In *Machine-Gun Kelly* (1958), the titular character (Charles Bronson) gets into a scuffle with another mobster. Kelly picks up his machine-gun, which the film has equated with his virility and masculinity, and announces that it's about time he killed someone. He shoves the barrel into the mobster's stomach and knocks the man down. As this character falls out of the frame, Kelly fires the gun, and its noise cues a sound edit to a close-up of a snarling tiger. Earlier in the film, Kelly had adopted the animal as a kind of pet and mascot. The cut comes at almost the same instant that Kelly fires the gun so that the viewer never actually hears much gunfire. The sound edit from gunfire to animal growl produces a continuity match in the acoustical realm because the two sounds are very much alike. Thus, while the images are disparate—Kelly shooting his gun, a caged tiger—the logic of the sound match is tight, and it makes the audio cut almost a subliminal one.

Furthermore, the audio cut works to prolong the act of violence but in a displaced realm. The cut takes us out of the murder scene to the darkened room where the cat is caged, but the continuity of sound that the cut establishes extends the duration of the shooting by transmuting it from a literal to a nonliteral level. It prolongs the machine-gun execution, which we only see and hear at its very beginning but whose associated meaning and sound carries over the cut into the shot of the cat. The sound of the spitting gun becomes that of the snarling cat, creating an audio extension of Kelly's violence.

This function of extending the machine-gun killing is an important one in the film because some of the force of the PCA's Special Regulations on Crime were evidently still in effect. Though Kelly's gun gets a lot of visual attention throughout the film he hardly ever uses it, and, when he does, it's invariably in a short, abbreviated burst. Thus, the use of metonymy in this scene reduces the level of brutality by taking us immediately away from the murder but does so in a way that increases the suggested duration of the killing beyond what is directly depicted. It's a strikingly evasive piece of editing that enables the filmmakers to do two somewhat contradictory things: extend the violence (into the nonliteral realm of the cat) and restrict it (by abbreviating imagery of Kelly shooting).

In *The St. Valentine's Day Massacre* (1967), Al Capone (Jason Robards) traps Aiello, one of his gangland enemies, in a small coach room onboard a train. Capone whacks him on the head with a handgun, and he collapses onto a seat. Capone pulls a straight razor out of his coat and leans forward to cut Aiello's throat. The editing omits this action, however, by cutting to the next scene before it happens. But the anticipated violence is displaced into a sound cue, which points toward it and lets the viewer know that Capone has proceeded with his plan even though the editing has removed the action from view. Before we leave the scene, the roar of an approaching train, sounding its horn, thunders on the soundtrack. This train remains off-screen; we never see it. As a result, the sound cue becomes more abstracted than if it were attached to a plainly visible source on-screen. Abstracted from a visibly referential source, the sound cue works to displace the suggested violence from the image track to the soundtrack and thereby to portray a violent action that will not be shown.

This elision of the razor violence demonstrates the durability of the PCA's policies regarding violence committed with sharp-bladed instruments. I have pointed out the policy disjunction that prevailed between violence committed with a gun and with a knife or other cutting or stabbing weapon. Representational restrictions were much tighter on scenes depicting wounds by stabbing, cutting, or slashing than they were with shootings. Released in 1967, *The St. Valentine's Day Massacre* reflects that era's loosening of Production Code restrictions. Its depictions of gun violence are quite explicit and bloody, though still not as graphic as *Bonnie and Clyde*. Characters are machine-gunned, blasted with shotguns, and pumped full of bullets from handguns at close range. Three Capone thugs, for example, shoot one gangster at close range, their pistols spouting flame, and the execution ends with a headshot. This occurs off-camera, but the victim is shown afterward with a gob of blood prominent on his forehead. The titular massacre goes on at some length and includes a fair amount of blood. Add in some other machine-gun massacres, and the film has a very high body count. The extent and ferocity of the mayhem are impressive, and this reflects a more relaxed era of greater permissiveness regarding gun violence. The film's abundant detailing of its many shootings, though, contrasts with the abrupt edit out of the throat-slitting scene. Severing a throat, even in 1967, was a more prohibitive kind of violence than riddling a man with a Tommy gun. Even two years later, Peckinpah had to abridge the climactic throat-cutting scene in *The Wild Bunch*, losing a side view of the action that showed a spectacular arterial spurt. A hierarchy of sanctions governed assaults on the body, with some kinds of assault deemed worse than others and subjected to greater restriction. Enduring for decades, this hierarchy even outlasted the Production Code. The Code was effectively gone by 1967; by 1969, it had been formally abolished. And yet the knife violence in *The St. Valentine's Day Massacre* and *The Wild Bunch* was still subject to greater sanctions than the startling gun violence in each picture.

Let us return now to further consideration of the audio components of metonymic displacement. *Sweet Smell of Success* (1957) features an especially swift and efficient use of the code. It uses picture and sound elements to substitute for a beating, which is not otherwise depicted. The powerful gossip columnist J. J. Hunsecker (Burt Lancaster) doesn't approve of the jazz musician that his sister is seeing, and he hires a pair of goons to beat up the musician. The fight is elided. The narrative action jumps over it entirely, but its occurrence is depicted in a displaced manner with cutaways to the musician's quintet, performing at a nearby jazz club.

As Hunsecker's thugs converge on Steve Dallas (Martin Milner) on a dimly lit street, the music of the band is heard from the nearby club where it is playing. When the cutaway occurs just before the assault begins, the musical continuity of the performance creates an unambiguous temporal link between the space on-screen (the club) and that off-screen (the street where Dallas is being beaten). The thugs surround Dallas, and when one calls to him, the action cuts to a low-angle dolly in on Dallas' face. It's an emphatic camera move that concentrates our attention upon him and suggests the forces that will be converging on him in the next moment. As the camera dollies in, the audio of the off-screen jazz band suddenly switches from long-shot to close-up sound perspective. This change is not just one of volume—the volume increases—but of proximity to the sound source. Although the camera perspective is outside on the street, the audio perspective is inside the club with the band. Image and sound reference different locations.

As the camera dollies in on Dallas, the off-screen trumpet soloist performs in audio close-up, hitting a couple of loud, shrill notes that prefigure the oncoming violence. These trumpet blasts are the lead-in to a drum solo, and the optical cutaway from Dallas to the jazz club occurs during this drum solo and specifically from a close-up of Dallas at the end of the dolly to a close-up of a drumstick smashing on a cymbal. The action then cuts to a master shot of the

40–41. Metonymic displacement keeps the beating scene off-camera in *Sweet Smell of Success*. The action cuts from the victim's face as his assailants close in to the drummer in a jazz band. The beating of drum and cymbal stands in for the off-screen violence.

band as the drummer finishes and is answered by the bass player, and then the scene dissolves out of this performance to a dialogue scene in another location. The two shots showing the band serve to displace the violence to an off-screen mode, and this happens with impressive speed, the shots lasting only a few seconds before the narrative resumes with a conventional dialogue scene. The abrupt and fast editing makes the moment of metonymic displacement very brief.

As I mentioned earlier, a similar scene in *The Set-Up* uses music performed in another location to substitute for a hand breaking. Mobsters surround and beat Stoker (Robert Ryan), an aging boxer, and to finish his career they break his hand. Before this happens, though, the action cuts away to a shadow play. A jazz band playing nearby has its silhouette thrown expressionistically onto the exterior wall of an alley building. A drummer beats his cymbal, the image and sound of which furnishes the substitute expression for the violence that is not depicted on-camera.

As these examples suggest, music is frequently a vital part of metonymic displacement, whether it originates from some source inside the story world or is composed and performed specifically for the film soundtrack. A splendid example of soundtrack music substituting for off-camera violence occurs in *Double Indemnity* (1944), during the murder of Dietrichson by his wife Phyllis (Barbara Stanwyck) and her lover, Walter Neff (Fred MacMurray). The murder takes place in a car. Neff, hiding in the back, springs up to kill Dietrichson on Phyllis's signal. Dietrichson and Phyllis are sitting in the front seat, and the camera stays on her during the killing. Although Dietrichson makes a few choking sounds off-camera—Neff is evidently breaking his neck—the killing's main indicator is provided by Miklos Rozsa's score. As the camera stays on a close-up of Phyllis, the music swells and surges to tell us about the struggle going on just off-frame, and when it subsides we know that Dietrichson is dead. The musical commentary compensates for the visually displaced action. It points to and embodies the violence that we do not see.

In earlier chapters, we saw how the new sound aesthetic of early thirties film was implicated in both the increasing stylistic amplitude of screen violence and in censorship action by the regional boards. Given the role that sound played in amplifying the domain of screen violence and efforts to suppress it, I have spent some time to show how filmmakers could use sound in a somewhat complimentary fashion—in metonymic displacement to minimize the duration or explicitness of episodes of screen violence. Obviously, though, metonymic displacement can cue creative image combinations just as it does those of sound.

In fact, metonymic displacement offers filmmakers opportunities for visually poetic expression that are greater than those of spatial displacement.

These opportunities are a function of the relationship that is created between the on-frame and off-frame material. With spatial displacement there is little or no symbolic relationship, and the on-frame/off-frame distinction mainly involves an issue of proximity and viewing angle. By contrast, using metonyms to substitute for violent action enables filmmakers to create imagery that shows violence resonating throughout the material world of objects, events and action. Violence becomes co-extensive with the material world that surrounds a shooting or stabbing and that reflects it back to the camera but in a disguised and secondary manner. Violence has its echo in the metonym—which, when carefully handled, can be more interesting, more poetic, than the sheer physicality of a violent encounter of a type the viewer has seen many times over. The possibilities for staging a fight, a shooting, or a stabbing are probably more limited than the metonyms that can be devised to stand in for them.

In Stanley Kubrick's *Killer's Kiss* (1955), his second feature as director, the hero, Dave Gordon, squares off in a fight against the villain, Rapallo. It takes place in a deserted warehouse full of plaster mannequins, which are in various stages of completion. Disembodied plaster heads, arms, legs, and torsos await their assembly into complete bodies. Other mannequins are nearly complete except for their arms. Kubrick establishes this rather bizarre environment before the fight begins, and it then furnishes a vivid mirror for the action. Rapallo wields an axe, and as he swings it viciously at Dave the mannequins all around them become a way of prefiguring Rapallo's intentions and a potential outcome of the struggle: Dave could be dismembered. While this potential outcome is not seriously scary or threatening—this is, after all, the mid-1950s, and the PCA is not about to let the film's protagonist meet such a fate—Kubrick uses the décor to plainly suggest that this is one eventuality.

Dave throws pieces of mannequin bodies at Rapallo, who chops them up with his axe, and Kubrick cuts away from this action at two points in the scene to show a table on which rest three heads without bodies—two upright, one toppled on its side. Above them, hanging from hooks, are two pairs of hands. This composition emblematically suggests the extreme degree of violence that the axe fight threatens. As filmed, the fight is reasonably free of brutality until the end. Rapallo proves himself to be quite clumsy with the axe and never gets close to hitting Dave with it. Thus it is in the décor, with all of its dismemberment, that the violence of the scene is lodged—a violence that for most of the scene is promise and potential if not actuality.

During the fight Dave picks up a pike, which he uses to impale Rapallo. Thus far the mannequins have embodied the potential for bloodshed. Now Kubrick uses them to transpose actual bloodshed and violent death. When

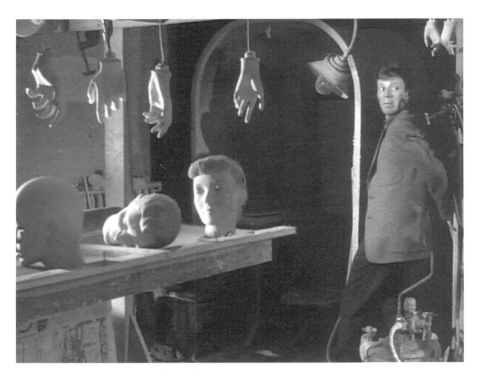

42. Metonymic displacement in *Killer's Kiss*. Disembodied hands and heads in a mannequin warehouse stand in for the violence threatened by an ax fight.

Dave rams the pike into Rapallo, Kubrick films the action in long-shot, with Rapallo in the background and our view of him blocked by Dave. As a result, the impalement is occluded, although we can infer what Dave is doing. Rapallo—little of whom can now be seen—screams, and Kubrick cuts away to a close-up of a mannequin's head, upside down, its mouth open, as Rapallo's screaming continues off-frame. The scene ends as Rapallo's scream dissolves into a train whistle and the shot of the mannequin dissolves into Grand Central Station, the locale for the next scene. The conclusion, then, gives us equally striking visual and audio metonyms.

Kubrick's use of the mannequins as a transposition device turns an ordinary movie fight into a memorably visual and poetic sequence. The violence in the scene is ordinary and unremarkable. The fight has little to recommend it as an action scene, and what violence it contains is not especially intense. But the visual environment that Kubrick creates for the fight *is* extraordinary, and he fully exploits it. The mannequins enlarge the scope of the scene's violence. They make it resonate throughout the visible world surrounding Dave and

229

Rapallo. As emblems of the violence passing between the characters, they enable Kubrick to go beyond this mayhem and to amplify it by suggestion and substitution. They supply the context that enables him to end the scene with a carefully motivated and striking instance of metonymic displacement, operating at both visual and audio levels.

INDEXICAL POINTING

Just as a filmmaker can manipulate the imagery of a scene to create metonyms, he or she can do so by creating indexes. Like the metonym, the index refers back to imagery and action that is occurring beyond the frame line or behind some obstruction on-screen. But, unlike the metonym that stands in for the absent imagery or action, the index directly points to it through a relationship of causality. The indexical image references an action that is subsequent to, and is caused by, the imagery of violence from which the filmmaker has averted the camera. Thus, there is a tighter relationship that connects the index to its referent—missing from the camera's field of view—than there is for the metonym. The dramatic connection is stronger, the affiliated emotion is more direct, and the arc of motion is shorter.

When Gaffney is shot in the bowling alley in *Scarface,* the camera pans away from him to show the metonym that will stand in for his body crumpling to the ground and for any subsequent movement or gesture that he might make as he dies. The pan follows his ball down the lane and into the pins, all of which fall except for the one that lingers a moment, spins, and then topples over. The behavior of this last pin refers back to Gaffney, now out of frame, and when it falls it seals his doom unequivocally and unambiguously. The relationship between the character and this bowling pin is entirely symbolic: Gaffney's dying did not cause the pin to behave in the way that it does. Its behavior references his death but is not caused by it. Thus, the associated meanings between the two events have some degrees of freedom. They are not bound inextricably to one another. For the metonym to exist, the viewer must make the connection, and it is a relatively explicit one.

Consider an alternative way that the scene might have been formulated. Gaffney is shot, but when he staggers and releases the ball it veers immediately into the gutter, shoots down the lane, and misses the pins entirely. In this case, instead of metonymic displacement we have an instance of indexical pointing. Being hit by the bullet causes Gaffney to loose his aim and miss his shot. In the metonymic formulation, he doesn't miss. It is the universe, instead, that mocks him and mirrors his end, registering it in an emblematic way. The gutter ball, by contrast, is directly tied into a relation of causation—

as the ensuing event to the shooting. It thus points back to the shooting. There are no degrees of freedom in this case. The subsequent event is bound unalterably to its antecedent.

As a result of this close tie, indexical pointing creates a somewhat different type of displacement than do the other codes. Of all the codes, spatial displacement has the most degrees of freedom. The filmmaker is free to move the camera or to cut as far from the violent act as he or she chooses. It is the displacement itself that counts, not its proximity to the omitted action. Working with metonyms, a filmmaker is more constrained by the need to find an appropriate emblem to substitute as one figure standing in for another. This task imposes pictorial, auditory, and dramatic constraints upon the filmmaker because the metonym needs to be connected to that for which it is a substitute.

These connections can work at a visual, auditory, or dramatic level. The metonym in *Machine-Gun Kelly* is satisfying because of the audio similarity between the roar of the Tommy gun and that of the tiger. Creating the metonym, however, depends on already having a tiger established in the narrative. Without this animal already being in the story, there is no metonym. Kubrick's thinking about the worst consequences of an axe fight—dismemberment—allowed him to create a memorable environment for the fight in *Killer's Kiss*, and that environment gave him a striking metonym at the end of the scene. But for the metonym to be available, he had to stage the scene on the set that he chose. If he had shot the scene elsewhere and inserted the shot of the mannequin face at the end, he'd have a kind of Eisensteinian effect—but it wouldn't possess the organic connection to the body of the scene that it now does.

Indexical pointing most constrains the filmmaker because the index typically needs to be something in the immediate spatial environment of the violent act. In order to register the assault or the death, the index needs to be bonded with the character or event; it needs to have an existential and physical connection. The act of displacement involves turning the camera upon this connection and revealing the object or action that is at the end of its causal chain. In our imaginary example Gaffney is shot, and his ball hits the gutter: this is a chain of action, with the index located at its end point. If the filmmaker is more constrained by the index, the tradeoff is that the viewer stays more closely inside the dramatic and emotional space of the violence. The camera's framing eclipses the mayhem but only just barely, or in such a way that the viewer sees what is happening but in a refracted or reflected form. Indexical pointing constrains the filmmaker more severely than the other codes—but, in compensation, it doesn't impose as severe a displacement upon the viewer, who typically remains in close proximity to the violent act.

In earlier chapters, we examined some striking indexes that point to violence in a reflected or refracted way. Although I did not identify them at the time as instances of indexical pointing, these were the shadow plays—the silhouettes of beatings, flayings, strangulations, and shootings in *G-Men* (1935), *Murders in the Rue Morgue* (1932), *The Black Cat* (1934), and *Scarface*. When the murderous ape strangles Dr. Mirakle, the camera frames the action in a way that keeps it off-screen, but not the shadows cast by the killing. In silhouette, the viewer sees everything: the ape's powerful arms gripping Mirakle's neck, his hands trying to break the animal's grasp, and his arms weakening and dropping as he dies. When Collins shoots Eddie Buchanan in *G-Men*, the viewer sees Buchanan's silhouette take the bullet and crumple. Verdegast's skinning of Poelzig in *The Black Cat* was too horrific for the camera to be pointed directly at it, but the shadow play enables the viewer to glimpse the horror.

To do so, the viewer must be imaginatively positioned inside the torture chamber with Verdegast, as the other scenes imaginatively placed the viewer in Mirakle's laboratory and on the street alongside Buchanan when he is hit. The index connects the viewer to the violence in a way that is more direct and

43. The shadow play as a form of indexical pointing—the killer ape strangles Dr. Mirakle in *Murders in the Rue Morgue.*

immediate, with less spatial displacement, than the other codes can manage. The index therefore is much better suited to conveying the existential qualities of violence—and more powerfully than the other codes. The index situates the viewer inside the causal arc of violent action. It stands in for an uninhibited view of the act, but it preserves the temporal flow that surrounds the act and, by doing so, it connects the viewer to the time and space of that act in a way that is more intimately related to the violence than what the other codes offer.

Contemporary filmmakers have used shadow plays as indexes of violent action, giving this code a long history and a resonance into the present period. When the surgically created human–animal monsters rebel against their creator in *The Island of Dr. Moreau* (1996), they kill the doctor's "daughter," who is one of his laboratory creations. He mutated her from a cat, and the monsters hang her like a cat—action that is staged off-camera but visualized on-screen as a shadow play. In *Married to the Mob* (1988), Jonathan Demme stages a gangland hit as an off-screen action by casting its silhouette on-screen.

Because of its immediate connection to an act of violence, the index is a more powerful marker of death or assault than the other codes. It punctuates the act of violence with absolute finality. In *The Postman Always Rings Twice* (1947), the adulterous lovers Frank (John Garfield) and Cora (Lana Turner), conspire to murder her husband, Nick. They take him for a drive, and Nick, who is drunk, begins to sing and call out into the canyon, which is a kind of echo chamber, playing his voice back to him. The echo amuses him, and, since he is calling when Frank murders him, it will mark the moment of his death.

Like the killing in *Double Indemnity* (though the action in that film was staged as metonymy), this one takes place in a car with the victim's wife present. Frank fractures Nick's skull with a bottle and then he and Cora send the car with Nick in it down the hillside, where it will look as if he has died in an accident. When Frank brains him with the bottle, Nick is off-screen and so is this action. The camera frames the bottle on the floorboard of the car in the back, where Frank is sitting. He picks up the bottle and his hand passes out of frame without the camera panning to follow. Off-screen, as we gaze at the floor of the car, we hear the bottle thud and break. More poetically, however, Nick's call into the canyon abruptly breaks off but the echo continues. When the bottle breaks off-screen and the ghostly echo of his voice replaces Nick's actual voice, the action cuts from the floorboard to a close-up of Cora. She reacts with fear and revulsion as the echo continues for a moment and then dies out. The moment of transition from Nick's real voice to the echo points to the assault that has occurred, and it suggests something fundamental about the nature of death: a person is not simply gone, but that in the moment of death and shortly thereafter a person leaves a trace, a lingering presence that persists and then, like a mist or an echo, fades away.

As in many film noirs, the universe in *Postman* is full of bitter irony. Frank and Cora get away with their scheme, but when things look brightest for them, Cora is killed in a car crash. The impact throws Frank clear of the wreck, and when he looks inside the car, the camera does not frame Cora. Instead, it frames a shot that shows the edge of the front seat, the floor and the bottom of the dashboard. After a moment, Cora's hand drops into view, holding a lipstick. The action cuts back to Frank, a medium close-up that shows him looking at the inside of the car, which is off-screen. He cries out "Cora," and the action cuts back to the previous framing of Cora's hand. Her hand relaxes, and she drops the lipstick, which hits the floor and rolls out of frame. As the shot ends, her hand hangs motionless above the floor.

This indexical manner of indicating her death provides another example of the way that substitutional imagery effecting visual displacement may elicit a relatively non-normative approach to shooting and editing. The shots of the interior of the car are point of view shots. They represent what Frank sees, and each one is preceded by a shot that shows Frank looking at the inside of the off-screen car. They are relative point of view shots rather than precisely subjective ones. They show us the same field of view that is arrayed before Frank, but since they are not subjective shots they do not suggest that we are literally looking through his eyes. Even so, the point of view relationships set up by the editing are very curious. Frank's view is not obstructed—or, at least, there is nothing about the wreckage that suggests that it would be. He should have a clear view of Cora, and yet his point of view shot is very restricted in its field. It shows only a small area inside the car and nothing of Cora, except for her hand. If we were to interpret the point of view relationships in the editing in literal terms, we would say that he does not look at Cora when he glances in the car, despite calling her name. He looks instead at the floor, which at the very moment he looks holds no trace of Cora (i.e., at the point where the shot begins). Her hand has not yet appeared in the frame.

This way of interpreting the point of view relationships, though, makes no narrative sense. Why would Frank not look at Cora? The only reason he would not do so is the same reason that the viewer is not permitted to see her on-camera: her injuries are too extensive for the screen to show, given the censorship policies of the period. But obviously, these need have nothing to do with what an imaginary character may see within the fictional narrative, only with what the viewer is allowed to see. What is interesting and somewhat deviant about the point of view editing in the scene is that it regulates the

44–45. Indexical pointing using unconventional reverse-angle shots in *The Postman Always Rings Twice*.

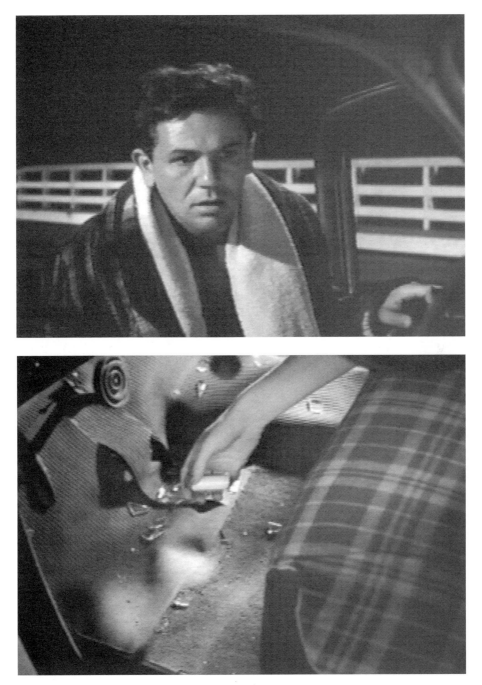

parameters of Frank's gaze according to the regulatory policies of the period. The framing of the action occludes Cora's injuries not only from the camera's and the viewer's field of view, but from Frank's as well.

The death of Lieutenant Jacobs in *Objective, Burma!* played off-camera and in a scene with an unconventional point-of-view structure, but in that case there was a clearly established disparity between what Nelson could see and what the film viewer would be permitted to see. We could see Nelson looking into the room where Jacobs lay and we could see Nelson from Jacobs's field of view, but we could not see Nelson's field of view. In this example from *Objective, Burma!* the politics of screen violence did not affect the imaginary character's access to direct sight of a horrifying episode—only the viewer's. The atypical point of view structure surrounding Cora's death, by contrast, implicates Frank's perspective in the operation of visual displacement. The politics of screen violence subject him to the same occluded view that they have forced upon the filmmaker and viewer.

Like Cora's drooping hand or Nick's echoing voice, indexes are often tied to the body or the physical presence of the afflicted character. This is one reason that they involve the viewer so immediately in the act of violence. Throughout the scene in *Objective, Burma!*, the camera frames Jacobs so that only his lower legs are visible, and when he dies, these register his passing. He groans off-screen, and his left leg, which had been flexed at the knee, relaxes and straightens. A burst of music simultaneous with this action creates a redundancy effect, underlining the index and marking it with finality.

In Anthony Mann's *Men in War* (1957), North Korean soldiers ambush a black American who has paused by the roadside to rest. The American soldier puts flowers in his helmet (an eerie moment that anticipates the events and protest of another war ten years later). He removes his boot and scratches his foot. His actions are intercut with shots showing the stealthy approach of two North Korean snipers, who get into position to take down the American with a bayonet. When the American is killed, the camera shows a close-up of his foot, which he has been scratching. It suddenly jerks, its spasm standing in for the bayoneting. His foot drops to the ground and lies still.

Tom Powers's execution of Putty Nose in *Public Enemy* (1931) takes place off-screen but uses sound to create the index. Putty Nose is at the piano when Tom shoots him. When Tom pulls his gun from inside his coat, the camera pans and dollies away from Tom to Matt, who is watching. Off-screen, Tom fires his gun, and we hear Putty make a gagging sound, then piano keys banging out of musical sequence, and a thudding noise. Putty has slumped onto the piano and then the ground.

Later in the film, Tom's assault on Schemer Burns's gang plays entirely off-screen, but its details are conveyed with indexical sound. Tom advances through the rain and enters the gang's headquarters while the camera holds the view outside. A cacophony of gunshots followed by the long, dying wail of a victim stands in for the absent action, and after a moment Tom, now wounded, staggers back outside. The scene in *Scarface* where Tony Camonte and his gang shoot up the Shamrock bar is staged in a similar fashion with the camera in the street outside, gunfire and vocalizations off-screen. With similar logic the dying, off-frame scream of an American lookout in *Bataan* lets us know his fate when he is shot by a sniper and falls, off-screen, from his perch in a high tree.

In later periods, when the PCA had relaxed its standards and its vigilance, the indexes could become more vivid—even as there was less overt need for them. When Draba (Woody Strode), the black slave in *Spartacus* (1960), bolts from the gladiators' arena and scales the wall, going after Marcus Grassus (Laurence Olivier), a Roman guard hurls a spear into his back. Draba, though, doesn't fall. He keeps on coming and grabs Grassus' leg. Grassus takes a dagger and plunges it into his neck. A cutaway to a medium close-up of Grassus serves to omit the dagger thrust into Draba's body. In the next moment, though, a blood spray hits Grassus in the face. While this index substitutes for a shot of the knife going into Draba, it is, arguably, more vivid than any such shot could be. It is not as explicitly violent because the camera is off the act itself, and yet the index in this case conveys the moment of brutality and its physical consequence with startling clarity and vehemence.

The index that shows the death of Buck Barrow in *Bonnie and Clyde* achieves the same result. Buck has been shot many times over by a passel of Texas vigilantes, and director Arthur Penn shows his death with a high angle shot that zooms down and in on Buck's twisted body, lying prone and surrounded by his killers. The zoom ends with a tight close-up of Buck's forearms, entwined, his hands and fingers jerking spasmodically. Buck's quivering extremities stand in for the larger event, the character's death. *Bonnie and Clyde* obviously was a key film in the amplification of screen violence, and Penn squibbed his actors with abandon to show their bodies being riddled with bullets. At the same time, he used indexical pointing to elide some of the features and moments of violence.

Used in this fashion, the code accompanied the dramatic expansion of filmmaking freedom in the late 1960s. Its poetic resources helped motivate its continuing use in contemporary film. Sometimes a greater effect is achieved by not showing the violent action or by doing so in an oblique manner. The motorcycle accident that kills T. E. Lawrence (Peter O'Toole) at the beginning of *Lawrence of Arabia* (1962) haunts the mind but not because we see the results of the crash. All we see are Lawrence's goggles dangling from a tree branch. Like the vanishing echo of Frank's voice in *Postman*, the goggles as index concentrate poetic force on this vestigial reminder of a life now gone to its violent end and on the mystery of the final passage.

Less is more: The oblique image can acquire greater resonance than the explicit one. This was always the paradox of screen censorship. By helping to foster the codes of substitutional value, the regulation of the screen in classical Hollywood helped augment the expressive and poetic capabilities of American cinema.

SUBSTITUTIONAL EMBLEMATICS

Unlike the codes we have thus far examined, this one does not involve a strategy for concealing acts of violence from the camera. Substitutional emblematics has its origin in the general ban in classical Hollywood film on imagery detailing wounds to the body. While squibs were occasionally used in such early films as *Bataan* (1943) and *Pride of the Marines* (1945), their widespread use did not come into vogue until 1967. Before that, it was permissible to depict gunshot wounds by showing either a small amount of blood or a hole in the actor's costume, but films generally did not visualize the bullet's impact on the body. In *Shane* (1953) and *The Killers* (1964), characters hit by a bullet are thrown backward by its force and impact (this, in itself, is rather exceptional), but the bullet itself remains relatively imaginary because it produces no visible damage on the body.

Many films, of course, did not depict, in even these small ways, the physicality of gun violence. As I have discussed in an earlier chapter, characters in Hollywood films often take a bullet at close range and show no evident response except general fatigue, a lassitude that compels them to sink slowly out of the frame. Their suit coats, uniforms, and white shirts remain immaculate. Violence committed with knives, spears, and arrows was more tightly constrained. When it occurred, it was often on the order of showing a stuntman taking an arrow in an obviously padded part of his costume.

Paradoxes and contradictions abound, however, in the history of screen violence. As I pointed out in chapter four, war films often pushed the limits of the acceptable. The World War II drama *Halls of Montezuma* (1950) features an on-camera stabbing of a Japanese sniper by an American soldier. The area where the knife penetrates his body is just beyond the frame line, so that it is displaced from view, but each of the several knife blows gets an audio effect. We hear the knife going into flesh and muscle. Furthermore, with each subsequent knife blow the blade is visibly bloodied. The dying Japanese fliers in

Flying Tigers (1942) vomit blood on-camera and in close-up. In *Objective, Burma!* we hear the moment of impact when a Japanese bullet strikes an American paratrooper. In *Bataan* and *Pride of the Marines*, actors are squibbed for headshots.

These are notable exceptions to the dominant trend, which was to preserve the human body in a relatively immaculate form regardless of the traumas and assaults to which it was subjected. The filmic practice of preserving the body as physically inviolate carried both an ideology and a metaphysic, but it did not contribute anything toward the *y*-axis expansion of postwar cinema. In fact, it operated antithetically to *y*-axis expansion. Much of the increase in the stylistic amplitude of modern screen violence is due to the numerous ways of detailing the convulsive and traumatic responses of the human body under force of violence. In this regard, Arthur Penn's seminal staging of the shooting deaths of Bonnie and Clyde was a definitive rejection of the ideal of physical inviolability that informed the clutch-and-fall aesthetic.

But while that aesthetic prevailed in American cinema, filmmakers experimented with various ways of muting its effects. Obviously, all the codes of substitutional value operate as alternatives to its effects. But one in particular does so with special reference to the body. Substitutional emblematics works to suggest a level of violence to the body that goes beyond what the images might explicitly show. Unlike the other codes, this one does not involve a visual turning away from the act of violence. It does not displace the act into an off-screen or occluded area of view. The violent act is depicted, but in a way or with details that suggest a degree of intensity and extent of bodily damage that the narrative content of the images does not explicitly reference. These details are emblems that point to this higher-order level of violence and substitute for it.

In light of the changes that *Bonnie and Clyde* brought to cinema in 1967, one of the peculiarities of *The St. Valentine's Day Massacre,* released that same year, is the lack of squibbing to show impact wounds. Gangster characters are shot on-camera and at close range with pistols, shotguns, and machine-guns, but bullet hits are not visualized. Blood only appears on the victims in a subsequent fashion, following a cutaway to their killers. The filmmaking shows no hesitation in dispatching large numbers of mobsters in brutal fashion—but the stylistics of the violence, in terms of damage to the body, reflect the norms of the classical Hollywood period rather than the new cinema of violence which was then emerging.

But if the body could not be depicted as torn open by gunfire, sets and props certainly could. The drive-by shooting was an old staple of gangster movies. A gang speeds down an urban street, hoodlums hanging out the windows of cars, spraying lead into restaurants and cafés, their patrons diving for cover. *The St. Valentine's Day Massacre* takes this conventional scene and amplifies it with gunfire of impressive ferocity and duration. Nobody in the restaurant is hit; all of the visible damage on-screen, and it is considerable, involves property damage. The characters are not squibbed, but the sets and props are. Bullets blow out chunks of masonry buildings along the street; they perforate the steel bodies of automobiles, splattering against windshields to leave a spider-web tracery of cracks; they shatter mirrors and storefront windows, explode crockery and vases, and splinter wooden countertops, raining a deluge of debris onto the floor and the characters cowering there.

The hundreds of bullet hits that shatter the sets and props, and the intricate electrical wiring and squibbing necessary to achieve the effect, stand in for what the film will not yet depict: bullet hits on the human body. As a unit of narrative, the drive-by shooting is overdone. It goes on too long and results in so much property damage that Bugsy Moran's gang comes to seem more interested—moronically so—in defacing property than in their ostensible purpose, which is to assassinate Al Capone inside the restaurant. The duration and ferocity of the shooting, and the lavish detailing of the bullet strikes on the environment, are a substitute, an emblem, for what the film is not going to show: impact wounds.

One of the most widely censored scenes in *Scarface* (1932) followed a similar drive-by shooting sequence (one that was much briefer). One of the drive-by shooters drops a machine-gun, and Tony Camonte retrieves it. The censored scene showed him firing the gun at the camera, its barrel spitting flame while he grinned with orgiastic delight. A reverse-angle shot showed the gun's bullets ripping up the walls of a poolroom and punching through the wood, splinters exploding from the impact. Once again, environmental damage substitutes for the gun's ultimate targets, the bodies of Tony's enemies. Censor boards around the country deleted the scene because it explicitly showed the carnage that could result from an automatic weapon in the hands of a sociopath. The boards did not like its extended visualization of gun damage in the terms that were depicted (the shredding of the pool hall) and in those that were implied (the gun shredding and disintegrating human bodies in a similar fashion).

This kind of substitutional emblematics—letting the environment absorb the damage that can't be shown on the body—is a very effective way of pumping up the level and intensity of screen violence. It can transform an ordinary shooting or other kind of assault into a violence that seems much harder and more physical than it would otherwise. When a victim is shot along with all of the environmental destruction, the gross level of property

damage can have an accretive effect on the gunshot victim and make those injuries seem more severe and extensive than what the images of the character's
body actually show.

Herein lies the key function of this code, and the reason for its great appeal
to filmmakers. Substitutional emblematics confers a level of damage on the
human body that exceeds the literal content of the images and the regulatory
terms by which shootings and other assaults were to be depicted. The PCA
was keenly attuned to script scenes featuring violence against persons that it
regarded as being too brutal or gruesome. Environmental damage, by contrast,
could be an effective substitute for brutality because it often was below the
agency's radar.

During the robbery that opens Anthony Mann's *Railroaded* (1947), a security guard exchanges shots with two burglars. Mann was a great stylist of
screen violence, and he staged this brief gunplay to strikingly harsh effect.
Suspicious that something is wrong, the guard draws his gun and prowls
down the corridor outside the office that is being robbed. One of the thieves
sees the guard's shadow on a window along the corridor, and he blasts it with
his shotgun. Mann films the thief firing at the camera, the gun spitting fire. A
reverse-angle cut shows the window shattering. The sound of breaking glass
from the window bleeds into the shattering glass of the office door as the
guard punches through it, so that he can work the knob and get in. The guard
fires through the broken door window and hits the robber in the throat. The
other burglar shoots the guard, and he crashes through the door, shattering
the remaining glass in the window and pulling the window shade down and
around his body as he falls through.

Only three shots are fired in the scene, and the low-key lighting and wide-
angle framing of the action keep the characters in the shadows and at some
distance from the camera. Accordingly, very little of the guard's body can actually be seen. When the first robber fires at the window, the guard is just a
shadow. With the second shot, he is little more than a shadow—only his gun
arm can be glimpsed extending through the broken door window. Rather than
using a prominent display of his body on-screen to register the force of the
gun violence, however, Mann uses sets and props. It is the pitch of the guard's
body through the glass panel on the door, the shattering of this glass, and the
wrenched and twisted window shade that convey the level of violence that he
sustains and which the lighting and wide-angle framing do not allow us to see
on his body itself. The set and prop substitute for the bullet-riddled body and
become their emblem.

During an era when bullet strikes produced little damage to the body, substitutional emblematics compensated for this and suggested otherwise. In

G-Men, during one of the film's numerous shoot-outs between the Feds and their main antagonist, the mobster Brad Collins, the agents have him cornered in an apartment. One agent, who is standing in the hallway, shoots through the door to the apartment. The action cuts inside the apartment to a composition showing the bullets hitting a mirror. Collins is reflected in that mirror, with his reflection positioned over the bullet holes. The bullets do not hit him, but as the slugs strike the glass the holes that appear there provide a kind of indirect means of squibbing the actor. The hits on the mirror *are* hits on Collins, displaced in the form of a substitutional emblematics. They show what the bullet trauma would look like if Collins were being hit.

This emblematic way of suggesting bullet hits is repeated at the climax of the film. As Collins speeds away from a government ambush, one of the G-men sprays his car with a machine-gun, killing the mobster. The action cuts to a close-up of Collins behind the wheel. The camera is mounted on the car's hood, with the windshield between Collins and the camera. This is where the camera has to be for the substitutional emblematics in the scene to work. With the rapid-fire force of an automatic weapon, the G-man's bullet spray hits the windshield. Seven bullets strike the glass: each hit is visualized, leaving a tracery of cracks, holes, and broken glass. Based on where the bullets hit the windshield, Collins is shot in the face and head. These wounds, of course, aren't depicted, but the strikes on the glass become substitute squibs for the actor, indicating in an emblematic way the nature and location of his wounds. As the camera films the scene, it is *as if* the bullets were visibly hitting Collins.

Substitutional emblematics may reference the body more directly than in these cases where aspects of the environment, which are separate from the body, function as stand-ins for bodily damage. Substances that are shown adhering to the body can become surrogates for blood or other physical fluids resulting from wounding or trauma. For this kind of emblematic to be effective, however, these substances must have a clear basis in the setting or dramatic action of the scene. In *Halls of Montezuma* (1950), an artillery shell wounds one of the American soldiers who are dug into trenches around the island. Every other soldier has been shown sitting on dry, parched, rocky terrain. After this soldier is hit, however, he crawls back to his comrades through water and mud. As he inches his way toward them, his passage makes a viscous sound across the moist terrain, as if he is bleeding out into the earth. When he reaches them his face, chest, and arms are darkened with mud as if with blood, and his face shines wetly in the dim light. As he chokes and cries out his last words, the dark mud and moisture on his face and chest are indistinguishable from blood and they give his grievous wounds a physical presence on-screen, even though the wounds themselves are not directly de-

46. Collins meets his end in *G-Men*. The simulated bullet holes in the windshield depict, via substitutional emblematics, the damage that is occurring to his body.

picted. The contrast of landscapes—the muddy ground through which he crawled and the dry landscape in which his comrades sit—serves to emphasize the substitutional emblematics that are at work.

The fearsome tortures inflicted by the Nazis on Bob Sharkey (James Cagney) in *13 Rue Madeleine* are never shown on-camera and are only suggested by the whipping sounds that come through the closed door to the torture chamber. When Sharkey does appear briefly on-camera, in two shots at the very end of the film, he is strapped to a chair, bare-chested, and has dark gashes on his chest and face. The two shots that reveal his condition are meant to be a revelation of horror to the audience, and it is a quick look because in the next moment the Allies' bombs fall and obliterate 13 Rue Madeleine and our suffering hero along with his Nazi captors. In that short moment of revelation, Sharkey's body glistens all over. He is drenched with sweat and water, which the Nazis have evidently used to revive him under torture. The water glistens on his skin in the light, soaks his pants, and pools on his stomach, on the chair between his legs, and on the floor under him. The moisture that covers Sharkey's tortured body and puddles under him gives his

243

skin a textured and a tactile presence that it would otherwise lack. The gashes on his face and chest do not drip blood, but the moisture that covers his body denotes blood and other bodily secretions. Its presence suggests the impact of torture upon his flesh.

At the climax of the chariot race in *Ben-Hur* (1959), Messala (Stephen Boyd) is thrown from his chariot, dragged over the coarse sand of the coliseum, and trampled by a team of horses. The sand that sticks to his torn and broken body and falls away from it as he is lifted helps to visualize the extent of the damage he has suffered. Very little of this is shown in a conventional way, in terms of blood or torn clothing. The sand that covers him in splotches, and that peels away from him, helps to compensate for this and makes him look quite ragged and shredded, even though this is not explicitly visualized.

By inflicting a level of violence on the environment that goes beyond what can be directed on the human body, and by adhering substances to the body to suggest a degree of assault or suffering that is not overtly shown, substitutional emblematics enabled filmmakers in the Hollywood period to evade some of the regulatory barriers to the depiction of violence. This code does not inevitably displace the camera's view of a wounded or dying victim or the act of violence itself; these things might remain on-camera. The code works to intensify the action on-screen by suggesting a level of trauma that exceeds what the imagery directly depicts. Doing so, it restores some of the mystery to violence and suffering by suggesting that these phenomena involve levels of meaning and experience that go beyond what the screen can show, what the eye sees, or what the casual observer notices. It suggests that in violence there is a depth of meaning that is terrible to behold and which transcends the most evident layer of experience visible to eye and camera.

EMOTIONAL BRACKETING

The strategies of substitutional meaning contained in the codes examined thus far are based on a relationship of discretion that exists between filmmaker and viewer. There were clear limits to what the screen would show in the Hollywood period. By displacing violence into an off-screen space, or into metonymy or index, a filmmaker could acknowledge these limits and implicitly shield the viewer from a direct confrontation with the details of brutality and death.

Emotional bracketing takes this relationship with the viewer a step further by opening a space inside the narrative where the viewer can recover and catch his or her breath following an episode of violence that is intense, startling, or with serious consequences for the narrative and one or more of its major characters. Instead of moving directly to the next scene, the narrative pauses for a moment while viewers collectively exhale from the impact of what they have seen and assess its consequences.

Because this code works to create a resting place for the audience inside the narrative, its presence in a film suggests that the filmmaker has retained artistic control of the violent material in the story and is exerting a moral perspective within that design. By contrast, the absence of emotional bracketing can suggest that a filmmaker is staging violence without a corresponding moral perspective on it. Indeed, the breathless pacing of many contemporary action films means that there is no pause whatever between violent episodes, as the narrative speeds from one massacre to another with the same relentless, automated response as the weapons used by hero and villain.

Emotional bracketing helps a filmmaker to shape the violent episodes of a narrative with a controlled artistic design and moral purpose. By activating and employing the code, a filmmaker is acknowledging that the violence on-screen is intended to have an emotional impact on viewers and that these viewers have the prerogative to recover from that impact and assess its consequences for themselves and for the characters in the film. This artistic approach, and its concern for the audience, characterized film violence in the Hollywood period: it contrasts with a more callous and brutal treatment of audiences by many contemporary filmmakers, who stage graphic violence with moral indifference and then rush on to the next narrative episode. This contemporary approach is based on a conception of desensitized viewers on whom extreme violence makes little impression. By contrast, emotional bracketing is predicated on, and proposes, the existence of sensitized viewers and a filmmaker's need to shape violence according to these dispositions.

The dramatic high point in *Pride of the Marines* is the foxhole combat with the Japanese that results in the blinding of Al (John Garfield). As we saw in chapter four, the violence throughout this scene is pitched at a keen level of intensity. Al and two other Marines wield a machine-gun and try to halt a relentless Japanese advance. Slowly the Japanese gain on them. Al's two buddies are hit. One is killed with a headshot, and the other is disabled with an arm wound. Each of these bullet strikes is visualized with squibs. Al is left alone at the gun, and as evening falls he gets rattled and anxious and doesn't see a Japanese soldier creeping up on his foxhole with a hand grenade. The grenade explodes at close range, in Al's face, and the detonation is visualized in a subjective shot from Al's perspective.

From that point on, spatial displacement keeps us from seeing Al's face. He's filmed from behind, his back to the camera, but his surviving buddy, Lee, sees the disfigurement and reacts with horror. Al pulls his pistol, and Lee, thinking Al is going to kill himself, pleads with him not to do it. But Al says he's going to kill the Japanese. He cries, "Tell me where they are, Lee, show me where they are, show me where they're coming from." As he says this with increasing hysteria, the action cuts from Al, his back to the camera, to a long-shot of the battlefield in front of the foxhole, littered with bodies. The camera tilts up to the sky as the musical score builds to a crescendo that drowns out Al's anxious pleading. The shot dissolves to another image of a very different set of clouds, brighter and more serene, and as the musical climax reaches resolution and diminuendo the camera tilts down to the skyline of Philadelphia. Ruth, Al's fiancée, begins speaking in voiceover: "I didn't hear from Al for a long time. Philadelphia seemed a long ways from the war." Another dissolve takes us inside the office where Ruth works as she gets a phone call informing her that Al is in a San Diego military hospital.

Following Al's blinding, the camera movements and the editing take us out of the combat sequence in a manner that is overtly marked as transitional. The musical crescendo, the matching shots of the clouds, the tilt up and tilt down from the heavens, and the dissolves explicitly mark this interlude as a moment between dramatic shifts in the narrative. The interlude takes us from one locale to another and, most critically, away from the violence that has maimed our central character and into a brief space and time where we can catch our breath before the next narrative segment, dealing with Al's rehabilitation, begins.

As this example suggests, emotional bracketing can be accomplished with standard editing transitions—frequently ones that require some duration for their execution, such as fades and dissolves. The duration required to complete a fade or a dissolve can be used to build and extend the moment of bracketing that punctuates the end of a violent episode and the point where a viewer can begin to respond in its aftermath. Cutaways, however, may also accomplish this bracketing of narrative episode and give the viewer opportunity to assimilate the violence that has just occurred. By creating spatial displacement and then extending it for some duration, cutaways can accomplish the same manner of bracketing that the dissolves and camera moves furnish in *Pride of the Marines*.

When a Japanese sniper claims a second American victim in *Bataan*—a headshot with the bullet strike visualized—the victim falls from a treetop perch. Spatial displacement abbreviates the fall, however, with cutaways to his comrades watching his death. A series of eight reaction shots show their emotional responses as they begin to realize the hopelessness of their situation, facing superior Japanese numbers on the island. It now seems likely to them that the Japanese will get them all. A long fade-out concludes the scene and punctuates the violence and their collective realization.

This kind of emotional bracketing coincides with standard points of narrative transition that mark certain scenes as pivotal moments in the story. The editing transitions, however, are not only marking narrative structure but bear a relationship to the violent content of the episodes. It is the violence as much as the editing markers that define these pivotal moments of narrative, and the interruptions created by the fades, dissolves, or cutaways are responses to the violence and its consequences for narrative and viewer. They punctuate narrative according to the significance and import of the violence that has been depicted. Emotional bracketing is a kind of narrative marker, which is why it is frequently accomplished by the standard optical transitions that punctuate other episodes of narrative. The key difference in instances of emotional bracketing is that the optical transitions are responses to violence, and shape the narrative in terms of the emotional impact that follows in its wake. This impact belongs as much to the viewers of the film as to the surviving characters within the story.

The violent death of the main character in *The Bridges at Toko-Ri* (1954) is meant to have a tremendous impact on the viewer, and, accordingly, it cues a significant moment of emotional bracketing. Harry Brubaker (William Holden) is a Navy pilot in Korea, reluctantly doing his patriotic duty in a war whose purpose he doubts. In the climax, he takes part in a daring attack on the titular bridges. He survives, but his fuel tank leaks and he doesn't make it back to the aircraft carrier. He ditches the plane and scrambles to safety as North Korean troops close in on him. A rescue helicopter comes for him; its pilot and crewman are two other major characters in the film. Things end tragically for all of them. The North Koreans shoot down the chopper, killing the crewman. After a short firefight, they kill the pilot and then Brubaker, who dies sprawled in a muddy ditch.

Brubaker's death activates an extended interlude of emotional bracketing, marked by a dissolve of extraordinary length—more than 14 seconds—that holds the overlapping compositions of his body in the ditch (the outgoing shot) and the aircraft carrier (the incoming shot), which is the locale of the next and concluding scene in the film. After the dissolve is completed, the shot of the carrier holds on-screen for another eleven seconds before the action cuts to the interior of the ship and the officers' reactions to the deaths of Brubaker and the helicopter crew. Counting the dissolve and the shot of the carrier once the dissolve is completed, this segment of emotional bracketing lasts for twenty-five seconds—a length of time that conveys the powerful impact that the deaths of Brubaker and the others are meant to have. Their lives have been consumed by a war about which the film expresses grave doubts, even as it affirms the importance of doing one's duty. The brutality

47. The death of Harry Brubaker (William Holden) in *The Bridges at Toko-Ri* is meant to be so disturbing that it cues a lengthy interlude of emotional bracketing.

and ugliness of Brubaker's death—as we last see him, he is sprawled awkwardly in the mud on a lonely plain—are meant to convey a sense of waste and to leave a strong impression on the viewer. The length of the optical transition out of this scene provides a clear measure of that intended impact.

As this example suggests, emotional bracketing may be cued by violence done to a significant character in the story. Alternatively, violence committed on even very minor characters may cue this transition if that violence is meant to be especially severe or disturbing. The famous scene in *Kiss of Death* (1947) in which Johnny Udo straps the old lady into her wheelchair and sends it down the stairs gives us a victim about whom we know next to nothing and, indeed, whom we have just met in this scene. The narrative presents her as a largely undefined character. As a result, viewers have no emotional investment in her, no attachment, but do presumably feel a generalized compassion since she is a helpless victim of Udo's cruelties.

It's the epic nature of his cruelty—throwing an old woman, and an invalid to boot, to her death—that compels the filmmakers to grant the viewer some space for recovery. Accordingly, after Udo shoves his shrieking victim down the stairs and the chair hits the floor, a long fade brings the scene to an end and leaves an interval of darkness on-screen before the next scene comes up. That interval gives viewers some respite.

Emotional bracketing punctuates narrative with a moral design, and in this respect the code was an integral part of the depiction of violence in the Hollywood period. The efforts of the PCA and the regional censor boards aimed to recuperate screen violence into a moral framework that transcended the limited capacities and perspectives of the gangsters, hoods, monsters, and mad scientists for whom violence was just a means of getting their way. Regulation of the screen in this period aimed to reclaim violence, which everyone agreed was necessary to narrative, with a higher moral purpose so that narratives would resonate with more than the mere depiction of mayhem. Sometimes the efforts were bone-headed—as in the injection of anti-gangster propaganda into *Scarface,* a film whose aesthetic clearly celebrated lawlessness and violence. A few scenes of propaganda attached to such a film would accomplish little. Emotional bracketing, however, was a more subtle method of recuperating violence into a moral framework. The operation of bracketing structures narrative according to an implicit moral dimension, which assumes that violence (at least some instances of it) can be so predatory, so cruel, and can result in such a waste of life that narrative needs to take a "time out" to provide viewers with a moment to reassemble their moral bearings. Witnessing vivid or horrific violence can scramble those bearings and confuse them. The operation of emotional bracketing stems from the realization by a filmmaker, or by a system of production such as that which prevailed during the Hollywood period, that the special vividness and emotional power of cinema—attributes that the Production Code formally acknowledged in its statement of general principles—mandated these "time outs."

As such, emotional bracketing provides a signal that a filmmaker is aiming to retain artistic control over the volatile material of screen violence. In these terms, the code retains its efficacy. It is not a dated artifact of a historical period, at least not for those contemporary filmmakers who handle violence with intelligence. One of the most appalling moments in James Foley's *At Close Range* (1986) comes when a father (Christopher Walken), a sociopath and career criminal, shoots and kills his son (Chris Penn) in a cold rage. The crime is meant to hit the viewer hard, and Foley uses spatial displacement and emotional bracketing to control the violence and grant the viewer some quarter. In the last moment of his life, the boy realizes what his father is about to do and pleads, "No, Dad!" The action cuts away from the boy and to the father. As soon as he fires the gun at his boy, who is now off-screen, the editing takes us out of the scene to a shot of the moon, which lingers for a few seconds, and then to a shot of the other

249

son (Sean Penn), waking in his bed in the moonlight. The editing omits all details of the killing except for the flash of the gun. There are no glimpses of the victim, and the editing takes us out of the scene at the very moment of violence. The cutaway to an emotionally neutral image gives the viewer a moment to recover from the awful violence that has just occurred.

This way of structuring the scene lets us know that the filmmaker is thinking about his viewers in relation to the violence that he is depicting. Emotional bracketing enables filmmakers to build this concern for viewers into the structure and fabric of a scene. In this regard, filmmakers in the Hollywood period found a code that was responsive to the regulatory pressures of those years and bequeathed it to succeeding generations of filmmakers as an essential tool of cinema.

CONCLUSION

My goal in this chapter has not been to provide an exhaustive inventory of all films that utilize these five codes of substitutional poetics. The goal has been to identify and examine these codes as a positive outcome of the screen regulation and censorship that prevailed during the classical Hollywood period. Within the regulatory climate of that period this system of visual rhetoric gave filmmakers an articulate and expressive way of handling problematic instances of screen violence—scenes that exceeded normative thresholds by virtue of the type or degree of violence depicted or the category of victim involved. Filmmakers had numerous ways of overcoming the PCA's opposition to proposed scenes of violence. The agency's own mode of operation—its commitment to serve production—entailed that it be flexible in negotiating solutions with filmmakers. Moreover, since the PCA scrutinized scripts and not actual productions, filmmakers were in a position to stylistically evade the agency's wishes.

But there was an overall logic and design that organized the maneuverings of filmmakers and the PCA. As a result, certain practices emerged in the craft of screen violence, and they could be counted on to guide the maneuvering over a proposed production and its filming. The body would remain inviolate. Bullets could visibly hit property but not people. The physical and emotional anguish resulting from violence would be minimized.

The predictive logic of these practices, backed up by the regulatory and censorship policies of the period, shaped in turn the rhetoric of visual forms. The legacy of screen censorship in the Hollywood period is often discussed in terms of negatives—in terms of the material that filmmakers couldn't show, the shots and scenes that were cut from films, the projects that were abandoned and not made. But restriction can sometimes be good for creative expression because it encourages a search for alternative forms. The rhetoric of screen violence in classical Hollywood cinema—a network of metaphor and metonymy expressed in camera positioning, editing patterns, and sound–image relationships—is a prime example of such a positive outcome. It enriched the range and stock of available creative expression for filmmakers and left its visual legacy deeply embedded in American film.

The regulation and censorship of the Hollywood period paradoxically demonstrated that violence in cinema lends itself especially well to poetically oblique expression. If this principle was most at home during the classical Hollywood period, contemporary filmmakers seem to believe that a more truthful approach to screen violence requires the relative suppression of this poetry in the service of an alternate principle—the numbing repetition of graphically unrestrained imagery.

6
After the Deluge

In 1968, the dike burst. The remaining vestiges of the Production Code were abolished and the Code and Rating Administration system took its place. The CARA system enabled filmmakers for the first time to make films aimed for an adult market, with large doses of graphic violence not intended for viewing by children without adult supervision. The R-rated films that followed—such as *Bullitt* (1968), *The Wild Bunch* (1969), *Soldier Blue* (1969), *The Godfather* (1972), and *Taxi Driver* (1975)—depicted gun violence with levels of blood and a detailing of impact wounds that no Hollywood film of preceding decades had been allowed to show. The long-term accompaniment of the shift to CARA and the fall of censorship was the permeation of graphic violence throughout contemporary visual culture.

No single factor was responsible for the film industry's transition to the CARA system. Numerous developments helped move the industry from the ideal of a mass, heterogeneous audience for motion pictures to the niche audiences that the G-M-R-X scheme presupposed. Most immediately, there was the threat that states or cities would adopt age-based policies regulating film admissions as a means of protecting children from rough screen material and that this development might extend the life of the regional censor boards. As we saw in the last chapter, *Ginsberg v. New York* (1968) and *Interstate v. Dallas* (1968) pointed in this direction.

Moreover, key players within Hollywood had become convinced that an age-based classification system would work better for the industry than the increasingly outmoded Production Code, rooted as it was in the mores and politics of the late 1920s. Recall that PCA president Geoffrey Shurlock said that he had become convinced in the 1950s that such a scheme was the way to go after seeing how well they worked in Europe.

252

By the time the industry implemented CARA, the Production Code Administration (PCA) had lost virtually all of its authority, in part because of the social disconnect between modern America and the morality incarnated in the old Code. The Code was exhausted, and filmmakers increasingly were simply ignoring it. The advent of television and the industry's loss of its theaters in the late 1940s accelerated this trend. Television replaced Hollywood as the new medium of the masses, and henceforth the film industry would learn to survive by niche-marketing its product.

Albert Van Schmus recalled how the deep commitment of the National Association of Theater Owners (NATO) helped to sustain the Production Code. To the extent that the Code helped to suppress objectionable material from films, it provided for the medium's appeal to the kind of wide audience that NATO wanted. By contrast, a G film and an R film were aimed at different viewers. MPAA President Jack Valenti, who helped implement the CARA system, remarked upon the changing audience demographics. "What you and I must understand is that there is, today, no mass movie audience. There are many audiences, each seeking different kinds of films, suitable to individual taste and temper and turn of mind."[1]

These "many audiences" included young viewers whose values and politics were more liberal and radical than those of previous generations, and a vital objective in implementing CARA was the pursuit of this demographic. As I explained in *Savage Cinema: Sam Peckinpah and the Rise of Ultraviolent Movies*, the MPAA pushed for CARA because of the new freedoms it gave filmmakers: in its public relations messages the MPAA defended these new freedoms and the revolution in content and style that late 1960s films embodied.

The inception of CARA was in response to all of these pressures. By implementing it, Hollywood sought to do an end run around the regional censor boards—to cope with the changed economics of production and distribution in a market where the industry no longer controlled the exhibition of popular visual entertainment, and to liberalize the content of American film in ways that could revitalize it and make it attractive to a young audience.

THE CONCEPT OF "VIOLENCE" EMERGES

CARA also coincided with a huge shift in the culture and in national politics that brought the subject of violence—in society and in the movies—to the forefront of the nation's consciousness. In this respect, the inception of CARA was also the inception of film violence, the launching of an era of heightened consciousness about this component of cinema. That era that has never closed; we remain in its grip. 1968 was a year of terrible assassinations—

Martin Luther King, Jr. and Robert Kennedy—accompanying riots and social unrest at home and the Vietnam War overseas. I discussed the links between the CARA system and this period of domestic turmoil in *Savage Cinema.* Rather than repeating that discussion here, I want to examine the MPAA's struggle to come to terms with the emergence of violence in American film and with the long-term consequences of this emergence.

In moving to CARA, Jack Valenti assured Congress and President Johnson that the new system would offer an industry response to public anger over perceived links between contemporary movies and social violence.[2] Because of the increasing level of violence in pictures like *The St. Valentine's Day Massacre* (1967), *The Dirty Dozen* (1967), and *Bonnie and Clyde* (1967), the National Commission on the Causes and Prevention of Violence in 1968 looked at whether Hollywood films might be helping to foster turmoil and increased aggression throughout society. Jack Valenti was scheduled for testimony on this issue.

The National Commission's focus on Hollywood, and the public controversies over movie mayhem that motivated it, put the topic of violence before the industry in stark terms. The industry's history, however, left it ill-prepared to address this topic. The PCA had regulated certain prescribed behaviors, but it had no fundamental concept or position on movie violence to guide it. Now, with the industry in the National Commission's sights, it had to come up with one.

Geoffrey Shurlock, PCA head from 1954 to 1968, was Code Administrator when Jack Valenti became president of the MPAA. Although he retired shortly thereafter, he and his office helped Valenti prepare for his appearance before the National Commission, and the correspondence surrounding this effort illuminates the agency's struggle to formulate a philosophy and policy for dealing with movie violence. The PCA had confronted the controversies over crime and gangster movies and passed the violence-related Special Regulations on Crime. But "violence" as a supra-category, demanding a special regulatory philosophy and policy—this was a new beast.

As we know, the Production Code featured an extensive moral philosophy that was woven into its list of Specific Applications and appeared as a long preamble. The Reasons Justifying the Code were a series of axioms about the nature of art and cinema and the necessity for upholding correct standards of life. Portions of this philosophy touched on depictions of violence, such as the injunction against structuring a story so that audience sympathy is given to wrongdoers and crime-breakers and the prohibition against justifying revenge as a motive in the drama.

But Hollywood's regulation of screen content did not necessitate the development of a super-arching philosophy about violence. Had it been developed, such a philosophy would have engaged many of the issues that preoccupy us today: the special characteristics of screen violence that are unique to cinema and are rooted in its means of expression, the capability of filmmakers to stylize violence in ways that make it hypnotic and fascinating, the differential effects on viewers of violence that is depicted as justifiable or that involves a deserving victim, or that is accompanied by depictions of pain and suffering or other physical or psychological consequence.

These questions are the legacy bequeathed to us by a century of escalating movie violence. The way that such ultra-violent pictures as *The Dirty Dozen* and *Point Blank* (1967) pushed violence to new levels of flamboyance and sadism disturbed many critics and viewers and prompted them to reflect upon the meaning of this new trend. Reviewing *Point Blank* in *Life* magazine, Richard Schickel confessed that he found the picture shocking, and he condemned its "gratuitous violence."[3] *Newsweek* objected to the film as "a symphony of vicious brutality."[4] Bosley Crowther, the film critic for the *New York Times*, described the new turn that screen violence had taken in the mid-1960s with pictures like *The St. Valentine's Day Massacre* and *The Dirty Dozen*:

> Something is happening in the movies that has me alarmed and disturbed. Moviemakers and moviegoers are agreeing that killing is fun. Not just old-fashioned, outright killing, either, the kind that is quickly and cleanly done by honorable law enforcers or acceptable competitors in crime. This is killing of a gross and bloody nature, often massive and excessive, done by characters whose murderous motivations are morbid, degenerate, and cold.[5]

THE MPAA AIMS FOR A POLICY ON VIOLENCE

It was in this context—movie violence pitched at new levels of blood and brutality and, in the world outside the cinema, the ongoing social and political violence—that the National Commission scheduled Jack Valenti to testify. The approaching date of his testimony, scheduled for December 1968, elicited a flurry of activity at the MPAA as it searched its files for information that would help him prepare for the questions that everyone anticipated and feared. These would likely focus on recent films with levels of violence that the Commission deemed egregious and on the MPAA's regulatory strategies. With regard to specific films, the MPAA worried about *5 Card Stud* (1968), in which Robert Mitchum played a vengeful preacher gunning down members of a card game in which he had been cheated. The picture's high number of killings and its conjunction of religion and sadism made it, in the MPAA's somewhat belated calculation, a ripe target for Commission inquiry. In researching its files on the picture, the MPAA found little evidence that the film had received any scrutiny of its violence during the script review process. If the Commission asked about the picture, this would be an embarrassing admission. In a memo to Geoffrey Shurlock, an MPAA staff member outlined the problem and asked if Shurlock had any information that might clarify how the picture had been handled by the Code office.

> Mr. Valenti has reason to believe that members of the Commission may have seen "Five Card Stud" and are concerned about the number of killings by the minister and the excessive violence in the picture. He has asked us to prepare a possible answer and defense . . . I have examined our picture file and find very little of help. Apparently, the picture was not SMA [Suggested for Mature Audiences]. Nor do I see any request for changes, either in the script or at any other level.[6]

The lack of correspondence about the picture's violence is very representative of Code files in the 1960s. The PCA had stopped responding to episodes of violence in the scripts it reviewed. The agency's complaints about *The Dirty Dozen*, for example, focused on profanity and depictions of prostitution, not violence. The lack of review given *5 Card Stud* was entirely in keeping with the PCA and MPAA's failure to engage filmmakers on the issues of violence in this period. The MPAA, however, did not wish to have to acknowledge this fact. Such an admission would be highly damaging and might even undermine the newly launched CARA ratings system. The agency's failure to stipulate that *5 Card Stud* go into release as an SMA picture was an additional embarrassment that pointed to the wayward, random affair that screen violence regulation had become in the 1960s.

One week following the memo to Shurlock, Eugene Dougherty responded that *5 Card Stud* would not be a problem film for the MPAA. He emphasized that the film's violence was not excessive, and the terms of the assurance he offered were fully reflective of the PCA's traditional approach—understandably, because Dougherty was an old hand in the Code office. That is, he found the violence neither quantitatively excessive nor the detailing of behavior to be unacceptably brutal or gruesome. "The number of killings is not excessive nor are they performed in any gruesome or brutal detail. They are merely Western-style vengeance of the tried-and-true variety."[7] The PCA's old genre-biasing is evident here, with the relatively greater latitude that was granted to Westerns. Dougherty added, "we rated it 'M' because of the subject matter, rather than any unpleasant details. . . . Mr. Valenti should have no serious complaints about this picture."

Dougherty went on to claim that application of the new G-M-R-X ratings system was being done with full care given to issues of screen violence. He claimed that the agency's scrutiny of the script for *The Night of the Following Day* (1968) resulted in the elimination of "excessively brutal, unusually gruesome . . . sex-oriented savagery" and that the film's R rating reflected its sexual (nonviolent) content. "Violence had ceased to be a concern in this film," he said, because the scripted brutality had been eliminated in the finished picture.

He was most effusive about the successful handling of violence in the World War II adventure-epic *Where Eagles Dare* (1968). Voicing again the PCA's traditional genre-biasing, Dougherty acknowledged that CARA was concerned with the picture's abundant violence, "but it is the less dangerous kind, in our opinion—war-related violence as compared to personal or criminal violence." Nevertheless, MGM had made extensive deletions in the film and had authorized CARA to state that the studio shared "our concern for excessive violence." CARA rated the film M.

In the end, the National Commission did not ask about *5 Card Stud,* but it did question Valenti extensively about *Bonnie and Clyde*—about whether he felt that picture's violence was excessive and about a murder committed by an eighteen-year-old who had just seen the film. Valenti dodged the question about the picture's level of violence by pointing out that the National Catholic Office of Motion Pictures (the former Legion of Decency) had voted it the "best mature picture of 1967" and called it "a great morality play."[8] Referring to the Catholic Church as "a great critic of senseless violence on the screen," Valenti said he would go along with their judgment of this picture. In regard to the apparent copycat crime he claimed that many things—virtually anything in fact—might trigger an already disturbed person and that films should not be made or restricted on the basis of the most disturbed members of a mass audience. He asserted that the screen must be free of censorship if it was going to flourish, and he promised that the new ratings system would be applied with full scrutiny given to depictions of violence. We will confront the limited effects of that promise later in this chapter when we review data on the incidence of violence in films across CARA's ratings categories.

As for *Bonnie and Clyde,* it would be very revealing to see the PCA's correspondence about the scripted violence in that picture. But, like some other key films—*Freaks* (1932) and *King Kong* (1933) among them—there is apparently no surviving case file on this picture. Geoffrey Shurlock, however, did reflect on the picture's violence in the oral history that he provided in 1970. His recollections suggest some of the considerations that would have gone into the negotiations over its violence—assuming that there were any, this being the low ebb of PCA engagement on that issue.

Surprisingly, he does not recall it as an especially inflammatory picture. The violence was carefully motivated in the story, and he regarded its overall level as being quite low. The number of killings and shootings was well below the huge body counts of 1930s gangster pictures. But the killings that did occur were bloodier than in the past, and therein lay the shock. The picture's violence, he said, "seemed to be in character and there did not seem to be too much of it. It was very violent when you saw it, but it was not a great deal of slaughter compared to what we have seen in fifty other gangster pictures where they just mow them down. There were very few people killed in *Bonnie and Clyde*. But there was a lot of bleeding and that was a shock."[9]

Beyond the danger that the National Commission would target specific films, the MPAA had another worry. Prior to Valenti's testimony, it was concerned that the Commission would ask hard questions about the MPAA's philosophy for regulating violence. In negotiations with filmmakers, how were depictions of violence assessed and evaluated? What considerations came into play when deciding whether a film got a PCA seal of approval or an M or R rating from CARA? This line of questioning could be especially dangerous because it would expose the ad-hoc nature of the industry's approach, its lack of an intellectual framework or philosophy to guide policy. The old terminology of "excessively brutal" or "gruesome" provided vague, subjective, and slippery standards for dealing with violence, and, as we have seen, the PCA was on the losing end of negotiations with filmmakers from the late 1940s onward.

The key development of the sixties was the emergence of "violence" as a discrete category disentangled from issues of behavior—from the considerations of criminality or genre that had subsumed it in previous decades. Facing this development, the MPAA lacked a sophisticated intellectual position on the issue, and it certainly can be argued that in the ensuing decades, it has never developed one. The many instances of egregiously mis-rated films—pictures with high levels of graphic violence carrying a PG rating—and the marketing of graphic violence to children, as detailed in the recent report of the Federal Trade Commission, suggest that the industry is still without a sophisticated understanding of the screen violence that it spends so much money creating and marketing.[10] Prior to Valenti's appearance before the National Commission, there was a flurry of activity at the MPAA as it struggled, in a last-minute fashion, to evolve a philosophy that he could offer as a basis for regulation.

An inter-office memo prepared for Shurlock less than a month before

Valenti's scheduled testimony tried to articulate some core issues that could guide CARA in making discriminations about the type and degree of violence in a given film. If this articulation of the issues could be refined, the memo's author suggested, then perhaps it could be presented as an appendix to Valenti's testimony, where it would serve to demonstrate that CARA was grappling with the issue of violence and trying to formulate policy around it. The memo unquestionably demonstrates an effort by the agency to think about issues of screen violence with a new level of detail.

It proposed a conceptual distinction between "personalized" and "nonpersonalized" violence. The relatively anonymous, large-scale violence in many war films could be considered nonpersonalized. The clutch-and-fall aesthetic exemplifies this conception of nonpersonalized violence. Personalized violence, by contrast, involved some degree of excessive brutality. "This is particularly significant with respect to the [CARA] ratings where the personalized aspect of the violence, i.e., sadism, brutality, etc., may be the factor which will place the motion picture in one category as opposed to another. Reference should be made to the attempt at the script level to secure changes so that the violence will not be 'personalized.'"[11] Implicit within this distinction is the notion that personalized violence is so-named because it involves some clearly depicted violation of the body—the "person" of a character—in contradistinction to nonpersonalized violence. Again, clutch-and-fall is the exemplar of nonpersonalized violence, so conceived.

A second key factor identified in the memo was the issue of consequences. Did a film show that violence had negative consequences for the victim and/or for society, or did it fail to show these? Was it better to depict screen violence in a clearly make-believe world (like the swordfights in an Errol Flynn swashbuckler), or was it more responsible for filmmakers, and better for viewers, to show violence with a more realistic depiction of its harsh consequences? The implication in the memo was that a depiction of consequences was preferable, but the MPAA was uncertain about the implications of changing its policy in this regard—about which mode of treatment it would be best to profess as agency policy. "A reference to the treatment of 'consequences' of violence, with perhaps a frank admission that the Code and Rating Administration is not sure whether the portrayal of the consequences and thus the removal of the violence from the unreal is more harmful than presenting the violence in a somewhat 'fanciful' or unreal setting."[12]

The MPAA's uncertainty about this question reflected a broader lack of consensus in the period about the effects of viewing screen violence and the characteristics of a film that are most implicated in those effects. The National Commission, for example, queried its witnesses extensively about *Bonnie and*

Clyde, Leonard Berkowitz, a social scientist who would become a prominent figure in the research on media effects, speculated that the ending of the film might have the effect of discouraging viewers from acting out what they had seen. According to this reasoning, the bloody montage depicting the deaths of Bonnie and Clyde showed the physical consequences of violence with a new level of explicitness and intensity. Berkowitz speculated that the film might have "a good effect of dampening the likelihood of the audience member acting aggressively himself, if he says to himself, yes, it can have this effect."[13]

Viewed this way, the film's graphic violence could be said to have a positive effect on viewers. As it turns out, however, the issue is a complex one, and it does not simply translate in practice to an equation of graphic violence with a chastened viewer. The induced effects of media violence depend on a host of factors. While *Bonnie and Clyde* does show the physical consequences of gun violence—the bullet strikes on their bodies are visualized in great detail—the film's style can be said to operate in an excitatory way on viewers, potentially working up aggressive predispositions in some viewers rather than dampening them. The montage editing and manipulation of different camera speeds creates an exciting and optically stimulating barrage of violent images. The effects of this style might prove to be more salient for some viewers than the film's depiction of the physical consequences of violence.[14]

Furthermore, without taking personality variables into account—viewers with personalities that show high levels of hostility may respond to film violence differently than viewers with low levels—and without assessing the stylistic design of violent episodes, an approach that focuses on a single variable such as "consequences" will fail to grasp the complex interactions between films and viewers. Personality factors are important because viewers differ in their reasons for watching movie violence and in the gratifications they derive from it. As Jeffrey Goldstein writes, "the attractions of violent imagery are many. . . . some viewers seek excitement, others companionship or social acceptance through shared experience, and still others wish to see justice enacted."[15] Still, though it is context-dependent, the issue of consequences is a very important one, and the MPAA was right to recognize it as a fundamental constituent in the depiction of screen violence.

The ideas floated in the memo were incorporated into a preliminary statement of CARA's position on screen violence and the philosophy guiding its classification of films. The statement said that while CARA accepted that violence was a necessary part of drama, it would pay close attention to certain aspects that might be worrisome. "Impersonal violence" was acceptable for general audience consumption. "War films have always fallen into this category. Who is going to be upset if the screen shows Teddy Roosevelt charging wildly up San Juan Hill and scattering the enemy like coconuts?"[16] When violence becomes "personalized and individualized," however, "legitimate combat scenes can degenerate into brutality." If such brutality is prolonged, then violence becomes sadistic. "Under the new rating system, a film containing such elements will be relegated to the 'R' and, in extreme cases, to 'X.'"

While the statement incorporated the idea that personalized violence was distinct from violence involving relatively anonymous members of a group, it was scarcely more precise than the old Code constructions of brutality and gruesomeness. A more interesting and systematic attempt to think through issues of screen violence and provide some guidelines for assessing its depiction appears in an informal handwritten memo to Shurlock. Its author emphasizes how important it is to think about violence on the screen and underlines the word "violence," a gesture that indicates the new salience that this term had acquired in 1968. "I have and have had over the years some very strong convictions about *violence*, or rather, the acceptability of violence on the screen." The memo then ranks categories of violence according to how acceptable or worrisome they are, with the most objectionable categories coming first.

- Where the aggressor virtually *enjoys* his violence, we should carry a big stick and be very stingy [i.e., impose a harsh rating like an R]. Barbara refers to this in her paragraph #3 when she uses the word sadism [see note 11].
- Where the aggressor is visually *indifferent* we should be a *little* more lenient. This is a gray area and difficult to define. We have had this in quite a few Westerns and gangster pictures.
- Where the aggressor *dislikes* his violence visually, we should be more permissive. This dislike can be very subtle shown by even slight facial expressions or body movements.
- Where the aggressor *loathes* his violence, we should be most permissive. This is rather rare but it has occurred several times. You know what I mean—closing your eyes and pulling the trigger.

The memo closed with a postscript: "As I read the above I find several holes. I haven't mentioned such vital things as provocation, self-defense or justification."[17]

The ideas in this memo go well beyond the diffuse and global categories of "brutality" and "gruesomeness" employed by the PCA. They represent an effort to create a scheme for analyzing and categorizing violence according to characteristics of the aggressor, and his or her emotional relationship to the violence being perpetrated. The assumption is that the manner by which the aggressor is depicted can make a moral statement about the violence that is portrayed in the scene, with more opprobrium being attached to scenes suggesting that the commission of murder or assault can be pleasurable than to scenes suggesting that aggression is being committed reluctantly. The scheme is also attentive to the visual depiction of the aggressor's emotional states (e.g., "closing your eyes and pulling the trigger"), and this attention provides for a more powerful analysis of cinematic violence than what the PCA was able to accomplish. In the old gangster films, for example, scene after scene showed gangsters gleefully blasting away at their enemies, while an anti-gangster message was conveyed in a woefully inadequate fashion through a few lines of dialogue spoken by police or other guardians of public safety. Audiences understandably responded to the élan of the killers and not the pulchritude of the public authorities.

As tentative as it is, the memo provided a promising start at creating a typology of screen violence relevant for the rating of films. It proposed an ordinal scale for ranking scenes of violence in terms of regulatory action. The unit of analysis—the aggressor's emotion—was conceptualized at four value levels, ascending from "loathes" to "dislikes" to "indifferent" to "enjoys," with a corresponding increase in the regulatory scrutiny that CARA would give to scenes as they ascended higher on the scale. But little of consequence evidently ensued from the ideas in the memo and the others floated during the flurry of activity that preceded Valenti's testimony before the National Commission.

In fact, an ad hoc approach to rating films has prevailed at CARA. It has been far more lenient in rating the violent content of films than in rating sexual content. In this respect, the thinking evident in the flurry of MPAA correspondence that surrounded the approach of the National Commission hearings proved to be of relatively short duration. Public outcry, for example, over high levels of violence in films rated PG—those to which children can be admitted without adult supervision—prompted the MPAA to reluctantly create in 1984 a new ratings category, PG-13, to serve as a mid-point between PG and R. Valenti said at the time, "if the violence is real tough, if it is persistent, it still will go into R. What we have now and didn't have before is a way station between R and PG. If there are any doubts about a picture being a little tough for a PG, it will be a PG-13."[18]

And yet CARA's failure to demonstrate a consistent and systematic approach to the rating of violent content persisted. A content analysis of the fifty top-grossing films of 1998, conducted by the Center for Media and Public Affairs, found that half of the most violent films in the sample carried a PG-13 rating rather than R.[19] This sample contained more than 2,300 scenes of violence (one scene might contain numerous acts of violence), and sixty percent of these scenes depicted serious violence causing severe injury or death.

In another study examining the amount of film violence in different ratings categories, the National Coalition on Television Violence found that there is no difference in the amount of violence in PG and PG-13 films, despite Jack Valenti's promise that PG-13 would be used to house "tough" and "persistent" depictions of violence. In a sample of more than a thousand movies rated by the MPAA from 1981 to 1992, PG and PG-13 films both had an average of twenty violent acts per hour as compared with thirty-three for R-rated films. Thus, although the CARA system uses four ratings categories, in practice there are really only three categories when violence is involved: G, PG/PG-13, and R.[20]

MOVIE VIOLENCE ON TELEVISION: *THE PROFESSIONALS*

With the inception of CARA and the fall of the Production Code, the film industry quite simply had abandoned its role as a gatekeeper regulating the flow of violent material into the culture—with the result that the outflow of violent imagery has now become a torrent. Ironically, however, as Hollywood relaxed its standards governing the production and marketing of violent movies, television assumed some of the traditional mission of the now-defunct PCA, at least in the time period that immediately followed the inception of the CARA ratings scheme. The hard-edged pictures that Hollywood began making in the late 1960s and early 1970s eventually found their way to network television, where they presented a problem for the network offices of program practices and standards. The films would have to be cut for broadcast, and the networks found themselves cast in the role of the now-defunct PCA, negotiating with filmmakers over cuts that would preserve the films as designed and yet diminish the duration, explicitness, and intensity of the depicted violence. Filmmakers now found themselves locked with the networks in the same kind of dialogue that they had maintained with the PCA.

Two examples will help to illustrate this development. Richard Brooks's *The Professionals* (1966) is a rollicking adventure about American mercenaries in Mexico during the revolution. The film does not contain the bloody squibs and slow-motion violence that became a cinematic norm a year later with *Bonnie and Clyde*, but there are abundant killings committed with bow and arrow, knife, machete, by strangling, and by gunshots to the head. Although the MPAA had revised the Production Code in 1966 to include a new SMA rating (Suggested for Mature Audiences) to designate adult-themed pictures, *The Professionals* failed to carry an SMA designation when it went to theaters, prompting the National Catholic Office of Motion Pictures to object that the picture's brutality merited this designation.[21]

When the picture was slotted to run on CBS in 1972, the network's vice president of program practices wrote to Columbia Pictures (the studio that produced and distributed *The Professionals*) to remind Columbia about "the overriding issue the subject of violence has become for the television industry" and about the network's efforts "to minimize violence on television."[22] The media violence controversies of the late 1960s had not diminished by 1972. In fact, that year the Surgeon General's Commission investigating violence on television had rejected the catharsis hypothesis (that viewing media aggression would provide a safe outlet for a viewer's hostile impulses) and concluded that the empirical evidence supported a connection between viewing television violence and antisocial behavior.[23] Feeling the pressures created by the violence controversy, the network wanted a strangling scene cut, which it deemed too violent, and another scene that showed the execution of Mexican government soldiers by the revolutionaries. Some are hung, and some are shot in the head at close range.

Richard Brooks, the film's director, tried to intercede with the network to protect the film from being cut, while pledging his cooperation and agreement that "the issue of violence in the entertainment media is indeed monumental."[24] He appealed to the network on the basis of artistic freedom in terms that reflected the new realities of post-PCA Hollywood. "I believe, however, that one of the principal objectives of an 'artist' is to mirror life—within the bounds of good taste. . . . Understandably, not *all* creative work is suited to *all* of the people *all* of the time." This was the philosophy of niche audience marketing—every film is not for all viewers—that had emerged with the collapse of the PCA and the transition to CARA. By the early 1970s, this philosophy was well established in cinema. Network television, by contrast, had inherited cinema's role as a mass medium catering to a mass audience. Consequently, it could not endorse this philosophy.

As a result, the scene where the film's hero, played by Lee Marvin, strangles a Mexican sentry was deemed too lengthy in its depiction of the murder. Television had no PG category in which it could house the scene or the film's exhibition. Faced with the disparity now prevailing between cinema and television, Brooks conceded, "the strangling of the guard may indeed be too violently *long* for children to see. Abbreviate it—do not delete it entirely." In regards to the execution scene, "perhaps some of the violence can be minimized as you suggest." But he again urged that the story required that much of the scene be left intact.

Exactly like the PCA had done in its efforts to tone down violence commit-

48. Since the silent era censors regularly deleted images of arrows or knives sticking into characters, and the PCA tried to limit such depictions. The problem continued to persist after the Production Code was retired. Director Richard Brooks was pressured by network television to cut arrow sticks from *The Professionals* when the film was slated for broadcast in 1972.

ted with sharp-edged weapons, CBS objected to images in the film showing arrows striking victims in the back and chest. The network wrote again to Brooks to suggest eliminating "the actual entry of the arrow into the back of the first guy, and minimize the second one as the arrow strikes his chest."[25] Brooks's position was to cooperate while maintaining his right to control the film's editing. "I *DO* believe we can agree on a version of 'The Professionals' for broadcasting purposes. At the same time, I have no intention of relinquishing my legal right to approve all cutting and editing of the movie, which right was granted to me by Columbia Pictures."[26]

As it had done in the Hollywood era and was now doing with television, hard-edged violence exerted a destructive force on the organic unity of a film's design. By inciting regulatory action and the editing of a film for other than artistic reasons, hard violence disintegrated the body of a film, scattering it in different versions across various distribution outlets. This is an enduring truth about the phenomenon of violence in cinema. It wounds the bodies of the characters in the story on whom it is perpetrated, and it wounds the films that harbor it by occasioning their mutation to satisfy the regulatory policies of varying distribution channels. In this sense, it can be argued that by filming hard violence filmmakers may be committing a kind of violence upon their own work, to the extent that they have occasioned the necessary alteration of that work across different distribution media and to the extent that they become complicit in that alteration. A vivid example of this process is provided the by rape–murder scene in Alfred Hitchcock's *Frenzy* (1972) and the elaborate negotiations that went on between Hitchcock and ABC in 1974 when the network was preparing to air the film.

MOVIE VIOLENCE ON TELEVISION: *FRENZY*

Frenzy is a supreme example of what Hollywood lost when it replaced the Production Code with the CARA ratings. Nearly all of Hitchcock's Hollywood films were made under the auspices of the PCA, when he had to use suggestion and oblique references to imply brutality or sexual behavior that he couldn't directly show. With an extended killing scene, *Torn Curtain* (1966) reflected the liberalized Code of the mid-sixties, and *Topaz* (1969) was released in the CARA period. But *Frenzy* was the first and only film in which Hitchcock luxuriated in the new freedoms available to filmmakers at that time.

The rape–murder scene is easily the most violent and repellent sequence that he ever filmed, and it was clearly designed for the niche audience segment that the R rating made possible. It isn't merely that the scene is violent; it features a new kind of violence depicted in a graphic manner not found in the classical Hollywood period: explicit and savage brutality and the commingling of sexual pleasure with sadistic cruelty. (As I noted in chapter four, scenes showing the torture and brutalization of women do recur in Hollywood film, often accompanied by a kind of free-floating sexual rage. But stylistic amplitude is a key discriminator. Those scenes are shorter and much less detailed than what Hitchcock shows in *Frenzy*.) We see Rusk, a serial killer, rape and then strangle Brenda Blaney, and the scene dwells in detail on the victim's terror and Rusk's savage pleasure. The rape is quite protracted, and so is the killing that follows. ABC television initially requested that the entire scene be deleted from the film, and this instigated a protracted and intricate series of negotiations with Hitchcock and Universal.

This development came as no surprise to the studio. Back in 1971, before the film went into production, executives at Universal evaluated the script and anticipated the problems that the picture would likely encounter when it went to television. As an inter-office memo acknowledged, "historically, the television networks have been extremely reluctant to show scenes of women being brutally assaulted or killed. NBC, especially, is quite sensitive about this, and we have been required to edit considerably such violence in order to de-emphasize the on-screen visual horror of a scene."[27] The memo listed the rape of Brenda, and another scene where a corpse is brutalized in a potato truck, as problem areas "for which production coverage might be devised in order to make the scenes acceptable for television release." In other words, the studio recommended that Hitchcock shoot inoffensive shots that could be substituted for problem footage in these scenes for network airing. Ironically, in this era of new cinematic freedoms, the studio's advice replicated PCA policy. As we have seen, the PCA occasionally advised filmmakers to shoot coverage when it anticipated that problems might arise in screening a film for clearance. A film's release for television was now producing the same pressures that theatrical release had incurred in previous decades.

In 1973, once the film had completed its theatrical run, Universal prepared a preliminary version of the film for television, using a cutaway to a telephone to cover deleted footage of the rape and nudity. Hitchcock rejected the use of this insert, fearing that it damaged the narrative sense and dramatic continuity of the scene: "This cut is a very bad piece of continuity because it creates the impression that Blaney is going to interrupt the murder [with a call on the phone]. It would be far better to stay on the murder and, if you wish to avoid the breasts, just show the tearing of the dress and use the big head of Rusk to cut away from it. Cutting away to the telephone absolutely ruins the dramatic continuity of the murder."[28]

When Universal worked on the scene to create a version that complied with ABC's suggested eliminations, multiple cutaways to the telephone were used to cover deleted footage, including the rape, the nudity, and much of the murder. When Hitchcock screened this version he objected to the inserts of the telephone, and he thereafter closely supervised the editing of the television version, trying to get a result that would be aesthetically acceptable and still satisfactory for ABC. "To start with, all the inserts of the telephone must be deleted. More to follow on this sequence."[29]

Hitchcock worked to create what was essentially a new sequence, omitting details of the murder but with proper attention to issues of narrative clarity and continuity. He strove for compromise solutions that would satisfy the network censors as well as his own filmmaking instincts. In the theatrical version, Hitchcock's camera stays inside the violence, playing it on the faces of the characters and in the face of the viewer. As the scene begins, Rusk removes his tie, prompting Brenda's terror-struck realization that he is the notorious necktie killer. Numerous close-ups of Rusk's savage face, Brenda's terrified

49. The rape and murder scene in *Frenzy* required much re-editing by Hitchcock in order to produce an acceptable television version of its violence.

reactions, her anguished prayer to God during the rape, Rusk's lunatic sounds of pleasure, the tie going around her neck and cinching tight, her eyes distending in fear, her fingers fluttering against the knot—Hitchcock weaves these shots into a montage that prolongs the killing and details it in vivid terms. After the murder, a grotesque close-up shows Brenda's dead face, her mouth open, her tongue horribly protruding. Rusk lingers in the office with the body, munches on an apple, then leisurely exits and walks down an alley and out into traffic. Brenda's ex-husband, Richard Blaney, then arrives at her building and heads for her office.

The new sequence that Hitchcock designed omitted all of the close-ups detailing the murder and used Brenda's reaction to the tie, as Rusk removes it, as a means for going out of the scene. The action would be as follows:

Close-up Brenda saying: 'My God, the tie.' Then go back to Rusk taking off his tie. Then a short (3 feet) DISSOLVE TO Rusk going out of the building. When the CAMERA PANS him up the alley toward the main thoroughfare—

and the CAMERA REMAINS STILL—CUT TO a 2 foot SUBLIMINAL FLASH of the dead woman—then go back to BLANEY in the alleyway and continue with BLANEY going up the staircase, etc.[30]

The detailed instruction to insert the subliminal flash of Brenda's corpse, at the point where the camera pan of Rusk in the alley had stopped, illustrates the care that Hitchcock was taking with this alternate version of the scene. He did not regard the new version as something to throw away on television. Inserting the subliminal flash when the camera had stopped moving would provide a smoother and less distracting transition point between the images than would be the case if the insert were simply dropped into the middle of the panning movement. Hitchcock even dispatched an executive from Universal to travel to New York and meet with ABC to discuss his suggestions. ABC, however, could not approve the flash insert of the dead Brenda because the shot was too gruesome. Her eyes were open, and her tongue was sticking out. These details were "too horrible" for the network.[31] The network did agree, however, to the use of an alternate and less disturbing image for the insert, "a ¾ side shot of her lying back in the chair—we can see very plainly that she is dead."

Hitchcock still wasn't finished tinkering with the scene. A month later, he fine-tuned the re-edit of "what used to be 'The Rape' sequence" by requesting two immediate changes:

1. As at present cut—Brenda says, 'My God, the tie' after Rusk is unpinning the 'tiepin.' Of course, this is incorrect. Rusk should unpin the tiepin—then start to take off his tie—then CUT to Brenda saying, 'My God the tie'—and:
2. Go out on her screaming, instead of going out on Rusk pulling off his tie as previously requested.[32]

Changing the positioning of Brenda's dialogue served to clarify that it is the action with the tie, not the tiepin, that betrays Rusk's true identity to her. Everyone in London knows about the notorious "necktie strangler," and Brenda now realizes her probable fate. Cutting out of the scene on the scream simply made for better filmmaking by creating an audio climax, giving the end of the scene a punch that it didn't otherwise have.

Other scenes in the film—the violation of a naked corpse in the potato truck and shots of a nude dead woman in Rusk's bed at the end—were rejected by ABC and occasioned re-editing by Hitchcock. In the film, police spy the body protruding from the back of the truck and give chase. The body falls off the truck, bounces on the roadway and is nearly hit by the police car. Even by today's standards, this imagery is exceedingly horrific. ABC wanted all views of the body deleted, which prompted Hitchcock to object that this would destroy the logic of the scene: "As now edited [with all views of the corpse deleted] there is no reason for the police car to follow the truck. We should see the body, which is in VERY LONG SHOT and cannot be offensive, from the policemen's POINT OF VIEW. We should also see the body fall off the truck. Also, please put back the shot of the police car pulling up against the body; this shot can be cut in half."[33] ABC agreed to put back the glimpses of the corpse as seen by the cops but would not agree to the body falling to the ground and bouncing on the pavement. As a result, the television sequence ended just as the police see the body and start to give chase. The shot of the dead woman in Rusk's bed at the end of the film was also too horrific for the network. It rejected Hitchcock's suggestion that the shot be trimmed and used in a subliminal fashion and proposed, instead, using a blow-up frame that would show only her chin and neck with a tie knotted around it.

The elaborately detailed negotiations between Hitchcock and ABC and the extended care he gave to the television edit of his film illuminate the significant disparity in the degrees of freedom under which Hollywood and network television now operated. The end of the Production Code served to increase the tendency for hard violence to corrode and dissolve the integrity of a film's finished design. While this had always been an implicit tendency under the Code, in practice the PCA worked to avoid this by front-loading all of its suggestions at the script stage. Thus, the tendency for hard violence to deform a finished film mainly came into play as the picture went into distribution and had to pass through regional and overseas censor boards.

While the problem was a persistent one throughout the classical Hollywood era, it gained renewed force with the institution of CARA and the sudden disparity that developed between theatrical film and the standards of broadcast television. The care that Richard Brooks and Alfred Hitchcock gave to the preparation of television versions of their films was predicated on their desire to minimize the bastardization of their work in television release. But all filmmakers did not enjoy this privilege. Hitchcock and Brooks were top guns in the industry in this period; less prominent directors did not supervise television edits of their work.

Broadcast television had inherited the PCA's mandate to make the medium acceptable to a broad audience. The film industry, by contrast, could now tailor adult material to select audience segments. Then, as now, the demographic for violent films principally includes young viewers, who tend to be male. When Warner Bros. was preparing to release Sam Peckinpah's *The Wild Bunch*, the studio's marketing surveys revealed that viewers who most approved of the film were males ages 17 to 25, and Warners resolved to go after this demographic in its advertising and promotion.[34]

MARKETING VIOLENCE IN CONTEMPORARY CULTURE

When the CARA system debuted and the restrictions of the Production Code were lifted, the public face the MPAA put on was the celebration of artistic freedom. Filmmakers would now be free to pursue mature subject matter, handled in a mature fashion for mature viewers. In practice, however, movie violence has become a saleable commodity for the film industry, and the ugly face of the niche marketing of film violence that has prevailed since 1968 is the targeting of young viewers. A 2000 report by the Federal Trade Commission clarified the extent to which the film industry currently aims its violent films at an adolescent audience.[35] The Commission studied the marketing of 44 violent R-rated films and 20 violent PG-13-rated films released by the majors between 1995 and 1999. It found that the marketing of 35 of the R-rated pictures (80 percent) targeted children under seventeen, using such tactics as placing advertising on radio and television shows aimed at young people, recruiting them for focus group research, and distributing promotional materials at "strategic teen hangouts" such as shopping malls, sporting events, and arcades. One studio described its plans for a violent picture thusly: "Our goal was to find the elusive teen target audience and make sure everyone between the ages of 12–18 was exposed to the film."[36]

The majors tested rough cuts of thirty-three of these R-rated films on audiences that included teenagers under seventeen, which is the cut-off age stipulated by the rating for admitting children into theaters unaccompanied by an adult. The majors, in other words, tested the films on viewers whose ages were inappropriate under the logic and provisions of the industry's own ratings code. One major studio's plans for a sequel to a popular R-rated film targeted 12-to-24-year-olds in its market research because that had been the core audience for the original picture, and the plan stipulated that half of the research sample be composed of 12-to-17-year-olds. But an even younger cohort was targeted. "Although the original movie was 'R' rated and the sequel will also be 'R' rated, there is evidence to suggest that attendance at the original [movie] dipped down to the age of 10. Therefore, it seems to make sense to interview 10 or 11 year olds as well."[37] Nickelodeon thwarted the plans of one major to air commercials for a violent PG-13 film on the cable network, whose audience is composed mostly of children under twelve. Nickelodeon objected that the trailer included things not found on the network's programming, such as gun

271

battles, fights, and exploding bombs. In explaining its attempt to air a violent trailer on the network, the studio's ad agency noted, "this film needs the audience Nickelodeon provides to be successful."[38]

The Federal Trade Commission also found numerous instances where trailers approved by CARA for 'all audiences' contained a sampling of an R-rated picture's violence. The trailer for *I Know What You Did Last Summer* (1997), a popular slasher film, contained verbal references "to decapitation and to a person 'being gutted with a hook,'" and the trailer for *Scream 2* (1997), another slasher film, contained "a verbal reference to mutilation (that a woman had been stabbed seven times) and several depictions of violence against women (women being pursued by a masked, knife-wielding killer)."[39]

These marketing efforts by the film industry point to a significant change in the medium of television since the period that surrounded the inception of CARA and the efforts of filmmakers like Brooks and Hitchcock to adjust their work to television terms. Since that time, television has drawn closer to theatrical film in the abundance and hardness of its violent programming. Television, too, has come to niche-market relatively graphic violence to viewers, and in both cinema and television the audience for violent entertainment has continued to skew toward the young and toward male viewers. An analysis of *Times Mirror* data, for example, on television viewing in 1993 showed that the heaviest consumers of violent programs were males aged 18–34, followed by females 18–34 and by males in the 35–49 category.[40]

The young adult audience provides one of the main props for today's film industry. It is prized by advertisers and by film industry executives because it has discretionary income and is highly driven to purchase consumer goods—and because it goes to the movies frequently. The Motion Picture Association's 2000 Motion Picture Attendance Study found that teenagers and young adults (ages 12–24) represented nearly half of the nation's frequent moviegoers (defined as going at least once per month) at the beginning of the 1990s and has hovered around 40 percent since then.[41]

Because this demographic is a key one for the industry, film and other media companies have been more than willing to feed its appetite for violence. This, in turn, has accelerated the profusion of violence in contemporary visual culture. Violent films today are conjoined with violence in other programming formats—made-for-television films (broadcast and cable), music videos, television series (broadcast and cable), and video games—to create a widespread popular culture of mayhem whose reach is nearly inescapable. The turn to graphic violence occurred first in theatrical film and has now spread, in greater and lesser degrees, to these other formats.

THE PREVALENCE OF SCREEN VIOLENCE IN CONTEMPORARY CULTURE

The degree to which media violence saturates the culture is indeed impressive. A content analysis conducted by the Center for Media and Public Affairs sampled multiple forms of popular entertainment in 1998 and 1999.[42] These included television series, broadcast and cable movies, theatrical films, and music videos. The sample of 284 television series episodes contained more than 3,000 acts of violence, with an average rate of 12 acts per episode. The sample of 50 television movies contained 865 violent acts, an average of 17 per film. The sample of 50 top-grossing theatrical films included 2,319 violent acts, an average of 46 per film. The sample of 188 MTV music videos carried 1,785 acts of violence—an average of 4 per video, which is quite high given the short running time of a music video.

Combined, the four popular culture formats featured an average of 31 acts of violence per hour. It would appear that, if a viewer watched equal amounts of television series and movies, music videos and theatrical films, that viewer on average would see a violent act every two minutes. But a significant trait that emerged from the data is that few films or programs featured an average amount of violence. They tended to cluster into high-violence and low-violence groupings. "This is not coincidental," the researchers point out. "Entertainment products are increasingly aimed at niche audiences or particular demographic segments of the population. Particular sub-genres, such as action-adventure TV series and slasher movies, are aimed at youthful audiences, particularly young males. So it is not surprising that much of the violence we coded was clustered in a relatively small portion of the sample."[43]

With regard to slasher films, these are hyper-violent cultural products, but the incidence of violence in the films is still startling. In a content analysis of thirty slasher films from 1980, 1985, and 1989, Molitor and Sapolsky found a total of 1,573 violent acts in the sample, an average of 52 per film.[44] 'Extreme' forms of violence (burning, dismemberment, beheading, bludgeoning or stabbing) typified more than a quarter (28 percent) of all violence coded across the sample.

Other components of the films accentuated the experience of violence. The researchers measured the expression of fear by victims and found on average that eleven minutes per film were devoted to the spectacle of victims in fear. Another study of slasher films found extended depictions of fear and a direct connection of this fear to violence. A content analysis of 56 films found that 474 characters were shown in fear of being killed, and 86 percent of these characters did not survive their ordeal of terror.[45] In a content analysis of the ten biggest-grossing slasher films, Weaver found that the average length of scenes showing the death of male characters was just under 2 minutes and those showing the death of female characters was just under 4 minutes, and that these lengthy intervals were accompanied by expressions of fear, terror, and pain.[46]

Slasher films furnish a compelling example of niche-marketed violence. Their primary audience is teenagers, and the appeal of the films lies in witnessing acts of slaughter. A 1990 survey of 220 teenagers found that 95 percent of them reported viewing slasher movies and that one of the prime motivations, not surprisingly, was enjoyment derived from watching blood and guts.[47]

Violent video games have borrowed and expanded the syntax of the slasher films. One of the features of slashers that provoked considerable dismay when the format began to proliferate in the early 1980s was the extended scenes that showed victims from the killer's point of view as he stalked them. Subjective camerawork simulated the killer's perspective for viewers. In the films, however, these subjective interludes are relatively brief. The optical perspective throughout most of a film—as is true for virtually all films of every genre—is third-person perspective, not tied to the literal point of view of any character.

In this regard, some of the violent video games that began to flourish in the 1990s seized on the most notorious visual device of the slasher films—the subjective shots simulating the killer's point of view—and replicated the device throughout the whole of a game, making it the structural foundation of its appeal to a player. First-person shooter games such as Mortal Kombat, Street Fighter, Wolfenstein 3D, and Postal enable the player to simulate killing and to feel the results at a physiological level. Elaborate graphics reward the player's successful "hit" with a splash of blood and viscera and the screams of the victim. Whereas the subjective camerawork of slasher films invites the viewer to identify with the killer, these subjective interludes are offset by the presence of other characters in the film, with whom the viewer can form alliances. By contrast, in the first-person video games, identification with the aggressor is more complete, providing the foundation of the game. The graphics replicate details of violence as seen from the killer's perspective. A shotgun victim blasted at close range, for example, may explode with more viscera and blood than is the case when the victim is shot from a greater distance. As media researcher Craig Anderson points out,

> In TV shows and movies there may be several characters with which an observer can identify, some of whom may not behave in a violent fashion. In most violent video games, the player must identify with one violent character. In "first person shooters," for instance, the player assumes the identity of

the hero or heroine, and then controls that character's actions throughout the game. This commonly includes selection of weapons and target and use of the weapons to wound, maim, or kill the various enemies in the game environment.[48]

Like slasher films, violent video games hold great appeal for young audiences. In a sample of fourth-grade children, for example, 73 percent of boys and 59 percent of girls reported that their favorite video games were violent ones.[49]

Slasher films and first-person shooter games attract their audiences with graphic presentations of violence: bodies exploding with blood and viscera, the screams of maimed and dying victims. While these media formats are striking examples of the expansion of violent entertainment in contemporary culture, in one sense at least they are not typical of the great bulk of violent material that now circulates through society. Most of the violence depicted in film and television is relatively pain-free and does not show serious consequences for its victims, such as damage to the body or emotional suffering. This mode of depicting violence has deep roots in American cinema. As we have seen, the PCA and regional censors were generally opposed to depictions of suffering and pain.

A content analysis conducted at the University of Southern California of the 100 top-grossing American films of 1994 found more than two thousand violent acts against people in the sample. Nearly 90 percent of this violence, however, showed no consequences to the recipient's body, even though the great bulk of the violence was committed with lethal or moderate force.[50] Nine out of ten violent scenes showed no bodily injuries such as bleeding, bruising, broken bones, or, at the greatest extremity, death or dying. The authors of the study comment, "in the film world, the human body's durability under violent attack is often greatly exaggerated, the links between injury causes and consequences appearing to have been suspended altogether."

The Center for Media and Public Affairs' content analysis found similar results: high rates of violence depicted as doing little or no damage to victims. Seventy-five percent of the violence on broadcast series and 68 percent on cable programs depicted no physical injuries. Psychological harm was even less frequent. Ninety percent of the violent acts on broadcast series and 87 percent on cable were shown as causing no distress to victims or to their friends or relatives. In made-for-television movies, upward of 60 percent of the violence was without physical or emotional consequences. In theatrical film, 79 percent of the violence lacked physical consequences and 84 percent lacked emotional consequences. Comparable rates prevailed for music videos. Summarizing these content trends, which were very similar across these visual media formats, the authors conclude,

> In the world of popular entertainment, bullets frequently miss their mark, heroes bounce back from beatings without a scratch, and few victims of violence are emotionally traumatized by the experience. Further, violence is often carried out by good guys who act out of laudable motives, such as self-defense or the defense of others. Finally, scripts almost never carry explicit criticism of the use of violence. In Hollywood's fantasy world, violence just happens, it happens often, and it often happens for a good reason.[51]

By showing violence as pain-free and abundant, it arguably becomes trivialized—and therefore more easily assimilated by viewers as entertainment and as a condition of screen reality that seems pervasive, inescapable, and without serious implication for either victims or viewer. Media violence researcher James Potter points out that such depictions of violence without consequences may be sending exactly the wrong message to viewers.

> The contextual web of realistic, serious, painful action that surrounds graphic portrayals of violence serves both to outrage viewers to complain about these portrayals and at the same time protects them from negative effects, especially of disinhibition and desensitization. In contrast, it is the nongraphic violence that is surrounded by the much more antisocial web of context. While viewers are much less outraged by this "other" violence—which is much more prevalent on television—they are much more at risk of learning that violence is fun, successful, and non-harmful.[52]

As violent movies, videos, and television shows have proliferated, the question that has lingered throughout the history of cinema now haunts contemporary society more strongly than ever. Does media violence influence some viewers to act violently? It is a dangerous question to ask because—like the question about whether smoking causes cancer—the answer threatens the product that industries invest millions of dollars creating and because it carries policy implications that require careful tailoring so as not to violate First Amendment protections on speech.

The question persistently arises with the problem of "copycat" crimes—violent acts that are apparently inspired by media programming. These crimes are often of a disturbingly extreme nature and typically appear to be transpositions of some scene in a film that the perpetrator has witnessed. In a previous chapter, I mentioned one of the earliest documented examples of a copycat incident, the killing in 1931 of sixteen-year-old William Gamble by a twelve-year-old playmate who was acting out a scene from a gangster film, *The Secret Six* (1931). But the history of classical Hollywood contains numerous other examples.

Protest letters from angry viewers and newspaper clippings contained in the MPAA's file archives recount other instances of copycat behavior. Among the clippings are incidents in 1946 from Iowa and New York. The *Des Moines Tribune* reported on the arrest of two boys, twleve and fourteen years old, for a string of burglaries. "Explaining they got the idea from "gangster movies," the boys told the sheriff they had committed at least 7 burglaries and an auto theft this week."[53] A boy arrested in New York was also an aspiring stickup man. "After seeing a movie show, a grimy-faced 10-year-old boy, trying to look like a hold-up man, walked into the Madison House in the Murray Hill district at Madison Avenue . . . flashed a toy pistol made of plastic material [and] announced 'This is a stick-up.' "[54]

One viewer who wrote to the MPAA felt distressed at hearing reports and rumors of apparent movie-inspired crime. "Not long ago, a murderer confessed that he brutally killed a young woman after seeing a horror show. He went immediately to another horror show and then killed his second victim. Many of these young criminals have admitted getting their ideas from pictures."[55] This viewer went on to relate an incident she had heard about in which a pair of adulterous lovers murdered the woman's husband after seeing *The Postman Always Rings Twice*, which was about just such a crime.

To the extent that the movies have inspired some of these incidents, they have done so through the vivid and exciting attention that they give to crime and violence. As y-axis amplitude has increased over the decades, this attention has become more vivid. Many of the viewers in the 1940s who wrote to the MPAA were upset about the attention that films gave to violent crime. Numerous writers complained about the high tide of violence in Hollywood film and pointed to the disparity between the incidence of violence in film and what they encountered in their own lives. Compared with the world they knew and inhabited, the film world was much more dangerous and violent. As a Brooklyn attorney wrote the MPAA in 1946, "this week I saw four movies that had a combined total of about 40 murders by pistol and dagger and a large number of sluggings that must have resulted in serious injuries and death. . . . I have never witnessed a killing in real life, yet must see at least one in two out of three movies I see."[56] The Cultural Indicators research project at the University of Pennsylvania has documented precisely this kind of disparity in the world of television, where the incidence of crime is much greater than real world crime rates and, the researchers suggest, leads some viewers to hold more anxious and fearful views of the world. The researchers term this the "mean world syndrome."[57]

Copycat incidents and attendant anxieties about the social effects of the movies helped motivate the Payne Fund Studies in 1933, the first extensive empirical look at the effects of Hollywood film on young viewers. Herbert Blumer, one of the authors of the studies, concluded that the excitement and appeal of cinema can overwhelm established modes of socialization such as school and the family. Blumer argued that movies about crime or sex can predispose some viewers to antisocial behavior, and he interviewed a number of young people arrested for petty crimes and found that many cited the movies as a key source that gave them ideas about committing the acts that got them into trouble. He wrote, "there are always a few delinquents and criminals who can trace in their own experience a connection between such influences and their own crime."[58] As we will see in a moment, much contemporary behavioral research on the effects of movies focuses on just this area—the ways that films can prime certain thought clusters and emotional associations that underlie aggressive behavior.

Copycat crimes are not new, and abundant examples from recent decades attest to the enduring nature of this phenomenon. The 1973 film *Magnum Force* apparently inspired the killing mode employed by two men who held up an audio electronics store in Utah. The robbers forced five employees to drink Drano and then put duct tape over their mouths. Three of the victims died, and one of the killers, who was later executed, claimed that they had gotten the idea from the film, which shows a pimp killing a prostitute by making her drink Drano.[59]

Famous cases involving television movies include *The Burning Bed*, which aired in 1984 and depicted a battered wife who set her husband and his bed on fire.[60] After the film aired, an Ohio woman shot her boyfriend, claiming he abused her like the husband in the film, and a Milwaukee man soaked his wife with gasoline and set her on fire. A few days after *Born Innocent* aired on network television in 1974, four teenagers raped a nine-year-old girl with an empty beer bottle on a San Francisco beach. The film depicted the rape of a teenager, played by Linda Blair, with a plumber's helper in a girl's reform school. The leader of the San Francisco gang said she had gotten the idea for the crime from the film.[61]

Other films from the 1970s linked to copycat crimes include *Taxi Driver*, which John Hinckley, Jr., who wounded President Reagan in 1982, had viewed numerous times. Hinckley modeled his behavior, clothing, and food intake on the film's psychopath, Travis Bickle.[62] The Russian Roulette scene in

The Deer Hunter (1978) inspired thirty-one copycat incidents in which hand-guns were used in rituals of Russian roulette between 1978 and 1982.[63]

Depictions of Russian roulette in subsequent films continued to exert a strong influence. A young man who shot himself in 1994 apparently was emulating the behavior of Mel Gibson's character in *Lethal Weapon* (1987).[64] Psyched up with suicidal longings, the Gibson character puts a semi-loaded gun to his head and defiantly pulls the trigger. Gibson survives; the viewer imitating this behavior did not. Another teenage victim of this ritual in 1998 may have been imitating a scene in the movie *one eight seven* (1997), where antagonists play Russian roulette in a deadly game of chicken.[65] Yet another victim of the ritual used a gun while watching a video of *Bad Boys* (1983), specifically a scene in which a cop puts a pistol to an informant's head.[66] Other suicides and related injuries that do not involve Russian roulette include the cases of three teenagers who were killed or injured after lying down in the middle of two-lane roads following the release of Disney's *The Program* (1993), which depicts similar daredevil stunts.[67]

A serial killer who took a knife to his victims cited the *Robocop* (1987, 1990, 1993) movies as his inspiration. "The first girl I killed was from a '*Robocop*' movie . . . with a man in it named Cain. I seen him cut somebody's throat, then take the knife and slit down the chest to the stomach and left the body in a certain position. With the first person I killed I did exactly what I saw in the movie."[68] Five people in Britain held a sixteen-year-old captive and tortured her with pliers for six days, and then set her on fire. During her captivity, the victim was forced to wear headphones and listen to an audiotape of a line from the horror movie *Child's Play* (1988): "I'm Chucky. Wanna Play?"[69] *Child's Play* was also implicated in the case of Martin Bryant, charged with killing thirty-five people in Australia and who liked to play act the role of the film's evil doll, Chucky, and more tenuously in the murder of two-year-old James Bulger by two ten-year-olds in a case that shocked Britain.[70]

In 1995, a gang doused a New York subway token booth clerk with flammable liquid and set him on fire. The incident occurred three days after *Money Train* opened in theaters—a film that depicted the torching of a Manhattan token clerk.[71] In 1995, two teenagers who were arrested in Britain for armed robbery after watching *Reservoir Dogs* (1992) told police they wanted to see what it would be like to be the characters in the film.[72] That film was also implicated in a 1999 case, where three teenagers in Britain lured a fifteen-year-old boy onto a field at night. They stripped him, then punched and kicked him in an assault that lasted over two hours, and finally tried to cut off his ear. One of the accused later said they were acting out the film's famous ear-cutting scene.[73] In March 1995, after immersing themselves in viewings of *Natural Born Killers* (1994), two Oklahoma teens murdered a man in Mississippi and shot and paralyzed a convenience-store clerk in Louisiana.[74] Other killings allegedly inspired by the film have taken place in Utah, Georgia, Massachusetts, and Texas.

Barry Loukaitis, a fourteen-year-old who killed three people in his middle school algebra class, talked about going on a killing spree like the characters in his favorite movie, *Natural Born Killers*.[75] Michael Carneal, arrested for a school shooting in 1997 that killed three Kentucky high-school girls, was a fan of *The Basketball Diaries* (1995), which included a scene where high-school boy in a trench coat shoots his classmates and teacher.[76] The infamous teenage killers at Columbine High School, dressed in their trench coats, reminded witnesses of a scene in *The Matrix* (1999), where Keanu Reeves, clad in a trench coat, blasts away at a lobby full of policemen. "One of the guys pulled open his trench coat and started shooting. It was a scene right out of the movie *Matrix*."[77]

This is an impressive litany of carnage associated with films. Although its history extends well back into the classical Hollywood period, the quantity of movie-inspired copycat crimes sometimes seems to have increased in recent decades—though this may be more a matter of appearance than of reality, due to more abundant reporting and publicity of these undeniably lurid incidents. An apparent increase might also be an artifact of the perpetrators' opportunism. Self-serving motives are doubtlessly at work in some of these cases. Saying "a movie made me do it" is a convenient way of avoiding responsibility for one's actions. A popular feeling that movies are eliciting copycat crimes is now deeply ingrained in the culture, offering miscreants a handy prop to rationalize their crimes.

Nevertheless, despite these caveats, the long history of such reported incidents—going back at least to the 1907 case of the adolescent girls arrested for shoplifting that I mentioned in chapter one—suggests that there may be a real phenomenon at work here, and one that is connected to the high levels of media violence now circulating in contemporary culture as well as to the greater levels of intensity and vividness with which contemporary media portray violence. As I have been suggesting throughout this book, the history of film violence plays out primarily on the *y*-axis, where the increases of amplitude work to intensify the viewer's emotional, psychological, and physiological responses. Sissela Bok, a professor of philosophy at Harvard, emphasizes this point:

By now, the vast assortment of slasher and gore films on video contribute to a climate of media violence different from that studied over the past four decades. So does the proliferation of video games offering players the chance to engage in vicarious carnage of every sort. These sources bring into homes depictions of graphic violence, often sexual in nature, never available to children and young people in the past.[78]

EMPIRICAL RESEARCH ON MEDIA VIOLENCE

This development is worrisome because the social science research on the effects of viewing media violence has demonstrated that it helps to induce aggressive attitudes and behavior in some viewers. The results of more than two hundred studies point in this direction.[79] The combined sample size of the participants in these studies is quite large and suggests that the consensus of agreement among the studies is nontrivial. The effects of aggressive media content have been studied in more than 43,000 individuals.[80] The consensus among researchers in this area—that media violence increases the propensity of some viewers to behave aggressively—is so strong that one prominent researcher has said that studies now "should no longer ask how much of an influence is exerted by aggressive portrayals in the media generally, but . . . should investigate the conditions under which these depictions have a greater or lesser effect."[81] The basic question—*is* there an effect—has been answered.

As I have suggested earlier, however, viewers differ in their reasons for seeking out movie violence and in the gratification they derive from it. Moreover, violent behavior is multi-factorial. Numerous factors combine to incline a person to be aggressive, and among the most important are family background and the availability of weapons. Media are not the most important factor, but they are in the mix. As one group of media violence researchers writes, "aggression is multiply determined; a variety of individual and social variables predict aggressive activity. We doubt that future investigations will find that exposure to violent media features prominently among the most important determinants of aggression in our society. Yet the impact of media violence on individual behavior is not trivial."[82]

The effects of media violence may be strongest with persons who are already predisposed to act violently. Such individuals, with high levels of trait aggression in their personalities, are more likely to choose aggressive films to watch and are more likely to feel angry afterward.[83] A study for the British Home Office looked at the reactions to violent films for two years of 122 young men between fifteen and twenty-one years of age. Fifty-four of the young men were violent offenders. Sixty-four percent of these selected violent films as their favorites, spent more time watching them, and had a better recollection of the stories. They also identified more closely with the stars of the

281

films, which included Sylvester Stallone, Jean-Claude Van Damme, and Arnold Schwarzenegger. The study's authors concluded, "the research points to a pathway from having a violent home background, to being an offender, to being more likely to prefer violent films and violent actors."[84] Further, "the implication is that both a history of family violence and offending behaviour are necessary preconditions for developing a significant preference for violent film action and role models." James Garbarino, a professor of child development at Cornell, found emotionally disturbed children at a Chicago school to be "absorbed with the imagery of violence from movies and television and video games. It is one of the truisms among those who work with troubled kids in America that they are hooked on the violent culture."[85]

The influence of violent media on receptive individuals seems to occur through processes of social learning, cognitive priming, and behavioral scripting. Social learning theory is primarily associated with psychologist Albert Bandura, who has examined the way that media characters and stories model values and behavior for viewers.[86] As the evidence from the Center for Media and Public Affairs and University of Southern California studies indicates, depictions of aggression in the media often fail to show negative consequences. Social learning perspectives suggest that a child viewing such depictions may learn the lesson that aggression can be a very effective means of getting one's way. Movie and television aggression is quick, efficient, and leaves little lasting damage on characters. As psychologist Craig Anderson summarizes these lessons,

> Children who are exposed to a lot of violent media learn a number of lessons that change them into more aggressive people. They learn that there are lots of bad people out there who will hurt them. They come to expect others to be mean and nasty. They learn to interpret negative events that occur to them as intentional harm, rather than as an accidental mistake. They learn that the proper way to deal with such harm is to retaliate. Perhaps, as importantly, they do not learn nonviolent solutions to interpersonal conflicts.[87]

The idea of cognitive priming has stimulated much research, primarily associated with the work of psychologist Leonard Berkowitz. This line of inquiry looks at the way media violence can "prime" the thought patterns of some viewers, increasing the likelihood for them to hold aggression-related ideas following the film or program.[88] Numerous studies have empirically demonstrated the process.[89] Over time these networks of thought may be more easily activated in viewers who are prone to aggression, and can be accompanied by physiological levels of response.

Cognitive scripting examines how repertoires of ideas and feelings, such as those connected with aggression, can coalesce over time and be organized as a scripted response which is increasingly resistant to modification.[90] A script is a kind of program for real or imagined behavior that has become automatized through repeated imagining or enactment. It suggests what is likely to happen in the world, how one should behave in response, and what the outcome is likely to be.

Each of these perspectives presupposes that a viewer cognitively processes media content by organizing it into mental models that carry affective labels and responses and correspond to the viewer's subjective picturing of reality. To the extent that the media influence these mental models, cognitive scripts, and socially-derived perceptions, contemporary media provide abundant opportunities for learning that aggression is an effective solution to problems and that it frequently does little harm. Moreover, aggression and violence are fun. Popular entertainment treats violence as a vehicle for pleasure. Movie violence is an object manufactured for consumption, and, as such, it is embedded with all of the pleasures connected to the rituals of movie-going and movie-watching. Lieutenant Colonel Dave Grossman, a soldier and psychology professor, has studied the mechanisms used by armies to condition soldiers to killing. He argues that by coupling graphic violence with consumer pleasure, contemporary movies are teaching the culture the lesson that killing can be fun.

> Producers, directors, and actors are handsomely rewarded for creating the most violent, gruesome, and horrifying films imaginable, films in which the stabbing, shooting, abuse and torture of innocent men, women, and children are depicted in intimate detail. Make these films entertaining as well as violent, and then simultaneously provide the (usually) adolescent viewers with candy, soft drinks, group companionship, and the intimate physical contact of a boyfriend or girlfriend. Then understand that these adolescent viewers are learning to associate these rewards with what they are watching.[91]

Filmmakers Edward Zwick and Marshall Herskovitz (*Glory* [1989], *Traffic* [2001]) point out that filmmakers today can depict anything: no disaster is too large, no amount of bloodshed too much. "We can reach in and touch that dark place in a viewer's heart, underscore it with rock 'n' roll, and fill theaters with teenagers howling as bodies are blown apart."[92] But, they ask, as filmmakers, "do we appeal to what is nihilistic in the audience or do we accept our responsibility as storytellers?" Cinematographer and director John Bailey believes, "we have a great responsibility to the people who see the images we create . . . If our own sensibilities [as filmmakers] are askew, if we have no moral compass to guide us, what point of view are we going to create?"[93]

Few filmmakers, however, are as outspoken about the relationship between film violence and the audience as Zwick, Herskovitz, and Bailey. Since the abolition of censorship and the PCA, film industry personnel have tended to construe the relationship between society and filmmakers in terms of freedom from restraint rather than in terms of responsibility toward the culture that consumes Hollywood's products. Today it has become old-fashioned and anachronistic to speak of what Joseph Breen and the PCA used to call the "voice for morality." As PCA scholar Gregory Black points out, in one of his first actions as PCA head Breen wrote a new definition for morally compensating values that films depicting crime or sex should include in order to counteract the appeal of vice. "To Breen this meant that these films must have a good character who spoke as a voice for morality, a character who clearly told the criminals or sinner that he or she was wrong."[94]

In practice, as we have seen, this policy was often ludicrously ineffective and sometimes led to wooden and stilted filmmaking—but it does demonstrate a line of thinking which guided the PCA in its script evaluations with filmmakers and which is singularly lacking in Hollywood today. To the extent that the PCA has come to be seen as a prudish institution, its policy of evaluating films with a moral compass has become tarnished. The victory over censorship led the industry to prize artistic freedom above everything else (except box office), and, it has evidently come to feel that the era of PCA regulation is a historical embarrassment that should never recur. The result has been the emergence of an ethic that might be termed "filmmaking-with-impunity," in which the highest and loftiest ideal to which the industry subscribes is the ideal of artistic freedom. The casualty in this evolution of sensibility and industry practice has been a guiding moral framework for evaluating filmmaking—currently there is none—and failure to sustain a recognition of the filmmaker's responsibility as a cultural worker.

In this regard, it is difficult not to feel that some of the assumptions and premises woven into the Production Code were rational and well-founded. They are sometimes disparaged as being mere symptoms of the Code's religious origins and therefore a kind of baggage superimposed on secular filmmakers. This is an unnecessarily restrictive and narrow view. They are among the reasons that the PCA worried about cinema's hold on viewers and worked to regulate film content.

These factors are enumerated in the section of the Code headed "Reasons Supporting Preamble of Code" and "Reasons Underlying Particular Applications" (see Appendix B) These sections contain many dogmatic assertions about life and art that are clearly motivated and bounded by a religious frame-work, but they also contain some very important first principles about the medium of cinema and factual descriptions of the medium's essential nature. These are worth remembering. They include the way that spectacle and action can arouse viewers and reach them in deep emotional terms, the recognition that expression in cinema depends on vividness of presentation rather than on the content of ideas or the logic of their presentation, awareness of the medium's pervasive social reach into big cities and small communities alike, and its appeal to mixed audiences of mature and immature viewers. "In general, the mobility, popularity, accessibility, emotional appeal, vividness, straightforward presentation of fact in the film make for more intimate contact with a large audience and for greater emotional appeal. Hence the larger moral responsibilities of the motion pictures." Most significant is this recognition: "The important objective must be to avoid the hardening of the audience, especially of those who are young and impressionable, to the thought and fact of crime. People can become accustomed even to murder, cruelty, brutality, and repellent crimes, if these are too frequently repeated."

VIOLENCE AND THE DEEP STRUCTURE OF CINEMA

These ideas illustrate the striking disparity between classical Hollywood and our own era. The PCA regulated violence in film because it took seriously the idea that film communicates values and ideas to viewers, and it feared that excessive "brutality" and "gruesomeness"—to use its operative expressions—would degrade those values to an undesirably low level. Herein lies the mixed blessing that the easing of regulation and the fall of regional censorship has produced. Today's industry is tremendously invested—creatively and econom-ically—in producing screen violence and, as a result, it seems unwilling to countenance the idea that such films might have socially undesirable effects. And why should it? The global box office is the industry's target because the cost of producing and releasing films has grown so large that expenses cannot be recouped from the domestic market alone. In year 2000, the two biggest films globally were *Mission Impossible 2* and *Gladiator*, each a paean to vio-lence. Filmmakers who traffic in screen violence typically reject the idea that their films might, as the Production Code put it, have the effect of hardening viewers and making them accustomed to brutality. Ensnared in the contro-versy over the copycat killing that followed the release of *Natural Born Killers*, director Oliver Stone said, "I regret the loss of life, I regret the paraly-sis, but I don't feel responsible for it. A movie is not an incitement to act. It's an illusion."[95] A Beverly Hills psychiatrist has pointed to the disconnect between filmmakers and their audience. "Producers, writers and directors don't want to acknowledge that their material can have such a strong psychological impact on viewers."[96]

If the makers of violent films are invested in denying a connection between movies and society, directors whose work is not tied to depictions of screen violence have been more forthcoming about their own conviction that a dynamic is involved between violent movies and those who consume them. Alan Pakula, director of *All the President's Men* (1976) and *Presumed Innocent* (1990), said, "movie violence is like eating salt. The more you eat, the more you need to eat to taste it. People are becoming immune to its effects. That's why death counts [in movies] have quadrupled and blast power is increasing by the megaton."[97] Over the past two decades, Hollywood has specialized in violent action films, marketed worldwide, that are full of big things blowing up. Fireballs and deafening explosions make for apocalyptic entertainment. The events of September 11 held an ugly mirror up to this fictional Armageddon. Reacting to the destruction of the World Trade Center by terrorists who used commercial airplanes as bombs, director Robert Altman voiced the feeling of many people who felt that the event, as captured on-camera, was eerily reminiscent of a Hollywood movie. "The movies set the pattern, and these people have copied the movies. Nobody would have thought to commit an atrocity like that unless they'd seen it in a movie. How dare we continue to show this kind of mass destruction in movies. I just believe we created this atmosphere and taught them how to do it."[98]

Despite the anti-violence feelings among some of the industry's filmmakers, today's Hollywood has been transformed so far from the assumptions about the medium written into the Production Code, and so far from the classical era when the industry was institutionally invested in restraining screen violence, that it seems like a totally different place altogether. The industry that once held filmmakers on a leash has now dropped it.

Violent behavior on-screen is more plentiful today than in the era of classical Hollywood. But it is not only quantity and range of behavior that distinguishes modern screen violence. It is not simply that there are more shootings and beatings and stabbings circulating through contemporary visual media. Of equal significance is the expansion of the y-axis, the stylistic domain. In chapters two and three, we saw how rapidly filmmakers learned to stylize violence in order to make it vivid and striking, and how rapidly they found effective audio and pictorial means for accomplishing this. They assimilated the lessons of sound filmmaking and quickly integrated sound with image in ways that magnified the intensity of violence: think of the metallic clatter of ejected cartridges hitting the floor from Loretta's machine gun in *Show Them No Mercy*.

But the PCA acted as the governor on the accelerating engine of screen violence, keeping its content and stylistic revolutions per minute well below the medium's real potential for visualizing carnage. CARA was the outcome of eroding that function. The results are evident in a genre like the slasher film, whose raison d'être is the simulation of slaughter.

But many other categories of film reflect the *y*-axis phenomenon. The two most prominent films about the D-Day landings—*The Longest Day* (1962) and *Saving Private Ryan* (1998)—show tremendous disparity in the stylistic emphasis they give to the violence of the Normandy invasion. *The Longest Day* employs the clutch-and-fall aesthetic, whereas, as everyone knows, the violence in *Saving Private Ryan* is horrific. Unlike the vast majority of violent movies and television shows, however, *Saving Private Ryan* is a serious work of art that aims to use violence as a legitimate part of its aesthetic and moral design. At the same time, Spielberg's effort to devise new techniques for visualizing violence—changing the angle of the camera's shutter, stripping the coating off the lenses—shows the extent to which he was determined to burst the boundaries of the existing stylistic templates. For Spielberg, this goal was inseparable from the historical and moral truths that he wanted to illuminate through the story. The horror of the violence would convey the magnitude of the sacrifice of those who died at Omaha Beach.

The contemporary expansion of screen violence manifests a greater continuity with the past than may at first seem to be the case. What changed after 1968 was the *means* whereby filmmakers could show what they now show, but their level of interest in doing so is not new. The preceding chapters have shown their abiding interest to think up new ways for characters to hurt one another and to devise novel cinematic approaches for depicting this harm. The earliest films examined in this study—*Public Enemy* (1931), for example, or *Murders in the Rue Morgue* (1932)—demonstrate this curiosity, with picture and sound treated as plastic elements to accentuate the baroque intensity of gangland shootings or sadistic torture.

A clear line of development connects the history of violence in classical Hollywood with the screen violence of our contemporary period. What has changed between the two eras, and what accounts for their apparent dissimilarity, is the relative freedom that permitted filmmakers after 1968 to pursue the dreams of their classical Hollywood counterparts. Hard and graphic violence *was* the dream of many filmmakers in classical Hollywood; they consistently pushed and prodded the Production Code Administration to accept depictions of violence that were harder and more brutal than it wanted. Often, when they defied the PCA, the agency acquiesced. In this respect, the excesses of our present period are really the development of a long-standing interest and fascination.

This historical continuity speaks to an imperative—an inherent dynamic within the forms of cinema that has given the history of screen violence the force of teleology. This formal imperative is at some tension with a prevailing view among scholars of film to understand film violence in primarily sociological terms: to see film violence as a screen that mirrors the power struggles, the social dynamics and tensions of the period in which a given film is made. As those tensions change, so does, according to this social-historical view, the nature of screen violence. Christopher Sharrett argues that the violence in post-classical Hollywood film reflects conditions of atomization and alienation in contemporary society, and that the violent image is a cultural "artifact embodying ideological assumptions."[99] J. David Slocum suggests that film violence manifests the struggle between "the forces changing society and those controlling it"; that it illuminates core social values and "the parameters of social order" within a given period.[100] This is a legitimate approach, and I have employed it to a degree in an earlier book, where I examined the films of Sam Peckinpah as seminal works of late sixties radical culture. But in that book I also worked from a close formal analysis of the films, and I argued that the formal structure of violence in cinema has its own dynamic and logic, poses its own ethical and moral issues, and offers inherent pleasures to filmmakers. These issues and pleasures tend to be minimized by the social history approach.

Those pleasures find their fulfillment in cinema's great capability for portraying mayhem vividly and in sensual terms. This capability is realized on cinema's y-axis and should be seen as an inherent property of cinema, like its capability for erotica. Sex and violence are often conjoined in problematic ways in discussions of cinema and censorship—but, in fact, each is something that cinema does supremely well and, more to the point, creating each experience gives filmmakers enormous satisfaction. Filming and editing violence is tremendously exciting for moviemakers, and this pleasure is lodged at the most immediate and basic level of their craft. It's a pleasure felt in dreaming up new ways of doing death. It's a pleasure manifest in editing shots to create a rhythm of destruction across a series of images in sequence. It's the pleasure of watching an entire magazine of film blast through a high-speed camera, knowing that it's capturing a gun battle in detail-laden slow-motion. Director Francis Ford Coppola has said that when he's doing a violent scene, everybody on the set crowds around to watch. These joys are rooted in the craft of moviemaking, and they transcend historical period just as the fascination with filming sex is deeply imbedded in the medium and has been present, and regulated as a source of controversy, since its inception. One of the first films ever made shows a man and a woman kissing. One of the earliest narrative films shows the gun battle surrounding a Western train robbery. The investment in these pleasures is the historical constant that links classical and post-classical Hollywood and which an emphatically sociological approach tends to minimize.

These pleasures, lodged in the forms of cinema and the work of filmmaking, are also why the problem of film violence will not go away. As long as there is cinema, filmmakers will seek the satisfactions of their craft that lie in this direction. In this regard, the medium's formal properties constitute their own history—they contain their own destiny and impose their own teleology on the cultures in which they unfold. The present period is distinguished by a host of factors working to exacerbate this condition, principally the economics of audience demographics and the global market for movie violence. This has led to a significant change in the industry, making it today more institutionally invested in the production of violence than in the classical Hollywood period.

After the terror attacks of September 11, debate throughout the country centered on whether that disaster spelled the end of the era of hyperviolent movies. When the planes hit the World Trade Center the imagery looked like a Hollywood action movie, and it made many people hope that the mindless violence of much contemporary film might finally diminish. After September 11, how could one watch a helicopter in *The Matrix* crash into a skyscraper and explode in a fireball? How could one watch the White House explode and New York skyscrapers erupt in *Independence Day* (1996)? How could directors make such images in the future? These questions have mainly a rhetorical force. The history of American film gives us the answers: people will. The appeal of all of this is undying. Ultraviolence is an embryo that lay inside the body of American cinema for six decades until it emerged. It had always been there, and, like the masked killers in slasher films that never lie down dead, it keeps coming on.

Appendix A: Primary Sample of Films

PRODUCTION CODE ADMINISTRATION CASE FILES

All Quiet on the Western Front (1930)
Bataan (1943)
Ben-Hur (1959)
Bend of the River (1952)
Big Heat, The (1953)
Big Operator, The (1959)
Black Cat, The (1934)
Body and Soul (1947)
Bride of Frankenstein (1935)
Brute Force (1947)
Case Against Brooklyn, The (1958)
Champion (1949)
Charge of the Light Brigade, The (1936)
Chase, The (1966)
Detective Story (1951)
Dirty Dozen, The (1967)
Dr. Jekyll and Mr. Hyde (1931)
Duel at Diablo (1966)
Frankenstein (1931)
Glass Key, The (1942)
G-Men (1935)
Gone With the Wind (1939)
Gun Crazy (1949)
Hatchet Man, The (1932)
Hombre (1967)
In Cold Blood (1967)
Island of Lost Souls (1933)
Killers, The (1964)
Killing, The (1956)
Kiss Me Deadly (1955)
Kiss of Death (1947)

Little Caesar (1931)
M (1951)
Machine-Gun Kelly (1958)
Major Dundee (1965)
Man from Laramie, The (1955)
Man of the West (1958)
Murders in the Rue Morgue (1932)
My Darling Clementine (1946)
Naked Spur, The (1953)
Objective, Burma! (1945)
One-Eyed Jacks (1961)
Party Girl (1958)
Phenix City Story, The (1955)
Point Blank (1967)
Pride of the Marines (1945)
Professionals, The (1966)
Psycho (1960)
Public Enemy (1931)
Raven, The (1935)
Raw Deal (1948)
Ride the High Country (1962)
St. Valentine's Day Massacre,
    The (1967)
Scarface (1932)
Set-Up, The (1949)
Shane (1953)
Show Them No Mercy (1935)
Spartacus (1960)
13 Rue Madeleine (1947)
White Heat (1949)
Winchester '73 (1950)

Appendixes

CENSORSHIP FILES FROM THE ALFRED HITCHCOCK COLLECTION

Frenzy (1972)
Psycho (1960)
Torn Curtain (1966)

CENSORSHIP FILES FROM THE RICHARD BROOKS COLLECTION

In Cold Blood (1967)
The Professionals (1966)

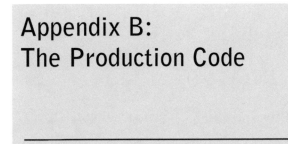

Appendix B:
The Production Code

A Code to Govern the Making of Talking, Synchronized and Silent Motion Pictures. Formulated and formally adopted by The Association of Motion Picture Producers, Inc. and The Motion Picture Producers and Distributors of America, Inc. in March 1930.

Motion picture producers recognize the high trust and confidence which have been placed in them by the people of the world and which have made motion pictures a universal form of entertainment.

They recognize their responsibility to the public because of this trust and because entertainment and art are important influences in the life of a nation.

Hence, though regarding motion pictures primarily as entertainment without any explicit purpose of teaching or propaganda, they know that the motion picture within its own field of entertainment may be directly responsible for spiritual or moral progress, for higher types of social life, and for much correct thinking.

During the rapid transition from silent to talking pictures they have realized the necessity and the opportunity of subscribing to a Code to govern the production of talking pictures and of re-acknowledging this responsibility.

On their part, they ask from the public and from public leaders a sympathetic understanding of their purposes and problems and a spirit of cooperation that will allow them the freedom and opportunity necessary to bring the motion picture to a still higher level of wholesome entertainment for all the people.

GENERAL PRINCIPLES

1. No picture shall be produced that will lower the moral standards of those who see it. Hence the sympathy of the audience should never be thrown to the side of crime, wrongdoing, evil or sin.
2. Correct standards of life, subject only to the requirements of drama and entertainment, shall be presented.

3. Law, natural or human, shall not be ridiculed, nor shall sympathy be created for its violation.

PARTICULAR APPLICATIONS

I. Crimes Against the Law

These shall never be presented in such a way as to throw sympathy with the crime as against law and justice or to inspire others with a desire for imitation.

1. Murder
   a. The technique of murder must be presented in a way that will not inspire imitation.
   b. Brutal killings are not to be presented in detail.
   c. Revenge in modern times shall not be justified.
2. Methods of Crime should not be explicitly presented.
   a. Theft, robbery, safe-cracking, and dynamiting of trains, mines, buildings, etc., should not be detailed in method.
   b. Arson must subject to the same safeguards.
   c. The use of firearms should be restricted to the essentials.
   d. Methods of smuggling should not be presented.
3. Illegal drug traffic must never be presented.
4. The use of liquor in American life, when not required by the plot or for proper characterization, will not be shown.

II. Sex

The sanctity of the institution of marriage and the home shall be upheld. Pictures shall not infer that low forms of sex relationship are the accepted or common thing.

1. Adultery, sometimes necessary plot material, must not be explicitly treated, or justified, or presented attractively.
2. Scenes of Passion
   a. They should not be introduced when not essential to the plot.
   b. Excessive and lustful kissing, lustful embraces, suggestive postures and gestures, are not to be shown.
   c. In general passion should so be treated that these scenes do not stimulate the lower and baser element.
3. Seduction or Rape
   a. They should never be more than suggested, and only when essential for the plot, and even then never shown by explicit method.
   b. They are never the proper subject for comedy.
4. Sex perversion or any inference to it is forbidden.
5. White slavery shall not be treated.
6. Miscegenation (sex relationships between the white and black races) is forbidden.
7. Sex hygiene and venereal diseases are not subjects for motion pictures.
8. Scenes of actual child birth, in fact or in silhouette, are never to be presented.
9. Children's sex organs are never to be exposed.

III. Vulgarity

The treatment of low, disgusting, unpleasant, though not necessarily evil, subjects should always be subject to the dictates of good taste and a regard for the sensibilities of the audience.

IV. Obscenity

Obscenity in word, gesture, reference, song, joke, or by suggestion (even when likely to be understood only by part of the audience) is forbidden.

V. Profanity

Pointed profanity (this includes the words, God, Lord, Jesus, Christ—unless used reverently—Hell, S.O.B., damn, Gawd), or every other profane or vulgar expression however used, is forbidden.

VI. Costume

1. Complete nudity is never permitted. This includes nudity in fact or in silhouette, or any lecherous or licentious notice thereof by other characters in the picture.
2. Undressing scenes should be avoided, and never used save where essential to the plot.
3. Indecent or undue exposure is forbidden.
4. Dancing or costumes intended to permit undue exposure or indecent movements in the dance are forbidden.

VII. Dances

1. Dances suggesting or representing sexual actions or indecent passions are forbidden.
2. Dances which emphasize indecent movements are to be regarded as obscene.

VIII. Religion

1. No film or episode may throw ridicule on any religious faith.
2. Ministers of religion in their character as ministers of religion should not be used as comic characters or as villains.
3. Ceremonies of any definite religion should be carefully and respectfully handled.

IX. Locations

The treatment of bedrooms must be governed by good taste and delicacy.

X. National Feelings

1. The use of the Flag shall be consistently respectful.
2. The history, institutions, prominent people and citizenry of other nations shall be represented fairly.

XI. Titles

Salacious, indecent, or obscene titles shall not be used.

XII. Repellent Subjects

The following subjects must be treated within the careful limits of good taste:

1. Actual hangings or electrocutions as legal punishments for crime.
2. Third degree methods.
3. Brutality and possible gruesomeness.
4. Branding of people or animals.
5. Apparent cruelty to children or animals.
6. The sale of women, or a woman selling her virtue.
7. Surgical operations.

REASONS SUPPORTING THE PREAMBLE OF THE CODE

I. THEATRICAL MOTION PICTURES, THAT IS, PICTURES INTENDED FOR THE THEATRE AS DISTINCT FROM PICTURES INTENDED FOR CHURCHES, SCHOOLS, LECTURE HALLS, EDUCATIONAL MOVEMENTS, SOCIAL REFORM MOVEMENTS, ETC., ARE PRIMARILY TO BE REGARDED AS ENTERTAINMENT.

Mankind has always recognized the importance of entertainment and its value in rebuilding the bodies and souls of human beings.

But it has always recognized that entertainment can be a character either HELPFUL or HARMFUL to the human race, and in consequence has clearly distinguished between:

a. Entertainment which tends to improve the race, or at least to re-create and rebuild human beings exhausted with the realities of life; and
b. Entertainment which tends to degrade human beings, or to lower their standards of life and living.

Hence the MORAL IMPORTANCE of entertainment is something which has been universally recognized. It enters intimately into the lives of men and women and affects them closely; it occupies their minds and affections during leisure hours; and ultimately touches the whole of their lives. A man may be judged by his standard of entertainment as easily as by the standard of his work.

So correct entertainment raises the whole standard of a nation.

Wrong entertainment lowers the whole living conditions and moral ideals of a race.

Note, for example, the healthy reactions to healthful sports, like baseball, golf; the unhealthy reactions to sports like cockfighting, bullfighting, bear baiting, etc.

Note, too, the effect on ancient nations of gladiatorial combats, the obscene plays of Roman times, etc.

II. MOTION PICTURES ARE VERY IMPORTANT AS ART.

Though a new art, possibly a combination art, it has the same object as the other arts, the presentation of human thought, emotion, and experience, in terms of an appeal to the soul through the senses.

Here, as in entertainment,

Art enters intimately into the lives of human beings.

Art can be morally good, lifting men to higher levels. This has been done through good music, great painting, authentic fiction, poetry, drama.

Art can be morally evil in its effects. This is the case clearly enough with unclean art, indecent books, suggestive drama. The effect on the lives of men and women are obvious.

Note: It has often been argued that art itself is unmoral, neither good nor bad. This is true of the THING which is music, painting, poetry, etc. But the THING is the PRODUCT of some person's mind, and the intention of that mind was either good or bad morally when it produced the thing. Besides, the thing has its EFFECT upon those who come into contact with it. In both these ways, that is, as a product of a mind and as the cause of definite effects, it has a deep moral significance and unmistakable moral quality.

Hence: The motion pictures, which are the most popular of modern arts for the masses, have their moral quality from the intention of the minds which produce them and from their effects on the moral lives and reactions of their audiences. This gives them a most important morality.

1. They reproduce the morality of the men who use the pictures as a medium for the expression of their ideas and ideals.
2. They affect the moral standards of those who, through the screen, take in these ideas and ideals.

In the case of motion pictures, the effect may be particularly emphasized because no art has so quick and so widespread an appeal to the masses. It has become in an incredibly short period the art of the multitudes.

III. THE MOTION PICTURE, BECAUSE OF ITS IMPORTANCE AS ENTERTAINMENT AND BECAUSE OF THE TRUST PLACED IN IT BY THE PEOPLES OF THE WORLD, HAS SPECIAL MORAL OBLIGATIONS:

A. Most arts appeal to the mature. This art appeals at once to every class, mature, immature, developed, undeveloped, law abiding, criminal. Music has its grades for different classes; so has literature and drama. This art of the motion picture, combining as it does the two fundamental appeals of looking at a picture and listening to a story, at once reaches every class of society.
B. By reason of the mobility of film and the ease of picture distribution, and because the possibility of duplicating positives in large quantities, this art reaches places unpenetrated by other forms of art.
C. Because of these two facts, it is difficult to produce films intended for only certain classes of people. The exhibitors' theatres are built for the masses, for the cultivated and the rude, the mature and the immature, the self-respecting and the criminal. Films, unlike books and music, can with difficulty be confined to certain selected groups.
D. The latitude given to film material cannot, in consequence, be as wide as the latitude given to book material. In addition:
   a. A book describes; a film vividly presents. One presents on a cold page; the other by apparently living people.
   b. A book reaches the mind through words merely; a film reaches the eyes and ears through the reproduction of actual events.
   c. The reaction of a reader to a book depends largely on the keenness of the reader's imagination; the reaction to a film depends on the vividness of presentation.
      Hence many things which might be described or suggested in a book could not possibly be presented in a film.
E. This is also true when comparing the film with the newspaper.
   a. Newspapers present by description, films by actual presentation.
   b. Newspapers are after the fact and present things as having taken place; the film gives the events in the process of enactment and with apparent reality of life.
F. Everything possible in a play is not possible in a film:
   a. Because of the larger audience of the film, and its consequential mixed character.

297

Psychologically, the larger the audience, the lower the moral mass resistance to suggestion.

b. Because through light, enlargement of character, presentation, scenic emphasis, etc., the screen story is brought closer to the audience than the play.

c. The enthusiasm for and interest in the film actors and actresses, developed beyond anything of the sort in history, makes the audience largely sympathetic toward the characters they portray and the stories in which they figure. Hence the audience is more ready to confuse actor and actress and the characters they portray, and it is most receptive of the emotions and ideals presented by the favorite stars.

G. Small communities, remote from sophistication and from the hardening process which often takes place in the ethical and moral standards of larger cities, are easily and readily reached by any sort of film.

H. The grandeur of mass settings, large action, spectacular features, etc., affects and arouses more intensely the emotional side of the audience.

In general, the mobility, popularity, accessibility, emotional appeal, vividness, straightforward presentation of fact in the film make for more intimate contact with a larger audience and for greater emotional appeal.

Hence the larger moral responsibilities of the motion pictures.

REASONS UNDERLYING THE GENERAL PRINCIPLES

I. NO PICTURE SHALL BE PRODUCED WHICH WILL LOWER THE MORAL STANDARDS OF THOSE WHO SEE IT.

Hence the sympathy of the audience should never be thrown to the side of crime, wrongdoing, evil or sin.

This is done:

1. When evil is made to appear attractive and alluring, and good is made to appear unattractive.
2. When the sympathy of the audience is thrown on the side of crime, wrongdoing, evil, sin. The same is true of a film that would thrown sympathy against goodness, honor, innocence, purity or honesty.

   Note: Sympathy with a person who sins is not the same as sympathy with the sin or crime of which he is guilty. We may feel sorry for the plight of the murderer or even understand the circumstances which led him to his crime: we may not feel sympathy with the wrong which he has done. The presentation of evil is often essential for art or fiction or drama. This in itself is not wrong provided:

   a. That evil is not presented alluringly. Even if later in the film the evil is condemned or punished, it must not be allowed to appear so attractive that the audience's emotions are drawn to desire or approve so strongly that later the condemnation is forgotten and only the apparent joy of sin is remembered.

   b. That throughout, the audience feels sure that evil is wrong and good is right.

II. CORRECT STANDARDS OF LIFE SHALL, AS FAR AS POSSIBLE, BE PRESENTED.

A wide knowledge of life and of living is made possible through the film. When right standards are consistently presented, the motion picture exercises the most powerful influences.

It builds character, develops right ideals, inculcates correct principles, and all this in attractive story form.

If motion pictures consistently hold up for admiration high types of characters and present stories that will affect lives for the better, they can become the most powerful force for the improvement of mankind.

III. Law, NATURAL OR HUMAN, SHALL NOT BE RIDICULED, NOR SHALL SYMPATHY BE CREATED FOR ITS VIOLATION.

By natural law is understood the law which is written in the hearts of all mankind, the greater underlying principles of right and justice dictated by conscience.

By human law is understood the law written by civilized nations.

1. The presentation of crimes against the law is often necessary for the carrying out of the plot. But the presentation must not throw sympathy with the crime as against the law nor with the criminal as against those who punish him.
2. The courts of the land should not be presented as unjust. This does not mean that a single court may not be presented as unjust, much less that a single court official must not be presented this way. But the court system of the country must not suffer as a result of this presentation.

REASONS UNDERLYING THE PARTICULAR APPLICATIONS

I. Sin AND EVIL ENTER INTO THE STORY OF HUMAN BEINGS AND HENCE IN THEMSELVES ARE VALID DRAMATIC MATERIAL.

II. In THE USE OF THIS MATERIAL, IT MUST BE DISTINGUISHED BETWEEN SIN WHICH REPELS BY IT VERY NATURE, AND SINS WHICH OFTEN ATTRACT.

a. In the first class come murder, most theft, many legal crimes, lying, hypocrisy, cruelty, etc.
b. In the second class come sex sins, sins and crimes of apparent heroism, such as banditry, daring thefts, leadership in evil, organized crime, revenge, etc.

The first class needs less care in treatment, as sins and crimes of this class are naturally unattractive. The audience instinctively condemns all such and is repelled.

Hence the important objective must be to avoid the hardening of the audience, especially of those who are young and impressionable, to the thought and fact of crime. People can become accustomed even to murder, cruelty, brutality, and repellent crimes, if these are too frequently repeated.

The second class needs great care in handling, as the response of human nature to their appeal is obvious. This is treated more fully below.

III. A CAREFUL DISTINCTION CAN BE MADE BETWEEN FILMS INTENDED FOR GENERAL DISTRIBUTION, AND FILMS INTENDED FOR USE IN THEATRES RESTRICTED TO A LIMITED AUDIENCE.

Themes and plots quite appropriate for the latter would be altogether out of place and dangerous in the former.

Note: The practice of using a general theatre and limiting its patronage to "Adults Only" is not completely satisfactory and is only partially effective.

299

However, maturer minds may easily understand and accept without harm subject matter in plots which do younger people positive harm.

Hence: If there should be created a special type of theatre, catering exclusively to an adult audience, for plays of this character (plays with problem themes, difficult discussions and maturer treatment) it would seem to afford an outlet, which does not now exist, for pictures unsuitable for general distribution but permissible for exhibitions to a restricted audience.

I. Crimes Against the Law

The treatment of crimes against the law must not:

1. Teach methods of crime.
2. Inspire potential criminals with a desire for imitation.
3. Make criminals seem heroic and justified.

Revenge in modern times shall not be justified. In lands and ages of less developed civilization and moral principles, revenge may sometimes be presented. This would be the case especially in places where no law exists to cover the crime because of which revenge is committed.

Because of its evil consequences, the drug traffic should not be presented in any form. The existence of the trade should not be brought to the attention of audiences.

The use of liquor should never be excessively presented. In scenes from American life, the necessities of plot and proper characterization alone justify its use. And in this case, it should be shown with moderation.

II. Sex

Out of a regard for the sanctity of marriage and the home, the triangle, that is, the love of a third party for one already married, needs careful handling. The treatment should not throw sympathy against marriage as an institution.

Scenes of passion must be treated with an honest acknowledgement of human nature and its normal reactions. Many scenes cannot be presented without arousing dangerous emotions on the part of the immature, the young or the criminal classes.

Even within the limits of pure love, certain facts have been universally regarded by lawmakers as outside the limits of safe presentation.

In the case of impure love, the love which society has always regarded as wrong and which has been banned by divine law, the following are important:

1. Impure love must not be presented as attractive and beautiful.
2. It must not be the subject of comedy or farce, or treated as material for laughter.
3. It must not be presented in such a way to arouse passion or morbid curiosity on the part of the audience.
4. It must not be made to seem right and permissible.
5. It general, it must not be detailed in method and manner.

III. Vulgarity; IV. Obscenity; V. Profanity

hardly need further explanation than is contained in the Code.

VI. Costume

General Principles:

1. The effect of nudity or semi-nudity upon the normal man or woman, and much more upon the young and upon immature persons, has been honestly recognized by all lawmakers and moralists.
2. Hence the fact that the nude or semi-nude body may be beautiful does not make its use in the films moral. For, in addition to its beauty, the effect of the nude or semi-nude body on the normal individual must be taken into consideration.
3. Nudity or semi-nudity used simply to put a "punch" into a picture comes under the head of immoral actions. It is immoral in its effect on the average audience.
4. Nudity can never be permitted as being necessary for the plot. Semi-nudity must not result in undue or indecent exposures.
5. Transparent or translucent materials and silhouette are frequently more suggestive than actual exposure.

VII. Dances

Dancing in general is recognized as an art and as a beautiful form of expressing human emotions.

But dances which suggest or represent sexual actions, whether performed solo or with two or more; dances intended to excite the emotional reaction of an audience; dances with movement of the breasts, excessive body movements while the feet are stationary, violate decency and are wrong.

VIII. Religion

The reason why ministers of religion may not be comic characters or villains is simply because the attitude taken toward them may easily become the attitude taken toward religion in general. Religion is lowered in the minds of the audience because of the lowering of the audience's respect for a minister.

IX. Locations

Certain places are so closely and thoroughly associated with sexual life or with sexual sin that their use must be carefully limited.

X. National Feelings

The just rights, history, and feelings of any nation are entitled to most careful consideration and respectful treatment.

XI. Titles

As the title of a picture is the brand on that particular type of goods, it must conform to the ethical practices of all such honest business.

XII. Repellent Subjects

Such subjects are occasionally necessary for the plot. Their treatment must never offend good taste nor injure the sensibilities of an audience.

Appendix C: Special Regulations on Crime in Motion Pictures (1938)

Resolved, that the Board of Directors of the Motion Picture Association of America, Inc., hereby ratifies, approves, and confirms the interpretations of the Production Code, the practices thereunder, and the resolutions indicating and confirming such interpretations heretofore adopted by the Association of Motion Picture Producers, Inc., effectuating regulations relative to the treatment of crime in motion pictures, as follows:

1. Details of crime must never be shown and care should be exercised at all times in discussing such details.
2. Action suggestive of wholesale slaughter of human beings, either by criminals, in conflict with police, or as between warring fractions of criminals, or in public disorders of any kind, will not be allowed.
3. There must be no suggestion, at any time, of excessive brutality.
4. Because of the increase in the number of films in which murder is frequently committed, action showing the taking of human life, even in the mystery stories, is to be cut to the minimum. These frequent presentations of murder tend to lessen regard for the sacredness of life.
5. Suicide, as a solution of problems occurring in the development of screen drama, is to be discouraged as morally questionable and as bad theatre—unless absolutely necessary for the development of the plot.
6. There must be no display, at any time, of machine guns, sub-machine guns or other weapons generally classified as illegal weapons in the hands of gangsters, or other criminals, and there are to be no off-stage sounds of the repercussions of these guns.
7. There must be no new, unique or trick methods shown for concealing guns.
8. The flaunting of weapons by gangsters, or other criminals, will not be allowed.
9. All discussions and dialogue on the part of gangsters regarding guns should be cut to the minimum.
10. There must be no scenes, at any time, showing law-enforcement officers dying at the hands of criminals. This includes private detectives and guards for banks, motor trucks, etc.
11. With special reference to the crime of kidnapping—or illegal abduction—such stories are acceptable under the Code only when the kidnapping or abduction is (a) not the main theme of the story; (b) the person kidnapped is not a child; (c) there are no de-

tails of the crime of kidnapping; (d) no profit accrues to the abductors or kidnappers; and (e) where the kidnappers are punished.

It is understood, and agreed, that the word kidnapping, as used in paragraph 11 of these Regulations, is intended to mean abduction, or illegal detention, in modem times, by criminals for ransom.

12. Pictures dealing with criminal activities, in which minors participate, or to which minors are related, shall not be approved if they incite demoralizing imitation on the part of youth.

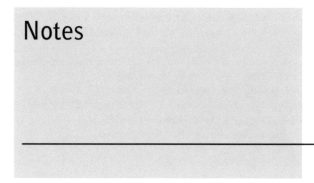

Notes

INTRODUCTION

1. See, for example, J. David Slocum, ed. *Violence and American Cinema* (New York: Routledge, 2001) and Christopher Sharrett, ed., *Mythologies of Violence in Postmodern Media* (Detroit: Wayne State University Press, 1999).
2. Richard Maltby, "The Spectacle of Criminality," in *Violence and American Cinema*, ed. Slocum, 117–152.
3. Lea Jacobs, *The Wages of Sin: Censorship and the Fallen Woman Film, 1928–1942* (Madison: University of Wisconsin Press, 1991).

ONE. CENSORSHIP AND VIOLENCE BEFORE 1930

1. *Show World*, February 26, 1910, Thomas A. Edison Papers, Microfilm Edition, Part IV, Document File Series, Motion Pictures—Censorship, 196:233, New York State Motion Picture Division, New York State Archives, Albany, NY.
2. Letter, Josephine Redding, June 9, 1910, Edison papers.
3. Letter, John Collier to Patents Co., July 1909, Edison Papers, 194:1.
4. In *Film: The Democratic Art* (Boston: Little, Brown, 1976), Garth Jowett covers these struggles in detail.
5. Quoted in Ira Carmen, *Movies, Censorship and the Law* (Ann Arbor: University of Michigan Press, 1967), p. 187.
6. *Block v. City of Chicago*, 239 ILL. 251, 87 N.E. 1011.
7. Ibid.
8. Quoted in Ibid.
9. Alan Dawley writes, "arguing for shorter hours and prohibition of night work, they invoked the special needs of woman as 'the mother of the race' and portrayed women and children as vulnerable to greedy male predators. This ideological set piece reprised the standard nineteenth-century paired opposites of corrupt masculine commerce and virtuous feminine domesticity." *Struggles for Justice: Social Responsibility and the Liberal State* (Cambridge, MA: Harvard University Press, 1991), p. 102.

10. For a summary of key cases, see Douglas Ayer, Roy E. Bates, Peter J. Herman, "Self-Censorship in the Movie Industry: An Historical Perspective on Law and Social Change," *Wisconsin Law Review* 3 (1970), p. 802.

11. Garth S. Jowett, "Moral Responsibility and Commercial Entertainment: Social Control in the United States Film Industry, 1907–1968," *Historical Journal of Film, Radio and Television* 10, no. 1 (1990), p. 3.

12. Robert Armour provides a summary of this conflict in "Effects of Censorship Pressure on the New York Nickelodeon Market, 1907-1909," *Film History* 4 (1990):113–121.

13. Nancy J. Rosenbloom, "Between Reform and Regulation: The Struggle over Film Censorship in Progressive America, 1909–1922," *Film History* 1 (1987), pp. 322–323; W. P. Lawson, "Standards of Censorship," *Harper's Weekly*, January 16, 1915, p. 64.

14. Rosenbloom, "Between Reform and Regulation," p. 310.

15. Ibid., p. 311.

16. *Mutual v Ohio*, 236 U.S. 230, 35 S. Ct. 387.

17. *Fox v Collins*, 236 Ill. App. 281 (1925).

18. Ibid.

19. Richard Randall, *Censorship of the Movies* (Madison: University of Wisconsin Press, 1968), p. 107.

20. Morris L. Ernst and Pare Lorentz, *Censored: The Private Life of the Movie* (New York: Cape and Smith, 1930), pp. 82–84.

21. Ibid., p. 39.

22. Ruth Vasey, "Beyond Sex and Violence: 'Industry Policy' and the Regulation of Hollywood Movies, 1922–1939," *Quarterly Review of Film and Video* 15, no. 4 (1995), p. 72.

23. Jonathan Munby, *Public Enemies, Public Heroes: Screening the Gangster from 'Little Caesar' to 'Touch of Evil'* (Chicago: University of Chicago Press: 1999), p. 145.

24. Gregory D. Black, *Hollywood Censored: Morality Codes, Catholics and the Movies* (New York: Cambridge University Press, 1994), p. 39.

25. Ibid., p. 239.

26. J. David Slocum, "Film Violence and the Institutionalization of Cinema," *Social Research* 67, no. 3 (Fall, 2000), p. 654.

27. Randall, *Censorship of the Movies*, p. 108.

28. Eliminations Bulletinss 1927–1965 of the New York State Motion Picture Division, New York State Archives, Albany, NY. Available on microfilm from New York State Archives, Albany, NY.

29. Eliminations Bulletinss, December 16–31, 1927.

30. Eliminations Bulletins, October 1927.

31. Ibid.

32. Eliminations Bulletins, September 16–30, 1927.

33. Eliminations Bulletins, May 16–31, 1928.

34. Eliminations Bulletins, June 16–30, 1928.

35. Eliminations Bulletins, October 1927.

36. Eliminations Bulletins, February 16–29, 1928.

37. Eliminations Bulletins, June 16–30, 1928.

38. Eliminations Bulletins, October, 1927.

39. Barrie Gunter and Adrian Furnham, "Perceptions of Television Violence: Effects of Programme Genre and Type of Violence on Viewers' Judgements of Violent Portrayals," *British Journal of Social Psychology* 23 (1984), p. 160.

40. Eliminations Bulletins, May 1–5, 1928.

41. Eliminations Bulletins, February 1–15, 1928.

42. Ibid.
43. Eliminations Bulletins, September 16–30, 1927.
44. Eliminations Bulletins, November 1927.
45. Eliminations Bulletins, January 16–31, 1928.
46. Eliminations Bulletins, October 1927.
47. Eliminations Bulletins, March 16–31, 1928.
48. Eliminations Bulletins, September 16–30, 1927.
49. Eliminations Bulletins, January 2–14, 1928.
50. Eliminations Bulletins, November 1927.
51. Eliminations Bulletins, June 16–30, 1928.
52. Eliminations Bulletins, January 16–31, 1928.
53. Eliminations Bulletins, September 16–30, 1927.
54. Eliminations Bulletins, September 1–15, 1927.
55. *His Day Off*, Eliminations Bulletins, October 1927; *Dummies*, Eliminations Bulletins, December 1–15, 1927.

TWO. CRUELTY, SADISM, AND THE HORROR FILM

1. James Hall, *Oral History with Geoffrey Shurlock*, p. 225. Unpublished manuscript, Louis B. Mayer Library, American Film Institute, Los Angeles, California (AFI, 1970).
2. Ibid., p. 76.
3. Quoted in David J. Skal, *The Monster Show: A Cultural History of Horror* (New York: Norton, 1993), p. 172–173.
4. Barbara Hall, *An Oral History with Albert E. Van Schmus*, 1993, p. 115. Unpublished manuscript, Margaret Herrick Library, Academy of Motion Picture Arts and Sciences, Los Angeles, California.
5. Analysis Chart, *Objective, Burma!* case file, Production Code Administration Case Files, Margaret Herrick Library, Academy of Motion Picture Arts and Sciences, Los Angeles, California.
6. Analysis Chart, *The Dirty Dozen* case file.
7. Letter, Jason Joy to Carl Laemmle, Jr., August 21, 1929, *All Quiet on the Western Front* case file, Production Code Administration Case Files.
8. Undated 1968 draft statement of CARA's position on-screen violence, MPAA Violence 1968 folder, AMPTP Collection, Margaret Herrick Library.
9. Alan Dershowitz, "The Danger of Seeing Movies Through a Censor's Eyes," *The Chronicle of Higher Education*, July 30, 1999, p. B7.
10. Leonard J. Leff and Jerold L. Simmons, *The Dame in the Kimono: Hollywood, Censorship and the Production Code*, second ed. (Lexington: University Press of Kentucky, 2001), p. xv.
11. Leonard J. Leff, "The Breening of America," *PMLA: Publications of the Modern Language Association of America* 106, no. 3 (1991), p. 435.
12. Barbara Hall, *An Oral History with Albert E. Van Schmus*, p. 102.
13. Ibid., p. 115.
14. James Hall, *Oral History with Geoffrey Shurlock*, p. 85.
15. Barbara Hall, *An Oral History with Albert E. Van Schmus*, p. 231.
16. Ibid., p. 102.
17. Randall, *Censorship of the Movies*, pp. 122–127.
18. John A. Vizzard, "Is the Code Democratic?," *Films in Review*, November 1951.
19. Letter, Joseph Breen to Harry Cohn, February 3, 1953, *The Big Heat* case file.

20. Excerpt from Van Schmus oral history, contained in email from Barbara Hall to the author, September 25, 2001.
21. Robert Vogel quote, ibid.
22. Barbara Hall, *An Oral History with Albert E. Van Schmus*, p. 239.
23. Ibid.
24. Certification Letter, April 21, 1943, *Bataan* case file.
25. Memo for the Files, July 6, 1949, *White Heat* case file.
26. Memo for the Files, Albert Van Schmuss, September 9, 1958, *Party Girl* case file.
27. Memo for the Files, Geoffrey Shurlock, April 5, 1960, *Spartacus* case file.
28. Letter, William Gordon to Edward Muhl, undated, *Spartacus* case file.
29. Memo for the Files, Jack A. Vizzard, February 22, 1960, *Psycho* case file.
30. Telegram re: Legion of Decency Cuts, May 17, 1960, Alfred Hitchcock Collection, Folder 590, *Psycho* (editing).
31. Telegram Attention: Donnenfeld, LaGrande, June 6, 1960, ibid.
32. Gregory Black has studied the PCA–Legion of Decency relationship and written about the Legion in depth. See *The Catholic Crusade Against the Movies: 1940–1975* (New York: Cambridge University Press, 1998).
33. Gerald Gardner, *The Censorship Papers: Movie Censorship Letters from the Hays Office, 1934–1968* (New York: Dodd, Mead and Co., 1987), p. xix.
34. Barbara Hall email to the author, September 25, 2001.
35. Phil Hardy, *The Western* (New York: Overlook Press, 1995), p. 240.
36. Letter, Joseph Breen to William Goetz, September 20, 1954, *The Man from Laramie* case file.
37. Jacobs, *The Wages of Sin*, p. 19.
38. David J. Skal, *The Monster Show: A Cultural History of Horror* (New York: Norton, 1993), p. 188.
39. Ibid., p. 182.
40. Barbara Hall, *An Oral History with Albert E. Van Schmus*, p. 102.
41. James Hall, *Oral History with Geoffrey Shurlock*, p. 254.
42. Barbara Hall, *An Oral History with Albert E. Van Schmus*, p. 130.
43. Ibid., p. 225.
44. James Hall, *Oral History with Geoffrey Shurlock*, p. 89.
45. Barbara Hall, *An Oral History with Albert E. Van Schmus*, p. 123.
46. Ibid., p. 130.
47. Letter, Aubrey Schenck to Joseph Breen, November 13, 1947, *Raw Deal* case file.
48. Letter, Breen to Schenck, November 14, 1947, *Raw Deal* case file.
49. Dougherty note to Aldrich, no date, DGA/Robert Aldrich Collection, Box #60, "Dirty Dozen" Kenneth Hyman folder, Louis B. Mayer Library, American Film Institute, Los Angeles.
50. Letter, Robert Aldrich to Eugene Dougherty, May 5, 1966, op. cit.; letter, Robert Aldrich to Geoffrey Shurlock, May 25, 1967, op. cit.
51. Barbara Hall., *An Oral History with Albert E. Van Schmus*, p. 114.
52. Ibid., p. 236.
53. Memo to Col. Joy from J. V. W., December 31, 1929; letter, Jason Joy to Jack Gain, January 2, 1929. Both from *All Quiet on the Western Front* case file.
54. James Hall, *Oral History with Geoffrey Shurlock*, p. 225.
55. Letter, Joseph Breen to Mark Hellinger, December 27, 1945, *Brute Force* case file.
56. Letter, Joseph Breen to David Stephenson, December 4, 1947, *Raw Deal* case file.
57. Letter, Joseph Breen to Harry Cohn, January 3, 1953, *The Big Heat* case file.

58. Skal, *The Monster Show*, p. 114.
59. Ibid., p. 117.
60. Letter, Jason Joy to Carl Laemmle, Jr., August 18, 1931, *Frankenstein* case file.
61. Letter, Fred W. Beetson to Laemmle, November 2, 1931, ibid.
62. Unsigned letter to Jason Joy, December 10, 1931, *Frankenstein* case file.
63. Leff, "The Breening of America," p. 441.
64. Eliminations report, Kansas State Censor Board, December 11, 1931, ibid.
65. Resume, December 17, 1931, unsigned, ibid.
66. Letter, Katherine Vandervoort to Carl E. Milliken, November 18, 1938, ibid.
67. Ibid.
68. Joanne Cantor and Mary Beth Oliver, "Developmental Differences in Responses to Horror," in *Horror Films: Current Research on Audience Preferences and Reactions,"* ed. James B. Weaver III and Ron Tamborini (Mahwah, NJ: Lawrence Erlbaum, 1996), p. 70.
69. Ibid., p. 72.
70. Ibid., p. 77.
71. Ibid.
72. "U Finds Ghouls Pay Off in Gold," *Variety*, July 26, 1941.
73. Letter, Joseph Breen to Katherine Vandervoort, November 26, 1938, ibid.
74. Letter, Fred W. Beetson to Laemmle, October 13, 1931, *Murders in the Rue Morgue* case file.
75. Letter, John Wilson to B.P. Schulberg, October 10, 1931, *Dr. Jekyll and Mr. Hyde* case file.
76. Letter, Jason Joy to Schulberg, December 1, 1931, ibid.
77. Letter Joy to Schlberg, June 3, 1932, *Island of Lost Souls* case file.
78. Letter, James Wingate to John Hammell, December 8, 1932, ibid.
79. Letter, Joseph Breen to John Hammell, September 18, 1935, ibid.
80. Letter, Breen to Luigi Luraschi, March 4, 1941, ibid.
81. D. Caroline Blanchard, Barry Graczyk, and Robert J. Blanchard, "Differential Reactions of Men and Women to Realism, Physical Damage, and Emotionality in Violent Films," *Aggressive Behavior* 12 (1986), pp. 45–55.
82. Letter, Jason Joy to Carl Laemmle, Jr., January 8, 1932, *Murders in the Rue Morgue* case file.
83. Letter, B.O. Skinner to Jason Joy, February. 20, 1932, ibid.
84. Letter, John Wilson to Ann Bagley, April 11, 1942, ibid.
85. Ibid.
86. Letter, Jason Joy to Will Hays, December 5, 1931, *Dr. Jekyll and Mr. Hyde* case file.
87. Letter, Joy to Hays, January 11, 1932, ibid.
88. Letter, Joseph Breen to Harry Zehner, February 26, 1934, *The Black Cat* case file.
89. Letter, Breen to Zehner, March 26, 1935, *The Raven* case file.
90. Letter, Breen to Zehner, March 11, 1935, ibid.
91. Letter, Breen to Zehner, March 14, 1935, ibid.
92. Letter, Breen to Zehner, April 12, 1934, *The Black Cat* cast file.
93. Letter, Breen to Zehner, December 5, 1934, *Bride of Frankenstein* case file.
94. Letter, James Whale to Joseph Breen, December 7, 1934, ibid.
95. Letter, Breen to Zehner, December 7, 1934, ibid.
96. Memo, Geoffrey Shurlock, February 9, 1935, ibid.
97. Letter, Breen to Zehner, March 23, 1935, ibid.
98. Ibid.
99. Ibid.

100. Memo for the Files, Joseph Breen, March 25, 1935, ibid.
101. Letter, Breen to Zehner, April 15, 1935, ibid.
102. Letter, Breen to Will Hays, May 8, 1935, ibid.
103. Ibid.

THREE. ELABORATING GUN VIOLENCE

1. Phil Hardy, ed., *The Gangster Film* (New York: Overlook Press, 1998), p. 28.
2. Richard Maltby, "The Spectacle of Criminality," in *Violence and American Cinema*, ed. J. David Slocum (New York: Routledge, 2001), p. 121.
3. Letter, Robert Pearson to Jason Joy, March 10, 1931, *Little Caesar* case file.
4. Letter, Jason Joy to Viola Montgomery, January 30, 1931, ibid.
5. Letter, Dr. Carleton Simon to Will Hays, January 26, 1931, ibid.
6. Letter, Jason Joy to James Wingate, February 5, 1931, ibid.
7. Letter, Jason Joy to Maurice McKenzie, January 30, 1931, ibid.
8. Letter, Joy to Albert Hawson, February 19, 1931, ibid.
9. Letter, Joy to John A. Cooper, February 21, 1931, ibid.
10. Ibid.
11. Letter, Joy to Wingate, ibid.
12. Letter, Joy to Hal Wallis, February 21, 1931, ibid.
13. Letter, Joy to Hawson, ibid.
14. Letter, Joy to Daryl Zanuck, January 26, 1931, *Public Enemy* case file.
15. Letter, Joy to Zanuck, March 17, 1931, ibid.
16. Ibid.
17. Memo, Lamar Trotti, April 24, 1931, ibid.
18. Letter, Darryl Zanuck to Jason Joy, January 6, 1931, ibid.
19. Letter, Ben Loenig to C. C. Pettijohn, June 4, 1931, ibid.
20. Letter, Jason Joy to E. B. Derr, June 4, 1931, *Scarface* case file, no. 1.
21. "Gang Film Plea Sent to Montclair's Mayor," *New York Times*, June 26, 1931.
22. Changes in these films are detailed in SRC letter to R. H. Cochrane, October 14, 1931, *Scarface* case file no. 1.
23. Memorandum in re: Scarface, A Brief of the Record, March 4, 1932, *Scarface* case file, no. 2.
24. Letter, Joy to Jack Wilson, June 3, 1931, *Scarface* case file no. 1.
25. Ibid.
26. Resume, Jason Joy, June 17, 1931, ibid.
27. Resume, Jason Joy, August 20, 1931, ibid.
28. Memo for the Files, Lamar Trotti, September 10, 1931, ibid.
29. Letter, Lamar Trotti to Kirk Russell, September 11, 1931, ibid.
30. Letter, Trotti to Maurice McKenzie, September 11, 1931, ibid.
31. Resume, Jason Joy, September 22, 1931, ibid.
32. Letter, Joy to Will Hays, September 30, 1931, ibid.
33. Letter, Lamar Trotti too Frank Wilstach, October 2, 1931, ibid.
34. Memorandum in re: Scarface, A Brief of the Record, *Scarface* case file.
35. Letter, John Wilson to Howard Hughes, June 4, 1931, *Scarface* case file no. 1.
36. Patrick McGilligan, "Clint Eastwood" in *Clint Eastwood: Interviews*, ed. Robert E. Kapsis and Kathie Coblentz (Jackson, Miss: University Press of Mississippi, 1999), p. 27.
37. Maltby, "Spectacle of Criminality," p. 121.
38. Letter, Joseph Breen to Will Hays, October 9, 1935, *Show Them No Mercy* case file.

39. Letter, Joseph Breen to Jason Joy, August 28, 1935, ibid.
40. Letter, Joseph Breen to Jack Warner, February 14, 1936, *G-Men* case file.
41. Letter, Breen to James Wingate, April 6, 1935, ibid.
42. Letter, Breen to Warner, ibid.
43. Ibid.
44. Ibid.
45. Ibid.
46. Ibid.
47. Letter, Breen to Jack Warner, March 1, 1935, ibid.
48. Letter, Breen to Warner, March 7, 1935, ibid.
49. Letter, Breen to Will Hays, April 10, 1935, ibid.
50. Letter, Breen to Luigi Luraschi, June 12, 1950, *Detective Story* case file.
51. Letter, Breen to Eric Johnston, August 4, 1950, ibid.
52. Leff and Simmons discuss this case but not the possibility of a relationship between the manner in which the PCA processed the film's two areas of problem content. *The Dame in the Kimono*, pp. 167–189.
53. Letter, Breen to Johnston, November 9, 1950, *Detective Story* case file.
54. Letter, Breen to Johnston, November 20, 1950, ibid.
55. Letter, James B. Harris to Geoffrey Shurlock, June 27, 1955, *The Killing* case file.
56. Letter, Geoffrey Shurlock to James B. Harris, July 1, 1955, ibid.
57. Letter, Harris to Shurlock, August 9, 1955, ibid.
58. Letter, Shurlock to Harris, August 10, 1955, ibid.
59. Letter, Stanley Kubrick to Shurlock, August 12, 1955, ibid.
60. Memo for the Files, Geoffrey Shurlock, August 23, 1955, ibid.
61. Letter, Shurlock to Harris, September 9, 1955, ibid.
62. Letter, Kubrick to Shurlock, September 24, 1955, ibid.
63. Letter, Joseph Breen to Franklin King, May 9, 1947, *Gun Crazy* case file.
64. Story synopsis, May 3, 1947, ibid.
65. Letter, Breen to King, ibid.
66. Ibid.
67. Examples include L. Berkowitz and A. LePage, "Weapons as Aggression-Eliciting Stimuli," *Journal of Personality and Social Psychology* 7 (1967), pp. 202–207 and Craig A. Anderson, Arlin J. Benjamin, Jr. and Bruce D. Bartholow, "Does the Gun Pull the Trigger? Automatic Priming Effects of Weapon Pictures and Weapon Names," *Psychological Science* 9, no. 4 (July 1998), pp. 308–314.

FOUR. THROWING THE EXTRA PUNCH

1. Letter, Geoffrey Shurlock to Robert Vogel, April 12, 1957, *Party Girl* case file.
2. Letter, Joseph Breen to William Goetz, September 20, 1954, ibid.
3. Letter, Joseph Breen to William Gordon, September 16, 1949, *Winchester '73* case file.
4. Letter, Joseph Breen to Jack Warner, March 26, 1936, *Charge of the Light Brigade* case file.
5. Letter, Breen to Warner, May 25, 1936, ibid.
6. Letter, Joseph Breen to William Gordon, September 16, 1949, *Winchester '73* case file.
7. Letter, Breen to Gordon, July 9, 1951, *Bend of the River* case file.
8. Letter, Geoffrey Shurlock to Charles Schneer, November 22, 1957, *The Case Against Brooklyn* case file.
9. Leter, Joseph Breen to William Gordon, July 9, 1951, *Bend of the River* case file.

10. Letter, Geoffrey Shurlock to James B. Harris, September 9, 1955, *The Killing* case file.

11. Letter, Stanley Kubrick to Geoffrey Shurlock, September 24, 1955, ibid.

12. The most extensive discussion of this standardization is David Bordwell, Janet Staiger and Kristin Thompson, *The Classical Hollywood Cinema: Film Style and Mode of Production to 1960* (New York: Columbia University Press, 1985).

13. An excellent discussion of the case is Gerald F. Phillips, "The Recent Acquisition of Theatre Circuits by Major Distributors," *Entertainment and Sports Lawyer* 5, no. 3 (Winter 1967), pp. 1–2, 10–23.

14. See, for example, Tino Balio, "New Producers for Old: United Artists and the Shift to Independent Production" in Tino Balio, ed., *Hollywood in the Age of Television* (Cambridge, MA: Unwin Hyman, 1990), pp. 165–184.

15. Michael Conant, "The Paramount Decrees Reconsidered," in Tino Balio, ed., *The American Film Industry* rev. ed. (Madison: University of Wisconsin Press, 1985), p. 544.

16. *1969 Film Daily Year Book of Motion Pictures*, cited in Ayer et. Al, "Self-Censorship in the Movie Industry," pp. 97–98.

17. *Variety*, January 22, 1958, cited in ibid., p. 10.

18. Barbara Hall, *An Oral History with Albert E. Van Schmus*, pp. 112–113.

19. Ayer et. al, "Self-Censorship in the Movie Industry," note p. 802.

20. Randall, *Censorship of the Movies*, pp. 42–43.

21. Ibid., p. 77.

22. Ayer et. al, "Self-Censorship in the Movie Industry," p. 814.

23. Ibid., p. 200.

24. Thomas Schatz, *Boom and Bust: The American Cinema in the 1940s* (New York: Scribner's, 1997), p. 36.

25. Ibid.

26. Letter from PCA to Luigi Luraschi, February 6, 1942, *The Glass Key* case file.

27. Ibid.

28. Letter, PCA to Luigi Luraschi, February 17, 1942, ibid.

29. Ibid.

30. Letter, T. P. Geoghegan to Joseph Breen, February 12, 1943, ibid.

31. Letter, Joseph Breen to Geoghegan, February 15, 1943, ibid.

32. Letter, Breen to Luraschi, April 9, 1943, ibid.

33. Clayton R. Koppes and Gregory D. Black, *Hollywood Goes to War* (New York: Free Press, 1987), p. 69.

34. Clayton R. Koppes, "Regulating the Screen: The Office of War Information and the Production Code Administration," in Schatz, *Boom and Bust*, p. 280.

35. Koppes and Black, *Hollywood Goes to War*, pp. 69–70.

36. Thomas Doherty, *Projections of War* (New York: Columbia University Press, 1993), p. 57.

37. Ibid., p. 136.

38. For more on this, see my *Savage Cinema: Sam Peckinpah and the Rise of Ultraviolent Movies* (Austin: University of Texas Press, 1998).

39. In her study of Hollywood's combat films, Jeanine Basinger points out that one of the cardinal rules of this genre is don't climb trees! He-who-does-dies. *The World War II Combat Film: Anatomy of a Genre* (New York: Columbia University Press, 1986), p. 57.

40. Ibid., p. 58.

41. *Bataan* review, *Variety*, May 26, 1943.

42. Letter, Joseph Breen to Jack Warner, April 19, 1944, *Objective, Burma!* case file.

43. See Doherty, *Projections of War*, p. 136.

44. Letter, Joseph Breen to Mark Hellinger, January 29, 1947, *Brute Force* case file.
45. Ibid.
46. Letter, Breen to Hellinger, December 27, 1945, ibid.
47. Letter, Breen to Hellinger, January 29, 1947, ibid.
48. Letter, Breen to Hellinger, June 2, 1947, ibid.
49. Letter, Joseph Breen to Jason Joy, June 16, 1947, *Kiss of Death* case file.
50. Letter, Joseph Breen to David Stephenson, November 10, 1947, *Raw Deal* case file.
51. Ibid.
52. Letter, Breen to Stephenson, November 12, 1947, ibid.
53. Letter, Breen to Stephenson, December 4, 1947, ibid.
54. Letter, Joseph Breen, Jr. to Eugene Dougherty and Harry Zehner, November 28, 1947, ibid.
55. Memo for the Files, M.E.H., February 5, 1947, *Kiss of Death* case file.
56. Letter, Joseph Breen to Jason Joy, March 6, 1947, ibid.
57. Letter, Joseph Breen to Harold Melniker, June 26, 1947, *The Set-Up*, case file.
58. Letter, Breen to Melniker, July 10, 1947, ibid.
59. Letter, Breen to Melniker, ibid.
60. Letter, Breen to Melniker, August 24, 1948, ibid.
61. Letter, Joseph Breen to Harry Cohn, February 3, 1953, *The Big Heat* case file.
62. Ibid.
63. Letter, Breen to Cohn, March 20, 1953, ibid.
64. Memo for the Files, Eugene Dougherty, February 11, 1953, ibid.
65. Memo for the Files, Albert Van Schmus, *Kiss Me Deadly*, case file.
66. Letter, Robert Aldrich to Albert Van Schmus, November 3, 1954, ibid.
67. Letter, Aldrich to Geoffrey Shurlock, February 11, 1955, ibid.
68. Letter, Aldrich to Shurlock, April 18, 1955, ibid.
69. Leo Braudy, *The World in a Frame* (New York: Anchor Books, 1977), p. 210.
70. Letter, Geoffrey Shurlock to Robert Aldrich, November 9, 1954, *Kiss Me Deadly* case file.
71. Ibid.
72. Ibid.
73. Screenplay, *One-Eyed Jacks*, section dated November 24, 1958, p. 103, Virginia Tech Library, Blacksburg, Virginia.
74. Ibid., section dated March 23, 1959, p. 140.
75. Ibid., section dated November 24, 1958, p. 143.
76. Letter, Geoffrey Shurlock to Luigi Luraischi, December 1, 1958, *One-Eyed Jacks* case file.
77. Ibid.
78. Ibid.
79. Letter, Shurlock to Luraischi, March 9, 1959, ibid.
80. Letter, Shurlock to Luraischi, March 12, 1959, ibid.
81. Letter, Shurlock to Luraischi, April 3, 1959, ibid.
82. Letter, Shurlock to Luraischi, April 8, 1959, ibid.
83. Letter, Shurlock to Luraischi, April 19, 1959, ibid.
84. James Hall, "Oral History with Geoffrey Shurlock," (Beverly Hills, CA: American Film Institute, 1975 rev. ed.), p. 168.
85. Ibid.
86. Louis Chapin, "New Movie Standards: General Film Code, Not Specific Bans," *Christian Science Monitor* (September 23, 1966), p. 5.
87. *Variety*, "'Vagueness' No Fatal Flaw: Dallas Flunked Only Rhetoric," May 1, 1968, p. 7.
88. Ayer et al., "Self-Censorship in the Movie Industry," p. 823.

89. Letter, Geoffrey Shurlock to Robert Vogel, September 23, 1965, *The Dirty Dozen* case file.

FIVE. THE POETICS OF SCREEN VIOLENCE

1. Vasey, "Beyond Sex and Violence," p 81.
2. Bordwell et. al, *The Classical Hollywood Cinema*, p. 5.
3. Letter, Joseph Breen to Jack Warner, April 15, 1944, *Objective, Burma!* case file.

SIX. AFTER THE DELUGE

1. Remarks of Jack Valenti before the Comstock Club of Sacramento, December 7, 1970, DBA/Robert Aldrich Collection, Box 9 (Motion Picture Association, 1968–1969).
2. "It's More Resolution than Noted," *Variety*, July 3, 1968, p. 5.
3. Richard Schickel, review of *Point Blank*, *Life*, October 20, 1967.
4. Review of *Point Blank*, *Newsweek*, September 25, 1967.
5. Bosley Crowther, "Movies to Kill People By," *The New York Times*, July 9, 1967.
6. Inter-office Memo, Barbara Scott to Geoffrey Shurlock, November 22, 1968, "MPAA Violence 1968," AMPTP Collection.
7. Memo, Eugene Dougherty to Ralph Hetzel, November 27, 1968, ibid.
8. *Mass Media Hearings, Vol. 9A: A Report to the National Commission on the Causes and Prevention of Violence* (Washington, D.C.: U.S. Government Printing Office, 1969).
9. James Hall, "Oral History with Geoffrey Shurlock," (1975), p. 138.
10. *Marketing Violent Entertainment to Children*, Report of the Federal Trade Commission, September 2000.
11. Inter-Office Memo, Barbara Scott to Geoffrey Shurlock, November 18, 1968, "MPAA Violence 1968," AMPTP Collection.
12. Ibid.
13. *Mass Media Hearings*, p. 43.
14. Dolf Zillmann's research has focused on the relation of excitatory responses and aggression. See, for example, "Excitation Transfer in Communication-Mediated Aggressive Behavior," *Journal of Experimental Social Psychology* 7 (1971), pp. 419–434.
15. Jeffrey Goldstein, "Why We Watch" in Jeffrey Goldstein, ed. *Why We Watch: The Attractions of Violent Entertainment* (New York: Oxford University Press, 1998), p. 222.
16. Undated, unsigned statement of CARA's position on-screen violence, "MPAA Violence 1968."
17. Unsigned memo, "Murf" to "Geof," ibid.
18. Will Tusher, "New PG-13 Rating Instituted by MPAA: Will Cover Some Pix That Would've Been R-Rated," *Variety*, July 14, 1984, p. 30.
19. S. Robert Lichter, Linda S. Lichter, Daniel R. Amundson, "Merchandising Mayhem: Violence in Popular Entertainment, 1998–99" (Center for Media and Public Affairs, June 1999).
20. James T. Hamilton discusses the NCTV data in *Channeling Violence: The Economic Market for Violent Television Programming* (Princeton, NJ: Princeton University Press, 1998), p. 16–17.
21. "Catholics and Code Watchful," *Variety*, November 23, 1966, p. 7.
22. Letter, Thomas Swafford to John Mitchell, June 23, 1972, Richard Brooks Collection, AMPAS Library, Box 35, The Professionals (to CBS).
23. Surgeon General's Scientific Advisory Committee on Television and Social Behavior, *Television and Growing Up: The Impact of Televised Violence.* (Washington, D.C.: U.S. Government Printing Office, 1972).

24. Letter, Richard Brooks to Swafford, June 28, 1972,Richard Brooks' Collection, Box 35.
25. Letter, Swafford to Brooks, July 28, 1972, ibid.
26. Letter, Brooks to Swafford, June 28, 1972, ibid.
27. Inter-office memo, Peter Saphier to Edd Henry, August 16, 1971, *Frenzy* case file, folder 337, Alfred Hitchcock Collection.
28. Memo, Peter Saphier to Peggy Robertson, April 3, 1973, ibid.
29. Memo, Peter Saphier to Petty Robertson, March 6, 1974, ibid.
30. Memo, Saphier to Robertson, March 8, 1974, ibid.
31. Memo to file, Peter Saphier, March 14, 1974, ibid.
32. Note to file re: Television version of "Frenzy," April 4, 1974, ibid.
33. Memo, Saphier to Robertson, March 6, 1974, ibid.
34. See Prince, *Savage Cinema*, p. 15.
35. *Marketing Violent Entertainment to Children*, pp. 12–20.
36. Ibid., p. 17.
37. Ibid., pp. 69–70.
38. Ibid., p. 71.
39. Ibid., p. 9.
40. Hamilton, *Channeling Violence*, p. 54.
41. MPA 2000 Motion Picture Attendance Study, available online at www.mpaa.org
42. Lichter et. al, "Merchandising Mayhem."
43. Ibid.
44. Barry S. Sapolsky and Fred Molitor, "Content Trends in Contemporary Horror Films" in *Horror Films: Current Research on Audience Preferences and Reactions*, ed. James B. Weaver III and Ron Tamborini (Mahwah, NJ: Lawrence Erlbaum, 1996), p. 42.
45. G. Cowan and M. O'Brien, "Gender and survival vs. death in slasher films: A content analysis." *Sex Roles* 23 (1990), pp. 187–196.
46. James B. Weaver III, "Are 'slasher' horror films sexually violent? A content analysis." *Journal of Broadcasting and Electronic Media* 35 (1991), pp. 385–393.
47. D. Johnston and J. Dumerauf, "Why is Freddy a Hero? Adolescents' Uses and Gratifications for Watching Slasher Films" cited in Patricia A. Lawrence and Philip C. Palmgreen, "A Uses and Gratifications Analysis of Horror Film Preference," in Weaver and Tamborini, p. 166.
48. Craig A. Anderson, "Violent Video Games Increase Aggression and Violence," Statement to U.S. Senate Commerce Committee hearing on The Impact of Interactive Violence on Children, available online at http://psych-server.iastate.edu/faculty/caa/abstracts/2000-2004/00Senate.html
49. D. D. Buchman and J. B. Funk, "Video and Computer Games in the '90s: Children's Time Commitment and Game Preferences," *Children Today* 24 (1996), pp. 12–16.
50. David L. McArthur, Corinne Peek-Asa, Theresa Webb, Kevin Fisher, Bernard Cook, Nick Browne, Jes Kraus, Bernard Guyer, "Violence and Its Injury Consequences in American Movies: A Public Health Perspective," *The Western Journal of Medicine* 173 (September 2000).
51. Lichter et. al, "Merchandizing Mayhem."
52. W. James Potter and Stacy Smith, "The Context of Graphic Portrayals of Television Violence," *Journal of Broadcasting and Electronic Media* 44, no. 2 (Spring, 2000).
53. "Nip Crime Career of 2 Iowa Boys," *Des Moines Tribune*, February 22, 1946, MPAA Breen Office Correspondence, MPAA/Vault 355, Box 1, Crime, Violence and Horror, AMPAS Library.
54. "Boy of 10 Attempts Hold-up in Hotel, *New York Times*, January 2, 1946, ibid.

55. Letter, Beatrice Mackie to Eric Johnston, March 14, 1947, MPAA Breen Office Correspondence.

56. Letter, Abram Glaser to Eric Johnston, March 31, 1946, ibid.

57. Numerous articles have been published from and about this project. See, for example, Nancy Signorielli, George Gerbner, Michael Morgan, "Violence on television: the cultural indicators project," *Journal of Broadcasting & Electronic Media* Spring 1995 vol. 39 no. 2, pp. 278–283.

58. Herbert Blumer, *Movies, Delinquency and Crime* (New York: Macmillan, 1933), p. 72.

59. Steve Garbarino, "Do Movies, Music Trigger Violent Acts?," *Newsday*, August 10, 1992, p. 38.

60. Ibid.

61. Juliet Lushbough Dee, "Media Accountability for Real-Life Violence: A Case of Negligence or Free Speech?" *Journal of Communication* 37, no. 2 (Spring 1987), p. 112.

62. Laura A. Kiernan, "Hinckley, Jury Watch '*Taxi Driver*' Film," *The Washington Post*, May 29, 1982, p. A1.

63. Wayne Wilson and Randy Hunter, "Movie-Inspired Violence," *Psychological Reports* 53 (1983), pp. 435–441.

64. Ruth Rendon, "2 Teen Shooting Deaths Probed," *The Houston Chronicle*, March 15, 1994, p. 15.

65. Richard Ruelas, "'A Nightmare: Russian Roulette Victim's Family Seeks Answers," *The Arizona Republic*, March 16, 1998, p. A1.

66. Michele Fleutsch, "Dead Teen Had Problems in School," *The Plain Dealer*, February 10, 1996, p. 1B.

67. Joan Kelly Bernard, "Lethal Risks: Young Copycats," *Newsday*, October 23, 1993, p. 20.

68. Karen Freifeld, "Tale of Death: Suspect Says *Robocop* Sparked Spree," *Newsday*, August 6, 1992, p. 3.

69. "Horror Fiction Became Reality," *The Independent*, December 18, 1993, p. 3.

70. "Massacre Suspect is Being Investigated in Several Murders," *The Houston Chronicle*, May 4, 1996, p. 25; Kim Senguptaa, "The Bulger Case," *The Independent*, March 14, 2000, p. 4.

71. Robert D. McFadden, "Token Clerk in Fire Attack Dies of Burns," *New York Times*, December 11, 1995, p. 1.

72. Tim de Lisle, "An Unhealthy Intimacy with Violence," *The Independent*, June 11, 1995, p. 27.

73. David Ward, "Youths Charged with Murder 'Copied *Reservoir Dogs*,'" *The Guardian*, July 5, 2000, p .8.

74. Michael Atkinson, "The Movies Made Me Do It," *Village Voice*, May 11, 1999.

75. Timothy Egan, "Where Rampages Begin," *New York Times*, June 14, 1998, p. 1.

76. Daniel Pedersen and Sarah Van Boven, "Tragedy in a Small Place," *Newsweek*, December 15, 1997, pp. 30–31.

77. Bob Harvey ad Christopher Guly, "Killings Chillingly Reminiscent of Scene from Hit Movie," *The Ottawa Citizen*, April 22, 1999, p. A1.

78. Sissela Bok, *Mayhem: Violence as Public Entertainment* (Reading, Mass: Addison-Wesley, 1998), p. 59.

79. A review of this literature is provided by Haejung Paik and George Comstock, "The Effects of Television Violence on Antisocial Behavior: A Meta-Analysis," *Communication Research* 21, no. 4 (August 1994), pp. 516–546.

80. Brad J. Bushman and Craig A. Anderson, "Media Violence and the American Public: Scientific Facts versus Media Misinformation," *American Psychologist* 56, no. 67 (June/July 2001), p. 484.

81. Leonard Berkowitz, "Situational Influences on Reactions to Observed Violence," *Journal of Social Issues* 42, no. 3 (1986), p. 93.

82. Wendy Wood, Frank Y. Wong, and J. Gregory Cachere, "Effects of Media Violence on Viewers' Aggression in Unconstrained Social Interaction," *Psychological Bulletin* 109, no. 3 (1991), p. 379.

83. Craig A. Anderson, "Effects of Violent Movies and Trait Hostility on Hostile Feelings and Aggressive Thoughts," *Aggressive Behavior* 23 (1997), pp. 161–178; Brad J. Bushman, "Moderating Role of Trait Aggressiveness in the Effects of Violent Media on Aggression," *Journal of Personality and Social Psychology* 69, no. 5 (1995), pp. 950–960; Richard A. Dubanoski and Colleen Kong, "The Effects of Pain Cues on the Behavior of High and Low Aggressive Boys," *Social Behavior and Personality* 5, no. 2 (1977), pp. 273–279.

84. Suzanne O'Shea, "Research Confirms Violent Videos as 'Pathway' to Juvenile Crime," *The Scotsman*, January 8, 1998, p. 5.

85. Quoted in Alan Kiepper, "What Does Hollywood Say Now," *The New York Times*, December 12, 1995, p. A27.

86. Albert Bandura, *Aggression: A Social Learning Analysis* (Englewood Cliffs, NJ: Prentice-Hall, 1973); *Social Cognitive Theory* (Englewood Cliffs, NJ: Prentice-Hall, 1989).

87. Craig A. Anderson, "Violent Video Games Increase Aggression and Violence."

88. Leonard Berkowitz, "Some Effects of Thoughts on Anti- and Prosocial Influences of Media Events: A Cognitive-Neoassociation Analysis," *Psychological Bulletin* 95, no. 3 (1984), pp. 410–427.

89. Travis Langley, Edgar C. O'Neal, K. M. Craig, and Elizabeth A. Yost, "Aggression-Consistent, -Inconsistent, and –Irrelevant Priming Effects on Selective Exposure to Media Violence," *Aggressive Behavior* 18 (1992), pp. 349–356; Anderson, "Effects of Violent Movies," pp. 161–178; Brad J. Bushman, "Priming Effects of Media Violence on the Accessibility of Aggressive Constructs in Memory," *Personality and Social Psychology Bulletin* 24, no. 5 (1998), pp. 537–545.

90. L. Rowell Huesmann and Laurie S. Miller, "Long-Term Effects of Repeated Exposure to Media Violence in Childhood," *Aggressive Behavior: Current Perspectives*, ed. L. Rowell Huesmann (New York: Plenum, 1994), pp. 153–186; L. Rowell Huesmann, "An Information Processing Model for the Development of Aggressive Behavior," *Aggessive Behavior* 14 (1988), pp. 13–24.

91. Dave Grossman, *On Killing: The Psychologist Cost of Learning to Kill in War and Society* (New York: Little, Brown, and Company, 1995), p. 309.

92. Edward Zwick and Marshall Herskovitz, "The Aftermath: When the Bodies are Real," *The New York Times*, September 23, 2001, p. AR11.

93. John Bailey, "Bang Bang Bang Bang, Ad Nauseum," in *Screening Violence*, ed. Stephen Prince (Rutgers University Press, 2000), p. 85.

94. Gregory D. Black, "Hollywood Censored: The Production Code Administration and the Hollywood Film Indutry, 1930–1940," *Film History*, vol. 3, p. 178.

95. Sam Whiting, "Casting Stones at Oliver," *San Francisco Chronicle*, August 18, 1996, p. 32.

96. Richard Leiby, "Movie Madness: Does Screen Violence Trigger Copycat Crimes?" *Washington Post*, December 3, 1995.

97. Quoted in Bushman, "Moderating Role of Trait Aggressiveness," p. 950.

98. "Altman Says Films Inspire Terrorism," Associated Press wire story, October 17, 2001.

99. Sharrett, "Introduction," in *Mythologies of Violence in Postmodern Media*, p. 10.

100. Slocum, "Film Violence and the Institutionalization of the Cinema," pp. 649, 651.

Bibliography

PRIMARY SOURCES

Most of the research and citations in this book derive from industry records, correspondence, and unpublished manuscripts housed in the following collections:

- Production Code Administration Case Files. The Margaret Herrick Library, Academy of Motion Picture Arts and Sciences, Los Angeles, California.
- MPAA Breen Office Correspondence. Margaret Herrick Library, Academy of Motion Picture Arts and Sciences, Los Angeles, California.
- Crime, Violence, and Horror Collection. Margaret Herrick Library, Academy of Motion Picture Arts and Sciences, Los Angeles, California.
- AMPTP Collection, "Media Violence 1968." Margaret Herrick Library, Academy of Motion Picture Arts and Sciences, Los Angeles, California.
- Barbara Hall, *An Oral History with Albert E. Van Schmus.* Unpublished manuscript, 1993. Margaret Herrick Library, Academy of Motion Picture Arts and Sciences, Los Angeles, California.
- The Richard Brooks Collection. Margaret Herrick Library, Academy of Motion Picture Arts and Sciences, Los Angeles, California.
- The Alfred Hitchcock Collection. Margaret Herrick Library, Academy of Motion Picture Arts and Sciences, Los Angeles, California.
- The Robert Aldrich Collection. Louis B. Mayer Library, The American Film Institute, Los Angeles, California.
- James Hall. *Oral History with Geoffrey Shurlock.* Unpublished manuscript, 1970. Louis B. Mayer Library, American Film Institute, Los Angeles, California.
- Thomas A. Edison Papers, Microfilm Edition, Part IV, Document File Series, Motion Pictures—Censorship, 196:233, New York State Motion Picture Division, New York State Archives, Albany, NY.
- Eliminations Bulletins 1927–1965 of the New York State Motion Picture Division, New York State Archives, Albany, NY.

SECONDARY SOURCES

"Altman Says Films Inspire Terrorism," AP wire story, October 17, 2001.

Anderson, Craig A. "Effects of Violent Movies and Trait Hostility on Hostile Feelings and Aggressive Thoughts." *Aggressive Behavior* 23 (1997), pp. 161–178.

———. "Violent Video Games Increase Aggression and Violence." Statement to U.S. Senate Commerce Committee hearing on The Impact of Interactive Violence on Children. Available online at *http://psych-server.iastate.edu/faculty/caa/abstracts/2000-2004/00Senate.html.*

———, Arlin J. Benjamin, Jr. and Bruce D. Bartholow. "Does the Gun Pull the Trigger? Automatic Priming Effects of Weapon Pictures and Weapon Names." *Psychological Science* 9, no. 4 (July 1998), p. 308–314.

Armour, Robert A. "Effects of Censorship Pressure on the New York Nickelodeon Market, 1907–1909." *Film History* 4 (1990), pp. 113–221.

Ayer, Douglas, Roy E. Bates, Peter J. Herman. "Self-Censorship in the Movie Industry: An Historical Perspective on Law and Social Change." *Wisconsin Law Review* 3 (1970), pp. 791–838.

Bailey, John. "Bang Bang Bang Bang, Ad Nauseum." In *Screening Violence*, ed. Stephen Prince. New Brunswick, NJ: Rutgers University Press, 2000, pp. 79–85.

Balio, Tino. "New Producers for Old: United Artists and the Shift to Independent Production." In *Hollywood in the Age of Television, ed.* Tino Balio. Cambridge, MA: Unwin Hyman, 1990, pp. 165–184.

Bandura, Albert. *Aggression: A Social Learning Analysis.* Englewood Cliffs, NJ: Prentice-Hall, 1973.

———. *Social Cognitive Theory.* Englewood Cliffs, NJ: Prentice-Hall, 1989.

Basinger, Jeanine. *The World War II Combat Film: Anatomy of a Genre.* New York: Columbia University Press, 1986.

Berkowitz, Leonard. "Situational Influences on Reactions to Observed Violence." *Journal of Social Issues* 42, no. 3 (1986), pp. 93–106.

———. "Some Effects of Thoughts on Anti- and Prosocial Influences of Media Events: A Cognitive-Neoassociation Analysis." *Psychological Bulletin* 95, no. 3 (1984), pp. 410–427.

——— and A. LePage. "Weapons as Aggression-Eliciting Stimuli." *Journal of Personality and Social Psychology* 7 (1967), pp. 202–207.

Bernard, Joan Kelly. "Lethal Risks: Young Copycats." *Newsday*, October 23, 1993, p. 20.

Black, Gregory D. "Hollywood Censored: The Production Code Administration and the Hollywood Film Industry, 1930–1940." *Film History*, vol. 3, pp. 167–189.

———. *Hollywood Censored: Morality Codes, Catholics and the Movies.* New York: Cambridge University Press, 1994.

———. *The Catholic Crusade Against the Movies: 1940–1975.* New York: Cambridge University Press, 1998.

Blanchard, D. Caroline, Barry Graczyk, and Robert J. Blanchard. "Differential Reactions of Men and Women to Realism, Physical Damage, and Emotionality in Violent Films." *Aggressive Behavior* 12 (1986), pp. 45–55.

Blumer, Herbert. *Movies, Delinquency and Crime.* New York: Macmillan, 1933.

Bok, Sissela. *Mayhem: Violence as Public Entertainment.* Reading, Mass: Addison-Wesley, 1998.

Bordwell, David, Janet Staiger and Kristin Thompson. *The Classical Hollywood Cinema: Film Style and Mode of Production to 1960.* New York: Columbia University Press, 1985.

Braudy, Leo. *The World in a Frame.* New York: Anchor Books, 1977.

Buchman, D. D. and J. B. Funk. "Video and Computer Games in the '90s: Children's Time Commitment and Game Preferences." *Children Today* 24 (1996), pp. 12–16.

Bushman, Brad J. "Moderating Role of Trait Aggressiveness in the Effects of Violent Media on Aggression." *Journal of Personality and Social Psychology* 69, no. 5 (1995), pp. 950–960.

———. "Priming Effects of Media Violence on the Accessibility of Aggressive Constructs in Memory." *Personality and Social Psychology Bulletin* 24, no. 5 (1998), pp. 537–545.

——— and Craig A. Anderson. "Media Violence and the American Public: Scientific Facts versus Media Misinformation." *American Psychologist* 56, no. 67 (June/July 2001), pp. 477–489.

Cantor, Joanne Cantor and Mary Beth Oliver. "Developmental Differences in Responses to Horror." In *Horror Films: Current Research on Audience Preferences and Reactions*, ed. James B. Weaver III and Ron Tamborini. Mahwah, NJ: Lawrence Erlbaum, 1996, pp. 63–80.

Carmen, Ira. *Movies, Censorship and the Law*. Ann Arbor: University of Michigan Press, 1967.

"Catholics and Code Watchful." *Variety*, November 23, 1966, p. 7.

Conant, Michael. "The Paramount Decrees Reconsidered." In *The American Film Industry* revised edition, ed. Tino Balio,. Madison: University of Wisconsin Press, 1985, pp. 537–573.

Cowan, G. and M. O'Brien. "Gender and survival vs. death in slasher films: A content analysis." *Sex Roles* 23 (1990), pp. 187–196.

Dawley, Alan. *Struggles for Justice: Social Responsibility and the Liberal State*. Cambridge, MA: Harvard University Press, 1991.

Dee, Juliet Lushbough. "Media Accountability for Real-Life Violence: A Case of Negligence or Free Speech?" *Journal of Communication* 37, no. 2 (Spring 1987), pp. 106–138.

De Lislie, Tim. "An Unhealthy Intimacy with Violence." *The Independent*, June 11, 1995, p. 27.

Dershowitz, Alan. "The Danger of Seeing Movies Through a Censor's Eyes." *The Chronicle of Higher Education*, July 30, 1999, p. B7.

Doherty, Thomas. *Projections of War*. New York: Columbia University Press, 1993.

Dubanoski, Richard A. and Colleen Kong. "The Effects of Pain Cues on the Behavior of High and Low Aggressive Boys." *Social Behavior and Personality* 5, no. 2 (1977), pp. 273–279.

Egan, Timothy. "Where Rampages Begin." *New York Times*, June 14, 1998, p. 1.

Ernst, Morris L. and Pare Lorentz. *Censored: The Private Life of the Movie*. New York: Cape and Smith, 1930.

Fleutsch, Michele. "Dead Teen Had Problems in School." *The Plain Dealer*, February 10, 1996, p. 1B.

Garbarino, Steve. "Do Movies, Music Trigger Violent Acts?" *Newsday*, August 10, 1992, p. 38.

Gardner, Gerald. *The Censorship Papers: Movie Censorship Letters from the Hays Office*. New York: Dodd, Mead and Co., 1987.

Goldstein, Jeffrey. "Why We Watch." In *Why We Watch: The Attractions of Violent Entertainment*, ed. Jeffrey Goldstein. New York: Oxford University Press, 1998, pp. 212–226.

Grossman, Dave. *On Killing: The Psychologist Cost of Learning to Kill in War and Society*. New York: Little, Brown, and Company, 1995.

Gunter, Barrie and Adrian Furnham. "Perceptions of Television Violence: Effects of Programme Genre and Type of Violence on Viewers' Judgements of Violent Portrayals." *British Journal of Social Psychology* 23 (1984), pp. 155–164.

Hamilton, James T. *Channeling Violence: The Economic Market for Violent Television Programming*. Princeton, NJ: Princeton University Press, 1998.

Hardy, Phil. *The Gangster Film*. New York: Overlook Press, 1998.

———. *The Western*. New York: Overlook Press, 1995.

Harvey, Bob and Christopher Guly. "Killings Chillingly Reminiscent of Scene from Hit Movie." *The Ottawa Citizen*, April 22, 1999, p. A1.

"Horror Fiction Became Reality." *The Independent*, December 18, 1993, p. 3.

Huesmann, L. Rowell. "An Information Processing Model for the Development of Aggressive Behavior." *Aggessive Behavior* 14 (1988), pp. 13–24.

——— and Laurie S. Miller. "Long-Term Effects of Repeated Exposure to Media Violence in Childhood." In *Aggressive Behavior: Current Perspectives*, ed. L. Rowell Huesmann. New York: Plenum, 1994, pp. 153–186.

Jacobs, Lea. *The Wages of Sin: Censorship and the Fallen Woman Film, 1928–1942.* Madison, WI: University of Wisconsin Press, 1991.

Johnston, D. and J. Dumerauf. "Why is Freddy a Hero? Adolescents' Uses and Gratifications for Watching Slasher Films." Cited in Patricia A. Lawrence and Philip C. Palmgreen. "A Uses and Gratifications Analysis of Horror Film Preference." In *Horror Films: Current Research on Audience Preferences and Reactions*, ed. James B. Weaver III and Ron Tamborini. Mahwah, NJ: Lawrence Erlbaum, 1996, pp. 161–179.

Jowett, Garth. *Film: The Democratic Art.* Boston: Little, Brown, 1976.

———. "Moral Responsibility and Commercial Entertainment: Social Control in the United States Film Industry, 1907–1968." *Historical Journal of Film, Radio and Television* 10, no. 1 (1990), pp. 3–31.

Kiepper, Alan. "What Does Hollywood Say Now." *The New York Times*, December 12, 1995, p. A27.

Kiernan, Laura A. "Hinckley, Jury Watch '*Taxi Driver*' Film." *The Washington Post*, May 29, 1982, p. A1.

Koppes, Clayton R. "Regulating the Screen: The Office of War Information and the Production Code Administration." In *Boom and Bust: The American Cinema in the 1940s*, ed. Thomas Schatz. New York: Scribner's, 1997, pp. 262–281.

——— and Gregory D. Black. *Hollywood Goes to War.* New York: Free Press, 1987.

Langley, Travis, Edgar C. O'Neal, K.M. Craig, and Elizabeth A. Yost. "Aggression-Consistent, -Inconsistent, and -Irrelevant Priming Effects on Selective Exposure to Media Violence." *Aggressive Behavior* 18 (1992), pp. 349–356.

Lawson, W. P. "Standards of Censorship." *Harper's Weekly*, January 16, 1915, pp. 63–65.

———. "The Breening of America." *PMLA: Publications of the Modern Language Association of America* 106, no. 3 (1991), pp. 432–445.

Leff, Leonard J. and Jerold L. Simmons. *The Dame in the Kimono: Hollywood, Censorship and the Production Code*, second ed. Lexington: University Press of Kentucky, 2001.

Leiby, Richard. "Movie Madness: Does Screen Violence Trigger Copycat Crimes?" *Washington Post*, December 3, 1995, p. G1.

Lichter, S. Robert, Linda S. Lichter, Daniel R. Amundson. "Merchandising Mayhem: Violence in Popular Entertainment, 1998–99." Center for Media and Public Affairs, June 1999. Available at *www.cmpa.com/archive/viol98.htm.*

Maltby, Richard. "The Spectacle of Criminality." In *Violence and American Cinema*, ed. J. David Slocum, pp. 117–152.

Marketing Violent Entertainment to Children: A Review of Self-Regulation and Industry Practices in the Motion Picture, Music Recording and Electronic Game Industries. Report of the Federal Trade Commission, September 2000.

Mass Media Hearings, Vol. 9A: A Report to the National Commission on the Causes and Prevention of Violence. Washington, D.C.: U.S. Government Printing Office, 1969.

"Massacre Suspect Is Being Investigated in Several Murders." *The Houston Chronicle*, May 4, 1996, p. 25.

McArthur, David L. Corinne Peek-Asa, Theresa Webb, Kevin Fisher, Bernard Cook, Nick Browne, Jes Kraus, Bernard Guyer. "Violence and Its Injury Consequences in American Movies: A Public Health Perspective." *The Western Journal of Medicine* 173 (September 2000), pp. 164–168.

McGilligan, Patrick. "Clint Eastwood." In *Clint Eastwood: Interviews*, ed. Robert E. Kapsis and Kathie Coblentz. Jackson, Miss: University Press of Mississippi, 1999.

MPA 2000 Motion Picture Attendance Study. Available online at *www.mpaa.org*.

Munby, Jonathan. *Public Enemies, Public Heroes: Screening the Gangster from "Little Caesar" to "Touch of Evil."* Chicago: University of Chicago Press, 1999.

O'Shea, Suzanne. "Research Confirms Violent Videos as 'Pathway' to Juvenile Crime." *The Scotsman*, January 8, 1998, p. 5.

Pedersen, David and Sarah Van Boven, "Tragedy in a Small Place." *Newsweek*, December 15, 1997, pp. 30–31.

Phillips, Gerald F. "The Recent Acquisition of Theatre Circuits by Major Distributors." *Entertainment and Sports Lawyer* 5, no. 3 (Winter 1967), pp. 1–2, 10–23.

Potter, W. James and Stacy Smith. "The Context of Graphic Portrayals of Television Violence." *Journal of Broadcasting and Electronic Media* 44, no. 2 (Spring, 2000), pp. 301–323.

Prince, Stephen. *Savage Cinema: Sam Peckinpah and the Rise of Ultraviolent Movies*. Austin: University of Texas Press, 1998.

Randall, Richard. *Censorship of the Movies*. Madison: University of Wisconsin Press, 1968.

Rendon, Ruth. "2 Teen Shooting Deaths Probed." *The Houston Chronicle*, March 15, 1994, p. 15.

Rosenbloom, Nancy J. "Between Reform and Regulation: The Struggle over Film Censorship in Progressive America, 1909–1922." *Film History* 1 (1987), pp. 307–325.

Ruelas, Richard. "A Nightmare: Russian Roulette Victim's Family Seeks Answers." *The Arizona Republic*, March 16, 1998, p. A1.

Sapolsky, Barry S. and Fred Molitor. "Content Trends in Contemporary Horror Films." In *Horror Films: Current Research on Audience Preferences and Reactions*, ed. James B. Weaver III and Ron Tamborini. Mahwah, NJ: Lawrence Erlbaum, 1996, pp. 33–48.

Schatz, Thomas. *Boom and Bust: The American Cinema in the 1940s*. New York: Scribner's, 1997.

Senguptaa, Kim. "The Bulger Case." *The Independent*, March 14, 2000, p. 4.

Sharrett, Christopher, ed. *Mythologies of Violence in Postmodern Media*. Detroit: Wayne State University Press, 1999.

Signorielli, Nancy, George Gerbner, Michael Morgan. "Violence on television: the cultural indicators project." *Journal of Broadcasting & Electronic Media* 39, Spring 1995, pp. 278–283.

Skal, David J. *The Monster Show: A Cultural History of Horror*. New York: Norton, 1993.

Slocum, J. David, ed. *Violence and American Cinema*. New York: Routledge, 2001.

———. "Film Violence and the Institutionalization of the Cinema." *Social Research* 67, no. 3 (Fall 2000), pp. 649–681.

Surgeon General's Scientific Advisory Committee on Television and Social Behavior. *Television and Growing Up: The Impact of Televised Violence*. Washington, D.C.: U.S. Government Printing Office, 1972.

Tusher, Will. "New PG-13 Rating Instituted by MPAA: Will Cover Some Pix That Would've Been R-Rated." *Variety*, July 14, 1984, p. 30.

Vasey, Ruth. "Beyond Sex and Violence: 'Industry Policy' and the Regulation of Hollywood Movies, 1922–1939." *Quarterly Review of Film and Video* 15, no. 4 (1995), pp. 65–85.

Vizzard, John A. "Is the Code Democratic?" *Films in Review*, November 1951.

Ward, David. "Youths Charged with Murder 'Copied *Reservoir Dogs*.'" *The Guardian*, July 5, 2000, p .8.

Weaver, James B. III. "Are 'slasher' horror films sexually violent? A content analysis." *Journal of Broadcasting and Electronic Media* 35 (1991), pp. 385–393.

Whiting, Sam. "Casting Stones at Oliver." *San Francisco Chronicle*, August 18, 1996, p. 32.

Wilson, Wayne and Randy Hunter. "Movie-Inspired Violence." *Psychological Reports* 53 (1983), pp. 435–441.

Wood, Wendy, Frank Y. Wong, and J. Gregory Cachere. "Effects of Media Violence on Viewers' Aggression in Unconstrained Social Interaction." *Psychological Bulletin* 109, no. 3 (1991), pp. 371–383.

Zillmann, Dolf. "Excitation Transfer in Communication-Mediated Aggressive Behavior." *Journal of Experimental Social Psychology* 7 (1971), pp. 419–434.

Zwick, Edward and Marshall Herskovitz. "The Aftermath: When the Bodies are Real." *The New York Times*, Sept. 23, 2001, p. AR11.

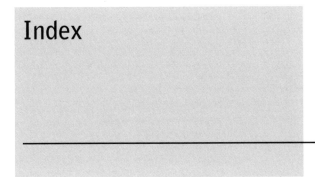

Index

About the Author

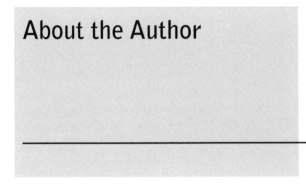

STEPHEN PRINCE, a professor of film at Virginia Tech, is a recognized authority on cinema violence. He is the author of *Savage Cinema: Sam Peckinpah and the Rise of Ultraviolent Movies* and editor of *Screening Violence* (Rutgers University Press).